Daniel Coit Gilman

The Organization of Charities

Being a Report of the Sixth Section of the International Congress of Charities,

Corrections, and Philanthropy, Chicago, June, 1893

Daniel Coit Gilman

The Organization of Charities
Being a Report of the Sixth Section of the International Congress of Charities, Corrections, and Philanthropy, Chicago, June, 1893

ISBN/EAN: 9783337254797

Printed in Europe, USA, Canada, Australia, Japan

Cover: Foto ©ninafisch / pixelio.de

More available books at **www.hansebooks.com**

THE

Organization of Charities

BEING A REPORT OF

THE SIXTH SECTION OF THE INTERNATIONAL CONGRESS
OF CHARITIES, CORRECTIONS, AND PHILANTHROPY,
CHICAGO, JUNE, 1893.

EDITED WITH AN INTRODUCTION BY
DANIEL C. GILMAN, LL.D.
President of the Charity Organization Society of Baltimore, Md.

BALTIMORE
THE JOHNS HOPKINS PRESS.
LONDON
THE SCIENTIFIC PRESS, LIMITED
128 Strand, W. C.
1894

THE WORLD'S CONGRESS AUXILIARY OF THE WORLD'S COLUMBIAN EXPOSITION.

The International Congress of Charities, Correction and Philanthropy.

PRESIDENT:
RUTHERFORD B. HAYES.

FIRST VICE-PRESIDENT:
FREDERICK H. WINES.

SECOND VICE-PRESIDENT:
ROBERT TREAT PAINE.

GENERAL SECRETARY:
ALEXANDER JOHNSON.

COMMITTEE OF ORGANIZATION:
FREDERICK H. WINES, JOHN G. SHORTALL, MRS. J. M. FLOWER.
NATHANIEL S. ROSENAU, SECRETARY.

SECTION VI.

THE ORGANIZATION AND AFFILIATION OF CHARITIES IN COUNTIES, STATES, CITIES, TOWNS AND VILLAGES, AND PREVENTIVE WORK AMONG THE POOR.

COMMITTEE OF ARRANGEMENTS:
Members Invited.

LEVI L. BARBOUR, Detroit, Mich.
CHARLES J. BONAPARTE, Baltimore.
JOHN G. BROOKS, Brockton, Mass.
MISS ANNA L. DAWES, Washington.
ROBERT W. DE FOREST, New York.
DANIEL C. GILMAN, Baltimore.
JOHN M. GLENN, Baltimore.
CHARLES C. HARRISON, Philadelphia.
J. W. JENKS, Ithaca, N. Y.
J. LLOYD JONES, Chicago.
MRS. C. R. LOWELL, New York.
RICHMOND MAYO-SMITH, New York.
MRS. MARY E. MUMFORD, Philadelphia.
ROBERT TREAT PAINE, Boston.
FRANCIS G. PEABODY, Cambridge.
MRS. W. B. RICE, New York.
MISS LOUISA LEE SCHUYLER, New York.
AMOS G. WARNER, Washington.
ALFRED T. WHITE, Brooklyn.
ANSLEY WILCOX, Buffalo.

TABLE OF CONTENTS.

	PAGE.
EDITORIAL NOTE	v
A Panorama of Charitable Work in Many Lands, by D. C. Gilman.	viii
The Problem of Charity, by Rev. Francis G. Peabody	xx

PROCEEDINGS :.
First Session: The Demarcation of the Field of Voluntary Charitable
Work 3
Second Session: Friendly Visiting 15
Third Session: The Relation of Public to Private Charity............ 31
Fourth Session: Labor Colonies, Relief in Work........................ 33

PAPERS ON CHARITY ORGANIZATION IN THE UNITED STATES:
History of Charity Organization in the United States, by Charles D.
Kellogg... 43
The State Charities Aid Association of the State of New York, by Miss
Louisa Lee Schuyler 57
The State Charities Aid Association of New Jersey, by Mrs. Emily E.
Williamson... 72
Are Labor Colonies Needed in the United States? by Mrs. Charles R.
Lowell.. 77
Labor Tests and Relief in Work in the United States, by Alfred T.
White 87
Registration of Charitable Relief, by Miss Francis R. Morse......... 99
Friendly Visiting, by Mrs. Roger Wolcott................................... 108
The Co-operation of Public with Private Charitable Agencies, by Alexander Johnson... 114
Public Subsidies to Private Charities, by Amos G. Warner........... 120

PAPERS FROM CONTINENTAL EUROPE ON PUBLIC AND PRIVATE RELIEF
OF THE POOR:
Charity in France and Belgium, by Herbert Valleroux.................. 135
Charitable Organizations and Charitable Work in Italy, by Egisto Rossi. 168
The International Treatment of Charity Questions, by Baron Von Reitzenstein 185
The Elberfeld System of Poor Relief, by Dr. Theodore Münsterberg.... 187
The Elberfeld System of Poor Relief and its Practical Application, by
Dr. Thoma.. 200
The Elberfeld System of Poor Relief, by L. F. Seyffardt................ 207
Co-operation between Public and Private Poor Relief, by Dr. Victor
Böhmert... 210
The People's Club, "Volkswohl", of Dresden; its Evening Entertainments and Homes for the People, by Dr. Victor Böhmert......... 228
The Organization of Charity in Russia, by Dr. H. Georgievsky........ 244

PAPERS ON CHARITY ORGANIZATION IN GREAT BRITAIN :   PAGE.
 Introductory Note, by C. S. Loch.. 250
 The West of London : S. Marylebone, by Rev. B. H. Alford. 253
 The East of London, by Rev. Dr. E. H. Bradby................................... 258
 Shoreditch, by C. N. Nicholson... 268
 St. Olave's, by C. P. Larner... 278
 Charity Organization in Islington, by Miss L. Sharpe........................... 283
 Co-operation of Charitable Agencies with the Poor Law, with Special
   Reference to St. George in the East, by T. Mackay....................... 290
 Manchester. Poor Law Relief and Charity Organization in an Industrial
   Town, by Alexander McDougall... 304
 The Charities of Bristol, by Miss Elizabeth Sturge................................ 312
 Rochdale. Industrial and General Characteristics, Poor Law Adminis-
   tration, and Charities, by R. A. Leach... 319
   Appendix : Report of the Work Done by the Rochdale Charity
     Organization Society 1880–1891, by Alderman Heape................ 338
 Helping the Poor in Aberdeen, by George Milne................................... 344
 The Problem of Poverty in an English Rural Union (Bradfield), by H.
   G. Willink... 350
 Charity Organization in Relation to Voluntary Effort, by Rev. Brooke
   Lambert.. 365
 Friendly Visiting, by Miss F. C. Prideaux... 369
 English Poor Law, by Baldwyn Fleming.. 377
 School Savings Banks, by Charles Henry Wyatt................................... 384
INDEX.. 391

EDITORIAL NOTE.

THE Conference on Charity Organization, whose proceedings are reported in the following pages, was one of the series of international assemblies held in Chicago during the Columbian Exhibition of 1893. It was projected as the sixth section of the International Congress of Charities, Correction and Philanthropy, and accordingly the initiative was taken by the officers of that body, Hon. R. B. Hayes, the late ex-President of the United States, Rev. F. H. Wines, of Illinois, upon whom devolved the presidency of the Congress, and Mr. N. S. Rosenau, who was in charge of the exhibit of Charities and Corrections during the progress of the world's fair. On their visit to Baltimore, in the early winter of 1892-3, while the National Prison Association was in session, this committee enlisted the cooperation of some of the members of the Charity Organization Society of Baltimore, and with them agreed to entrust the plans of the sixth section to a body of ladies and gentlemen, selected from many different cities. An active correspondence then began, and presently three committee meetings were held in New York, to give unity and directness to the various suggestions which had been made by those who were consulted.

Several persons who were invited to become members of the committee of arrangements were prevented, by distance or by other engagements, from active cooperation,—among them, Mr. Ansley Wilcox, of Buffalo, Rev. J. Lloyd Jones, of Chicago, Professor Jenks, of Cornell University, Miss Dawes, of Washington, and Rev. J. G. Brooks, of Brockton, Mass.

The persons below named attended one or more of the meetings, held in New York, and so constituted the acting

COMMITTEE OF ARRANGEMENTS.

LEVI L. BARBOUR, Detroit,
CHARLES J. BONAPARTE, Baltimore,
ROBERT W. DE FOREST, New York,
DANIEL C. GILMAN, Baltimore,
JOHN M. GLENN, Baltimore,
CHARLES C. HARRISON, Philadelphia,
MRS. C. R. LOWELL, New York,
MRS. MARY E. MUMFORD, Philadelphia,
ROBERT TREAT PAINE, Boston,
FRANCIS G. PEABODY, Cambridge,
MRS. W. B. RICE, New York,
MISS LOUISA LEE SCHUYLER, New York,
RICHMOND MAYO-SMITH, New York,
ALFRED T. WHITE, Brooklyn,
AMOS G. WARNER, Washington.

The officers, chosen by the committee, were these.
President: Daniel C. Gilman, Johns Hopkins University, Baltimore.
Secretary: Richmond Mayo-Smith, Columbia College, New York.
Treasurer: Charles C. Harrison, Philadelphia.
Executive Committee: Messrs. A. T. White, of Brooklyn, R. W. De Forest, of New York, and F. G. Peabody, of Cambridge, with the President and Secretary.
Finance Committee: Messrs. R. T. Paine, C. C. Harrison, and C. J. Bonaparte, and Mrs. C. R. Lowell.

The executive committee perfected the arrangements for the meeting in Chicago, and (with the exception of one member) were present during the deliberations. The finance committee collected an amount sufficient for the payment of the incidental expenses, and for the assurance of the publication of this volume. This pecuniary support came chiefly from active upholders of the principles of charity organization in Boston, Brooklyn, New York, Philadelphia, and Baltimore.

The special arrangements for the meeting, including a very large part of the foreign and domestic correspondence, devolved upon Professor Mayo-Smith, of Columbia College, New York.

The Congress assembled in Chicago, June 12, 1893. The opening address was delivered by the Reverend Professor Peabody, of Harvard University, which, at the request of many persons who heard it and of many who heard of it, is reprinted in this volume. At the same meeting, a discourse commemorative of ex-President Hayes, who died in the preceding January, was delivered by Reverend F. H. Wines, since published in the report of the National Prison Congress. Another address of general interest was given by the Hon. Robert Treat Paine, of Boston, which has since been published in a separate volume.

The section on Charity Organization held four sessions, over which Mr. Robert W. De Forest, President of the Charity Organization Society of New York, Mr. Jeffrey R. Brackett, and Mr. John M. Glenn, of Baltimore, presided. The debates which followed the reading of the papers are reported, not so perfectly as might be desired, in the following pages. Those who heard the communications and the comments upon them, were unanimous and hearty in their expressions of satisfaction and in their desire to impart, to those who could not be present, the impressions of this encouraging and stimulating conference.

It is to be regretted that a valuable paper by Mr. Levi L. Barbour on "The Demarcation of the Field of Voluntary Charitable Work" is omitted. It was not forwarded by the reporter and has not since been found.

The delay which has occurred in the publication of this volume is due to the necessity of sending to England the proofs of the very valuable papers contributed through the kind agency of Mr. C. S. Loch, Secretary of the Charity Organization Society of London. As the authors were widely separated, much time was consumed in receiving the return proof sheets. Special acknowledgments are due not only to Mr. Loch, but also to the Rev. John G. Brooks, who was actively interested in securing communications from continental writers.

The care of seeing this volume through the press was assumed by Mr. John M. Glenn, one of the managers of the Charity Organization Society of Baltimore. The Index has been prepared by David I. Green, Ph. D., recently called to the oversight of the Charity Organization Society in Hartford, Conn.

BALTIMORE, *January,* 1894.

A PANORAMA OF CHARITABLE WORK IN MANY LANDS:

BEING A REVIEW OF THE PAPERS SUBMITTED TO THE INTERNATIONAL CONGRESS IN CHICAGO, JUNE, 1893.

BY DANIEL C. GILMAN.

In the volume to which this essay is an introduction the reader will find an expression of opinions upon the organization and administration of charities from many thoughtful students and observers in England, France, Germany, Italy, Russia, and in many states of the American union. Most if not all the writers are persons who have devoted years to the study of human sufferings and delinquencies, and to the agencies by which the strong endeavor to bear in part the burdens of the weak. Many of the contributors, if not all, are officially concerned in the administration of public or private charities. Not a few of them are known far beyond the borders of their own country as authorities or experts in the treatment of pauperism and the prevention of misery, vice and crime. Their collective essays afford a sort of panorama of the charitable work of Christendom, at the close of the nineteenth century. The panorama, however, is not complete. Hospitals, dispensaries, and institutions for the relief of the aged, the protection of the young, and the restoration of the feeble do not come within the present survey. Nor are educational, reformatory, or penitentiary establishments discussed in this volume. But the methods now employed in Europe and America for the prevention of pauperism, the relief of poverty, and the orderly administration of beneficence, are here succinctly set forth with all the variety of expression that is suggested by spontaneous efforts, in different conditions, under various traditions and laws, and described by men and women who are unacquainted with the views of their collaborators. In all this diversity a remarkable unity of principles will be soon discovered. Four principles are generally recognized as wise and correct, and in some places are indeed so familiar that they appear elementary.

First, the nature and influence of charitable works and the comparative values of different modes of procedure, are as worthy of exact study, as the facts and laws of political economy. If humanity is still far from having worked out "a science of charity," it has taken the first steps toward the establishment of a systematic and trustworthy system; it has undertaken to collect the facts and to make some generalizations upon the information thus brought together. Organized charity proceeds upon the assumption of the unity of human nature, so that although laws, religions, traditions and usages differ in different lands, like causes every where tend to produce the like effects. It examines the methods which have been employed for the relief of necessities in the light of these consequent results. It records and compares the experience acquired in towns and villages and country places. It notes the rise and fall of individual characters, and the uplifting or the degradation of families and neighborhoods. It observes particularly the effects of good and bad financial laws and ordinances; good and bad sanitary regulations; good and bad religious and moral influences. As it makes these studies, charity organization is not at all alarmed if it is called in a sneering tone "scientific," for history is full of examples of the taunts that have been thrown upon the beginnings of a science. Nor is charity organization dismayed by being opposed as cold and unsympathetic. The medical and surgical arts are constant witnesses to the truth that severe remedies are sometimes the most efficacious, and that to be truly helpful to a sufferer, the adviser must be intelligent, calm, firm, and self-controlled. As the analogy between the diseases of the human body and the failures of human society is apparent, so too are the analogies of treatment. There must be a science of pathology, which ascertains and describes the characteristic lesions, before empirical methods can be superseded and the true principles of hygienic and sanitary science be established. In social as in bodily ailments the art of healing must be based upon ascertained facts and on accumulated experience.

Secondly. It is another principle of charity organization that there shall be no needless expenditure of force, no dissipation of energy. Four agencies, which are at work in almost every community—civil, ecclesiastical, associated and individual beneficence—must be brought into such harmonious relations, that there will be no overlapping or duplication of charitable support. The State has its legitimate province; so has religious sympathy and good will; so has associated or institutional activity; so has private generosity. The effort of charity organization is to protect each of these humane influences and likewise to prevent their rivalry and conflict. There are two dangers ever hovering over a charitable community,—that the expenses of administration will be disproportionate to the good accomplished; and that for the lack of adjustment and co-operation, the recipient of aid will be so amply supplied that he becomes permanently dependent or pauperized. It is only by careful comparison of the facts that the benevolent forces of any community can be wisely and economically administered. Co-operation in charity is of prime importance.

Thirdly. Charity, to be really and permanently efficacious, must always (except in emergencies, like fire, accident, and sudden illness), be guided by personal acquaintance with the wants that are to be relieved. Indiscriminate almsgiving at the door or on the street; the free bestowal of food "no questions being asked;" spasmodic liberality one day and crisp parsimony the next; the avoidance of particular inquiries in respect to the conditions of those who seek assistance, may satisfy the conscience of a tender-hearted person, but his alms will probably aggravate in his beneficiaries the distresses that ought to be healed. No process is more favorable to the encouragement of improvidence, laziness and intemperance, than the heedless generosity which gives to all who ask without discrimination. Nevertheless, busy people, especially in large towns, are often unable to make domiciliary visits. Here come in the associated charities. A central office with its auxiliaries, and especially with its staff of agents and visitors, will investigate for those who cannot make their own enquiries every apparent case of need.

Fourthly. The best of all charities is not that which gives something for nothing; but that which gives something in return for industry, labor, economy, self-sacrifice and self-help. Work, for the strong and healthy, is better far than a dole. Useful labor, fairly requited, uplifts the needy man by perpetuating the consciousness that he does not belong to an impoverished class; bounties carelessly bestowed, without any return, tend to place the recipient in the ranks of the pauper. This principle does not prevent generous treatment of those who are dependent, good pay for their work, and special help in times of sickness and distress; nor kindness to those who are rearing and teaching young children, to those who are in sorrow, to those suddenly thrown out of work. The effort is always to be made to keep from sinking lower those who by misconduct or misfortune are on the verge of permanent shiftlessness and distress. But the main stay of every family, as of every individual, must be work, unless age or infirmity intervenes; and those who are charitably disposed do the greatest service to the needy by providing for them tasks of a useful character for which a moderate payment can be made.

In short, Education, Registration, Co-operation, Visitation, and the Provision of Employment, are the five-fold agencies upon which the leaders in charities are united.

From these general considerations let us proceed to notice the papers contained in this volume. First comes an admirable statement of the office of Charity set forth in an address delivered by the Rev. Francis G. Peabody of Harvard. This is followed by a report of the discussions elicited after hearing the essays read to the conference in Chicago. Many of the most intelligent workers in the charity organization societies of this country took part in these debates, and often in the familiar phrases of their off-hand expression, pithy statements and concrete illustrations were brought forth. They illuminated many sombre chapters of accumulated experience. Then come ninety pages on the work of charity organization in the United States, introduced by a very valuable compact history of the movement, by Mr. C. D. Kellogg, Secretary of the Charity Organization Society in New York. Twenty years ago there were no such associations in America. Now there are ninety-two in this country and Canada. No one is better qualified than Mr. Kellogg to make such a review. The communication unabridged is to appear in the report of the Twentieth National Conference of Charities and Correction.

The examples of associated charities are introduced by an historical paper on the State Charities Aid Association of New York by one of the original and chief supporters of that work, Miss Louisa Lee Schuyler. It is a remarkable exhibit, in most respects unique, of the possibility of enlisting friendly, voluntary agencies, in the visitation of public institutions without awakening the opposition, but rather with the welcome, of the governing authorities. This is only a part of the good work accomplished by the association. The acquaintance thus acquired in respect to the needs of the State enabled the managers to suggest and support many independent agencies of beneficence,—such as the training of nurses for hospital and for private service; the collection of books and papers for public institutions; the opening of temporary homes for needy children; the provision of immediate aid to the injured;

the establishment of a municipal lodging house in New York; and the abolition of the poor-house system of caring for the insane.

New Jersey is the only state which has endeavored to follow the example thus set by New York, and the story of the Charities Aid Association of New Jersey is told by Mrs. Williamson. This society is only seven years old, but its value is demonstrated by the simple statement of what has been accomplished in that brief period.

Indeed, as one reads the narrative of these two societies, so full of sensible, judicious and practical suggestions in respect to the possible co-operation of official authority and private philanthropy, it appears strange that the example has not been more widely followed. Doubtless this clear summary of experiences will suggest to the citizens of other states the value of kindred organizations. The consideration, the tact, the devotion and the intelligence enlisted gratuitously in the public service are above praise.

Mrs. Charles R. Lowell of New York next discusses the question whether labor colonies are needed in the United States, describing the experiment at Plainville, N. J., from 1874 to 1888, contrasting it with kindred European colonies. Her conclusion is that labor colonies are not needed in this country to provide an opportunity to work, but that they are needed for training, and that to be successful they must be under public control.

The methods by which unskilled labor has been employed in various American cities are next described by Mr. Alfred T. White, President of the Bureau of Charities in Brooklyn, who presents in a few concluding sentences the results of a great deal of experience and observation.

The next paper is a discussion of "Registration," that is to say, of the practice so prevalent in charity organizations of keeping records of the relief furnished by the various co-operating agencies of any city. Those who are unfamiliar with this most important feature of modern charitable work in large towns, will here find the advantages of it explained and the objections answered in a paper prepared by Miss F. R. Morse of Boston.

Friendly Visiting is essential to the effective relief of the poor, and this work is probably better done in Boston than any where else in this country. The requisites of such service are set forth in a paper by Mrs. Roger Wolcott of Boston. She does not favor perfunctory or official visitations, like the Elberfeld system, nor even what is commonly known as the "district" plan, but she shows what good may be accomplished when an intelligent and kind-hearted person becomes the friend of one or two families and gains their confidence.

The next two papers are supplementary to one another and relate to a fundamental question, which has not yet received its final solution, at least in this country. The doubtful point is the extent to which public contributions, that is allowances from the treasury of a city or a state, may be given to charities that are supported and controlled by private individuals. Mr. Alexander Johnson, of Indianapolis, points out the difficulties which may arise in the mind of an overseer of the poor, when he is asked to co-operate with a private charitable organization, shows how these difficulties have been and may be overcome. Professor Warner (lately at the head of the public charities in Washington), opposes, with a vigorous argument, the policy of granting subsidies to private charities. "As a transition policy for growing communities and for new and developing varieties of benevolent work, it may have its place", but as a rule "all that can be said against subsidies in general can be said against this form of subsidies, and more, because here we have to deal with religious, medical and social sectarianism."

The second section of the volume before us is devoted to the papers which exhibit the practice of Continental States in the relief of the destitute. Mons. Valleroux, an advocate of Paris, presents an historical survey of French charities as administered in three epochs,—before the Revolution, during the Revolution, and since the Revolution. In the first period he says that private beneficence did every thing; in the second, the government assumed full control, even to the extent of prohibiting private charities; in the new régime, charity is exercised both by the public authorities and by individuals. At the present time, he notes a growing tendency to put every thing into the hands of the government, "and to replace the ancient form of charity, done by the faithful with their money and for the safety of their souls, by a charity done by the administration with the money of taxpayers and for electoral purposes." Mons. Valleroux adds a few pages upon Belgium, where the historical antecedents are akin to those of France. The present tendency of legislation is toward an alleviation of the burdens of the communes and the increase of those of the central government.

Signor Rossi discusses the charitable organizations of Italy, giving a brief historical preface, and introducing elaborate statistical tables, most of which are based upon the government returns of 1880. One of the most interesting parts of this essay is the analysis of the Poor Law of 1890. If the benevolence of the middle ages was almsgiving, modern charity is "work and education", and "the new law of Italy is imbued with this spirit."

A paper by Baron Von Reitzenstein of Freiburg, Baden, which was prepared for the first section of the Congress, is here presented in an abstract. This is far from doing justice to an extended and suggestive paper to which the student must be referred. It gives a comparative view of the methods of relief employed in different countries, and it praises the charity organization societies of England and America, while the Elberfeld system of Germany receives the highest place among existing methods, because it reserves to the township the administration of relief, while it also makes the freest use of the unpaid services of responsible private citizens.

This is a good introduction to the two papers which come next, on the Elberfeld system of poor relief, prepared by Dr. Theodore Münsterberg of Hamburg, and by Dr. Thoma of Freiburg. "Organization," says Münsterberg, "is the magic word which alone can solve these difficult problems." Good results depend "upon the consideration and treatment of each individual case." This principle of "individualization" was brought to life, forty years ago in Elberfeld, and now stands in Germany "as the type of a good and appropriate system of poor relief." After giving some details in respect to the methods of this system, the author states that other large and small cities, Leipsic, Dresden, Königsberg, Frankfort o. M., Cologne, etc., have adopted the Elberfeld plan, and he shows particularly the results attained in Hamburg, a city of 600,000 inhabitants, where some noteworthy modifications of the plan were adopted in 1893, with signs of great promise.

Dr. Thoma, reminding the reader that an overseer or visitor of the poor, has at most but four cases to look after, describes the success of the Elberfeld system in Freiburg, Breisgau, where it was introduced in 1879. While he admits that there are here and there weak points which come to light only in practice, he is persuaded of the excellence of his plan and believes that "the splendid results achieved since 1853 indicate that the system will hold its position in the future, not only in Freiburg, but in all Germany."

To these two papers a noteworthy addition is made by Herr Seyffardt, who is the presiding officer of the charity administration in Crefeld.

In reply to an inquiry from our colleague, Rev. John Graham Brooks, as to whether it was often found necessary for the central board to overrule the decisions of the local overseers or visitors, he admits that some such supervision is sometimes requisite, but he deprecates any action which would "weaken the very vital nerve of the Elberfeld system,— the moral responsibility of the overseer for the poor whom he has to take care of."

Two important communications came from Dr. Victor Böhmert, chief of the Royal Statistical Bureau in Saxony. In the first, he presents an argument for the organization of public poor relief and for the supervision of private charities, and he quotes as applicable to the large towns of Germany this remonstrance from the Board of Charities in Paris. It is instructive to notice that the evils so apparent in American cities are equally apparent under other forms of government and administration. These are the words quoted from Paris: "The same persons are relieved twice and oftener; much money and labor is squandered; the capital is overwhelmed with the destitute from the provinces and abroad, who can neither be properly relieved nor sent back to their homes." Dr. Böhmert briefly indicates the attempts made in Prussia and Austria to secure co-operation among the public and private agencies for the relief of distress; and in greater detail he brings out the experience of Dresden, the capital of Saxony, a city of 276,000 inhabitants. Here in 1880 the Elberfeld system was adopted. Four hundred official overseers were appointed, to each of whom not more than five cases were assigned. A society for the prevention of pauperism and mendicancy soon enrolled 4,000 members, and soon established a rent savings bank, workshops for residents and transients out of work, and an employment bureau. Finally the public authorities instituted a central bureau of information and called upon all the voluntary organizations "to join in the officially prepared plans and enter into closer relations with one another, as well as with the public relief." The particulars of this movement are very suggestive and instructive, but an American reader cannot fail to notice that similar action on the part of our municipalities, in the present unfortunate conditions of city government, would certainly be fruitless. At present we must strive for co-operation by the forces of moral suasion and not of city ordinances. Dr. Böhmert firmly believes in the co-operation of public and private agencies, and commends the experience of Elberfeld and Crefeld, "two model cities in the organization of poor relief."

The second paper of this able writer, describes the *Volkswohl,* or People's Club of Dresden, for the promotion of evening entertainments, lectures, concerts, refreshment rooms, homes for girls, homes for apprentices, and other agencies for the alleviation of the lot of those who are not impoverished, but are bread winners on small pay and without access to the comforts and recreations that are enjoyed by the more favored classes. This paper is an excellent concrete illustration of the way in which the life of those who are humble and destitute, but not downcast or forlorn, may be enriched and elevated.

A brief paper from Dr. Georgievsky of St. Petersburg gives a summary of the charitable works of the Russian capital, and indicates the inception of a scheme for introducing a special bureau of information, like that which has been successful in Dresden.

The third section of our volume is devoted to Great Britain. To the efficient co-operation of Mr. C. S. Loch, Secretary of the Charity Organization Society of London, the Chicago Congress is greatly indebted. By his kind mediation, papers have been brought together illustrating the opinions of men and women respecting charity organization in the metropolis. The experience of Marylebone, a west end district, where begging abounded and benefactions overlapped until better methods were employed, may be contrasted with a plain and unembellished tale of Whitechapel. Shoreditch, St. Olave's, and Islington also furnish memoirs. The London chapter concludes with a paper by Mr. T. Mackay on co-operation between the public and private charitable agencies. The aims of the society to secure reforms of the Poor Law are distinctly brought out. This section concludes with a similar series of papers from industrial centres,—Manchester, Rochdale, Bristol, Aberdeen,—and from Bradfield, a rural union, "where outdoor relief has almost reached the vanishing point, and where some of the principles of charity organization were formulated as far back as 1834, although there is no charity organization society."

The writers of the British papers are these: Mr. C. S. Loch, Rev. B. H. Alford, Rev. Dr. Bradby, Mr. C. N. Nicholson, Mr. C. P. Larner, Miss L. Sharpe, Mr. T. Mackay, Mr. Alexander McDougall, Miss Elizabeth Sturge, Mr. R. A. Leach, Mr. George Milne, Mr. H. G. Willink, Rev. Brooke Lambert, Miss F. C. Prideaux, Mr. B. Fleming and Mr. C. H. Wyatt.

To this review, which is intended to facilitate the perusal of a rather complex collection of papers, some conclusions may be added.

These essays embody the most recent observations, experience and suggestions of some of the ablest promoters of associated and organized charities in Great Britain, on the continent and in this country. They are written for the direct purpose of enlightening and helping the great hosts of benevolent persons who are so humane as to be devoted to the relief of the distressed and cast down, and who are at the same time so intelligent that they wish to work upon the best plans, with the greatest prospects of success. The careful study of these papers, with the critical and suggestive comments, may be commended to the members of charity organization boards throughout this country. The papers are undoubtedly technical, devoted to matters of fact. For this very reason they will well reward the careful reader. But it is hoped that another class of persons will be helped by this volume, the students of social economics and the writers of articles on pauperism and charities, and also the administrators of almshouses, workhouses and the other manifold establishments which deal with the unfortunate and neglected.

In the bestowal of charity and in the prevention of misery, the world has reached a new epoch. It is clearly perceived that some measures afford only temporary gratification to the giver and the recipient, while others promote the permanent improvement of character. Kind sentiments are not dulled by the study of facts. On the contrary, they are not most devoted to the poor who drop a quarter or a nickel in the hand of every beggar, but those who take pains to follow up each applicant, personally or through some vicarious friend, until the real needs of the applicant are discovered, and the measures of permanent relief are applied. "Not alms but a friend," "not doles but employment," "not help for an instant, but permanent relief," "not degrading but uplifting aid" are the watchwords of modern charity. Thus the needy are kept from becoming paupers, and those who are striving to do their best are helped upward and onward. Nobody doubts that material relief, food, fuel, clothing, must be given away, and in times of emergency, when hard times prevail, the bounty of the forehanded must be bestowed on those who are suffering. But one method will aggravate the disability; another method will remove it. Co-operation between all private and church associations, and where possible with the public authorities, leads at once to the careful registration of what is done and what remains to be done. Then comes personal investigation with sympathy and counsel for those who will accept it. Relief can always be secured when necessity is apparent. Those whose degradation and wickedness prevents their response to these elevating influences must pay the penalty of their habits and be placed in the almshouse or the infirmary or the prison.

Social reforms go very slowly. It is much easier for men to walk in the ways to which they are wonted than to mark out and traverse better routes. But by persistence reforms are accomplished. Science, which is only another word for exact knowledge, always has the worst of it in its first struggle with ignorance and prejudice; but it always wins in the end. Science has only just taken up the problem of relief. It has not yet made a careful survey of the situation. The subtle but pervasive influences of religion, legislation, administration, finance, custom, prejudice and tradition are factors, the significance of which is not fully understood, and will not be for generations to come. But meanwhile a good deal has been ascertained, and upon these ascertained facts very good working plans may even now be built. Human suffering can be greatly relieved, if it cannot be prevented or exterminated.

The human race seems likely to replenish its fallen ranks with a certain number of the incompetent, the inefficient, the weak-witted, the vicious. It will always be a problem how far such persons are to be dealt with by the severe methods of the law, or by the gentler agencies of kindness. But the denizens of the lower stratum are not nearly so numerous, nor so difficult to deal with, as those who have been fairly well off, but who now (it may be by their own faults,—it may be by the faults of others,—it may be by circumstances and conditions which human analysis cannot reveal), have entered on the downward road, or are in danger of making that fearful descent. These we can reach. Organization, co-operation, and friendly visitation are the general agencies which in each particular case of need will bring out the abundant resources of a charitable community.

THE PROBLEM OF CHARITY.

BY REV. FRANCIS G. PEABODY, PROFESSOR OF CHRISTIAN ETHICS, HARVARD UNIVERSITY.

The first and the most interesting thought with which one faces an assemblage like this, is the thought of the special quality and character of life which it represents. Other Congresses in this great series will gather here many of the world's most conspicuous names and most famous leaders, but the meeting which begins to-day does not depend on reputation or fame to fulfil its rich opportunity. It is not a Congress of those who are achieving great names for themselves or famous deeds for their country; it is the Congress of self-sacrifice, the meeting of those who are content to be unknown if only the world in which they live can be made better through their service. It stands for quiet self-forgetfulness and unassuming devotion. It is a Congress whose special motto might be that strange word of the Christian gospel: "He that would be the greatest among you shall be the servant of all." I see the delegates to such a Congress gathering here from all their different works of self-effacing benevolence; I see you coming from your asylums and reformatories, from your charity offices with their pathetic clients, and from your beautiful visitations in many a sunless home; and yet, as you meet, I see in your faces not the weary look of those who have borne with much hard duty, but the unaffected happiness which comes to men and women only through a life of generosity and service. I congratulate you on this great privilege of your chosen work. It is a great joy to feel sure, as you may, that in your vocation you are dealing with the central problems of this modern age.

The fundamental law of the naturalist is said to be the survival of the fit; the much more fundamental law of the charity worker is the revival of the unfit; and this revival of the fitness to survive in the degraded and outcast, the unfortunate and defeated in the competition of life, is the new science for whose transforming power the world is waiting, and whose ministers it is your happy privilege to be.

Many of you, no doubt, are so immersed by the details and routine of your daily life that you hardly realize the nature of this extraordinary spiritual movement in which you have your part. If in these days, as of old, the Master of the spiritual life should come to you in your daily work and say: "I was an hungered, and ye gave me meat; I was naked, and ye clothed me; sick and in prison, and ye came unto me," you would, I doubt not, answer with the same surprise which others of the old time felt: "Master, when saw we Thee hungry and fed Thee, or sick, or in prison, and came unto Thee?" No such great task as this is given to us to do. And yet, I think that He, who knew what was in man, if He could stand in the midst of such an assemblage as this with its devoted workers and generous administrators, would say, as He did of old, and with a deeper sympathy perhaps than He could feel in many a church that bears His name: "Inasmuch as you have done it unto one of the least of these My brethren, ye have done it unto Me."

To an audience thus composed I do not presume to come with any word of practical advice. I do not propose to offer counsel about charity to those who know her and serve her best. In all such questions of past history, or present administration, or future programme, we are soon to listen to wise counsellors of many nations and tongues, and I do not anticipate the themes which are to be presented to us in these busy days. And yet, before we separate to these varied deliberations, it may be well to pause a moment in the region of more general thoughts, and to give one quiet look together over the whole range of the work which you have given your lives to do. Let us for a moment stand off from the details of the task, as the artist now and then stands off from the work over which he lovingly and laboriously bends, that he may the better see how each part is related to one harmonious whole. Or rather, let us go up—as officers of an army go up—out of the smoke and conflict of the battle they are fighting, to some remoter hill-top where the plan of the whole campaign lies less obscured beneath their feet; and then, perhaps, we may go down again and take our places in our own special battalion, and fight our own little battle against social wrong, with a renewed and a more patient hope.

Standing thus together, then, at this point of general view, I wish to ask with you the most general question which our subject can possibly suggest: What is this phenomenon of charity, I enquire, in which each of us has his special part? What is the nature of this field of service which we see stretching away about us on so many sides? How can we define the work with which modern charity undertakes to deal? What is the problem of charity? That is the elementary question which I ask you to consider. And the first and most general answer to this most general question is this,—that the problem of charity in the modern world is a vastly larger thing than either the name or the history of charity might lead one to expect. For many centuries charity has occupied a very limited and special field. Its sphere has been bounded by the practice of alms-giving for temporary relief. It has needed but two elements; on the one hand, the tender-heartedness of the giver; and, on the other, the mendicancy of the receiver. The prosperous have felt ill at ease while their neighbors suffered, and have mitigated the lot of the unfortunate by doles of money or material support. That has been the work of charity. Let us recognize the beautiful impulse which such a work represents. It is an impulse which has its historical beginning with the birth of Christianity. Along with other mighty truths then entering into the world there came a new deal of human nature, a sense of value in each human soul for its own sake, however degraded or forsaken that soul might be. Out of the new faith in the Fatherhood of God flowed this other new faith in the brotherhood of men, and it made one of the great transitions in the evolution of the human race. The poor and rejected, the submerged of mankind, were regarded in a wholly new light when they were thus accepted as essential parts of the one body in Christ. The solidarity of the race became a practical belief. If one suffered, all suffered with him. The "Caritas" of the Christians gave a quality and color to human relations which classic civilization never knew. Poverty was no longer a bar to brotherhood. It was rather an invitation to the new fraternity. Through the custom and worship of the early Christian Church there ran this golden thread of practical faith, that relief of a brother's want was the first test of a true Christian life. And yet, beautiful as this new sense of value was, it brought with it its own new danger. The new zeal for charity came to demand the poverty on which to spend itself. The new philanthropy created a new mendicancy. Poverty grew by what it fed on. Mendicancy came before long to be a profession, and unproductive idleness to be one mark of a saint. The workers of the world had to support an increasing number of these sacred unemployed. There seemed to be little virtue in making one's honest living, but great virtue in giving alms to those who did not make their living. Thus Christian charity threatened to become, for the rich, little more than the sentimental atonement for prosperity; and for the poor a grave temptation to indolence, pauperism and fraud. How slowly any change was to come in this conception of charity is to be seen even now in many an Oriental nation, where alms-giving and mendicancy are still all that represent the work of charity, and where the notion of a Congress of scientific students to discuss the principles of charity would seem simply absurd. But in western Europe and the countries populated therefrom, partly through a better understanding of Christianity itself, and partly through the growth of the scientific spirit, a new range of opportunity has by degrees opened before the work of charity. The new forms of industrial life, the vastly greater social complexity, the increasing wealth, the manifold inventions and the democratic spirit of the last fifty years, have made for us a new social environment, with new problems calling for new rules of conduct. Just as our methods of trade have been transformed by steam and telegraph so that the sailing-vessel to the Indies and the merchant's letter of advice are now like ancient history to us, so modern charity has by degrees left behind it the elementary relation of giving and receiving, and has become a part of the great complex unity of modern life. It is not that the earlier ideal has had to be out-grown, but that it has had to be intelligently directed. We inherit from the past of philanthropy this great spiritual force, which has proved itself a natural part of human life just as the force of steam or of electricity is a natural part of the physical world, and we are now called, not to the repression of this impulse to charity, but to the discipline of it for the service of the world. The scientific mind fastens on this dynamic capacity of the love of man, just as it takes possession of the electric current and harnesses it to the machinery of modern life; and then this force of Christian feeling which in its undisciplined use threatened peril to society, for the first time discloses the many directions in which it can be profitably applied, and the larger service it was designed to do. Just as the electric flash is applied to its scientific service of heat and light and motion, so the instinct of charity, instead of being an occasional sentiment lighting up here and there the selfish world as an electric flash lights up a midnight sky, becomes the foundation of a science and is practically utilized in ways of which the earlier world did not dream. The old charity was simply the unreflecting expression of the sheer emotion of pity; the new charity directs this emotion along definite economic lines. The old charity satisfied the feelings of the giver by alms; the new charity educates the receiver to do without alms. The old charity was temporary relief; the new charity is continuous education. The old charity had but one way of expression; the new charity has a thousand channels. Often the most charitable course is that which has the least so-called charity about it. It is better charity to find work than to relieve want, better charity to teach a trade than to encourage the trade of mendicancy, better charity to provide stimulus for thrift than to make thrift unnecessary. The old charity met the drunken beggar on the street and gave him the means for his further degradation; the new charity meets a drunken woman on the crowded thoroughfare—as did one fair girl in one of our great cities not long ago—puts an arm round the poor bewildered wretch, passes down the busy street hand locked in hand, puts the woman to bed, and then watches the patient from day to day until at last the demon of drink may be driven out by the expulsive power of a new affection, and the body and soul of a human being may be saved.

Such is modern charity in its new summons to its larger work. And now I go on to ask once more for a definition of the conduct thus described. What is the problem of charity as it thus opens before us in this new breadth and scope? It is, I answer, a twofold problem—the same problem which meets any man who has at his command a special force with which to work, and a special work given for that force to do. Here, on the one hand, is this power of a great spiritual idea, and here, on the other hand, is the mighty mechanism of modern life with its awful contrasts, its pitiful competitions, its tragic incidents; and to apply this ideal to this reality—that is the problem of charity. It is, in short, ethics applied to economics; the sense of duty introduced as a dynamic into the complex machinery of the modern world. And what does this problem demand of charity? It demands two elements, each perfectly distinct and each absolutely essential. One element is the method of charity; the other is its motive. The method must be the method of business. It must not conflict with economic principles; it must conform to them and reinforce them. The motive, on the other hand, must be that of ethics—the same sense of brotherhood which once satisfied itself with almsgiving, precisely as active in its influence, but disciplined in its use. And here at once appear the two risks of modern charity—risks which are equally familiar and equally misleading. Charity may, on the one hand, be unbusiness-like, so that the motive lacks method; or charity may become wholly a matter of business, so that the method lacks motive. You may introduce the power carelessly, and then your machine will be shattered; or, you may trust to the machine to run itself, and then the machine will stop. Here, then, are the two cardinal principles of charity—its economic method and its supra-economic impulse. The one gives to charity its science, the other preserves to charity its sentiment. Science without sentiment is like an engine without steam; beautifully adjusted it may be in all its parts, but practically a lifeless structure. Sentiment without science is like steam which is unapplied to its proper work or unchecked in its expansion. The moment one considers the nature of any modern movement of charity, he sees these two opposite aspects of the case. Take, for instance, the work—now so widely and beneficently undertaken—of providing improved lodgings for the poor. The first test of such a scheme is, as you are well aware, the business test. To be wise charity, such an undertaking must, first of all, be good business; and the demonstration that security, privacy and cleanliness can be provided for the poor on strictly commercial terms and with business success, makes perhaps the most conspicuous triumph of scientific charity. But turn the same case round and the other side of the problem appears. What is it, after all, that makes such dwellings financial successes? It is that they express the thoughtfulness, considerateness and justice of those who built them. Put them in the hands of unscrupulous owners, and the very elements which induce good tenants to seek them—the safety, the privacy, the inducement to thrift—disappear, and with these disappears also the commercial advantage. Thus the motive which distinguishes such lodgings from the surrounding rookeries is, after all, what gives them their business. Philanthropy rightly directed has economic value. Wise charity is good business. Benevolence has a place in the modern industrial world. Or, observe again this same twofold character in your associated charities system : It has its mechanism, and that mechanism is disciplinary, negative, stern. But this machinery only performs its service that there may work through it the mission of the friendly visitor, bearing a moral motive to the poor. The two sides of this system are essential to each other. Take away the machinery, and the friendly visitor has no security from fraud; take away the friendly visitor, and the system tempts one to look for fraud and little else. The business method runs the risk of hard-headedness, and the kindly friend the risk of soft-heartedness, and the twofold nature of wise charity is the essential basis and strength of the whole scheme. In the book of the prophet Ezekiel there is a wonderful picture of the world of heaven. It was to him a vision of many and bewildering wheels. "The appearance of the wheels," says the prophet, "was like unto the color of a beryl, and their work was, as it were, a wheel in the middle of a wheel." But within these wheels, as the prophet saw them, there were living creatures, "and when the wheels went, the living creatures went, and when the living creatures had the spirit to go, the wheels were lifted up, for the spirit of the living creatures was in the wheels." It is a picture of the visions which so many earnest workers have to-day of the future of philanthropy. Wheels there must be, and wheels in the middle of wheels. But the wheels are set in motion by the spirit of life, and the spirit of the living creatures is in the wheels.

Such seems to be the problem of modern charity—a twofold problem, partly of economics, partly of ethics, its method of the head, its spirit of the heart. This problem, however, carries with it large consequences. From these two elements, thus defined, there issue a whole series of practical rules, to which wise charity must conform. Each principle involves several corollaries. There are some rules which are laid upon your charity by its demand for economic method, and there are some which flow directly from its moral motive, and together these corollaries make up the condition of all effective work. It is these working rules of wise charity which you, in your different sections, are now to discuss and reinforce in all their variety of application to the special theme which will engage you. But before we separate to these special tasks let us notice a few of the most elementary of such rules which thus proceed from the two principles I have laid down, first from the business method of charity and then from its ethical impulse. On the one hand there seem to be three most general demands laid on our charity by the principle of business method. And first among such I name knowledge— the comprehensive and scientific knowledge of the material with which one in charity has to deal. It seems to be rather an elementary truth to say that business method needs accurate and comprehensive knowledge. A man, for instance, who deals in cotton must first of all know all about the visible supply, the probable crop and the movement of trade in his special business. The person who deals in charitable relief in any community ought first of all, we should suppose, to know the real extent, the exact nature and the world-wide movement of his subject. Yet as a matter of fact, I ask you, how much charity has behind it this kind of comprehensive knowledge? Who knows, for instance, in his own city with entire precision the total dimensions of destitution, the types to be dealt with, their relative size and special character, the occupations represented, the total number of the unemployed, the cost of living and the migration into the city and away from it? Yet it is precisely such knowledge which would give to charity work, as it gives to all other business, its grasp and decision, and would insure for it public confidence. Charity guaranteed by knowledge is like the exploring of a dangerous country with a chart of it in your hands. It changes a series of incidental and fragmentary observations into a systematic campaign. Fortunately for us all, we have before us a monumental example of this kind of charity coast survey work in the elaborate and costly research of Mr. Charles Booth, of which, says the London *Spectator*, "it is not too much to say that it has done more to help the solution of the social problem than any man, or indeed any institution or agency of the time." To have the whole life of a great city laid down on a chart, with the nature of its population, its strata of social classes, and the various rocks, dangers and obstructions which hinder the movements of reform all plainly indicated—what help to navigation in such troubled waters can be greater than this? It is safe to say that among the many works of mercy which every city needs, there ought to be included this work which seems rather remote from mercy—the scientific survey of the field to which mercy is to be applied. Certainly here is a great opportunity in any city for an individual or institution with the money, skill and inclination for scientific sociology. Sooner or later every large town must be dealt with in this way, and it is an encouragement to think that hardly any other such investigation will ever have to be so vast or so complicated as this which has led the way.

I name next, as a second obvious demand of business method, the union of the forces applied to charity. Consolidation in business may have its perils, but it is essential to effectiveness in modern life. It is equally true in charity. Scattered and unrelated charities run two leaving many cases uncared for at all. The unworthy are tempted to risks,—the risk of duplicating many cases of relief, and the risk of deceive, and the worthy find themselves often beyond the technical purposes of these special institutions. A complete understanding among all who are concerned in charity is essential both to justice and to mercy. And this business aspect of charity has its importance for the givers as well as for the receivers. Scattered and disconnected organizations are enormously extravagant. There is more than one institution to-day in most of our large cities calling itself a charity, where at least half of the total income goes to support the person who collects the funds. The institution, that is to say, practically exists to give the collector a living, and the collector, pleading at your door for such a cause, weakens the plea which you ought to answer in another. Still further, this very multiplicity of demands makes many persons shrink altogether from their duty. They are never safe from these irregular appeals, their giving becomes unsystematic and spasmodic, and finally they begin to harden their heart toward the whole subject. It is interesting, therefore, to inquire whether even without consolidation there cannot be some "pooling of issues" in such affairs, and some degree of unity attained. The most important experiment of this kind has been tried for some years past in the city of Liverpool, and I trust that in some one of your sections attention will be called to this Liverpool system of collection. In the year 1873, as many of you, no doubt, are aware, the charity experts of that city noticed the accidental and unsystematic way in which relief was administered, and the subscription lists of 38 of the principal institutions and agencies were overhauled with the following surprising results. Out of a total number of persons in that city estimated at twenty thousand, who were believed to be able to contribute to charity, only 6,600 had subscribed to these 38 principal methods of help. The total number of subscriptions given under these 6,600 names was 19,000, or an average of three subscriptions by each giver. But, again, of the 6,600 names, more than 50 per cent. appeared but once, and 16 per cent. but twice. The bulk of the giving, that is to say, was done by about one-third of the givers. Indeed, out of the 19,000 subscriptions, more than 10,000 were made by about 1,000 persons. Half the habitual giving, in other words, to the charities of Liverpool was done by these 1,000 persons, the same names re-appearing on a great number of the lists. On the basis of these facts, a simple business method was proposed. The various charities were not united in administration, but they were induced to present their claims through one office and on one sheet. At the beginning of each year a list of charities, now amounting to ninety-eight, and guaranteed by a central committee as worthy of help, is distributed to some 15,000 citizens, and on this sheet each subscriber sets down and divides at his discretion his charity subscription for the year. From those who are well-disposed but unacquainted with any special form of charity, a general subscription is asked, to be distributed at the discretion of the central committee. Such a plan is, at any rate, economical, for it dispenses with a large number of collectors; and it is trustworthy, for it eliminates unworthy institutions. But should we expect it to increase the total giving? Would most people give more by sitting down at the beginning of the year and counting the cost, or by careless yielding to repeated demands? I think we might at first suppose that more could be got by repeated appeals and by good-natured, unsystematic giving. But such is not the teaching of the Liverpool scheme. The more business-like charity has been made, the more the public has been willing to invest in it. In 1877, the Liverpool Society received £4,641 for 18 charities; in 1892, it received £25,899 for 98 charities. I commend this business system to any large city. The charities of Boston are at this moment practically supported by a small fraction of those who are able to help them, and who, under judicious method, would be willing to help. In the case of any one of our more general societies, half the list of annual subscribers, and among them the largest givers, could probably be named with tolerable certainty without consulting the report. What we need is that broader constituency which, rightly approached, would be glad to do its share, but which demands a business method guaranteeing a reasonable investment.

I shall name but one other rule of good business method in charity, which follows directly from the knowledge of the facts involved and from the union of the forces engaged. It is, of course, the thoroughness of system pursued. On this subject, as on many others, the Germans, who are the system-makers of the world, have the great lesson to teach. The charity of a German town is a much more limited undertaking than with us, with much less pretentious institutions and much less extravagance; it is often perhaps too plodding, cautious and conservative in procedure, but it has at least the one distinguishing trait of thoroughness. I do not now enter into the discussion of the space-system of relief as usually employed in Germany, compared with the case-system, as customary with us. Indeed, I do not see why the advantages of both may not be welcomed. In some German cities, the public municipal relief is by space, each visitor covering like a sentinel his own little beat; while the voluntary and private charity is by case, with the adaptation and friendly interest a case-system permits. But what, much more than its system, concerns one in the German plan is the enlistment of enough competent people to make either system effective. Municipal charity with us scarcely pretends to use thorough and personal scrutiny, and even our associated charities system, with its adaptation of the Elberfeld model, has to depend on voluntary offers of assistance and is rarely equipped with an adequate supply of competent visitors. Germany, on the other hand, enlists each year by actual draft and selection an army of its most responsible citizens, and commits to them the oversight of the poor as a part of their good citizenship. A citizen of a German town serves his term in the friendly army of poor relief just as he serves his term in the army of national defense. This is what ensures a thorough business-like system. Conservative, plodding, over-official, may be German ways in charity, as in most other things; but they have at least the virtue of thoroughness. There is complete centralization of direction, and complete individualization of relief. I do not wish to be understood as desiring to see such a plan of compulsory charity service accepted as yet in our very large cities. Where cities are already grossly misgoverned and over-governed, I do not propose to favor an extension of the power of appointment. But there are, on the other hand, scores of towns in this country, of moderate size and of reasonably good local government, where a thorough system of visitation might be successfully maintained. It should be made a part of one's citizenship to be ready for a summons to serve one's town. We have long accepted the principle in the case of jury-service. Why should not the prosperous be trained to this other and much more fundamental function of public duty? It would be a blessing to many an empty—and to many an overcrowded life—to be thus called away from its own interest to this public and generous work; and it would be a fortunate town which, before its growth became unmanageable, should educate its rich citizens to do something for the needy, and its needy citizens to do something for themselves. Such a town would be free from many of the abuses and burdens of institutional charity. It would be a good town for the thrifty poor to live in, and a town which the undeserving would avoid. It would be a town in which prosperity brought with it responsibility for others, and poverty was sure of a chance of self-help. It would be a place in which Christian preachers could with better hearts select such texts as: "Bear ye one another's burdens," and "No man liveth to himself,"—a town over whose gates might be written: "The rich and poor meet together. The Lord is the Maker of them all."

I have dwelt long enough on the rules of conduct in charity which issue from its first principle,—the method of business, and now I have but a few moments in which, finally, to indicate the chief rules of conduct which issue from the other principle,—the principle of the moral motive. Here I turn from all these questions of method, and think of charity at its source, as an expression of the personal and moral life. The individual life finds itself incomplete until it passes over into union with the common life. That is the ethical statement of charity. Freedom finds its fulfillment in service. That is the motive of charity, and without such a motive charity becomes simply dead officialism and machinery. Misguided sentiment may pervert charity, but lack of sentiment kills charity. And into what rule of conduct does this fact open? Plainly into this,—that there is no charity which is not personal. You cannot be charitable by machinery. You cannot give in charity unless you give yourself. I do not mean that giving in money is never charity. Money may be the best expression you can offer of the self-sacrifice and sympathy which charity represents. But it is not charity because it is money; it is charity because it is money given with personal thought and discretion and feeling. Money given on other terms is not charity. It is sometimes self-display; it is sometimes self-deception, calling itself charity; it is sometimes a ransom for being let alone. Charity means that a person takes his own place by money or by work in the social organism of poverty; and no one else can take the place which belongs to you. It is a campaign in which you cannot buy a substitute. That is the first rule of conduct which this side of the problem dictates. The call of charity is a personal call.

And now, given this personal relation of life with life, how does it affect the conduct of each person involved? It operates in what is really a most curious manner, bringing to the two lives concerned precisely opposite effects. Its first effect on the receiver of charity may be described as the education of wants, and its first effect on the giver of charity as the simplification of wants. The two are easy to distinguish. What, on the one hand, is the first thing which you can do for the poor, when you put away charity as a matter of money and think of it as a matter of personal relationship? The first thing you can do is to start a new ambition. The first obstruction to your help is the fearful absence of wants which is so often found among the poor—what Lasalle called the "verdammte Bedürfnisslosigkeit"—the cursed habit of not wanting anything. The saddest feature of many degraded lives is their content. They do not care to be clean; they do not miss fresh air; they do not crave good food; and the first gift which the charity visitor can bring them is the gift of a new want. This good angel sweeps the room, or washes the child's face, or cooks the dinner; and at the next visit the mother has done these things herself, and the first step toward self-help is taken. But now turn the same story round and consider the giver's life. To him or to her there comes the opposite and no less blessed gift,—the simplification of wants. In the presence of poverty and human need other ambitions drop away. Self-indulgence and social folly grow simply uninviting. Life is simplified of its complexity. One is delivered from the absorbing problems which centre about one's self by this natural interest in others. The quality of mercy blesses those who give as well as those who take. Here are the two opposite gifts, a new ambition and a new simplicity, the multiplication of wants and the simplifying of them. I suppose that people must often wonder at the pleasure which others seem to find, or the peace of mind which they themselves discover in works of charity. Looked at as a practical undertaking, charity is often very dull and sometimes very disheartening. The poor are, as a rule, not very picturesque or very noble; they are often stupid and often unresponsive. Whence then comes the peculiar interest of such endeavor? Much of it comes, no doubt, from this simplifying of one's own wants, and much comes, on the other hand, from contributing to others a new ideal. It is a great joy to be delivered from one's self, to be freed both from idleness and from meagreness of life, to pass from the complexity of modern civilization to the simplicity of unambitious service. That is one source of great happiness. It is another great joy to find that you have the power to communicate a motive, that even so ineffective a life as you had supposed your own to be can do a better thing for another life than any money-help can do for it,—the imparting of a new ambition, the miracle of calling another soul to life, the joy of helping another human being not to lie down in mendicancy, but to rise up into self-help. It is with such charity to-day as it was with Peter and John at the beautiful gate of the temple where the lame man lay—as the passage says—to receive an alms. And Peter fastened his eyes on him and he gave heed, "expecting to receive something." But Peter said, "Silver and gold have I none, but what I have that give I thee. In the name of Jesus Christ of Nazareth, rise up and walk."

PROCEEDINGS
OF THE
SIXTH SECTION
OF THE
INTERNATIONAL CONGRESS
OF
CHARITIES, CORRECTION, AND PHILANTHROPY,

Subject:
CHARITY ORGANIZATION.

PROCEEDINGS.

International Congress of Charities, Correction and Philanthropy.

SIXTH SECTION.

FIRST SESSION, JUNE 12, 1893.—2 P. M.

The sixth Section of this Congress assembled at 2 o'clock P. M. The chair was taken at the request of the Committee of Arrangements by ROBERT WEEKS DE FOREST, Esq., of New York, President of the Charity Organization Society in that city. The Secretary was Professor R. MAYO-SMITH, of Columbia College, New York.

The CHAIRMAN, in calling the meeting to order, spoke as follows:

This is purely a business meeting, and when I say business meeting I mean that we meet here, not simply for the purpose of talking, but in order, if possible, to get at some results. As most of you know, we unfortunately have not the pleasure of the presence of the presiding officer of this particular section, President Gilman of the Johns Hopkins University. He is unable to be present here by reason of the closing exercises of his university, and it therefore devolves upon me to preside.

In the first place, I would suggest that the Secretary read a letter which President Gilman, as Chairman of the Committee of Arrangements, has addressed to the members of the Congress. This is properly the first act in the proceedings of what I will call for short the Charity Organization Section of this Congress.

The Secretary thereupon read a letter from President Gilman, dated Baltimore, Md., June 6, 1893, rehearsing the various steps that had been taken in making the arrangements for this section of the Congress, and in securing appropriate papers.

The CHAIRMAN.—That is the keynote to the plans of this particular section of this Congress. We aim, as you see by this letter, not simply to have a number of papers read here, amid all the distractions that must necessarily attend a meeting of this kind, and with all the other papers that are being read on so many different topics at the same time in the other sections of this Congress. We aim to print a volume, or volumes, which shall contain whatever there may be of permanent value in the papers presented to us. This Congress, as perhaps it is wise to remind ourselves, is an international one, and the front seat naturally belongs to those of our foreign friends who are present. Now, unfortunately, our foreign friends are very few in this meeting, and that is the reason why the majority of those who speak at our sessions will be Americans. But, on the other hand, it must not be supposed that because our foreign friends are not here in person they have not a deep interest in this Congress, and in this particular section of it. We have a large number of papers from different foreign countries, from gentlemen of the highest standing and reputation ; and those papers we propose to present in the printed volume.

We have for this particular sectional meeting the following foreign papers ; a paper on Charity Organization in Germany, by Professor Victor Böhmert, of Dresden ; on Compulsory Organization of Charities in Italy, by Dr. Egisto Rossi, of Rome ; on Scientific Charities in Germany, by Baron von Reitzenstein, of Freiburg ; on Relief of the Poor in Russia, by Professor H. Georgievsky, of St. Petersburg ; on Charity Organization in Relation to Voluntary Effort, by Rev. Brooke Lambeth, Vicar of Greenwich, England; and additional papers are promised. We have also a number of important communications from our own countrymen.

The first subject of our meeting is "The Demarcation of the Field of Voluntary Charitable Work." It is a pretty broad subject, and is intended to bring out a free discussion as to the proper scope of voluntary and governmental effort in charities in general, and, it may be, of the proper scope of charity organization societies in particular. The first paper will be from Levi L. Barbour, Esq., of Detroit, Mich.

The Chairman then introduced Mr. Barbour, who read his memoir on the subject above named.

After the conclusion of this paper a discussion followed, introduced by the presiding officer, Mr. De Forest.

The CHAIRMAN.—It is interesting to note that this first American paper brings out and lays down what may be called the fundamental principle of American charity, namely, that our charities should be supported by the people by voluntary contributions and not by the government with public funds. That is an important and broad doctrine, and I do not suppose it can be discussed as applicable to mankind in general. I suppose it is a question that must be discussed in relation to a particular country. Not long since I had the pleasure of showing a friend around our New York institutions, and I took him to see a hospital. He said : "Is this private?" "Yes, this is private." He seemed to be somewhat surprised. Then we went to an orphan asylum. That was private too. And so pretty much all the charitable institutions of the city were found to be private. He was very much amazed. It was a situation of affairs for which he was not at all prepared, and so absolutely different from that of similar institutions in his own country, that he could hardly realize it. So I am glad to have one of the keynotes of this discussion struck at such an early stage.

Now, the more this is a conversational meeting, the better. We have not, as I said, a definite program. We may read more papers, and we may read fewer papers. So far as the speeches are concerned, I propose, with your approval, to strictly enforce the ten-minute rule, and to reserve the right on the part of the Congress to make that ten minutes five.

If Dr. Warner will favor us, we shall be glad to hear from him on this particular topic.

Professor A. G. WARNER, lately of Washington, D. C., and now of the Leland Stanford, Jr. University in California, was then introduced to the Congress by the chairman. Professor Warner said:

I agree with the suggestion of the chairman that no particular principles can be laid down for the guidance of all countries in the matter under discussion. The experiment of substituting church relief for public relief at Glasgow showed what could be done under the management of a man like Thomas Chalmers. When the attempt was made to substitute public relief for church relief at Elberfeld, it was shown that that was the very system for a city in Germany at that particular time, the system of public relief there working much better than that organized and administered by the churches. In fact, the church relief system had broken down when the Elberfeld system was introduced and developed to its present condition. In Italy, also, private charities have recently been secularized. The great endowments for the care of the poor in Italy have been so badly administered that they have been secularized by the Italian government, and from private administration they have changed to public administration.

We find, looking at the matter historically, that, as a rule, churches and private associations have been the experimenters. It has been through the church or through private enterprise that new ideas in charity have been developed, and the community has been educated up to a position where it insists upon having large work steadily done. In the work of Bourbonnais on the charities of France he shows that almost all of them originated under church influence, and were, for a long time, administered by church officials, and then he exclaims against the present system where the bureaus administer even a very large share of the endowments left by private persons. He thinks that the transfer to the state of the function formerly discharged by the church is a usurpation, and that the power of administration should be restored to the church. These charities were instituted especially by the church, or by private associations under church influence. And yet it may be that the author is not right in saying—after it had been shown that a large block of charitable work must be done, and after the methods of doing it have been reduced to a routine—that it should then be left to private associations or enterprises.

Look at this country. What used to be considered the education of the deaf and dumb, the education of the blind, and farther back, perhaps, the care of the insane also—all these were first done by private enterprise.

It was through the influence of these private enterprises that the community was educated up to the point where it insisted upon having these blocks of charity done; but that point being reached, a steadier income, a firmer administrative grasp, and a more general and systematic arrangement of the work were necessarily called for. Hence the control passed from the hands of the private inventors of the new charities to the hands of the State. At the present time, where the hospitals become very large, where the orphan asylums become very large, (as they have in the places of which mention has been made), it has been found that while the management remains in private hands, the money frequently comes from the public coffers, and the constant tendency is to transfer the work to the public management. For instance, the administration of outdoor relief in European countries is found to be well done by the local communities under a system by which a large number of unpaid officers are brought into the work. In this country it is found that we cannot administer outdoor relief in such a manner without the degradation of the poor and the corruption of local politics. It is a question, then, of administrative or governmental skill on one side, and on the other of the possibility of collecting from individuals the money necessary to support large charities, when they have developed to such an extent that it requires a large and constant revenue to maintain them. The function of private enterprise in charitable work will, as it seems to me, remain this: if the state is large and opulent, it can do something after you say it must and show it how; but it is not inventive, it is not progressive, and it is to private enterprise that we must look for the doing of new work. The public and private officers of charitable institutions react upon one another through mutual supervision. In America public officials very seldom supervise private charities, and yet I think it is a plan we shall have to come to, (as the European countries have), when the incomes are very large. The possibilities of abuse are so great, that public officials will have to supervise private work, and then, returning that compliment, private enterprises like the state charitable organizations of the country can return the debt by supervising the public institutions and seeing that they are wisely administered.

The CHAIRMAN.—We should all like to hear a few words from Professor Henderson of the University of Chicago.

Professor CHARLES R. HENDERSON was then introduced to the Congress, and he said:

I should like to emphasize (though it would be impossible to give added emphasis to it) the forcible presentation of a thought contained in a sermon delivered yesterday by Dr. Gladden. The whole problem of charity organization is to bring together the person who can help and the person who needs help. Mr. Rosenau, in a paper read at the University, at one of the dinners of our Associated Science Clubs, gave a chart in which he represented all those who needed help, all those who come before the charitable organizations, and then finally those who were not remanded to permanent institutional help, but were brought into individual contact with some benevolent person. I should like to see this chart printed and published because of its suggestiveness. If this principle of individual helpfulness were carried out it would modify, though it would not necessarily abolish, in this country official outdoor relief. Anyone can see that the present system is as far as possible from that enunciated by Dr. Gladden yesterday. Let any of you go to the offices of the county or township trustees and notice that long, mournful row of paupers coming for relief, and you will see that, though they are very near the embrace, they are really as distant as the sky. Never touched, spoken to, or befriended by word or look, but in the coldest possible official way thrust apart from those who would be glad to do all they could, and who could easily be led to do them good. But this is not only true of official outdoor relief. It is also true of our church charities, which are almost as much open to this objection as the official outdoor relief.

Churches, on the whole, are doing very little in the way of giving money in this country. Most of the relief of the pauper class comes through the officials. Of course many localities may be named as exceptions, but I think this is the general rule.

We have waited fifteen years for a promised book by Herbert Spencer, and now that it has arrived it is simply "a small mouse" indeed. Perhaps I have not comprehended him; but if I understand him in his book on Positive Benevolence, it is about the most negative thing I ever read. He says the only thing that we are obliged to do by the law or by duty, is to help some one who may come across our path and be in need. The people, for instance, in the West End of London are the people who are able to help the poor. The people in the East End are those who most need assistance. The people of the West End could say: "I never meet these people and it is no part of my duty to go and find them." So there are a great many people who would be neglected. But it is undoubtedly true that under the system of absolute individual help a great many people would give indiscriminately.

The desire to do good, to help the unfortunate, to assist the hungry, is a real social force, something that can be counted on, and people are going to give—if not wisely, they are going to give nevertheless—for the hunger of the world is too deep to be assuaged by anyone. There remain one or two methods in the immediate future. One is the Elberfeld method and the other the association of charities. I understand that the latter method is before us this afternoon. The Elberfeld method may at some time be applicable to our conditions. It certainly is not in the immediate present; but I think the societies already organized according to this method are showing that it is possible to pass the bounds which now limit us. Now in Chicago, Buffalo, Detroit—in nearly all the large cities, in fact—how many people are aided? A great many friendly visits are made, it is true, some more successful than others. But we shall never reach the ideal until we have given to one person as many of the poor as he can befriend in the best sense of the word—following up the work carefully, watching month after month, and year after year, until out of hopelessness and wretchedness have come prosperity and happiness. It is a long, weary road. We must remember that for centuries these people have been going down and the weight of centuries of heredity is upon their shoulders. We cannot befriend them by simply flinging a gift to them in passing. We must do the best we can, until, perhaps, a wider outlook may open in the years to come and the government be induced to use its instrumentalities to assist in the work.

The CHAIRMAN.—Following in the line of Dr. Warner's address we are interested in noting historically the development of methods in charitable work. In the medieval period nearly all charities were church charities. But a change has taken place in almost all European countries, where now almost all charities have become state charities. Even in England a large part of the charitable relief is given through the government, by taxation. Now we Americans ought to stand in the forefront of what may be called the modern tendency. It is interesting to note that in our own country, at the present time, the strongest charities, those that have (if I may use the words) the greatest life, are those which are not connected with the government or with the church. I do not mean that those who take part in our charities are not religious people or church members. On the contrary, most of them are members of the various churches; and I do not think it is arrogating too much to ourselves to say that the most active, aggressive persons in the charitable societies at the present time are members of the churches. But the movement is, nevertheless, strictly undenominational.

The gentleman who will next address you on this subject is Dr. J. W. Walk, of Philadelphia.

Dr. J. W. WALK, Secretary of the Society for Organizing Charity of Philadelphia, was then introduced to the congress by the chairman. Dr. Walk said:

As an old member of the Conference, with which I have been connected for eleven years, I desire to ask your indulgence if I should transgress for a minute or two the length of time allotted me, for this reason. It will be of no value if I give you propositions without the arguments by which they are supported; but I fear I cannot do that in the brief time at my disposal. It is of the very first importance that we should have clear ideas of the matter in hand before we begin to work. Much of our work is worthless, because we go off with the idea in a hurry, without due consideration.

Now, there is a classification, to which I wish to call attention at the start, of the whole field of effort for the dependent portion of the population. It is being adopted by many different societies. By this classification the dependent poor are divided into delinquents, defectives, and destitutes. Now, what is the demarcation between charity and official care? What is the demarcation between charity and the control of these three classes?

First, as to the criminal, the vicious, and the insubordinate. If government means anything, it means protection from crime. As John Stuart Mill said: "Civil government exists to resist force and to prevent fraud." Governments were first instituted to resist encroachment from the outside. When they are not in danger from this source, they must resist encroachment from enemies on the inside. So it seems to me that the government should take care of its criminals and insubordinates, the latter being delinquent children. I do not think any one, by private means, should attempt to set up a house of correction, and I doubt very much the expediency of giving police powers to private societies, like the Society for the Prevention of Cruelty to Children. It would be better for the government to do that work as it supervises murder and theft. It is a risky thing to give police powers to private societies. There is one possible exception—that is with regard to delinquent children. The children's aid societies of Philadelphia and other cities, are trying now to educate delinquent children, who were formerly placed in reformatory schools, and they endeavor to improve and save them by family influence. It is an experiment. I wish it well. But there are a great many difficulties in dealing with bad boys and girls in families; there is danger of their doing more harm than good. There is one function, it seems to me, that private charity has in regard to these penal, reformatory institutions—that is the function of voluntary inspection, as pursued by the State Charities Aid Associations in New York and elsewhere.

Now, as to the next class,—the defectives, including the blind, the deaf-mutes, the feeble-minded, the epileptics and the inebriates. As far as the care of the blind, deaf-mutes, and feeble-minded goes, during the period of training in childhood and youth, I think that should be taken out of the field of charity and placed among the educational endeavors of the country. My thought is that the government should give to every child a fair public school education. Ordinarily it gives it in the public schools; but if the child be blind, a deaf-mute, or feeble-minded, and is not suited for instruction in the public schools, then instruction ought to be given in schools suited for the purpose. When we come to the adults, many of them become self-supporting, and, after proper training, are no longer charges on the state. Then, as regards those who are not self-supporting. The question is whether the care of them should be private or by the state. When we come to the insane, again, I believe we should have them cared for by the state or the county—by the government in some form, because, after all, the insane are put inside the institutions more for the good of the community than for their own sake. We must not forget this even though no charge of crime attaches to them. The same general principles apply to inebriates and epileptics.

I come last to the destitutes, including the aged poor, the infant poor, the sick poor and the wounded poor.

Here is a great field for organized charity, for church, individual and society work. I believe this is the field to which we should ultimately confine ourselves, and from which we should ultimately exclude the government and the state, for two reasons. First there is the ethical reason, that it is not, under any proper theory of government, for the best interests of the people to have the state take care of these classes. Mere destitution has no claim on the government. There is no reason why money should be taken out of your pocket to give to me, simply because I am destitute. I believe that is a field for Christian sympathy, but not for government aid. If the charitable effort of the country were concentrated upon this class of dependents, we could soon care for them all, and it is in caring for this class that state aid is real relief work. The state can properly care for the criminals, the vicious, the insubordinate, and the defective, but when the state begins to care for destitutes, trouble begins.

There is one class of the sick whom the state should provide for—not for their sake, but for ours. Those are the sick with contagious diseases. In case of cholera, for instance, the state may take them, not for their own sakes, but for the safety of the community.

Outdoor relief, where given by the state, is wrong in principle and pernicious in practice. It should be abolished.

I would like to supplement the facts given by Mr. Smith of Buffalo, last night, to the extent of saying that a comparison in Buffalo of twelve years with outdoor relief, with twelve years without outdoor relief, showed a saving of $700,000, and, wonderful to relate, a saving also of $400,000 in indoor relief. So there was a saving in twelve years of over a million dollars. And to-day, in the institution of which I have charge, we have fewer paupers than we had fifteen years ago—almost entirely due to the abolition of outdoor relief. But I hope for something more. I hope the day will come when private and associated charities, separate from governmental support, will take up the indoor relief question. If we would center our efforts on this one subject, I believe the time would soon arrive when we could substitute for madhouses, hospitals, and asylums, institutions supported and maintained by churches, by private societies, and by individuals.

The Chairman next introduced to the congress Miss Zilpha D. Smith, General Secretary of the Associated Charities of Boston, who said:

I should like to say a few words on the subject of churches and charities. It is more sad than stupid to hear people connected with churches say they should start a certain charity because others have done so. There is an institution in Boston in whose prospectus appears the statement that it was started because the denomination under whose name it operated had not previously undertaken any large benevolent work. Of course such a charity is rotten at heart. Fortunately, all church charities are not of that character. The church that is made up of both rich and poor finds its way easy. But most of the churches to which we belong, I fancy, are of another class. They are made up of people who are able and willing to take care of themselves. If they want to help others, they must go outside their church connection to do it.

Mr. A. W. CLARK of Omaha, was introduced to the congress, and spoke as follows:

I wish to say a word in regard to omitting in our work the criminal classes. This is the first time I have heard such a clear statement of that view, and my own experience is that this would be a great mistake. My experience in the Rescue Home has led me to believe that a large number of these brothers can be rescued, and that the officials are not working in the direction of saving them. During the winter——

Dr. WALK.—I do not want to be understood as stating that the function of punishing criminals is a state function. I did not mean that a man, after he gets out of prison, should receive state assistance, but that the function of correcting his crime, putting him in prison and training him, is a function of the state. After he gets out of prison we ought to help him.

Mr. CLARK.—Well, perhaps I misunderstood. One night I asked two of our detectives to examine those that we had as lodgers. One hundred and seventy or more were there that night, and we had fifteen known to be criminals. One of them had been for eight years in the Michigan State prison. We have succeeded in rescuing a large number of those people during the winter. A short time ago a man was locked up. The police were after him. I said: "You let me have him for forty-eight hours and if I can't control him during that time you can take him." The police consented. The man was saved from going to the city jail, and now is in a good position in our city.

On the point of children, I do not believe it is an experiment. In Omaha and other places it has been shown that many of these boys can be saved by our means, by placing them in homes, instead of leaving them to the state.

Professor E. W. BEMIS of Vanderbilt University, (Tenn.) was asked to speak, and, being introduced, spoke as follows:

In this particular department of work I have made no discoveries, and there is little I can say. I would rather your time should be taken up by those who have made original studies. I have great interest in this work. I think the state is doing a great deal in preventive measures; but when it comes to the actual appearance of the evil in adult life, I have no doubt that private charity must do it through organized effort.

Mr. A. O. CROZIER of Grand Rapids, Mich., was next introduced, and said:

I presume I belong to one of the youngest charity organizations in the United States—an organization effected only a few weeks ago at Grand Rapids, Mich. I have not been with you a great while, but I find that my old-fashioned notions are very fast disappearing; and I fear, if I sit here much longer, I won't have any of them to take back.

We used to have in Grand Rapids (where, by the way, we spend $35,000 to $40,000 a year for outdoor relief in a city of less than 100,000 inhabitants,) a splendid idea, that to give money in charity was the end of it. For years we had a thanksgiving demonstration of the charity people, and we used to advertise in the papers that we would practice charity upon all applicants on that day. Of late years we have been very much surprised at the number of applicants. We supposed there were very many people there who needed relief, and at our last Thanksgiving demonstration of charity the line was half a mile long. I am a member of the Gates Committee of the new society. They have been holding meetings in our offices, and they have been going through the books. They investigated our work, and on the Gates Committee we are cutting off nearly 50 per cent., and we are fortunate in having a Poor Director who listens to our advice. We elect a Poor Director and put him under bonds for the conduct of his office. Then the board of aldermen turn around and appoint a Poor Committee, and that committee takes from the Poor Director almost all his duties, especially that of purchasing supplies. The chairman of the committee told me the other day that a member of the committee came to him and said he had a friend who was running a grocery store, and he had been at him a good deal to get some orders from the city. He said: "If you haven't any objection, just give me a little order." The chairman said he had no objection, and supposed he was going to give him an $8 or $10 order. Under that license that member bought $300 or $400 worth of groceries that cannot be used inside of four years. Then he at once turned around and O-K'd the bill, and that binds the city, for any member of the poor committee can O-K a bill. Now, if this new work is carried out the way you gentlemen propose, I fear it is going to take away from us a great deal of the strength and interest of the various charities in that city. But we are very green and we have much to learn, and we are glad to be dropped into a furnace of this kind, where we can be warmed up and dried out so soon.

Miss RICHMOND, General Secretary of the Charity Organization Society of Baltimore, was introduced and spoke as follows:

The question of the demarcation of private and public charity is after all a question of expediency, and I cannot formulate any one great moral principle that is involved in the division of the work. If it is simply a question of expediency, do not let us get into the habit of feeling that private and public charities are in any sense opposed to each other. I think that is a possible tendency, and a very fatal one. It has occurred to me that one function of a charity organization society may well be to create an intelligent public interest in public charities. No public charity can be a success without that. Public officials are just like other people. Unless they have some one interested in what they are doing, their interest flags. There is no way of getting at what public charities are for and what they do, and do not do, so promptly as to take an intelligent citizen and interest him in the welfare of some particular family, and then let him touch our public charities from the relation of our public charities to that family. Take an intelligent man and give him a family, where there are two or three small boys. He cares for the public schools then as he never cared before. He cares for every public institution that affects the lives and welfare of those boys. That is a form of education which seems to me most practical and efficient, and one that the charity organization societies still have to develop. We are doing it, but not to the extent we should. Another question arises: Aren't we getting ourselves into the same difficulty that the clergymen are in? They say, "All your charities are springing up and you are taking away our workers; we are losing in concentration." You can't blame them. They want to keep their people about them and make their churches powerful. It is natural; but until a man rises above that, he is not the useful citizen and Christian that he should be. A charity organization society is only doing the right thing when it puts its members into right relations with every other charity in the community, public and private.

The CHAIRMAN.—We will hear from the president of the first charity organization society in the country, Mr. T. Guilford Smith of Buffalo.

Mr. T. GUILFORD SMITH of Buffalo, N. Y., was then introduced, and said:

It is very cheering, indeed, to see so much interest in the abolition of outdoor relief. I said the same thing last night, and some gentlemen came to me afterwards and asked me if I meant public or private outdoor relief. Of course I meant public outdoor relief. I have in my pocket a valuable paper, which will be read. I believe, at one of our public sessions, from the clerk of the Whitechapel Board of Guardians in East London. We know what Whitechapel is. We know it is one of the worst parts of the East End, and we know what the gulf is between the East and West end of London. This paper shows how outdoor relief ought to be curtailed, how it can be, and why the results are so gratifying when it is curtailed. In the city of Buffalo we are hoping that the millenium may arrive, when we shall have no outdoor relief. Mr. Kellogg, in his report in 1873, endeavored first to have the municipal government insist that all outdoor relief, and every other relief by the city, should be subject to investigation. The mayor at that time said he did not know about soap, candles, groceries and shoes, but he would be quite willing that coffins should not be given out without investigation. That was the first ordinance, and coffins became by law subject to inspection and all that. We did find one or two cases where people applied for coffins, who did not have any corpse, but wanted to speculate in coffins. That led to the passage of an ordinance under which all outdoor relief is now subject to police investigation. As we think two men are always better than one, the Charity Organization Society of Buffalo had an ordinance passed, according to which the mayor sends to us every morning a copy of all the applications for outdoor relief. We send our agents to supplement the work of the city agents and the result is that sometimes there is a difference of judgment as to whether the relief is wise or unwise. We keep a carefully tabulated statement every day as to how much money the city has in its hands; and we take pleasure in showing the authorities how much, in our opinion, has gone wrong. In due time we hope by this method to get outdoor relief absolutely abolished. But it is a long, hard row, and whether we shall be able to accomplish it or not, I do not know. I think the whole charity organization movement cannot do better than to keep on preaching that doctrine until the desired object is attained.

A DELEGATE.—I wish to call attention to the immense amount of public charity in this country which seems utterly ignored by the charity organizations. It is practical charity to a large degree. I refer to our national pensions. I know they are often given in order to get grocery bills paid. Merchants will secure a pension for a man in order to secure payment of the debts due them. Many such instances have come to my attention; and I wonder if any attempt has been made to scientifically investigate the matter. It is going to be an important matter in the future.

Mr. ANSLEY WILCOX of the Charity Organization Society of Buffalo, N. Y., was next introduced to the congress, and said:

On behalf of Section 1, of this congress, I feel personally repaid, and I am sure all those who have been drawn here this afternoon have been repaid for the loss of our own sectional meeting, or the postponement of it, by the opportunity afforded to listen to the thorough and brilliant discussion on this subject which has taken place here. It has been opened up well. The discussion this afternoon has prepared the way for the papers which will be read this evening, and papers which will be presented in Section 1 tomorrow morning. This evening papers will be presented on the question of the proper boundaries of public and private relief, and upon the subject of poor relief in large cities, and questions of that kind, which are directly in line with the discussion this afternoon. Tomorrow morning we shall have a paper, which has come to us only to-day, by Baron von Reitzenstein, of Germany, and which I know will prove of great interest. I ask that this meeting adjourn to tomorrow morning in order that the members may have an opportunity to listen to this paper of Baron von Reitzenstein.

The Section then adjourned.

SECOND SESSION, JUNE 13, 1893.—2 P. M.

JEFFREY R. BRACKETT, ESQ., of Baltimore, in the Chair.

The CHAIRMAN.—I have been asked to tell you that of the four papers put down upon the program, two by your leave, will simply be read by title, namely, the paper on the Elberfeld system, by Dr. Thoma, Burgomaster of Freiburg, and the paper on friendly visiting, by Dr. Münsterberg, of Hamburg. We have left a paper on friendly visiting by Mrs. Roger Wolcott, of Boston, and another paper on the same subject by Miss Prideaux, of London. We all agree in this, that conference meetings are much more interesting when but few papers are read and we have the opportunity of hearing short, terse speeches from a number of practical people. Therefore, by your leave, we shall read one paper and part of another, and then we shall have several brief addresses by various ladies and gentlemen. The meeting will begin with a paper on friendly visiting by Mrs. Roger Wolcott, of Boston, to be read by Miss Frances Smith, of Boston.

Miss Smith then read that paper. At its conclusion the Chairman said:

Dr. Ayres, Secretary of the Charity Organization of Cincinnati, has very kindly consented to read Miss Prideaux's paper and to call our attention especially to those points which apply to work in American cities.

Dr. Ayres then read the paper prepared by Miss Prideaux of London on friendly visiting.

Dr. AYRES.—I had the pleasure recently of reading a very full account in the English papers of the Charity Organization Conference held in London on the 20th of May last, in which all the charitable organizations of Great Britain were represented, and they had a three days' conference, holding morning and evening sessions, and visiting institutions in the afternoons. The papers were upon investigation and registration and the work of charity organization committees. One gentleman from one of the district committees of London described at great length the details of registration. I imagine that their registration is done with more system and with greater care than in many American cities. Another described in great detail the principles of investigation. I remember this point, that they should inquire of the neighbors and of the parish priests, and in the retail stores, and of the relatives of the family in other cities, as well as at home, and so on, all as a part of the regular investigation to be gone through in every case. I suppose that some of our societies in this country take this much care, but others do not. At any rate, in London this part of their work is very carefully done. But when I came to the friendly visiting, I was rather surprised to see that the idea did not seem to take; at least, the ideas which I thought were strong, from an American point of view, were not marked in the newspaper with the word "applause," as were so many others. The only time that I saw "applause" at the end of a remark relating to friendly visits was after a remark that investigators and other members of the committee should visit the poor in their homes for the sake of getting the chief information from the family rather than from neighbors, retail storekeepers or anybody else.

I feel that the missionary work in London has been very well carried out, but the spirit of friendly visiting, as we have it in this country, is not so prevalent as appears to be illustrated in this paper by Miss Prideaux.

That leads me to one other remark. There is in friendly visiting a vast power. It arouses, as somebody else has said, a great longing on the part of all who engage in it to do something for their poorer neighbors. My remark is, that if the charity organizations do not undertake this service, there will be a thousand other agencies that will take it up, for it is a force that cannot be neglected. In London we see that the Charity Organization Society did not take up friendly visiting and we find that other societies are taking it up. It cannot be neglected, and so, if the Charity Organization Society in any city in this country do not take up this great earnest work then other people will. It is true that in some places such friendly visiting through charity organization societies has met a certain antagonism from churches which have not understood the movement. The good people of the churches do not enlist as visitors because their pastors do not teach them to do so, and the pastors do not teach them so because the theological seminaries have not so instructed them. And if we can take the opinions of two leading professors in two leading schools of Chicago, who have co-operated in this Congress, then we may be sure that to the seminaries we must look for influences which will eventually lead the church members into this work.

The CHAIRMAN.—I think that you will all agree with me that we cannot spend our time better than in listening to short, practical talks by practical people. We must all agree on the desirability of friendly visiting. I don't think there can be any question about that. If I may make a suggestion, what we most need is to be helped by being told how far the charity organization societies of this country are living up to their motto, "Not alms, but a friend." I do not think we should be pessimistic as to this branch of charity organization, but I do feel (if you will allow me to express my own opinion, derived from a short experience on that side of our work) that it is not as plain sailing as on the other side, the side of official work. The "not alms" part is much easier to fulfill than the "friend" part. Now let us have some practical definite suggestions as to how we can get visitors and how we can keep them and how we can make them do their best work.

You must allow me just one moment more, for I want to speak of the great responsibility which an organization assumes, when, in print, before the public, it says, "Turn over to us the cases that deserve relief."

We heard last night, in a remarkably eloquent and profound discourse, from Mr. Robert Treat Paine, that he did not see how some cities got on without friendly visitors, and I know we shall all be delighted if Mr. Paine, one of the original advocates of charity organization in this country, will tell us something of the work in Boston, how they have gotten large numbers of good visitors there and the methods which they use.

Mr. ROBERT TREAT PAINE.—I wish I could answer the question. It is a perpetual struggle. We have about 800 visitors in Boston and they are passing out of the ranks all the time and there is a steady occasion to fill up the gaps. Just how it is done you must ask Miss Smith. It is always easy to turn over to somebody else the reply to hard questions. If I may say just one word, our friendly visiting began and the work was promoted chiefly by two ladies who started the preliminary organization of "co-operative visitors" with a degree of fine enthusiasm that was really wonderful. It was made social, it was delightful, instantly the thing grew, and growing spread, and in spreading has prospered. We must bear in mind that you must get visitors in different parts of the city and I do not see how you can enforce upon them rigid and cast-iron rules. We have not had many rules in Boston, but the idea has been to allow each conference to grow up in its own natural healthy way. Some of the conferences have meetings in the evening at the house of a member where its friends meet on a certain evening. The executive committees meet there and the visitors come and talk over their cases. They soon have very friendly relations with each other and it is very easy then for a lady to bring in one friend this month, and another friend the next month, and so the conference will grow and spread. Conferences rise and fall like the tides. Sometimes there will be an emigration of some of the ladies to Europe and then there is a desperate struggle to fill up the ranks. It is a perpetual effort, and I am going to say with just a little bit of candor that it is not perfectly sure that any particular ward or small city will be able to keep up the energy of friendly visiting which it may start with. It is absolutely sure that it ought to be kept up. If the energies fail in one direction or at one time, they must be replaced and re-invigorated by new blood and by new energy and by new methods, as soon as possible.

I have sometimes said that this friendly visiting is a vast evolution, and that just a little bit before the millenium comes we shall have something better; that is, if we can have the whole community educated up to these ideas of friendly visitors, so that when they know of any family that is in need, the first person that learns of the distress will go there in a patient, thorough, persistent and devoted way, there will not be so much need of an organization. Yet that is something coming in the millenium, and it is a long way off.

One of the questions that comes up with us is, how far church organizations should work with or should supplant friendly visitors in the different wards. Now, in my own church in Boston, Trinity Church, the largest Episcopalian church in the city, there was an organization of friendly visitors which grew up there, and it drew a great deal of the visitors' life blood right out of my own conference (Ward 12) and transplanted it to the church organization, because the ladies preferred to work with the church rather than with the conference. And yet the church work was done miserably. I did not go to the church meeting, but my wife did and a number of other persons. But they did not happen to have any brothers who put into that work energy enough to give the work thoroughness and scientific foundations. So it was a failure, and the result is that the church visiting society has vanished and the conference is left. We shall get those same ladies into the conference before long. Thus I am trying to convey the impression that there is not a uniform, cast-iron method, but a plan must be adapted to the circumstances of each ward and city and must be made thorough. Ladies (almost nine-tenths of the visitors are ladies) must bring in their friends, one after another, and get them to see that the friendly visiting of the poor is a consecrated work, and besides, that there must be a great deal of friendly pleasure put into it. Some of the pleasantest relations of social life in Boston cluster around these little groups of friendly visitors in the different wards. This gives them a great power. I do not see why such relations should not always be relied upon.

Mrs. GLEN WOOD of Chicago.—I would like to ask whether your friendly visitors are gathered from among the young people, the unmarried ladies and gentlemen, and I would like also to ask if they are all ladies, or ladies and gentlemen who do this visiting.

Mr. PAINE.—There are men, but not one in ten. The men are very busy. Sometimes you may get a good visitor for a year or two and then he drops out ; but with ladies there is not so much danger of this. Young ladies come in and, of course, families are selected where a young and inexperienced lady can do just the right sort of work. We have a great many young ladies and a great many, of course, of middle age.

Mrs. M. A. HOPKINS.—We have what we call a Rector's aid society in our church. He gives us certain names and a certain district to visit, and we report every week to him, and the society has been very successful indeed in a social and friendly way. We report everything we do to him because we meet together and are sent out from the church.

The CHAIRMAN.—Mr. Paine has told us something that makes us men ashamed of ourselves and feel that we should take a back seat in this conference ; so I think it would be well to hear from one of the ladies in Boston where so many friendly visitors are engaged. Will Miss Birtwell of Boston tell us something of the work there and of her ideas about it?

Miss BIRTWELL, of the Associated Charities, Boston.—I will only speak of a few details. Life is made up of little things and the success of the work in our district always depends more or less upon practical common sense brought to bear upon what might be called comparatively petty details.

One of the most difficult things, I think, that the salaried agent has to contend with is the introduction of these young ladies, these inexperienced visitors, to the work. She is placed in a position of the teacher who has a new pupil every week and cannot give individual attention to that pupil, so as to bring her up to the standard of the rest of the class. That is really necessary ; and here is a place in which the Executive Committee and the experienced visitors can be of very great value. It is my custom, when I have a new visitor, to give her as much time and attention the first week or two as I possibly can. Then I am likely to invite her to one of the meetings of the Executive Committee and I introduce her to all the members of the committee and I watch very carefully to see which member of the committee she takes a particular fancy to, or which member takes a particular fancy to her, and then I place her under the wing of that particular person. When an emergency arises in the family that is assigned to her to visit, I perhaps ask this member of the executive committee to call upon her and talk it over with her, instead of my writing a business letter about it ; and in that way the pleasant social relations to which Mr. Paine has referred are formed and the relation of the new visitor to the conference is strengthened, her interest and enthusiasm are aroused, and she will do much better work. The members of the executive committee can also give her a great deal of insight into the work such as the agent has not possibly the time to give. An inexperienced visitor needs that very much. When we assign a family to an experienced visitor we do not have to give her any instructions about it. We simply say, take this family and study it and see what the trouble is and what you can do about it. But that general instruction is not enough for an inexperienced visitor. She wants to know what she must do and she wants a very definite object; and then she is apt to lose sight of everything else. Perhaps there is a child to be gotten into the eye and ear infirmary, and after she has gotten the child in, she is very apt to come back and say, "Now I have done that, and I have not anything else to go for, and when I go, the woman wonders what I have come for." She has lost sight of the chief end and she needs to be warned against this mistake. She may go with the definite object of getting the child into the infirmary, but at the same time she must not lose sight of the fact that while she is doing that, her main object also is to establish a friendship with that woman, so that after the definite object is accomplished her visits may be continued in a perfectly natural manner and be looked forward to with more pleasure than when there was a definite object in them.

A good deal is said about the exchange of sympathy and experience, but I do not think we make enough of that after all. We talk about it a great deal, and yet we do not make it definite enough. Now, we want to exchange experiences, to enlarge the horizon of these poor people by sharing our pleasures with them, but I think it goes deeper when we share our sorrows with them. We are very willing to tell them about our joys, but our sorrows are sacred,—not any more sacred, however, than theirs. I remember calling on a woman once whom I had not seen for three years. She looked up as I came in, and she said, "How do you do? How is the little orphan niece?" I had entirely forgotten that I had ever told her of any sorrow in my own life, and yet that was the thing she remembered the moment she caught sight of my face.

I remember one of my visitors whom I thought a little too business-like, as she was a very energetic woman. I managed once, when she was present, to suggest this idea of telling the people more of our own lives, and she evidently took it to heart. The next time she went to visit a certain woman, she told her of her contemplated trip to Europe and her plans for enjoyment for the summer. The woman looked at her rather bitterly, and said, "Oh, yes, it is very fine for you to go to Europe and have a good time," and the visitor said to me afterwards that that plan did not work. But this summer the lady is in Europe, and I called on the woman and she said to me, "Yes, Mrs. So-and-So was telling me one day of her life as a young girl, and she said that she could not always go to parties with the rest of the girls, because she did not have such pretty dresses as they did, and she always had to wear the same dress. She told me that, because she wanted me to know she felt for me in my sorrow."

I think it will go deeper if we share our sorrows than if we share merely our joys.

Another point in connection with our visitors is their lack of patience. Somebody has said that the virtue most to be admired is patience. This is especially so with young people and in their visiting they get discouraged because they are so impatient of results. They expect to make half a dozen visits on a poor family inside of a month and see them helped. Now, which one of us ever had our lives strongly influenced by a friendship of a month's standing? We are apt to say that these people are very easily influenced. Well, many times they are, and it is very touching to see their responsiveness, and it often shows the poverty of friendship in their lives when we see how very readily they respond to slight acts of friendship. But after all a real deep friendship is a thing of slow growth, and these young visitors must learn that they must work long and patiently for results.

I once heard a sermon which made an impression on my mind that has remained with me for many years. One of its main ideas was to get your influence before you use it. Many people seem to think that if they can visit a poor family, by virtue of their superior education and culture they must immediately have a very strong influence. They do not get it that way. They must get it just as our friends get an influence over us, by long, patient contact, and by the slow, natural growth of friendship.

There is another point which I should like to refer to. Sometimes the visitors and their families do not get on particularly well. The visitor does not get very much interested in her family, and, what is more important, the family does not get interested in her. Now, I might just as well take two persons in this room and say, "Now I want you to be intimate and confidential friends at once," as to expect that a successful friendship is going to be established simply because a well-to-do person is sent to a poor person. It does not follow necessarily. The law of congeniality holds in these relations as in the ordinary relations of life, and if the visitor and the family do not prove congenial, it seems to me a mistake to force it, and to insist upon the visitor continuing her relations with that family. We will not give up too easily, but it is wiser to make the change and try again. Of course, those who assign the visitors to the families must have rare insight into human nature and human character in order to assign cases successfully; but everybody will make mistakes, and those mistakes can easily be removed by recognizing the fact of human nature. It seems to me wise not to be too persistent. American women have the reputation of adaptability in all the relations of life. There is no qualification more necessary for successful work in the line of charity.

The CHAIRMAN.—Mr. Paine, I am sure, astounded many of us by telling us that there were so many friendly visitors in Boston. Now, we know that many other cities are not so fortunate. New York, for instance, although an enormous city, has, compared to Boston, few friendly visitors. Of course, we must bear in mind the peculiar geographical position of New York city. There are gentlemen present who can tell us more of the work in that city.

I should like to ask, what do we mean by friendly visitors? The phrases that we use are like a great many tables of statistics that we read. We can read the figures, but we do not know all that is behind the figures. One hundred good visitors, who can be relied on to do prompt and effective work, are infinitely better than three hundred visitors on whom we cannot rely, but who are simply enrolled on the lists of those who occasionally work with us. I do not mean to imply that the eight hundred in Boston are not every one just as good visitors as Mrs. Roger Wolcott, but I know that in Baltimore, my own city, there is a great difference in visitors.

Now, I know we should all be glad to hear something on friendly visiting work, on the numbers of friendly visitors and why we cannot get hold of them, in the largest city of the country, where the problems, (as Mr. Paine said last night) are most pressing and are going to be most pressing, if this work is going to do what we claim that it shall do. We shall all be delighted to hear from Mr. De Forest, president of the Charity Organization Society of New York.

Mr. DE FOREST.—I think my Boston friends know that New York does not like to be interrogated on this subject. Now, I confess that I have listened to this paper of Mrs. Wolcott's, this portrayal of the ideal friendly visitor, with very much the same feelings as when I have read descriptions of the marvellous architecture of the World's Fair. If I had not come here and seen for myself this wonderful symmetry, this harmony of form and color, which produces the grand architectural effect, I certainly could not have believed it possible; so if I had simply read Mrs. Wolcott's paper, and had not attended these conferences and seen this row of Boston women sitting with pencil in hand, taking down everything that was said, and if I did not know something about the actual situation in Boston, I should say that this ideal could not be realized.

I do not know how it is in smaller cities, but I do know how it is in New York. To speak with perfect frankness, we have extreme difficulty, I will not say in getting this ideal friendly visitor, because I have never seen the ideal friendly visitor realized in New York, but in getting fairly good friendly visitors. Now, I say that frankly, because some of our brethren in other large cities may be unduly discouraged by this story of Boston success. It should not be put down entirely to lack of effort, because I know there have been conscientious efforts made to secure a much larger number of friendly visitors than we have.

We have different conditions in New York city, from those in Boston and I take it that different conditions exist almost everywhere.

We have tremendous preoccupation.

Then we do not have separate homes for the poor. We have a tenement house system. And I speak of it for this reason, because many young women whom we should naturally secure as friendly visitors and who would probably be secured, if they lived in other places, could not be asked to go by themselves into New York tenements.

After all the question before us is a practical one, and I believe in giving a practical bent to this talk. We all want to know what to do. We are all agreed as to the beneficence and as to the desirability of friendly visiting. We are all agreed that this ideal of Mrs. Wolcott's should be lived up to as far as possible. Yet some of us feel that we must put up with what we can get, instead of insisting upon that ideal. The great question is, how to get the friendly visitors and that question, so far as my own knowledge of charity organization work in this country is concerned, has been more nearly solved in Boston than anywhere else.

Now, if you are asking me for my opinion as to why it is difficult to find friendly visitors, I wish you would bear in mind first the question of environment. I do not think there ought to be any excuse in a village or in a small town (and when I say a small town, I do not know but that I should include a pretty large town), I do not think there ought to be any difficulty in such a place, with organization and energy, in getting an excellent corps of friendly visitors. There is usually such an absence of pre-occupation in smaller places that good people have time to attend to this kind of work. Yet Boston is a large city. It has been successful in obtaining friendly visitors and the Boston lesson, to most of us, is that success in friendly visiting is a question of management, a question of organization. If the rest of us were able to place in control of our societies—I was going to say such men, I think I would prefer to say such women—as the Boston society is composed of, we should hear very much less complaint about the difficulty of getting friendly visitors.

Now, in connection with New York, if you will pardon me for making a suggestion, there are two representatives here, a gentleman and a lady who stand at the head of one of the largest societies in New York. The gentleman is Mr. John Paton and the lady is Mrs. Fullerton. The society to which I allude is "the New York Association for Improving the Condition of the Poor." It stands to the Charity Organization Society of New York as the older relief societies do to the younger charity organization societies in other cities. If you want any further information as to New York you will be rewarded by applying to them.

Mrs. R. H. HAYES of Galveston, Texas.—I do not hear anybody speak for my portion of the country. I do not think we are represented here at all. You have got no further south than Philadelphia, and I came from Galveston, Texas. I belong to four or five organizations and when we joined them we expected to make friendly visits. The question never comes up about friendly visits. We expect them. That is a part of our duty, and in that way we have raised women and children from poverty and degradation. I only want to say these few words, because you seem to keep it all up north to yourselves, and I want to let you know some work is done down south of Mason and Dixon's line,—although I was born in Illinois and was raised in Springfield.

The CHAIRMAN.—I know you would all like to hear a few words about the work in New York from Mr. Paton, President of the great Society for the Improvement of the Condition of the Poor of that city.

Mr. PATON, President of the Association for Improving the Condition of the Poor, New York.—It is only an hour since I arrived direct from London, where I had a sort of roving commission from my society to investigate the work of relief in the slums, and I have spent considerable time in that interesting study. I, therefore, was quite unable to prepare a paper for this congress, but I hurried here direct from the steamer in order to have at least the satisfaction of being present.

One speaker, whose remarks interested me very much, referred to the Charity Organization Society of London. In the course of my work last winter I saw a great deal of that most excellent society and of its exceedingly able secretary, Mr. Loch, who is well known, at least by name, to many here. If Mr. Loch were present, I do not think he would contradict me when I say that, in the matter of friendly visiting and in the investigation of needy cases and in the detail work, his society does not begin to compare with what is done by the splendid organization presided over by our friend Mr. R. W. De Forest,—the Charity Organization Society of New York. The London society does its work in a different way, and it does not do nearly so much in the way of friendly visiting.

The work of friendly visiting is one of the deepest interest to the society of which I have been president for a good many years, the New York Association for Improving the Condition of the Poor. We have been at this work for nearly fifty years, and before long we shall celebrate our jubilee. We endeavor to cover a pretty large field, the city of New York from the Battery to the Harlem River, probably as large a field as is covered by any society in the United States, and we investigate and give relief, of course, without distinction of creed, of color or race. When I became connected with this society in 1880 we enjoyed the services of about 350 friendly visitors. Well, some of them were doing admirable work, but about that time the New York Charity Organization Society began to throw light upon the subject of giving relief to the poor. and I unhesitatingly say that we owe to that society the new, and I think improved method, in which we carry out our work.

Gradually, with many a vote of thanks and many a kindly expression, we have dropped from our list all our 350 visitors. Some of them, as I have said, were doing splendid work, but there was a most awful waste of charity. We were spending thirty or forty thousand dollars a year, and this amount was given away, in the days when New York was not so large as it is now, with a free and lavish and very generous hand. We were, I do think, helping to build up a gigantic system of pauperism. We were pauperizing the recipients by the indiscriminate and thoughtless and at the same time, kindly and generous way in which our relief was given. Our friends of the Charity Organization Society taught us an admirable lesson and we have never ceased to study their methods and to work, as Mr. De Forest will tell you, in the greatest harmony and co-operation with them. We gradually got rid of our 350 visitors and we now do our work more thoroughly and more efficiently with a small corps of trained visitors of our own, most of them educated and brought up in our own office, our salaried officers. We believe in skilled, trained visiting. I believe there is no more kindly visiting in the city of New York than that of our visitors. We know them intimately, every one of them. We studied their characters before we gave them these important appointments. They are women of kindly sympathy, but they are skilled and trained in the work. We have divided the city of New York into districts. I wish Mrs. Fullerton was present here, and she could tell you better about the work. Each one of these women has charge of a great section of the city, at least as far as the cases reported to us. Every morning at nine o'clock they meet in the superintendent's office, and there is no more interesting place in New York to study the methods and modes of charitable working than in our office between nine and ten, when you may hear the reports and see the work which is done. The visitors then give in their reports of the cases which they have seen upon the previous day, the new cases are handed over to them and at ten o'clock they go out upon their rounds, all over that vast city, returning next morning with the reports of the new cases and to receive again the fresh ones. We profess, whenever it is desired, to give within twenty-four hours a written report on any case that is sent to us by any clergyman, by any society, by any subscriber, in fact, by any friend. We also go a step further. We undertake the charge of the family or of the individual, and I do not think that you will find that we let them go until they are set upon their feet or no longer require relief.

The CHAIRMAN.—Now we have heard from large cities and we have also heard that it is probably easier to develop the work of friendly visiting in smaller cities. I know you will all like to hear some words from a smaller city, and I am going to ask Miss Starr, of Burlington, to tell us of her work, and of the success in Burlington of the friendly visitors.

Miss M. E. STARR, Secretary of the Charity Organization Society, Burlington, Iowa.—Our society is only a year and a half old, and I do not think with its youth and limited field and its inexperience that it will be of any value here. But Mr. Brackett has asked me whether or not we have been able to secure a sufficient number of visitors who would visit their families often enough and earnestly enough. While believing heartily in friendly visiting and hoping that it will one day accomplish what it aims to do, I must answer that thus far we have not been successful. I attribute the failure to two reasons. One is that the visitors have too many families to care for. We have had during the last year about 130 families and about 70 visitors, but the number of working visitors is so small that many have had five families to visit and some more. With an average number of demands upon a visitor outside of her friendly visiting I do not think that she can care for more than two families in a way that will tend to raise them above the need of relief.

Then another difficulty has been a lack of definite information on the part of many visitors as to what was expected of them; this is partly due to a failure to attend the meetings. How to remedy that I do not know, and I wish some one could tell me. It may be also partly due to a lack of sufficient communication between the visitors themselves.

Mr. GEORGE D. HOLT, Secretary of Associated Charities, Minneapolis.—I think the matter of friendly visiting, considering the limited time in which we have engaged in it, is very far advanced. Our city has a population of 171,000 and we have slums and everything of that kind, with individual cases that are probably just as depressing and as hard to reach as in any city, but of course not so numerous. The thought has occurred to me, as this discussion has gone on as to the great city of New York, why it would not be a good idea to adopt the plan we have in our city in reference to the liquor traffic, called the "Police Limits," where no liquor is allowed to be sold. Why could not this friendly visiting be introduced into some section of New York and made a complete success there and then spread out? I think that is the reason why we have succeeded so well. We did not district the city all off and establish a conference in every one of the districts, but we simply started with one and were very careful in selecting the workers to start with, and now it has spread into four conferences covering the entire city and the money to meet all expenses was in sight before we attempted it. I think that if the matter is started in this way it will be successful, and I speak of this for those who are just starting in the city work. Raising money has not been difficult in Minneapolis. The gentleman from New York spoke about the pre-occupied condition of the citizens. I think you will find that eminently true of the citizens of the north-west. They are pre-occupied, and that is one of the hardest things to overcome.

Dr. J. W. WALK, of Philadelphia.—There have been, during the discussions of the congress, several references to Philadelphia which I would, like to explain, if possible. Mr. Paine, I think, referred to the fact that Philadelphia had once had a large number of visitors, but had not kept up the number, and the chairman of the Charity Organization committee of the National Conference in making his report said that Philadelphia did not report its visitors. Well, I want to make a very frank admission. I will tell you exactly what is the matter.

When Philadelphia began the charity organization work, as you know, it began with a great many district organizations, which were relieving agencies, and which are yet relief agencies. The visitors at the very start in many of the organizations became almoners of relief. The visitors gave relief and even where they did not give it they made recommendations to the superintendent, which soon came to have the force of commands, so that a visitor in going to a family was recognized as some one who could give an order for food or clothing or for the payment of rent or for other things.

Now, I think every one in this room will agree, and I think the gentleman who is president of the New York Society for Improving the Condition of the Poor, and Mr. De Forest, President of the Charity Organization Society of New York, will agree with all the others that when relief is to be given at all, it should be given by an expert, specially qualified to judge the conditions which require relief, and to discriminate among the people who are to have it, so that he does not give the treatment for consumption to the man who has rheumatism.

Now then, what is our position in Philadelphia? After the first few years we had hundreds of visitors, who were acting as almoners of relief, either directly or otherwise. That was the condition when Mr. Kellogg, who at that time held an official position in Philadelphia, went to New York. We found that that condition could not continue and gradually our visitors fell off. I have made no report this year, because I want to tell the exact truth, and it was very hard to tell the truth about that condition of things; I mean, hard to express it in a way that would not be misunderstood. We have more than 500 names of visitors on the list, but I did not report them, because I am afraid a great many of them are simply names.

I hope that a time will come, when Philadelphia will have—(because we are not "pre-occupied" there; we have plenty of time to eat and sleep in Philadelphia; we get along nearly as well as the people that work 25 hours a day)—now, I hope the time will come when we shall have a body of about 1200 visitors there, who are friendly visitors exclusively, carrying sympathy, counsel, and encouragement to the poor. Their influence is not at all belittled and injured by the idea of alms, but you can see that, having started wrong, it will take us a good while to get right. That is the condition in Philadelphia, but I ought to say, in justice to the work, that we have a great many visitors who are still working and some excellent ones, or we could not carry on our work at all.

The CHAIRMAN.—I am sure that the remarks of our friend from Philadelphia and of Mr. Paton only prove to us all the more that the friendly visitor is a failure when allowed to dispense alms.

Miss FRANCES SMITH of Boston.—I should like to say a few words as to some of the questions which have been brought up this afternoon. As to the difficulties of securing visitors for certain parts of New York city, I wish to say that Ward 7 is a part of Boston in which not a single visitor lives. We have to draw all our visitors from other parts of the city, and I want to tell you that some of our visitors come just as far as they would have to go if they were living in New York. Some of our best visitors come from Meriden and Lexington, some of them from twenty miles away. Now, it is no use to dwell upon the difficulties of the situation. My people always say, and that is my own idea, "if we ought to do a thing, we can do it, and we will find a way to do it."

Now, as to getting the young people, I think they said that there are young people in New York whom they might get, if it were not for these dreadful tenement houses. Well, we have a similar difficulty in Boston. Almost all the people in the district where I am at present live in tenement houses, and it raises a difficult question. They have brought up the question of having young people, and discussed it, and they have always said that their youth is not the trouble. It simply depends upon the character. If they are people of fine and noble character, they go down and visit in these tenement houses without any hesitation. And I am proud to say that we have a great many young lady visitors in our ward and not one has ever met with the slightest sign of disrespect. There are just as many good people in Ward 7 as on Back Bay, and if anyone attempts to show disrespect to a lady there, the poor people are just as ready to come to her assistance as any gentleman on Beacon street.

Another difficulty is that their people at home do not want them to visit and that is the chief trouble. There are a great many of these young ladies who would come gladly but for their fathers and mothers, and, I am sorry to say, husbands sometimes. Well, how shall we get around that? We have got to bring young people up. The way one lady found was this. We bring them in and let them see what we are doing and we get them interested in the details, and gradually they feel some confidence in themselves. The most important thing to do is to let a young lady copy on your cards or records the reports of the visitors, the result, perhaps, of the investigations of the visitors. They learn from that how to do the work and they do not get so much an idea of the red tape as they might if you gave them other parts of the work to do. Well, now, you can gradually get one of these young ladies from office work into visiting. They become interested in their work, and they go home and get their families interested and then there is no further difficulty.

I suppose New York has some colleges. We get young men and young ladies from colleges to come and help us in our work. It is not quite so satisfactory as other visiting in some ways, as they remain only one or two or three years, when they move and the family loses them, but still we have had very good success. It is extremely interesting to find that these college-bred young people pop up in other cities at the head of other charitable societies and come back to us and read us papers on what they have seen in England and other countries, and bring back to us the benefits of their own experience.

Well, then, about the churches and the liking of people to visit in the churches. Now, I take it that the duty of a charity organization society is to do its work so well that people will find, unless the church does exceedingly good work, that they would much better come back and work with the charity organization society. I have often had people who left us for the church societies come back and say "We would rather work here, because the work is done well, and we like to do good work."

There is one other point. Do not go too fast in your work. Make the first thing in your charity organization work the finding and training of visitors. Remember always that you must have a visitor for each family. I do not think it is half as important that we should go out into the other work, important as it is, until we have first been able to get visitors for all the families.

Another way in which we have been very successful is for each visitor to get another visitor. Now, you must not say to them in the abstract, "I want you to get another visitor," but you must tell them about a certain family and ask them if they cannot get a visitor for that family. In other words personal interest is important.

Next let me speak of a way in which we have been most successful in getting visitors, because I do not know that any other conference has tried it. We used to write up the whole history of the family. But whoever got acquainted with a person by hearing the family history first? Who ever got acquainted with people by being told all their faults, the one thing we used to dwell upon? We used to give all the bad things about families. Now, we must act in a natural way in charity organizations as well as elsewhere. Now all we put on the list is a very brief statement. I will suppose a case: "Family of Mary and John Sullivan; live at 149 Front street; they have three children, two boys of ten and twelve years and a girl of seventeen. A friendly visitor is very much needed; can introduce herself by saying that she comes from Mrs. Simons." I am supposing that Mrs. Simons referred this family to us. But suppose we heard of it in an indirect way. Suppose that the girl of seventeen is out of work. Then we might write, "You can introduce yourself by saying that you have heard that Mary is out of work." "A visitor can aid very much by helping Mary and advising her how to get work." "The visitor will find herself very useful to the family as time goes on from month to month." Add something like that. You must not let her think that there is only one thing to do. Now, that is all put on paper, and that is all that is given. What is the advantage of it? It is that the friendly visitor goes to that family and forms her own ideas of it. She feels the same interest in them that I felt in the very first family that I visited. They were horrible people, but I did not know it at the time. I did not know anything about them, but I went in to see them and I never have taken more interest in any family. If I had known what they were, I do not believe I should have cared so much for them. Remember this, that, as a rule, all the people in the family are not bad. As a rule, it is only one or two of them, and the good that you do to a family is usually by bringing out their good points and by cultivating them. It is, therefore, very bad to introduce a family to a visitor by telling bad things about them. In this way we have no difficulty whatever in getting visitors in Ward 7 for the very worst families. Of course if a person asks not to be sent to a certain kind of family we respect his wishes, but otherwise we send him as I have stated, and let him find out what the family is.

It is very important to encourage a visitor. If you see one who is disheartened, you must find something to keep him at work. Visitors are often discouraged because they do not see immediate results. They may be doing a very good work, but the poor people, as a rule, do not know how to express themselves; they do not say to the visitor what they feel. Hence an inexperienced visitor will be discouraged. It is, therefore, a good plan, whenever you hear any good thing that a poor person has said about the visitor, to repeat it.

Mr. PAINE.—I have been asked whether we have any poor people among our visitors. It is a very interesting contrast that, whereas among the Associated Charities we have almost none, yet among the St. Vincent de Paul visitors of the Roman Catholic Church the visitors are almost wholly of that class, and they do beautiful, faithful and devoted friendly work. I have had occasion to see more or less of this in Boston, and it is a surprise and delight to me to see how thoroughly and devotedly the poor, plain working people, who are Roman Catholics, will give their evenings to friendly visiting after they have been working hard for their own support during the day.

Dr. AYRES.—In Cincinnati we have found that the plain visitors sometimes do the most excellent work, and we have been able to bring them into conferences with people of higher social culture with admirable effect.

Mrs. HAYES of Texas.—I want to say that you have all been on the top of the ladder, but we have commenced at the lower round. Our city is small and it is a very simple thing to have friendly visitors in a small city. In all our organizations, as I have said before, it is distinctly understood when we join that friendly visiting is a part of our duties. Our president, or whoever is at the head of the organization, appoints a committee, and that committee (that is, in several societies that I belong to) appoints the friendly visitors, taking them from those who are the most capable, having most of the requisite qualifications.

Mr. DE FOREST.—I spoke about the question of getting friendly visitors, and said that in my judgment success depended on the management. I do not want any better illustration of the truth of that conclusion than what was said by Miss Frances Smith. She showed, in an admirable manner, what good management is. Perhaps it is not our fault if we cannot obtain equally good management. We deal with men as we find them and take what management we can get. There is another conclusion, which may occur to the minds of some members of the conference, namely, that the trouble in cities other than Boston is possibly this, that the Smith family is not large enough.

The section then adjourned.

THIRD SESSION.—TUESDAY EVENING, JUNE 13TH, 1893.

ROBERT W. DE FOREST, Esq., of New York in the Chair.

The CHAIRMAN.—As you see from the programmes the special topic to-night is the Relation of Public to Private Charity, and the first paper will be that of Miss Louisa L. Schuyler, of New York, entitled "Voluntary Unofficial Supervision of Public Charitable Institutions in Co-operation with Official Boards."

This is a description of the work which has been accomplished by the State Charities Aid Association of New York, and having had an opportunity to read it, I will say that it is very interesting. It is a history of what a single society has done, yet it has a broad interest. It is an object lesson, showing what can be accomplished by a comparatively small body of earnest men and women. I take great pleasure in introducing to you Miss Schuyler.

Miss SCHUYLER, of New York.—The subject of my paper is Voluntary Unofficial Supervision of Public Charitable Institutions in Co-operation with Official Boards. I am obliged to add that owing to a weak voice I am not able to read it. I will therefore ask Mr. Wilcox to do so.

Mr. ANSLEY WILCOX then read the paper. At its conclusion, the following remarks were made:

The CHAIRMAN.—We have with us Mr. Oscar Craig, President of the Board of State Charities of New York, the official organization of the state. I will ask him to speak a few words if he will.

Mr. CRAIG.—The paper which you have heard needs no commendation; the statements commend themselves; they are simply statements of facts. I shall confine my remarks to one topic introduced by this paper—the appointment of visitors with authority to go into the institutions of the state. The State Board of Charities has the power by statute to appoint visitors in every county of the state to go to the eleemosynary and correctional institutions of the state, which are not controlled by the state government. That includes 500 corporations. The State Charities Aid Association has the power to apply to the Justice of the Supreme Court for the appointment of visitors to all the charitable institutions of the state, except private corporations. During my experience of fourteen years as a member of the State Board of Charities and of several years as its president, I have learned that visiting, in the several counties of the state, can be better accomplished under the supervision of a voluntary organization, the "State Charities Aid Association," than by the official body, the "State Board of Charities;" therefore for several years I recommended that the visitors appointed by our board should be, by voluntary consent, transferred from our board to the voluntary association. That has been accomplished in most of the districts of the state; and in my own district (for which I am primarily responsible) it has been accomplished in every county except one. An official body is limited by its official dignity. It cannot go to the public press and proclaim abuses and evils as a voluntary organization can. The State Board of Charities, an official body with power to examine under oath and report to the state legislature, might be compromised by the opinions expressed in the public press, before such examination had taken place; but there is no such limitation to a voluntary organization. This paper is, indeed, an object lesson for other states; every state which has such an official body as a State Board of Charities, should interest itself in securing also a voluntary association like the State Charities Aid Association of New York.

The CHAIRMAN.—I ask General Brinkerhoff, Chairman of the State Board of Charities of Ohio, to step to the platform and speak a few minutes.

General BRINKERHOFF of Ohio.—I have been familiar for many years with the splendid work done by the State Charities Aid Association of New York, and perhaps for New York it is the best form; but in Ohio (and perhaps in other states without a dominant city like New York) I think we have a better method of reaching the same end. This is the Ohio system. A law requires the Court of Common Pleas in each county to appoint a Board of County Visitors, consisting of six persons, three men and three women, and not more than three of each party, and they are required to visit all the places of charities and correction in the county where they belong. They have the power to visit them at least four times during the year; in fact they make many more visits. They report to the Court of Common Pleas once a year, and they send the report also to the Board of State Charities. The courts also require that whenever any child is to be proceeded against, in order that it may be sent to a reformatory, notice shall be given to the Board of County Visitors, who shall appoint a guardian *ad litem* for the child.

We have held two annual conferences on the subject of charities and correction, and have gathered audiences as large as this and sometimes larger. The annual reports of these conferences are published, and are weighty and useful. I could talk to you by the hour of what has been accomplished by these boards of county visitors; they are appointed for two years, and two members go out each year. The judges take the greatest interest in these matters. We have eighty-eight counties in the state, and you may imagine the result.

The CHAIRMAN.—The next paper is by Mrs. BENJAMIN WILLIAMS of New Jersey, on the State Charities Aid Association of New Jersey.

This was followed by a paper by Mr. ALEXANDER JOHNSON, of Indiana, on the Co-operation of Public with Private Charitable Agencies.

FOURTH SESSION.—JUNE 14TH, 1893, 2.15 P. M.

JOHN M. GLENN, Esq., of Baltimore, in the Chair.

The CHAIRMAN.—The first paper is by Mrs. Charles R. Lowell of New York, entitled "Are Labor Colonies needed in the United States," which will be read by Miss Richmond of Baltimore.

At its conclusion, the following remarks were made:

The CHAIRMAN.—I ask Dr. Warner to give his views of this paper and to tell us also something of his work in Washington in connection with the municipal lodging house of that city.

Dr. WARNER, lately of Washington and now of California.—Those who remember Mrs. Lowell's paper at the St. Louis conference will observe that to-day she has presented almost exactly the same view of the pauper treatment of the male vagrant that she then presented of the treatment of vagrant men and women. The central thought which she has given us is expressed in the phrase "sterilization of the unfit," the idea being to prevent by segregation their increase in the community; while their lives will be attended to with great kindness, their stock shall end with their death. As to the character of the unemployed in this country, as she states it, those who have worked with free labor bureaus, or have sought in other ways to find employment for the unemployed, will agree with her estimate of the character of the unemployed in this country. At least they will agree that it is very nearly correct. When a gentleman of Brooklyn was asked if he found it difficult to find work for the faithful and efficient he said "yes, for the faithful; yes, for the efficient; but for the faithful and efficient, no." That is a conclusion similar to what is set forth in Mrs. Lowell's paper. Those who have simply thought about the matter and have seen but a few of the unemployed at their back doors, and have perhaps had but a very brief acquaintance with them, may feel that there is some injustice where faithful and efficient men cannot find work. We must not jump at the conclusion that they are efficient. The industrial conditions that existed years ago may have thrown the faithful men out of work, and idleness may have become a habit; so if you come to deal with them, you will find that they are not faithful. At the same time we cannot say that it is the fault of the individuals, but the result of their environment, and that they are out of harmony with their environment. And we can but feel that their inefficiency must be recognized.

It seems to me that Mrs. Lowell ignores one function of the labor colony. She says in this country we do not have faithful and efficient men who are out of work; and second, the unfaithful men will not stay in the colony; and third, the function of the labor colony as it exists in Germany is that of oppression to the community. There are places where men will be given hard work for little pay, and that should be the rule of action of these colonies. The great army of tramps of this country (and I have seen a new genus on the Pacific Coast) should be put at reformative work and long sentences. People have been harping on this ever since Howard wrote about it a hundred years ago. This needs to be taken hold of in a practical way by those who appreciate the condition of the criminals. The jails are thoroughly, essentially and entirely bad in most counties of the United States. The longer sentence and reformatory work should be introduced. That will do more to discourage tramping and vagrancy than anything else. As to the city work in Washington I do not care to speak about that; what is to be said of it, will be found in the Charities Review. It is better to keep the subjects separate.

Mr. L. L. BARBOUR.—In Michigan we have a colony without the labor attachment, and we have poor-houses without any labor attachment. In February or March between three and four hundred inmates were in our poor-house who had been there most of the winter. The physician and an officer of the State Board went out to investigate the poor-house. It was suggested that they ascertain how many inmates of the institution were able bodied. After a thorough investigation made, both men concluded that at least one hundred of the four hundred inmates were perfectly capable and able to earn their own living. It was found that in a large quantity of cord-wood in the yard adjacent to the poor-house, some 150 cords had been cut, but not sawn up. The keeper of the poor-house was asked if the men did not have any work; and replied, "They wouldn't do any work." It was suggested that he tell them after breakfast the next morning to go out and saw a given quantity of that wood before they could have any dinner. The next day he informed the two visitors that eighty-seven took to the road immediately after breakfast. If some provision of that kind could be prescribed for this class of laborers, (of whom we find so many in our poor-houses during the winter throughout the country,) it would undoubtedly relieve us of this class.

Miss AMES.—I met an American who had traveled in thirty-two states for eight months as a tramp; he said he did it "to make a study of sociology." This gentleman said he estimated that there were about 50,000 professional tramps in the United States. I asked him how he lived during this period; he said "I lived just as well as you do: I never lived better in my life." At one time in Milwaukee he tried to see how many dinners he could get; he got four dinners and then he stopped. He said they gave what they call "Hand-outs," and they gave out what they call "Sit-downs." He said as long as they did that, these tramps continued to be tramps. He had never found a single tramp who could not read or write, and he had found three college graduates. He said he was thrown in jail for sleeping on a freight car. He said that with exceptions, the jails are just as bad as possible. I think he spoke of Pennsylvania as a perfect paradise for tramps. I learned a great many valuable points from him on this subject.

I have visited the labor colony in North Berlin; there it was not compulsory with the inmates to stay, yet they were not allowed to come and go as they pleased; if they wanted to look for work, they were allowed to do so. Many of the inmates there were well educated, and one was a man of rank: some had been brought down by drink or had fallen through some other means. They were there working for very small wages; among other things at brush-making. I tasted the soup allowed them and it was excellent. This was one of twenty-two labor communities which have been started with varying success in Germany.

Dr. AYRES.—I would like to ask how the deficiency was made up if the colonies were not self-supporting?

The SPEAKER.—I think a part came from private funds and a part from the state.

Dr. AYRES.—Under whose control was the colony? Of a society or of the state?

The SPEAKER.—I cannot answer definitely.

Dr. AYRES.—Most of us who have had experience in dealing with homeless men and homeless women try to find work for these people; we do find work for them, and they work while the spasm of goodness lasts. I suppose most of you have noticed that they do have these spasms of goodness and that during that time they are very good indeed. If we have a place where men can come for a few days and get their living by hard work, and then pass on to the next city, that may be bad for the men and for the city. Let me give one or two illustrations. I knew some young fellows who were in the Cleveland wood-yards where they have to work hard, and I have seen them saw wood before they could get a night's lodging. Some of them would stay in the wood-yard five days, and when they had stood it as long as they could and found it was getting to be real work, they came to Cincinnati; but when it got to be cold weather they went back to Cleveland where they could get food and lodging by hard work. You heard Mr. Johnson say that when he first established the wood-yard in Chicago he found a man from the country who came to Chicago and spent the winter at hard labor, because he said he would have to work hard on the farm and he thought it was preferable to spend the winter in Chicago, even if he did work hard. It is hard to say where the evil begins and where the good commences. I feel as if we had made more progress in dealing with fallen women than we have with fallen men.

The CHAIRMAN.—I ask Miss Rogers, one of the Overseers of the Poor of Boston, to tell us of their work in Boston.

Miss A. P. ROGERS.—We have in Boston a free lodging house for men, a temporary home; and they work in the wood-yard which is attached to the home. They are obliged to cut and saw and split wood in a certain quantity for a night's lodging. We had last year 32,000 lodgers. This includes duplication, for a good many men come over and over again. Much care is taken in finding work for these men, and therefore a good many of them come many times in the winter. The rule of the home is that the men should not stay there over three days, but a few, old men and incompetent, are allowed to stay longer. We also have a temporary home for women where women can come, generally towards night, and receive lodging of the most simple kind, and the plainest of food, and for that they do the work of the house,—a certain amount of cleaning and washing for the home. They also bake all the bread of the two institutions. They may stay in the home a week or sometimes longer, if the matron has a good reason for keeping them. They come there to find work and at times we find work for them, but they generally find work for themselves. The women have not been very successfully supplied with work until lately; now there is a more strict rule, and we are endeavoring to find out the character of the women who come. Until last year we have never known definitely how many have come. Last year we knew that 1,283 different women came to the home and 744 children. The statistics will show that out of the 1,283 women, 587 came the first time that year, and that 802 came only once during the whole year; 223 of the women who came, had been in the Home "on and off" since 1882, so that the labor test had not kept them from being constant habitués at the home.

A DELEGATE.—How long do you allow the women to stay?

The SPEAKER.—Not more than seven days without some good reason; there are many women who are incompetent and the matron, who knows them well, often allows them to stay longer.

A DELEGATE.—I wish to ask what per cent. of the cost is paid by the allowance for the wood-yard?

The SPEAKER.—The wood account is kept by itself; the wood-yard simply pays its running expenses.

A DELEGATE.—It does not pay all the running expenses, does it?

The SPEAKER.—No.

THE CHAIRMAN.—We have the good fortune to have with us the Rev. E. J. Dupuy of the Maison Hospitalière, Paris, France. We shall be glad if he will kindly tell us about this work.

Mr. DUPUY of Paris.—We have in Paris what we call a hospital house; you might almost call it a home. Two Englishmen came to Paris and lost their papers and money. The police did not know what to do with them; so they were sent to a pastor, who thought he would start a house for such men. He put one in as superintendent and the other as chief clerk and opened a small house. We have a like system in other cities in France. Men are taken in and the first day are set to chopping wood. Usually there are about 50 per cent. of these men that will take lunch the first day and will quit the next morning, because they do not want to work. Of the other half there are many who remain longer. Some prefer to go away after two or three days, and it is very rare to keep them in our house more than a week. We keep a few of them a fortnight, and some of them have remained there a month; two of them have actually been in the house two years. They are employed as a foreman and as a collector of bills. Almost all have had some difficulty with justice and have a prison record; some have been forgers and burglars, but some are good men who have been led astray by drink and bad habits. This house has just been enlarged through the liberality of some friends and can accommodate from fifty to a hundred men. Very many have been attracted to the large cities by the wood-yards. In 1878, 1879 and 1880, when a number of people were frozen to death in the streets because they had no home, the private charities opened "asylums;" applicants were obliged to give their name and the state whence they came, and they could have free lodging for three days. Immediately the number of tramps and beggars increased in Paris. Since then they have opened wood-yards and the number still increases. In the case of women it is quite different; we would not keep a tramp twenty-four hours, but with a woman it is quite different, especially in France, where they have the law against them. When we can keep her we do so, and give her moral strength and courage and help her along, and then she is sent out into the country. We have laundries for the women. The Sisters of St. Charles are working with us, the police take great pleasure in helping us, and even the state gives us money. In Marseilles they give them a certain amount and tell them to go and lodge in town. This is simply giving an income to vagrants and sometimes to the most disreputable men. I think no money ought to be allowed to these people, because when they have no more money they will try to find work. Whereas, if they are given fifteen or twenty cents, they know where to get rooms for four cents, and they have sixteen cents to enjoy themselves with. But what are we going to do with these men? In November and December of last winter I saw more than 300 men pass through these houses. Of these 300 men I am sure that about 250 had been in jail, on an average, from six to twelve months. The wood-yards are very good now, but I think they will be later on a source of evil.

Mr. PATON.—I am free to confess, after a winter's study of the charities of London, that in America we are very far behind the English in the matter of labor tests, but in some respects I think we excel. Our charity organizations and societies, particularly in New York (the ones with which I am most acquainted), are far superior to anything they have in England; but I am free to say that we come far short of London and other parts of Europe in the matter of labor tests. Let me give you an instance. The New York Poor Association is very far from being wholly a relief society. The relief work is the smallest part of the operation. For example, we have the baths. We can give a thousand baths a day. I think in the hot weather we can come up to that. We are sending 25,000 people down to Coney Island to get a change of air and the sea breeze; we are opening convalescent homes for sick children; but we are doing very little in the matter of labor tests, and that is one reason why I went to Europe and spent a good part of last winter in the slums of London, although I did not attempt to go through Loch's handbook of charities, for there are 1,100 charities in London described in that work. In this matter of labor tests I should unhesitatingly place at the head of the list the large army of high church ritualists. We have our wood-yards in New York, and I am thankful to Mr. Kellogg for his wood-yard, but I hope he will have something a thousand times better in the labor homes. They are carrying on twenty different kinds of industries. Every man, as far as possible, is put to the kind of work for which he is most fit. In one of these homes I saw three men—one a broken down lawyer, one a minister, and the third a valet. They carried on twenty or thirty different kinds of work in this labor home, and every man there has to work, and work hard, just as if he were earning daily wages. He is kept five or six months until they make a man of him. Of course he can go out at any moment if he so chooses. In London there were admirable "rescue homes," of which one at least is limited to sixteen girls, in order that every girl may be a study to the matron. I think there are fifteen or sixteen of those schools in London.

Next to the two institutions I have spoken of comes Booth's social wing of the Salvation Army; I visited it; there are every night in London about 500 men and women under their roofs; they gather them into the shelter; each man is supposed to pay two pence; they get a leather mattress to sleep on and two good meals, and there is a rousing meeting going on in the adjoining room, to which they are invited but not compelled to go. They have their "elevators," and here comes in the most successful part of the social army; the elevator is a place where they take a man from the gutter and put him upon his feet and try to make him a useful member of society. There is a constant invitation to go into the "elevator."

A successful industry is what they call "cabinet-making;" they make all the furniture, bookcases, etc., needed by the Salvation Army, besides a vast deal for sale. I have not the statistics with me.

Mr. WILCOX of Buffalo.—If this subject is still open for discussion, I would like to say what occurred to me in listening to the very interesting remarks of Mr. Paton. I suppose the idea which is embodied in the phrase labor test is a twofold idea, starting with the proposition that there are certain classes of men in the community who belong to the general class of tramps and beggars, who claim that they cannot get work to do. Such a person must be furnished with work which he can do, and with a compensation for it which will save him from immediate starvation; but if you give him a fair compensation for the work he does, it ceases to be "a test." Now, of course, the circumstances which Mr. Paton has described do not apply to the class that is underpaid. In Buffalo we have never succeeded in establishing a labor test. We tried the wood-yard, but that work is exceedingly simple; anybody can do it; in fact so far as I know there are only three kinds of work that have ever been suggested as "a test," sawing wood, breaking stone and cleaning streets. If there is any other kind of work that is more simple, I do not know what it is. We successfully established a wood-yard about twelve years ago. We raised the necessary sum of money and started with an overseer, and we said that we would furnish a man with a day's work at a rate which would save him from starvation. That worked well for a short time, but we soon found that we had a large stock of wood left on our hands; we were entirely unable to sell our wood. The use of natural gas, which has met the demand for kindling wood, is now so common, that we find it impossible to run a wood-yard on a large scale. We still have what we call our wood-yard, and we have arrangements with local dealers by which they will employ a limited number of men, and we keep it up on a very limited scale, but we have been swamped and have a great deal of wood which we cannot sell at all.

The meeting then adjourned.

PAPERS

ON THE

WORK AND PROBLEMS

OF

CHARITY ORGANIZATION

IN THE

UNITED STATES.

HISTORY OF CHARITY ORGANIZATION IN THE UNITED STATES.

1872—1893.

BY CHARLES D. KELLOGG, SECRETARY OF THE CHARITY ORGANIZATION SOCIETY OF NEW YORK.*

Under more than a score of names there may be enumerated ninety-two associations in the United States and the Dominion of Canada as in existence in 1893, which profess loyalty to the principles characteristic of the movement known as the Organization of Charity. Of the whole number sixty-five have made returns, with widely varying precision and completeness, to the "Committee on the History of Charity Organization" of this Conference, and upon these returns this report is based.

HISTORY.

Conditions Twenty Years Ago.—Twenty years ago, in the sense of an agency for bringing charitable and municipal relief organizations into concert of action, there were no Charity Organization Societies in America. There were, in many cities, voluntary general relief societies professedly ready to undertake any sort of humane task within their ability. In some instances they laid claim to most approved maxims of work, but as they were invariably distributors of material aid this function submerged all others, and they sank into the sea of common almsgiving, appealing to their patrons for support on the ground that the money given to them would enable them to enlarge the number of their beneficiaries or increase the amount of their gifts, and attracting the needy to their doors with the hope of loaves and fishes. In many quarters there was no lack of judicious reasoning, or of admission that

---

*This is an abstract of a paper prepared by Mr. Kellogg as chairman of the committee on charity organization of the twentieth National Conference of Charities and Correction. The paper is published in full in the report of that conference.

the moral nature and the social lot of the poor were large factors in the problem of pauperism; but the efforts to extirpate it were feeble and incidental, not dominant. On every side the current of public sentiment was that every penny spent in administration was so much abstracted from the poor, and that the best management was that which entailed the least cost in getting bread and soup to the hungry, and shelter, fuel, and clothing to the cold.

Relief Twenty Years Ago.—The practice of legal or public out-door relief differed greatly in different communities. But from every quarter testimony arises that the system was without adequate safeguards of investigation, tests of destitution, means of hindering duplication of relief from several sources simultaneously, or of making the relief adequate to the necessity. Private almsgiving was profuse and chaotic, while still behind the demands made upon it; and was dispersed in tantalizing doles, miserably inadequate for effectual succor where the need was genuine, and dealt out broadcast among the clamorous and impudent. Twenty years ago those in the United States who thought that the function of relief would be lifted above temporary material aid were few in number and but just beginning to be heard. Indeed, it is the industrial depression following the commercial crisis of 1873, throwing multitudes out of work and making a heavy draft upon the benevolent, which seems to afford the starting point for the examination and reformation of the prevailing methods of charity.

Beginnings.—In 1872 the nearest approximation to charity organization to be found in the United States was the Chardon Street Building in Boston, erected in 1869 by joint contributions from the city and personal subscribers, in pursuance of a plan first promulgated by Hon. Robert C. Winthrop in 1857. Under its roof are the offices of the official boards, and the principal voluntary relief societies of the city; and the existence of this building facilitated the subsequent systematic development of registration and co-operation in that city.

Charity organization had independent and almost simultaneous initiation in Buffalo, New Haven, Boston, Brooklyn, Philadelphia and two or three other cities, an account of which is given in the full report submitted to this Conference, but which the brevity of time allowed to this committee forbids us to read.

This movement found an expression of its unity in the National Conference of Charities and Correction, which is itself an outgrowth of the American Social Science Association. It is first mentioned in the proceeding of the Chicago Conference of 1879, where Mr. Seth Low presented a description of the work in Brooklyn, and a committee was formed to report upon charity organization. Two years later, at Boston, nineteen societies reported to the Conference, and the committee grew to a section, which published a separate report of its own proceedings.

Suppression of Out-Door Relief.—Simultaneously with the beginning of charity organization, and promoted by the same men, there was a repression, in important cities, of official out-door relief. Returns from four cities for that time, show that the amount saved to taxpayers in 1880, was $396,403. This event attracted wide attention in watchful official circles and was the beginning of a wiser administration of the charitable funds raised by taxation in many communities.

Ten Years of Growth.—In 1882, there were twenty-two charity organization societies known to exist in the United States, and ten others which had adopted some of the leading features of this movement, and were enrolled as correspondents with the former societies. They embraced cities and towns having a population of 6,331,700, or twelve per cent. of the total of the United States, and among them were the chief centres of influence in the country. Of these societies ten were in or had just completed the first year of their operations, administering in incorporated populations of 2,363,138. From this point it is practicable to make tables and comparisons which exhibit the growth of the charity organization movement in the United States.

At the close of the year 1892, there were ninety-two charity organization and affiliated societies, an increase of two hundred and seventy-eight per cent. in ten years; and they were located in cities and towns comprising a population estimated at 11,080,766. In nearly every instance the motive leading to these organizations is declared to have been discontent with the prodigality and inefficiency of public relief, and the chaotic state of private charity.

Two Types.—Classified by their relation to almsgiving, twenty-five report that they do not give material relief from their own funds; twenty that they do relieve; nine, that they do so only in emergent cases, and of these two say they do so in order to avoid official outrelief. In 1881, there were but twelve non-relieving and seven relieving societies reporting.

Lapsed Societies.—It is known to this committee that thirteen charity organization societies have been formed and dissolved. A few are practically in suspension. Various causes may be assigned for the creation of this delinquent and lapsed list. For the most part the nascent society yielded to the opposition of the friends of the old system, or was planted on a community not prepared to comprehend and maintain it. Probably the lack of trained and capable superintendents, and of suitable friendly visitors prepared to bear the restraints of charity organization, is the chief cause of miscarriage.

On Reports from Societies.—The last ten years of the history of charity organization, the amplified report will exhibit in tabulated statistics appended thereto, merely calling attention to their salient points and results. For its preparation a circular letter was prepared and sent to every society known to your committee. It is to be regretted that many of the returns were very imperfect. From the material furnished the following exhibit is made:

Changes of Method.—Relief Adopted:—In a movement so recent there has been small room to judge of the effects of various methods and to devise new plans of work. There are three distinct phases of development to be detected in the growth of their work: (1) the adoption of material relief; (2) the abolition or reduction of such relief; and (3) the expansion of friendly visiting and provident enterprises. Four societies report a change from organizing and co-operative work by adding thereto the distribution of some form of alms. From statements made to us the inference is that alms relief has been for the most part taken up in a very restricted way, and but few charity organization societies, which did not begin with it, have since adopted it.

Relief Withheld.—On the other hand, several of our societies have distinctly receded from the work of material relief, to seek it by co-operation with other benevolent agencies. Notable is the history of Cincinnati and Detroit, where their several independent district associations were abolished, and a board of trustees were put in complete charge of the administration. From the important city of Philadelphia, where the society began with its sovereignty lodged in ward associations, the report comes that the central board has gained in influence and authority over the ward administration and is now enforcing the charity organization theory more vigorously than was possible at first. In Pueblo and San Francisco direct relief has receded, and been replaced with better systems of investigation and co-operation with other charitable agencies. Syracuse has restricted its material relief to the merest tiding over of emergent cases until some judgment can be reached on the better disposition of an applicant for aid, and this society enrolls itself as a non-relieving association.

Finance.—In extenuation of the enormous percentages of contributing support, it must be remembered that this review embraces only fourteen organizations in 1882, several of which were in their first year, and compares them with fifty-four societies reporting ten years later. In the last ten years the number of societies trebled; individual contributors quadrupled; contributing churches and societies increased more than three hundred and seven per cent. The income of forty-eight societies increased three-fold in 1892 over that of seventeen in 1882, and reached an aggregate of $263,421. Fourteen societies report the beginning of invested funds, and together hold property and securities valued at $409,038.

Real Estate.—Endowments began in Buffalo in 1880, when through the generosity of a single individual the Fitch Crèche was established, at a cost of about $40,000. To this gift Mr. Benjamin Fitch added much other property, conveying it by deed of trust to the society for the purpose of encouraging provident schemes. The Fitch Institute, completed in 1883, not only affords offices for the accommodation of the society, but within it are comprised an accident hospital and a training-school for nursery maids and domestic servants. Very noble is the admirable and imposing United Charities Building of New York, erected by Mr. John S. Kennedy, and dedicated March 6th, 1893. It was deeded to four of the principal charity societies of the city, who manage it through a board of trustees chosen by them. Each has an equal share in the use and income of the structure, and one of these is the Charity Organization Society. As it cost over $600,000, the equity of this society is valued at $150,000. The Charities Building in Chardon street, Boston, was already in existence when the Associated Charities of that city were organized, and here that society has always had its headquarters free of rent. The Bridgeport society owns a building valued at $11,000; that of Cleveland, one valued at $23,000, and New Haven has a fund of $30,000 dedicated to a like purpose. These edifices are centres of conference, co-operation and exchanges of information, and virtually add an estimated value of about $220,000 to the invested resources of charity organization in the United States, making a total of $630,000.

Internal Organization.—Fifty-two societies report placing in the field of administration and personal service of the necessitous in 1892 an army of 5,476 men and women. This number is below the actual fact, since seventeen of the societies make no return of their administrative officers, and eight, none of their friendly visitors; while Philadelphia fails to enumerate the officers and visitors of its eighteen large district societies, with which several hundred visitors are connected. The total number is doubtless over 6,000. In administrative work 763 men, an increase of 157 per cent. in ten years, and 511 women, an increase of 220 per cent., were engaged in 1892; of paid officials the same year there were seventy-seven men (increase 220 per cent.) and 135 women (increase 250 per cent.) in the service; while of friendly visitors 456 men (increase 1,400 per cent.) and 3,534 women (increase 165 per cent.) toiled in the homes or over the ill fortunes of applicants for aid. As 74,704 cases came under the notice of the societies, this would give an average of 17.6 cases to each visitor, a number altogether too large for effective work. Fifteen societies control one hundred subordinate district conferences or associations, and twenty-nine avail themselves of conferences among officers and visitors to consider methods in the disposition to be made of cases. The conferences range from weekly through monthly and quarterly sessions. A notable example of kindred work lasted through the first eight years of the Philadelphia society. There once a month an assembly of the whole society was held and numerously attended, at which papers were read and practical discussions maintained on the problems of charity; and the effect of them was incalculable in educating the workers, and even the community, in a sense of responsibility for their poor brothers and sisters.

Lines of Work Developed—Repression—Public Out-door Relief.—It would be gratifying, if the statistics were to be had, to show what charity organization has done directly in lightening the tax-payer's burden; but this is a matter of minor significance compared with the more humane remedial aims of the movement. Only eight societies have supplied definite figures, and the results are a present annual reduction in municipal out-door relief in Brooklyn, Buffalo, Burlington, Ia., Hartford, Conn., Indianapolis, New Haven, Conn., Omaha, Philadelphia, Syracuse and Taunton, Mass., of $409,480. There has been no out-door public relief in New York during the past twenty years.

Besides this sum, in Cincinnati and Minneapolis municipal out-door relief has diminished one-half, notwithstanding the increase of population. Albany and Portland, Ore., note its decrease. In Detroit its distribution has been turned over to a special commission appointed by the Mayor, and presumably removed from partisan political control. In Newark, N. J., it has been restricted to bread and coal tickets during the three winter months, but is continued to widows and the aged the year round.

Street Begging.—From fifteen important cities information comes that street begging has been perceptibly diminished. In five of these cities it is pronounced suppressed, which means, at least, that mendicants no longer flaunt their rags and deformities before the eyes of the citizens, or wail their dolorous cant in the public ear. New York employs two special officers to deal with this class of cases. An analyzed record is kept of the cases, and in 1892, 63.4 per cent. were found to be inmates of cheap lodging houses and police stations; 20.7 to have homes, and 2.9 not to be traced to any abode. Of these, 21 per cent. were maimed, sick or aged, and 79 per cent. able-bodied. To give to these maimed and aged on the streets was unmixed cruelty, as it kept them from the more humane provision of the almshouse. These are the only records within reach that permit a study and classification of the street-beggar genus, and probably the ratios here given will hold good for the whole class throughout the country. In many cities the suppression of street begging is hindered by the vicious custom of the civic authorities to issue licenses to thinly disguised beggars to play musical instruments and to peddle small wares in the streets, as, *e. g.*, Boston, Buffalo and New York.

Vagrants.—In the repression of vagrancy three resources have been employed—the police, for the incorrigible and dissolute; labor tests, as a means of discriminating those who have abandoned themselves to a predatory career from those who are willing to use the means afforded for reaching self-support; and lodgings, where wayfarers may abide temporarily while in search of employment. Some of the wayfarers' lodges employ labor tests, and the favorite form of such tests is the wood-yard. The oldest and most systematic of these combined lodges and tests is in Boston, where the city took up the work in 1879. It at once relieved the police station-houses of the casuals, and spared the unfortunates, who were desirous of self-maintenance, the humiliation and contamination of police stations. Here, too, the purification of persons and the clothing of the beneficiaries is scrupulously attended to, accompanied by the strong reinforcement of that cleanliness which restores one's self-respect. This system has also been carried to a wide extent in Philadelphia, where the Charity Organization Society performs at its own expense for the city the work of relieving the station houses and streets from the casuals. The work of the society in the rural district of Bryn Mawr is chiefly of this kind. It is reported to us that twenty-seven of our societies, in dealing with this vagabondage, lodged 71 per cent. and subjected 26 per cent. to labor tests. This distinction between lodging and labor tests does not, however, seem trustworthy; since, as a rule, both are practiced in combination.

In addition, 117 cases of fraudulent schemes, especially those pretending to be organizations for charitable purposes, were detected and exposed, and in many cases broken up, in 1892; by far the greater part of this suppression having occurred in New York.

Co-operation.—Co-operation is one of the most difficult attainments. It is a thing of slow growth, but each advance made and held is a distinct and decisive triumph of organization of ideas. Out of forty societies embraced in this branch of our inquiry, thirty-one claim a co-operation, more or less complete, with municipal agencies of relief. The ratio thereof is the high one of 97 per cent. The returns of thirty societies show that together they have established a practical co-operation with one-third of the charitable agencies and institutions in their cities. In thirty-four cities co-operation has been attained with 44 per cent. of the churches located in them.

Registration.—It is a singular mark of the general and deep impression upon the public mind concerning the imposture and worthlessness of applications for relief, that registration and investigation should be regarded as a sort of detective and repressive system. But their detective and repressive effect is only incidental to them under present social conditions. Their true purpose is far greater and grander; and were all imposture and dishonest design to cease, there would still be need of these two processes. The information accumulated by them not only lays bare imposture but maintains the cause of the upright poor, and supplies their credentials of sympathy and help. It would not abolish overlapping, but adjust it, so that the alms from one source may complement the alms from another, and so concert them that they may be timely, appropriate and adequate. Above all, it is the key to co-operation. The records of the registration bureau enable the charity organizationist to say to all who toil for the relief of penury, "We have that information which is invaluable to you, if you would do your work wisely and efficiently. We cannot compel co-operation, but we can serve you, and by service become your auxiliary and friend."

There are two sides to registration. Societies and individuals may make use of our archives for guidance in administering their own relief, and they may also enlarge our efforts by reporting the families and persons whom they aid. The first form of co-operation is by far the more common; it is much rarer for churches, societies and private almsgivers to report to us their own operations. Often this default is simply owing to the need of adopting unwonted methods, and to the labor required in a systematic exchange of information. Were our bureaus of registration replenished and used as the charity organization theory requires, the active benevolences of society would fall into alignment and move as a disciplined army, animated with a common purpose to the conquest of the problems of penury, misery and degradation.

Administrators of public official relief recognize that they are responsible to the public for the way in which they perform their work, and hence they are most willing to open their records to our societies. In eleven large cities it is claimed that the bureaus of registration are working in unrestricted harmony and completeness with poor-law officials. Indianapolis and New Haven estimate that their records cover nine-tenths of the municipal relief cases; in Albany, Buffalo and Rochester the ratio ranges from one-quarter to three-quarters; and in three other cities this form of co-operation is returned as partial or considerable. Registration for voluntary societies would appear to be for fifty-nine per cent. of them in twelve cities. Fourteen societies have registered for churches, attaining to the service of from 10 to 80 per cent. of the whole number in their communities, New York taking the lead. Such service for asylums and similar private institutions is naturally restricted. For eight societies, the registration service has extended from 5 to 75 per cent. of the whole number of such institutions, New Haven leading.

In 1877 a plan was proposed in Buffalo of a central registration bureau for all the charity organization societies, which should confine itself to recording travelling and professional mendicants. It was a scheme for the suppression of the tramp nuisance, but proved to be premature.

Social Slate.—Another important plan was devised at the same time for the classification of applicants for relief according to their family relations, ages and nationality. It went into fairly general operation in 1889, when the blank forms were agreed upon and published by action of this National Conference. It is based on the joint experience of the American societies and elicited the approval of the First International Conference of Charities, held in Paris.

A word may be said here to enforce the value of keeping uniform records. Our societies are the only agencies in the United States through which authentic statistics can be gathered, not only covering a census of relief-seekers, but eliciting the results of various methods of dealing with them. This sort of information, if carefully collected and collated, will soon become a treasury of details to which the sociologist will confidently resort, and on which legislators, reformers and workers among the poor have already begun to base their course of conduct.

Classified Disposition of Cases.—From the beginning charity organization societies in the United States have followed a plan of recording the disposition made of applicants whose cases came under their charge, which conformed in a general way to that of the great parent society in London. There are 44 of them whose reports have been received, and these embrace the treatment given to the huge number of nearly 75,000 cases. With the exception of a few cities, this number embraces only new and not recurrent applicants, and hence represents the fresh expansion of the work in the year 1892. Owing to the different method of keeping their records, and in making the returns compiled in the reports of the various societies, exact deductions cannot be made, and the same cases must appear in two or more classes. It is probably that a tide of over 100,000 families and individuals flowed through the conduits of the charity organization societies. If they are grouped in large generalizations it may be affirmed, as approximately true, that three-tenths of this vast array of alms-seekers really need material succor, and an equal number do not need it at all. Of the charge of one-tenth, our societies have been wholly relieved by placing them in other care. For nearly one-fifth co-operation of other societies and of individuals and municipal officers has been obtained; and for one-fifth relief by employment was found adequate. It is probable that these ratios fairly represent the experience thus far of those engaged in charity organization work.

Provident Schemes.—Graduation from dependence to self-maintenance is an expression familiar to all engaged in this work throughout the United States. It describes the aim of this reform, and the degree of achievement in it is a supreme test of our principles. If there is to be no elevation of our wards into self-support, then charity organization societies only add to the alms-doling, the consequences of which have been so pernicious to society. In cities where charity organization societies have been planted and acquired their characteristic influence, there has been a very conspicuous contemporaneous growth in the number and variety of provident societies. And our societies claim that this is not a mere chance, but the direct result of their teachings, and generally the result of the personal labors of their own members.

Saving Funds.—These are of four sorts—simple provident societies, taking small deposits at the counter; stamp banks, where deposit stamps are sold at stations in different parts of the city; banks to receive small deposits gathered by visitors who call at houses for them, as in Newport, R. I., and Castleton, S. I.—an ingenious system, which combines with great effectiveness the work of the friendly visitor with the encouragement of savings; and fuel-funds, by means of which the deposits of the summer secure deliveries of wood and coal in the winter at cost price. Eighteen such provident fund organizations were known to exist in 1892 under the auspices of our societies, gathering in the savings of 33,826 depositors.

Special Lines of Development.—Attitude toward Relief.—As each community has its distinctive characteristics, so each charity organization society inevitably adjusts itself to them, and diversities of practice and development spring up. These variations are desirable as enlarging the number of experiments tried, and as throwing side lights upon special problems. In one particular there is a growing unison of judgment. In the returns of the sixty societies contributing to this report, there is no advocacy or defense of relief-giving from their treasuries. On the contrary those societies which practice it either deprecate it or excuse it. All this testimony is a distinct indication of the advance of our principles, and of an intelligent perception of the function of charity organization. The matter is of prime importance, for upon this rock of almsgiving many a society has been wrecked.

Emergencies.—A peculiar and severe test of charity organization societies has come in the demands made by special emergencies. The Chicago Relief and Aid Society reached a position of commanding influence and was led into the adoption of many charity organization principles by acting as the distributor of large funds contributed for the aid of sufferers by the great fire of 1871. Boston was moved to the steps which resulted in her Associated Charities by the suffering consequent upon the great fire of 1872, and on the commercial crisis which began in 1873 and brooded over the land for two or three years. The Malden, Mass., society was formed to alleviate the distress caused by a great fire in 1875. At the time of the terrible Johnstown flood, the District of Columbia committee to gather aid for the sufferers, sent the secretary of the Associated Charities of Washington thither as their agent. In 1889 a disastrous fire swept over an area of twenty-five acres in Lynn, rendering 175 families homeless, and putting seven thousand persons out of employment. The information accumulated by the Associated Charities, covering many families, was instantly available; the skill of its visitors, agents and managers came into immediate requisition; a delegation of experienced visitors came from the society in Boston, and during the six days in which a more general relief committee was taking form and acquiring funds and stores, the Associated Charities was giving order and shaping methods which alleviated immediate distress and facilitated subsequent operations. The tornado of Louisville in May, 1890, by which seventy-six lives were lost and two hundred persons were injured, created great suffering. The Board of Trade Relief Committee expended $156,000 in alleviating it, and employed the visitors and agents of the Charity Organization Society as its investigators and almoners. In the Park Place disaster in New York in May, 1891, when sixty-three persons were killed or injured, those in charge of the Mayor's Relief Fund invoked the aid of the Charity Organization Society, and within a week the particulars of each case were collected and recommendations made which were followed in the distribution of the fund contributed for the sufferers. By the same means the $7,000 collected by the New York Herald for the same disaster was disbursed. This capacity to act in emergencies cannot seem strange to those who consider the advantages of a pre-existing registration bureau, of a large staff of trained agents and visitors familiar with the aspect of want, and of a co-operative scheme which embraces the whole field of benevolent work among the destitute.

Legislation—Not the least of the labors undertaken in this movement are the efforts to amend legislation. In Massachusetts, the separation of the pauper from the criminal class in public institutions has been accomplished; there and in New York strenuous and sometimes successful efforts have proceeded from our societies to restrict the sale of alcoholic liquors; the poor relief laws have been amended: in the same states the statutes have defined tenement-houses so as to bring a larger number under official inspection; new requirements have been imposed by sanitary laws, and in Boston an alliance has been made with the Technological Institute to secure reports on the violation of sanitary principles. In New York a law, unfortunately not yet in operation, has been obtained requiring the city to open municipal lodging houses to relieve the station houses of wayfarers and secure their cleanliness; immigration has been made a subject of careful investigation, and recommendations prepared for submission to Congress. In several societies there is a department of legal advice, in which professional service is rendered gratuitously to prevent injustice or secure the poor in their rights.

Education.—Seminaries or departments for the investigation of sociological questions have been established at Harvard, Yale, Johns Hopkins, Cornell, Pennsylvania, Vanderbilt, Leland Stanford, Chicago and many other Universities, at the State Universities of Ohio, Michigan and Nebraska, at Amherst and Bryn Mawr Colleges; and in connection with some of these institutions occasional or serial papers are published from time to time. Representatives of our societies have been called upon to lecture on these themes in several colleges and theological seminaries, especially in the prominent ones in or within easy reach of the leading cities, and also before audiences assembled in churches.

NECROLOGY.

Some few of the many whose memory and example remain as benedictions to their associates, must have a tribute here to meet the demands of our hearts.

Hodge.—With happy sagacity the Philadelphia Society called Dr. H. Lenox Hodge to be its first president. Of honored lineage, of high professional eminence, of winning sweetness of disposition, he uttered judgments so wise and conciliatory that the divergent opinions of his associates melted into unison before them. His great influence was a tower of strength to the nascent society, and his name entrenched it in public confidence. He embodied that "sweetness and light" which Matthew Arnold thought to give the soul its noblest excellence. He died in the strength of his manhood, and while president of the society.

McCulloch.—In Indianapolis the Rev. Oscar C. McCulloch was a magician of philanthropy. His was a scholar's diligence and enthusiasm in the study of the alleviation of human misery. No man was more dexterous in detecting the dictates of true charity and following them through the complexities and discords of social benevolence; for in his heart was the divine instinct which "beareth all things, believeth all things, hopeth all things." The Charity Organization Society of Indianapolis, founded under his leadership, is his monument, and to future generations may it long transmit his honored fame.

Preston.—Vicar-General Preston was an earnest and useful friend of the society in New York, and an efficient intermediary in all negotiations with the authorities and agencies of the Roman Catholic Church.

Brooks.—By the death of Phillips Brooks the Associated Charities of Boston lost one of its most loved and inspiring friends. He was on the first committee appointed to report a plan of organization and co-operation, and on the provisional council until the society was organized. That society records that "his eloquence and his great influence have been repeatedly exerted in the society's behalf. His ability and still more his personal character were such that whatever he touched gained from him beauty and dignity. His eloquent words at the various public meetings of the society set forth the scope of its work and the spirit that should pervade it, in a way that exalted and ennobled it for all who heard him."

Buzelle.—Of George B. Buzelle of Brooklyn it was declared, as his body was laid to rest, "he was one of God's noblemen." He had caught the spirit of his Master's words "Whosoever shall be great among you shall be your minister; whosoever of you shall be chiefest shall be servant of all." He was not an hireling; he was not an official; he was a man and a brother. No one could have known Mr. Buzelle without being impressed with his faithfulness. Nothing could stand between him and his duty. The chairman of this committee, as his nearest neighbor in like responsibility, and all who have known him in these conferences, and especially in the painstaking and eminently successful labors of this chairmanship a year ago, will testify that these words cover no exaggerations.

It would be a grateful task to linger over these tributes to the memories of departed colleagues who live still in our esteem, but time forbids. These were among many others we would name, by priority of labors or by eminence of influence, of so wide note that they could not be passed by in silence. Others have wrought with no less consecration of heart, no less generosity of thought and hand. Gratitude for the inspiration of their example, for the quickening touch of their noble personality, follows them beyond the tomb. We love to think of these souls, so radiant here with pure charity, having done their humane work to the least of these His brethren, as having entered into the joy of their Lord.

THE STATE CHARITIES AID ASSOCIATION OF THE STATE OF NEW YORK.

1872—1893.

VOLUNTARY, UNOFFICIAL SUPERVISION OF PUBLIC CHARITABLE INSTITUTIONS IN CO-OPERATION WITH OFFICIAL BOARDS, AS ILLUSTRATED BY THE WORK OF THE STATE CHARITIES AID ASSOCIATION OF NEW YORK.

BY MISS LOUISA LEE SCHUYLER, MEMBER OF THE ASSOCIATION.

The State Charities Aid Association of New York was organized in May, 1872, with the object of bringing about reforms in the poorhouses, almshouses and state charitable institutions of the State of New York, through the active interest of an organized body of volunteer visitors, acting in co-operation with, and as an aid to the local administration of these institutions, and the official state boards of supervision.

Upon nomination of the State Charities Aid Association, through its board of managers, justices of the Supreme Court are authorized to grant to the visitors of the association orders to enable them to visit, inspect and examine, in behalf of the association, any of the public charitable institutions owned by the state, and the county, town and city poorhouses and almshouses within the State of New York; such visitors to be residents of the counties from which these institutions receive their inmates. The association reports annually, on or before the 1st of December, to the State Board of Charities and to the State Commission in Lunacy, upon matters relating to the institutions subject respectively to the inspection and control of these two official bodies. The full text of the law is given as an appendix to this paper.

The association entered upon its work in 1872, not in any spirit of criticism of officials, but with the wish to assist them towards the reforms they themselves desired, by the creation of a strong local public sentiment in favor of these reforms; knowing also that for much that was at fault the system, and not the men who administered it, was responsible. The association was, however, equally determined to expose abuses and corruption wherever found. What measure of co-operation, what degree of public support has attended this conception of the attitude towards others sought to be maintained by the association, the following pages will show. It may, however, be mentioned here that an experience of twenty-one years has taught us that wherever our visitors have been welcomed by the local authorities, there earnest and honest men have been found in charge, with nothing to conceal and everything to gain from outside interest and support; whereas, where the visitors are not welcomed, it has become almost a sure sign that in these institutions are practices and management which will not bear the search-light of independent, fearless vision.

That the people have the right to visit and inspect the public institutions of charity owned and supported by themselves is a cardinal point of our faith; and the association in its membership has sought to make the lines so broad that it may fairly claim to represent the people. In its ranks are found men and women, young and old, rich and poor, the farmer, the merchant, the medical and legal professions, all political parties, the Protestant, the Catholic, the Hebrew. And this claim of the association, that it represents the people in its volunteer work, has again and again been recognized by the legislature of the State of New York: first of all by providing for the visitors of the association, as already mentioned, a right of entrance into all the public charitable institutions in the state; and secondly, by the enactment, sooner or later, of every measure of reform, requiring legislative action, which the managers of the association have applied for. It is thoroughly understood that the association, composed entirely of volunteer workers, desires no administrative powers for itself, fearing to divide or impair the responsibility of the local authorities for the good management of their respective institutions. The association desires only to see, and to speak of what it sees. This is power enough, in a country where the press is free and where public opinion is all-powerful.

The frame-work of organization upon which the association rests is very simple. It is governed by a board of managers of fifteen members, men and women, elected annually from those members of the association who reside in the city of New York, known as members of the Central Association, and numbering to-day 220. The officers of the County Visiting Committees vote also for managers at the annual meeting. The board of managers, by act of incorporation, has full power to direct and control the affairs and funds of the association, and is responsible for its good government.

The officers of the association, president, vice-president, treasurer, secretary and librarian, are, except the secretary, elected annually by the incoming board from its own members; and the president and secretary of the association are also chairman and secretary of the board. The secretary is the chief executive officer of the association, and is appointed and removed by the board of managers. The librarian, in addition to the duties appertaining usually to this office, collects for the library, by donation, books and pamphlets upon subjects connected with the work of the association. These books are available to all members, and are also loaned to other students who may apply for them.

There are four standing committees of the Central Association: upon Children; upon Adult Able-bodied Paupers; upon Hospitals; and a Finance Committee.

The duties of three of these standing committees are defined in the by-laws of the association, as follows:

"*Committee on Children.*—It is the duty of the Committee on Children to keep itself informed of the number, condition and disposition of the pauper children of the state; and to urge the adoption of such measures in the care and training of these children as may tend effectually to destroy hereditary pauperism, and as speedily as possible restore them to the family-life of the community.

"*Committee on Adult Able-bodied Paupers.*—It is the duty of the Committee on Adult Able-bodied Paupers to keep itself informed of the number of able-bodied pauper men and women in the almshouses of the state, and the character and value of the labor performed by them, and the Committee shall advocate reformatory treatment for all persons of this class. The Committee shall endeavor to have the laws for the arrest and commitment of vagrants enforced, shall advocate measures obliging all adult able-bodied paupers to work, and promote all efforts which tend to abolish beggary and vagrancy; and it shall endeavor to bring about the abolition or reformation of the system of official out-door relief.

"*Committee on Hospitals.*—It is the duty of the Committee on Hospitals: 1st. To keep itself informed of the number and condition of the sick, insane, epileptic, blind, deaf and dumb, idiot and aged paupers in the New York institutions of public charities, and to urge the adoption of such measures as are best adapted to restore their health, alleviate their sufferings, and secure their humane care. 2d. To collect and impart information in regard to the most approved plans for the construction, ventilation and disinfection of hospitals and asylums, and for their administration; and to prepare plans for the organization of their kitchen, linen, laundry, nursing and supply departments. 3d. To keep itself informed of the organization and management of the dispensary and ambulance service, and to suggest and advocate any modification thereof that may seem desirable."

The *Finance Committee* collects, through voluntary contributions, the small amount of money needed annually: for rent of headquarter office in New York city, and for clerical assistance; for printing, postage and office expenses; for the salaries and traveling expenses of the secretary and assistant secretary. Less than $10,000 is needed for these purposes. No money is received from public sources; nor will this be accepted, as we wish to be independent of all outside influences.

COUNTY VISITING COMMITTEES.

It is the special duty of the secretary, in person and by correspondence, to organize County Visiting Committees throughout the state, who receive their appointment from the board of managers and who work under its direction and control. Composed of both men and women, these committees number to-day forty-eight, comprising 750 members.

It is the duty of the visiting committees to visit the poorhouses and almshouses of their respective counties, reporting monthly to the board of managers, through the secretary at the headquarter office in New York city. Such portions of these reports as may have reference to children are referred to the Standing Committee on Children of the Central Association; those which relate to vagrants to the Standing Committee on Adult Able-bodied Paupers; those having reference to the sick, the insane, epileptics, idiots, the blind, deaf and dumb, and the aged to the Standing Committee on Hospitals. The members of these three standing committees are experts and students of the subjects referred to them. It is their duty to inform themselves of the best form of care which each class of dependents should receive, to gather this information from every country in the world, from every other state of our Union whose enlightened methods are superior to our own, to originate ways and means to meet the difficulties referred to them, and then to place this information at the disposal of the visitors in such form as to be of practical use to them. Sometimes the questions asked, being the same from many quarters, are answered by the publication of handbooks, for Visitors to the Poorhouse, Visitors to Hospitals, Visitors to the Insane, by treatises upon nursing, training-schools for nurses, hospital laundries, upon legal subjects, etc. Sometimes a simple method for ventilating a hospital ward is asked for; and again, plans for altering an old poorhouse or building a new one, or for the erection of a new hospital. Thirty-four such publications (the authors of all but one being members of the association), besides leaflets and circulars innumerable, have been issued to meet the demands of our visitors and others for special information.

It will thus be seen how the student members and the active visiting members of the association act and react upon each other. The former help the latter by their expert knowledge; the latter prevent the former from becoming mere theorists by applying to their theories the test of practical application.

The remedies to be applied are most of them local in character, intended to improve the condition of those inmates of poorhouses and almshouses who legitimately belong there; and the accomplishment of these reforms depends upon the influence of the visiting committees in their own counties, with their own boards of supervisors, with their own city commissioners of charities, or superintendents of the poor. For other classes of inmates the heroic treatment of removal to other institutions and other surroundings is necessary. This often calls for legislative action; and such action, when determined upon, is always undertaken and controlled by the board of managers. A thorough study is given the subject, extending at times over one or more years, the best legal talent is sought, and the bill, when drafted, is placed in the hands of a special committee to secure its enactment; while members of the association in all parts of the state are called upon to interest their representatives in the legislature in its behalf.

The remedies, it will thus be seen, are of a two-fold nature; some of them general, requiring the intervention of the legislature, others local, to be sought at home.

RESULTS.

What has this system accomplished through these twenty-one years, since the association began its work in 1872?

Much that will never be known; the many acts of kindness to individuals, the rescue of little children from pauperizing influences, the assistance given convalescents when leaving hospital, the happiness brought into many a maimed and broken life—all this, going on quietly day after day, can never be recorded; nor the sympathy and support given by our visitors to the overworked wives of poorhouse keepers, to the keepers themselves. These are not small things. They lie deep in the very foundations of our work. From the desire to alleviate suffering, to help the helpless, to fight for the oppressed, have sprung all the reforms of the State Charities Aid Association, dignified sometimes by high-sounding names, but all going back to the simple recognition of brotherly love to the individual man,' or woman, or child we have known and cared for in the poorhouse.

The following are named as direct results of the work of the State Charities Aid Association. And, in stating them, we wish it borne in mind that what has been accomplished is equally due to the co-operation of the local authorities. In addition to this, and where this has not been attainable, the co-operation of the State Board of Charities and the State Commission in Lunacy have been invaluable. At times the association as been obliged to carry its reforms single-handed, but these instances are fortunately rare.

1. A higher standard of care has been introduced into every poorhouse and almshouse in the state. This means better nursing, special diet for the sick, improved hospital accommodation, separation of the sexes, suitable food, proper clothing, and many little comforts for the aged and infirm. It is impossible to enumerate the small and the great benefits conferred upon the inmates of these institutions through the presence of a few humane and intelligent visitors, commanding the confidence and respect of their own communities and sure of a powerful backing from headquarters.

2. *Training-School for Nurses*, 1873.—This school, attached to Bellevue Hospital, one of the largest pauper general hospitals of the city of New York, was established by our New York County Visiting Committee, who raised the necessary $20,000 with which to begin it, opened the training school on the first day of May, 1873, and to whom is due its efficient management and great success. At first governed by a special committee, the school increased so rapidly in importance that it was soon incorporated as a separate society, merely reporting annually to the parent association in recognition of its origin.

The whole number of patients nursed by this school, from 1879 to 1893, is 50,059.

Its graduates number 424; of these, 45 are now holding positions in hospitals, 19 as superintendents of training schools, 10 as matrons, and 16 as head nurses.

In New York city they have been employed in the New York, Mt. Sinai, Charity and Post-Graduate Hospitals, and in the Hospital for Ruptured and Crippled; at Chicago, in the Cook County Hospital, St. Luke's, and the Presbyterian; in the City Hospital of Boston, the Johns Hopkins at Baltimore, the Brooklyn City Hospital, and the Protestant

Episcopal Church Hospital at Philadelphia. One graduate is in Louisville, one in Indianapolis, one in St. Louis, one in Savannah; one in England, one in Italy, two in Canada, and two in China. The number of private cases nursed by the graduates may be inferred from the fact that there were 1,336 calls for private nurses made during the past year through the registry kept by the Bellevue school.

The school has therefore not only accomplished its primary object of obtaining good nursing for the patients of Bellevue hospital, but has opened a new profession to women; has supplied private families with well-trained, competent nurses, and has furnished district nurses for the sick-poor in their homes.

The above is one illustration of a local remedy sought for and applied at home by a county visiting committee; but destined, as a pioneer school established on a basis unknown at that time in this country, to become so far-reaching in its effects that almost every state in the Union has been benefited thereby.

3. *Hospital Book and Newspaper Society*, 1874.—Boxes for the reception of fresh daily newspapers are placed, by this society, at the railway stations, the ferry slips, the exchanges, etc., in New York city, whence the papers are collected every day and taken to the hospitals, to be immediately distributed through the wards. In 1892 these daily papers numbered 158,417. Books and pamphlets are received at the office of the society, and are sent every week to hospitals, asylums, poor-houses, prisons, life-saving stations, light-houses, etc., often forming the nucleus of a small library. During the year 1892 the society distributed 7,716 books, 15,944 magazines, and 54,020 illustrated and weekly papers. The Hospital Book and Newspaper Society, at first a committee of the association, is now a branch, with independent membership and treasury.

4. *Farming Out the Poor Abolished*, 1875.—In one of the counties of the State of New York there yet remained, when the visiting committee of that county was organized, a remnant of the barbarous system of farming out the care of the poor to the lowest bidder. The abuses connected with this practice can well be imagined. Through the exertions of our visiting committee, this system was speedily and completely abolished.

5. *Temporary Homes for Children*, 1877–85.—In 1875 the New York State Board of Charities secured the enactment of a law, known as "the Children's Law," which made obligatory the removal of all children

over two years of age from the poorhouses and almshouses of the state. In this great reform the board had the full sympathy of the members of the association throughout the state, who have also been active in promoting the enforcement of the law. To provide a suitable place (the poorhouse being very properly forbidden) where temporary lodging for children could be had, pending their removal to homes in families, the visiting committees of Ulster, Westchester and Queens counties established three Temporary Homes for Children, in 1877, 1880 and 1885.

6. *Tramp Act*, 1880.—In several counties it was found to be the direct pecuniary interest of the Overseers of the Poor to encourage vagrancy, as they received from the county treasury fifty cents *per capita*, often more, for each night's lodging given a tramp. It required three years to obtain the necessary remedial legislation; but since the enactment of this deterrent measure, the State of New York has been less attractive to tramps. (Laws of New York, 1880, Chap. 176.)

7. *First Aid to the Injured*, 1882.—The serious condition in which accident cases were received at the hospitals in New York city, owing to ignorance of what should be done before a physician could be summoned, induced the organization, by the Hospital Committee of the association, of a Society for Instruction in First Aid to the Injured, modeled upon the English societies of like nature. This society, since its formation, (at first as a committee of the association,) has given 264 courses of lectures, of which 62 were to pay-classes and 202 to free-classes, to the police, railroad employees, working girls' clubs, and to members of the Young Men's Christian Association and Young Men's Institute, making a total of 6,595 persons thus instructed, of which number 3,545 received diplomas qualifying them to render first aid to the injured. During the eleven years of the existence of the society, it has received over one thousand testimonials from members of the police force and others, attesting the value of the instructions received.

8. *Trained Nurses for the Insane*, 1885.—Acting in co-operation with the Bellevue Training-School for Nurses and the City Commissioners of Charities of Kings County, the Association secured for six graduates of that school a special course of training at the Kings County Insane Asylum. Later, one of these nurses was the first principal of a training-school for nurses for the insane, established at the Hudson River State Hospital.

9. *Municipal Lodging Houses,* 1886.—The association obtained the passage of an act for the establishment, by the New York city authorities, of one or more municipal lodging houses, with the object of diminishing the number of tramps and vagrants at present sheltered without charge by the city in the police station-houses, and of providing decent lodging for respectable persons in temporary distress; labor to be exacted in return for shelter.

The act, being permissive and not mandatory, has never been put in operation. An amendment will doubtless be applied for by the Committee on Adult Able-bodied Paupers, to remedy this defect.

10. *State Care for the Insane Act of* 1890.—*State Care Appropriation Act of* 1891.—For over fifty years it has been the policy of the State of New York to provide hospital treatment and care for its dependent insane. State asylums were first established for acute cases of insanity, to be succeeded later by state asylums for the reception of chronic cases from the poorhouses. Seven large state hospitals have thus been erected and equipped, for the purpose of giving the insane skilled medical treatment and suitable care. It was owing to an infringement, in recent years, of this humane policy, a backward step of the legislature, through which county after county was authorized to retain its milder cases of insanity, until one-third of all the counties of the state had been exempted from the general law, that brought about the necessity, in 1888, of applying for legislation which should restore to the state its old-time policy, and at one stroke completely abolish the poorhouse system of caring for the insane.

It is not necessary to speak here of the condition of the insane in the poorhouse asylums. Nearly all the reports, official and unofficial, of the years 1887–91, unite in condemning it. The remedy proposed by the association was the division of the state into insane asylum districts, one for each of the seven state hospitals; the insane from the poorhouses to be sent to the hospitals of their respective districts. To accommodate them comparatively small, inexpensive buildings were to be erected on the grounds of the existing state hospitals, to contain each not more than 150 nor less than 10 patients; the cost of building, including equipment, (heating, lighting, ventilation, fixtures and furniture,) not to exceed $550 *per capita.* It was made obligatory upon the State Commission in Lunacy to cause the removal of all patients from the poorhouses as soon as state accommodations for them could be provided, and the poorhouses were forbidden to receive further cases of insanity. New

York, Kings and Monroe counties were to be excluded from the provisions of the bill, simply because they had asylum grounds and buildings of sufficient magnitude to be transferred to the state, and reorganized as state hospitals, whenever these counties might wish to come under the provisions of the proposed measure.

In 1888, when the association, single-handed, and in the face of a most formidable opposition, entered upon this great reform, there were over 2,000 insane persons scattered through the poorhouse asylums of the state. That first year, as a matter of course, our bill was lost, public opinion not having yet been sufficiently educated to sustain it; the second year the bill was again lost, but, owing to increased popular support, and the strong advocacy of the president and other members of the State Board of Charities, it was passed by the senate and made great progress in the assembly; the third year the measure received the unanimous and powerful support of the newly-created State Commission in Lunacy, and became a law, after a prolonged and bitter contest. It is known to-day in the State of New York as the State Care Act of 1890. (Laws of New York, 1890, Chap. 126.)

The following year, upon figures furnished by the State Commission in Lunacy, and again acting in concert with the State Commission and the State Board, the association introduced its State Care Appropriation bill, asking for a grant of $454,850 for buildings and equipment. More than this was not needed, owing to the near completion of the St. Lawrence State Hospital. Again there was opposition, but, by this time, owing to the support given the reform movement by the entire press, the people had become fully aware of the condition of the insane in the poorhouses, and would no longer tolerate delay. Every dollar we needed was granted, by unanimous vote of the senate, by a large majority vote in the assembly. This ended the contest—the long four years' battle had been fought and won! (Laws of New York, 1891, Chapter 91.)

Further than this, the State Care Act declared that when accommodations had been provided by the state for the insane from all the poorhouses, the state should bear the cost of their entire maintenance. Last winter, the necessary conditions having been fulfilled, Governor Flower recommended, in his annual message, that an appropriation for this purpose of $1,300,000 be made, to be raised by special tax of one-third of a mill. This appropriation was granted by unanimous vote of the legislature of 1893.

To-day the insane from the poorhouses of fifty-two counties are under state care, leaving but three counties whence they await removal. The Monroe County Asylum has become the Rochester State Hospital; and it is hoped that New York and Kings counties will before long join in bringing the entire state under one uniform system. By the first of October next, we are assured by the State Commission in Lunacy, the insane will all have been removed from every poorhouse in the state of New York.

Time does not allow us to dwell upon other important features of the State Care Act. But enough has been said to show how a general reform, pronounced by experienced men impossible of accomplishment, owing to the organized opposition of the county officials of one-third of the entire state, was finally carried by the determined efforts of a volunteer association, sustained by the press and the people, and heartily supported by the State Commission in Lunacy, and commissioners of the State Board of Charities. No better illustration could be given of the value of official and volunteer co-operation.

In the twenty minutes allotted to this paper it is not possible further to chronicle the work accomplished by the association, nor to speak of that now under way or yet to be undertaken. In the near future we look to the establishment of a state colony for epileptics, to the finding of family homes for dependent children, and the supervision of the children in those homes.

Promotion of the Work of Charity Organization.

One large and important department connected with the earlier work of the association has not been mentioned, and must be briefly spoken of. Before the days of charity organization societies in this country, our visitors were constantly aware of the need of preventive work. They found inmates of poorhouses who might have been saved from becoming paupers, had a helping hand been extended them at some crisis in their lives. It was to meet this need that a standing committee, "on the elevation of the poor in their homes," was added to our original plan of work. To this committee is due the organization of district visiting among the poor in several of the smaller cities of our state; the initiation, in 1879, of the tenement house reform movement in New York city; an act restricting the imprisonment of witnesses in 1883; and the formation, in 1884-85, of the first Working Girls' Clubs in the city of New York. Perhaps, most important of all, an extension of the knowledge of the work of the Charity Organization Society of London, with its principles of self-help and self-support, as also the beautiful work among the poor of Miss Octavia Hill. Miss Hill's papers, scattered through many English magazines, were, with the consent of the author, collected and published by the association in 1875, under the title of "Homes of the London Poor," this being their first appearance in book form.

For eleven years, from 1875 to 1886, this committee did most important service, and then, in accordance with our principles of not duplicating work, disbanded to pass over to the charity organization societies of the State of New York, whose existence it had done so much to promote, the unfinished business of the committee now properly belonging to those societies.

Touching lightly upon this, we revert to the original purpose of this paper, which, prepared for the International Congress of Charities, Correction and Philanthropy of the World's Congress Auxiliary of the World's Columbian Exposition, aims to illustrate the measure of success which attends all philanthropic work, when official and volunteer bodies join forces and co-operate in behalf of reform.

Co-operation between Voluntary and Official Bodies.

The only effective co-operation between volunteer and official bodies is that of mutual good will, and the more independent each is of the other, in organization and in manner of work, the closer will be the co-operation in behalf of a common object, where the right spirit prevails.

Many years ago, as far back as 1873, when the science of organization for philanthropic purposes was less well understood than at present, the association hoped that closer co-operation with our State Board of Charities could be obtained by giving to that board, to whom we already reported annually, the legal right to appoint visitors, it being understood that the visitors appointed should be nominated by the association. The visitors were to make duplicate reports to both bodies. This clumsy contrivance was actually thought well of by us at the time, and the legislation we asked for to put it into operation was granted. Certainly it required no prophet to see that visitors, working under two masters, both, it is true, desiring the same reforms, but with inherently different methods of work, must sooner or later receive conflicting instructions. The plan did not work well. The present arrangement by which, since 1881, our visitors have received their appointment from justices of the Supreme Court, has worked satisfactorily in every respect. The association reports annually to the State Board of Charities; both support each other's measures of reform, while neither is responsible for the other's action, and a closer co-operation now exists between these two bodies than ever before.

As an illustration of the cordial relations which exist to-day between our volunteer association and, I may say without exaggeration, the state officers and official boards of the entire state, I will instance a bit of legislation granted the association by the legislature which has just closed its session.

Up to the present time, while our visitors had a legal right of entrance into the town and county poorhouses and city almshouses, they had no legal right to visit the charitable institutions owned by the state. We had always wished to visit the state institutions, but when the insane were removed from the poorhouses, we especially desired to follow their welfare into the state hospitals; not in any critical spirit, but as their friends, as friends also of the state medical superintendents, with whom we had worked so harmoniously in behalf of state care legislation for the insane. We desired, therefore, an amendment to our right-of-entrance law of 1881, to enable us to visit the state institutions.

Let me state briefly the support this proposed amendment received. It had the recommendation to the legislature of the Statutory Revision Commission, in whose revision of the law the amendment was included; the approval of the State Commission in Lunacy; of the president of the State Board of Charities; and last, but certainly not least, one of the oldest and most respected of our state medical superintendents himself wrote to the legislature, warmly advocating a measure which was to give us the right to inspect his own state hospital. No voice was raised in opposition; the bill was passed by the unanimous vote of both houses of the legislature, and received the approval of the Governor on the 6th of May last.

One more instance of the degree of co-operation secured by the association. In the interest of the welfare of the insane we had been obliged to antagonize the superintendents of the poor of one-third of the counties of the state—four years of weary strife, ended only two years ago. To-day we are invited by these same men to attend their annual convention, and our secretary goes from this Congress to meet with them; they are now among the most earnest supporters of state care for the insane; and this spring we joined hands in behalf of legislation to establish a state colony for the epileptics now in the poorhouses, working together for this purpose.

No law will make co-operation possible: "for the letter killeth, but the spirit giveth life."

The association at present commands the respect and confidence of the people, the support of the entire press, and of the leaders of both political parties. Its strength lies in its integrity of purpose, its careful study of all reform movements before entering upon them, its industry, its freedom from all outside influences and its absolute fearlessness.

As I am to be followed by a paper from our sister society, the State Charities Aid Association of New Jersey, organized in 1886, whose successful career in these few years deserves to be recorded at this time and in this place, I will say no more. But I cannot close without a strong plea in behalf of the establishment of State Charities Aid Associations in every state of our Union. No one knows better than yourselves how much they are needed. My object, in this paper, has been to place before the experienced minds and sober judgment of those who hear it, an evidence of the enormous power for good which can be obtained through the co-operation of our State Boards of Charities, our State Commissions in Lunacy with volunteer associations like the one described. We need organized bodies of visitors for every one of our public charitable institutions everywhere, "whose visits, inspections and examinations," in the words of our charter, "are hereby declared to be for a public purpose, and to be made with a view to public benefit."

APPENDIX.

AN act in relation to the State Charities Aid Association. *Approved by the Governor, May 6, 1893.* State of New York, *Laws of* 1893, *Chap.* 635.

The People of the State of New York, represented in Senate and Assembly, do enact as follows:

Section 1. Any justice of the supreme court, on written application of the State Charities Aid Association, through its president or other officer, designated by its board of managers, may grant to such persons, as may be named in said application, orders to enable such persons, or any of them, as visitors of such association, to visit, inspect and examine, in behalf of said association, any of the public charitable institutions owned by the state, and the county, town and city poorhouses and almshouses within the state. The persons so appointed to visit, inspect and examine said institution or institutions shall reside in the county or counties from which said institution or institutions receive their inmates, and such appointment shall be made by the justice of the supreme court of the judicial district in which said visitors reside. Each order shall specify the institution to be visited, inspected and examined, and the name of each person by whom such visitation, inspection and examination shall be made, and shall be in force for one year from the date on which it shall have been granted, unless sooner revoked.

§ 2. All persons in charge of any such institution shall admit each person named in any such order into every part of such institution, and render such person every possible facility to enable him to make in a thorough manner such visit, inspection and examination, which are hereby declared to be for a public purpose, and to be made with a view to public benefit. Obedience to the orders herein authorized shall be enforced in the same manner as obedience is enforced to an order or mandate made by a court of record.

§ 3. The State Charities Aid Association shall make annual reports of the results of its visits and inspections, made under this act, to the State Board of Charities upon matters relating to the institutions subject to the visitation of said Board; and to the State Commission in Lunacy upon matters relating to the institutions subject to inspection or control by said Commission. Said reports shall be made on or before the first day of December for each preceding fiscal year.

§ 4. Chapter three hundred and twenty-three of the laws of eighteen hundred and eighty-one is hereby repealed.

§ 5. This act shall take effect immediately.

STATE CHARITIES AID ASSOCIATION OF NEW JERSEY.

BY MRS. EMILY E. WILLIAMSON, OF ELIZABETH, NEW JERSEY.

This association was organized in Morristown in the year 1881, and from that time until the year 1886 work was done in that county alone in a quiet unostentatious manner.

The greatest achievement of the county society was the organization of the Morris County Children's Home, a noble charity which has deservedly prospered. To it the children in the almshouse, three years old and over, were at once removed, and to this home the freeholders continue to send all pauper children, paying for each child one dollar and a half per week. It was determined by this county society to enlarge the field of operation to cover the entire state, and to this end a notice of incorporation was issued by the county society signed by the officers, Henry W. Miller, president; George H. Danforth, vice-president; Julia K. Colles, secretary. It was stated in this notice that the general object of the society "is to promote the improvement of the mental, moral and physical condition of the inmates of all charitable and penal institutions in the state of New Jersey, and in particular of all state institutions, county poorhouses and city almshouses, prisons, jails, penitentiaries and reformatories, lunatic asylums, orphan asylums, and of all places where, for charitable, penal or reformatory purposes, any individual is supported at the public charge, and to induce the adoption by the community at large of such measures in the organization and administration of both public and private charity as may develop the self-respect and increase the power of self-support of the poorer classes in society."

Thereafter the following bill was introduced into the senate by Hon. James C. Youngblood, March 22d, 1886, and was signed by Governor Abbett, April 16th:

An act to confer upon the State Charities Aid Association of New Jersey, an association incorporated under the provisions of the act entitled "An act to incorporate benevolent and charitable associations, approved April ninth, one thousand eight hundred and seventy-five," the power to visit, inspect and examine the county and town poorhouses, jails, asylums and other public reformatory and penal institutions of this state.

1. *Be it enacted by the Senate and General Assembly of the State of New Jersey*, That any justice of the supreme court of this state is hereby-authorized to grant, on a written application to him of a majority of the board of managers of the State Charities Aid Association of New Jersey * * * to such person or persons as may be named in such application, an order enabling such person or persons to--visit, inspect and examine, in behalf of such association, any of the county, town, township, or city poorhouses, prisons, jails, penitentiaries, reformatories, and lunatic or orphan asylums, located within any of the counties in which said justice may be appointed to hold the circuit court thereof; and every such order shall specify the institutions to be visited, inspected and examined, and the names of the person or persons by whom the visitation, inspection and examination are to be made, and shall be in force for one year from the date on which it shall have been granted, unless sooner revoked.

2. And be it enacted, That it shall be the duty of any and all persons in charge of each and every poorhouse, prison, jail or other institution embraced in the order specified in the first section of this act, to admit any or all of the persons named in the said order of the justice of the supreme court into every part of such institution, and to render the said person or persons so named in said order every facility within their power to enable them to make, in a thorough manner, their visit, inspection and examination, which are hereby declared to be for a public purpose, and to be made with a view to public benefit; obedience to the order herein authorized shall be enforced in the same manner and with like effect as obedience is enforced to any other order or mandate made by such justice.

3. And be it enacted, That it shall be the duty of the said association to make an annual report to the legislature of this state.

4. And be it enacted, That this act shall be deemed a public act and shall take effect immediately.

Approved April 16th, 1886.

After the passage of the bill creating the state association the work went vigorously on, and to-day ten of the most important counties of the state are included in the organization. As will be gathered from the reading of the bill, the association has under its jurisdiction the penal institutions of the state, making its duties far more complex than those of the New York organization. The association from the first has numbered among its members prominent men and women, who have given their influence to all proposed reforms, working not only in the interest of the pauper and criminal classes, but also with a desire to protect the taxpayers.

Public opinion has been aroused on many important questions, and it is found that the association is recognized everywhere as a power for good. The state prison has from the first been opened to the association. A great deal has been done for the prisoners, principally from an educational standpoint, religious and secular. The parole bill now in operation in our state was drawn at the suggestion of this association.

The board have in many ways, by petitions, &c., urged the building of an intermediary prison on the plan suggested by the commission appointed by the Governor two years ago, of which Charlton T. Lewis, LL. D., was chairman.

Governor Wertz, in his first annual message, January, 1893, urges the legislature to appropriate money for the intermediary prison; an appropriation will undoubtedly be made by the next legislature for this purpose. At the meeting of the association held in Trenton, May 14th, of the present year, the following extract was read from a letter written by warden Patterson to the secretary:

"To the subject of providing for discharged convicts, I have given a great deal of thought, and it seems to me that no more laudable thing could be done in our state than that of providing some way to ameliorate the condition of those who have been unfortunate enough to be placed under our control. Other states are making suitable provisions for this class, and all of the states are considering the subject."

A committee was immediately appointed to consider and report upon the best plan for taking care of discharged and paroled prisoners. This committee will complete its work and report to the Governor in December next.

An act was drawn by the law committee of the association, which became a law in 1888, providing for the separate confinement of youths under sixteen years of age from older criminals, in the jails, workhouses and penitentiaries. Clause 3 of the same act provides for the separate detention of youths in the station-houses and lockups.

It has been found difficult to make the various boards of freeholders conform to the provisions of this act, owing to the fact that alterations in the jails, costing money, were required. But by degrees, under strong pressure, the requirements of the law will be fulfilled.

The distribution of magazines and proper books in the jails seems in itself a little matter. But in every case, and they are many, where it has been faithfully carried out, the result has been good. Wardens who have been at first opposed to the plan, acknowledge the good results.

The establishment of religious services in many of the jails has been of great benefit to the prisoners.

The station-houses in our large cities have been greatly improved through the influence of the association.

The county asylums have been carefully inspected and many suggestions made by the association carried out.

In the few almshouses of our state where insane persons are kept, they are well cared for, except in the matter of special medical attendance, which is, of course, of great and vital importance.

In the city hospitals, many good results have come from suggestions made, such as the adding of new wings for alcoholic patients and better sanitary arrangements.

In our state are forty-one almshouses of a public character. Twelve are county almshouses supported by a county tax. In twenty-nine townships are township poorhouses, a few of which are private. Great abuses have existed in many of them. The work of this association has nowhere shown better results.

When the committee began their investigations, as a rule the almshouses were found to be dirty, with no sanitary regulations or conveniences, and no such thing as separation of sexes. The list of those included in the above description is growing less each year, owing to the work of the association. The four almshouses that were from the first found to be in first class condition, with separation of the sexes, were the Newark and Paterson city almshouses and those of Cumberland and Hudson counties.

An act for the better regulation of the almshouses of this state was passed May 6th, 1889, and amended March 12th, 1890, at the special request of the association, calling for the complete separation of the sexes in all parts of the buildings and yards, an exception being made in favor of old married people living together as man and wife. It is found almost a herculean task to enforce the requirements of this law. It is being accomplished slowly, but it requires the greatest watchfulness on the part of the state and local committees and the general secretary. In the small almshouses it will be evaded, if possible. The treatment of women in our factories, shops and stores is another point that a special committee from the board is considering. The condition of the tenement houses and districts has also received special attention.

The secretary is in receipt of letters from all parts of the state, calling attention to abuses and violations of the laws. This last is one of the most important questions now receiving the attention of our members. The laws as they stand are, many of them, all that is needed, but never having been enforced, they have become obsolete. The secretary is preparing for the use of the members of the association, a complete list of all laws regulating the care of paupers, the insane and criminals. Such a list will greatly aid the reformatory work already begun. It is best to begin by enforcing the laws, rather than to ask for further legislation.

The great success of the association is largely due to the fact that it has from the first been wisely guided; sentimental criticism has at no time been allowed; facts with practical results have governed the board of managers, upon which are representatives from each county and town.

ARE LABOR COLONIES NEEDED IN THE UNITED STATES?

BY MRS. CHARLES R. LOWELL, OF NEW YORK.

The term labor colony, as used in the following paper, means a farm managed by a charitable corporation or a municipality, and having for its object the training of the laborers who work upon it, with a view to their being fitted eventually to earn a living elsewhere.*

The Cedar Hill farm, of 200 acres, at Plainville, New Jersey, was established in 1874 by Mr. Joseph W. Drexel, of New York city, for the purpose of helping men from New York, and was maintained until 1888.

Rev. John Dooly, who was connected with the management, writes in regard to it:

"We had no trouble to get men to go. They worked willingly ten hours each day, were obedient and gave good satisfaction to us and to those who took them. The average cost per day for the time the farm was running was about 20 cents per man. If we had kept an average of twenty men on the farm, the cost would not have been over 10 cents a day. * * The men received no pay and were taught the rudiments of farming, which accounts for the large number who went to farm work.

"The farm could accommodate 20 men at one time, but the numbers were kept down to *save* expense, which was very unwise.

"The expense of administration was for superintendent $480 per year; for hired woman for work $180; for postage and other incidentals, in all about $100; total about $760, and the subsistence of three persons, superintendent, wife and girl, or woman, $219; total $979. The cost of above was taken into account in estimating the expense per day.

"Mr. Joseph W. Drexel bought and owned the farm and met *all* the expense of the same.

The men signed an agreement when they went there, to work for their board and such instruction as they should receive in farming. This was to guard against any claim for wages. Working clothes were provided for all, their own clothes were cleaned and mended and laid aside till they left the farm. A Sunday suit was also provided for them,

---

*I know of but one experiment of the kind having been made in the United States.

and all who wished went to church and sat with the superintendent's family in the family pews provided by Mr. Drexel.

"An opportunity was presented and an offer made to Mr. Drexel for the purchase of the farm in 1886, by which he would have received all he had spent and at least 7 per cent. interest."

The following statistics for five years are all that can now be furnished:

CEDAR HILL FARM, PLAINVILLE, SOMERSET CO., N. J.

STATISTICS REGARDING MEN.	1883	1884	1885	1886	1887
Number of different men	38	36	33	32	44
Total number of days	1534	1778	2036	1340	1614
Average number of days per man	40½	49⅞	61	41$\frac{11}{16}$	36$\frac{1}{4}$
Men sent to situations on farms	18	20	13	12	22
Returned to trade or friends	5	4	1		1
Returned to New York	9	7	13	16	16
Men on farm December 31st	6	6	5	4	5
Total number of men per day	4⅓	4⅞	5⅔	4	4$\frac{11}{17}$
Died	...	...	1	...	...

It must remain a question whether a constant population of twenty suitable men could have been found for the farm.

All successful experiments even approaching the labor colony in character, hitherto attempted in this country, have contemplated the permanent settlement of the persons to be benefited upon the land they have helped to develop, and however philanthropic such enterprises have been in intention, they have, I believe, invariably been managed upon business and not upon charitable principles, depending upon the character and enterprise of the settlers for success, building thus upon a sure foundation.

The description or consideration of such enterprises does not come within the scope of the present paper, nor within that of the sixth section of the International Congress.

The German labor colonies, of which twenty-two have been established during the past ten years, and the Hadleigh colony of the Salvation Army in England, belong to the type of enterprises I have in mind. These were established to benefit two classes of men:

1. Those able and willing to work, but for whom there is no work; or in other words, those who, through bad social conditions, are unable

to find any means of earning a living, the farms being intended to give to such men an opportunity not to be found elsewhere.

2. Those who, by their own faults and weaknesses, have been driven from the natural channels of occupation, the farms being intended as places of refuge for such, where they will be trained and developed, so that they may become, eventually, self-supporting members of society, either in their own or some other country.

The plan is a most alluring one. It seems to solve the problem which most distresses the modern conscience, "What can be done for the man who wants to work, but for whom there is no work?" For in approaching this problem it is always assumed that the majority of those to be provided for are of this class. The existence of the second class, of the men with faults and weaknesses which make them unable and unwilling to work, is practically ignored. There is an extreme haziness of mind in dealing with the whole subject of help to the "unemployed." It is so much easier to mould circumstances than character that the temptation always presents itself to do the easy thing and trust that the difficult thing will do itself. In this case the assumption is, that, when the opportunity is given to work and to learn, a large proportion of the men to be helped will be ready to profit by it.

This I do not believe to be the fact, at least in the United States.

I do not believe that labor colonies are needed in this country to provide an opportunity to work, and although I do believe that they are needed for purposes of training, I think that they must be under public control or they will fail in every sense of the word.

My object in this paper is to sustain the above position by facts and by argument.

However true it may be that in European countries, and even in England, there is a large class of able-bodied men who want to work, and know how to work, and yet cannot find any work to do, I do not believe that there is any such *class* of men in this country. That in New York or in any large city there are always certain individuals so situated, must, of course, be true; but the natural agencies are sufficient to dispose of them, and gradually each man finds the place that needs him and there is no necessity for the intrusion of any unnatural means of providing work for such men.

There can be no question that in New York, if anywhere in this country, must be found the greatest number of men out of work; and yet in New York it is not able-bodied, intelligent, competent men who seek the aid of charitable societies to provide them with the means of earning a living.

So far as I have been able to learn, it is the experience of such societies that the men who seek vainly for work are usually either unable or unwilling to earn a living by regular labor.

To the question "To what do you ascribe the inability to find work of the men who apply to your society for help?" the following answers were given:

From the superintendent of the United Hebrew Charities: "Unwillingness to accept positions offered and their love of large cities. We could place most all our protegés, especially unskilled, if they would leave the city."

From the superintendent of the Christian Aid to Employment: "Intemperance and incompetence."

From an ex-superintendent of the Bowery Branch of the Young Men's Christian Association: "Many are intemperate or inefficient, or do not have a trade perfectly, or are clerks. The majority of the unemployed have worked at light work."

From the general agent of the Association for Improving the Condition of the Poor: "Old age and sickness, laziness, incompetency, intemperance."

From the German Society of the City of New York: "Suspension of work on buildings and all kinds of out-door labor. Strikes and closing of factories."

From the superintendent of the Bowery Branch Young Men's Christian Association: "Dissipation."

From the officers and agents of the Charity Organization Society:

1. "I think that, in general, the inability of men who apply to the C. O. S. to find work may be ascribed to general shiftlessness and indisposition to work, and to lack of any training which would enable them to do anything well."
2. "An indisposition to work regularly and to keep at it."
3. "Physical ailments, intemperance and shiftlessness."
4. "Intemperance, incapacity and shiftlessness."
5. "They are generally lacking in energy and are not skilled in any branch of work. If Jews, 75 per cent. are suffering from some physical weakness; other nationalities usually are brought to the condition in which we find them through drink. I believe that prenatal influences have a great deal to do with their condition."
6. "Lack of skill, incompetency (lack of ability to acquire skill), unreliability. During certain seasons the cessation of such work as the applicants are able to perform—mostly laboring work—and dullness of

trade. The latter class usually have steady work during nine months of the year."
  7. "Intemperance and inefficiency."
  8. "Intemperance, shiftlessness and roving disposition."

In regard to the average time during which an able-bodied, intelligent man, speaking English, would be out of work in New York City, I have received the following statement of opinion:

From the superintendent of the United Hebrew Charities: "He should not be out of work over one week."

From the superintendent of the Christian Aid to Employment: "If directed promptly to the proper channels, about forty-eight hours, unless he is *hopelessly* incompetent."

From an ex-superintendent of the Bowery Branch of the Young Men's Christian Association: "Depends on his business. A *laborer* soon finds work. The trades are difficult to get work in. Unions and strikes limit the opportunities."

From the general agent of the Association for Improving the Condition of the Poor: "One month; but, if skilled, he would often have to resort to unskilled labor first."

From the German Society of the city of New York: "Men who are able and willing to do all kinds of work, only a few weeks, except in the winter months."

From the officers and agents of the Charity Organization Society:
  1. "I should think that the average time that such men would be out of work in this city would be, if skilled, ten to fourteen days; if unskilled, twenty to twenty-five days."
  2. "Perhaps a week or two. It depends largely upon the man himself, of course. Many such men would get work again immediately; others might not get it in six months or a year."
  3. "Several weeks."
  4. "If the labor conditions are normal, one or two weeks."
  5. "Less than three months."
  6. "We can always find employment for such exceptions at once."

Before proceeding, I wish to guard against the error of assuming that the above testimony from the charitable societies of New York proves more than it does. Fortunately, the able-bodied, honest and industrious man has a deep-rooted distrust and dislike for all means of help which savors of what is technically called "charity," and therefore the fact that the societies I have quoted receive requests for aid from such men very rarely, does not prove conclusively that there are none needing help, or who ought to be helped in their efforts to find employment; but it does prove that such men cannot be reached by any enterprise founded and maintained as a "charity," and consequently that no labor colony of the kind considered in this paper could be of use to them. Labor bureaus, or exchanges, maintained by employers and workmen as a means of mutual convenience, or by labor unions, (in either case purely as a business matter) have been suggested as one means of dealing with the difficulties which undoubtedly do exist even for the able-bodied, intelligent and industrious man, who is temporarily out of work; but here I am trenching on matters foreign to the theme I have undertaken to discuss.

It seems to me, however, that it is safe to assume that the above testimony proves that in New York there is no *class* of able-bodied, intelligent and industrious men seeking work who cannot find it, and that individual men of the character and in the situation described, could not be helped by any "charitable" enterprise, and also that what is true of New York city is true of the rest of the United States. In other words, that, however bad the social conditions in the United States may be, they are not yet so bad that men, able and willing to work, cannot generally find employment through the usual channels; and consequently it must be acknowledged that there is, as yet, no necessity and no field for any artificial means of providing work for such men.

This conclusion makes it unnecessary for me to consider Labor Colonies so far as they are intended to furnish an opportunity to work to men able and willing to earn their own living. Such men in the United States have the opportunity and use it, with how much unnecessary attendant hardship it is not our province to stop and consider. That a wiser system of taxation, that a more highly developed sense of justice among men who now control the opportunities to work, and among working men themselves, would undoubtedly result in a very much better and happier condition for the industrious and able-bodied man, both while he seeks employment and after he has found it, can not be doubted; but those are questions of greater importance than any presented to us to-day and are to be considered by students of social and political economy and not by students of charity and correction.

Since, then, it appears that the bulk of the men in the United States who cannot find permanent employment, are in that position because of some fault in themselves, or in other words, because they cannot offer to the community any work which is worth paying living wages for, the problem to be solved by us is not that which so troubles the European and English philanthropist, but one much narrower and more simple.

That there are many men out of work in the United States is true. That they should have work is equally true.

The problem before us is, how shall this be brought about, and in order to reach the answer, it is necessary to take up the question of the reason why these men are out of work more in detail.

The answers given above may be classed under four heads, the deficiencies named being physical, mental, moral or industrial. It appears that a man may be too weak, too foolish and ignorant, too lazy and vicious, or too incompetent, to secure permanent work.

What then shall be done to meet the evils of his remaining out of work, which is a condition disastrous to himself and others?

The physically weak must be relegated to the care of the hospital, the convalescent home or the poorhouse. We cannot consider his needs until he is cured, and then he will naturally fall into one of the other classes, unless he finds his own work normally, as a man should and as most men do.

For the other men incapable of earning a living, for the ignorant, the lazy, the incompetent, it appears that there is but one remedy, education, training, development—they must be taught to work and be taught to want to work—their minds, their hands, their wills must be trained. But how? The natural answer would seem to be "In a labor colony."

But should the proposed labor colony be under the management of a private charitable corporation, the two horns of the dilemma presented would be the following: On the one hand the colonies might be managed upon principles which would make them agreeable places of residence to those for whose benefit they were established, in which case they would certainly flock to them. The object of the colony, however, would be the training of the inmate for future independent life and his final passing out of the colony into such a life, and he could gain no such training in any place where strenuous exertion was not required and strict self-control inculcated—that is in any place where his comfort or pleasure were considered before his real good. But, on the other hand, were the colony managed so that his real good was sought, he, being unused to exertion, to order, to self-control, would find the process intended for his benefit so extremely unpleasant that he would leave, if at liberty to do so, and the labor colony would soon find itself without laborers.

Either result would be a complete failure.

Can this dilemma be avoided? Can labor colonies of such a character as will benefit the lazy, the vicious and the incompetent, and in which they will nevertheless stay, be maintained in the United States? Only by employing compulsion to retain the inmates, and this can be done only by putting the labor colonies under public control.

In every state of this Union there already exists some system by which the local government deals with the lazy, the vicious and the incompetent, when, for whatever cause, it is thought worth while to deal with them at all, instead of leaving them to go to destruction without an added impetus from official cruelty and folly.

The jails and the poorhouses all over the United States (with some exceptions in New England) seem to be carefully prepared to do as much harm as human ingenuity could devise to the unhappy beings who are condemned to enter them. They have not even a deterrent influence upon the bulk of their inmates—they present all the features which attract and degrade them, and none which would repel and might elevate them.

As a rule, the persons sentenced to jail or poorhouse as a punishment are weak in body, mind and character. What they desire is food, warmth, shelter and companionship, provided all these can be gained without exertion on their own part. Their muscles are flabby and unused to exercise, their minds are low and empty, their characters wanting, so far as appears, in all moral attributes. What they need is *training*, careful and prolonged; years would scarcely suffice to develop them physically, mentally and morally into human beings capable of self-respect, self-support and self-development. What is the practice in almost every state in the Union? Such beings as I have described are shut up in jail or poorhouse for a term of from ten days to six months, in complete idleness, in bad air, in dirt, and among companions of the same nature as themselves, and this is repeated sometimes several times in one year. The wonder is that the ensuing degradation is not more rapid and more marked even than it is.

What system should be adopted in place of this hideous travesty of justice and common sense?

In every township or county a large farm should be bought, on which all men, who by begging or vagrancy confess themselves to be unable to provide a fitting livelihood for themselves, should be *trained* with care, for months or even for years, should it appear necessary. The object of the institution should be the education of the inmates in every direction. The advantages of farm labor over other kinds of work are many. It is healthier, it does not interfere with the work of men outside, men trained in farm work can get employment away from cities, a farm supports in part, at least, those engaged upon it. In a large part of the United States indoor occupation must also be provided for the inmates during a portion of the year when outside work is not possible, and this should be provided with the object of the further development of the faculties of the inmates, one of the most important being the *faculty of persistent application*. Mr. R. L. Dugdale in his "Study in Crime, Pauperism, Disease and Heredity" called "The Jukes," says (p. 59) "After disease, the most uniformly noticeable trait of the true criminal is that he lacks the element of continuity of effort. Steady, plodding work, which is the characteristic not only of honest and successful individuals, but also of all nations that have made a mark in history, is deficient in him, and needs to be organized as a constituent of his character."

This applies equally or more strongly to the pauper or vagrant. Many men who will work for a day or two, or even a week or two, will not continue at any regular occupation. Their bodies and their wills are equally deficient and equally in need of training.

That labor colonies are needed in the United States for the training of men unable and unwilling to work, and that in order to accomplish their object they must be under public control, I think I have proved. And I claim still further, that it is the duty of the community to substitute such colonies for the present cruel and wasteful jail and poorhouse method of dealing with the criminal and pauper vagrant.

The fact that the common county jails of the United States are in but few respects any better than the jails found and reported upon by Howard in 1776 in England and elsewhere, and that they bear a strong resemblance to the prisons now existing in Russia, ought to inspire the people of the various states to renewed exertion to wipe out such a stain and disgrace.

There is another kind of labor colony which is greatly needed in all communities. It is that described by General Booth of the Salvation Army as an "Asylum for Moral Lunatics" and no words can better paint the need or scope of such an institution than the following extract from "Darkest England" with which I will close my paper:

"It is a crime against the race to allow those who are so inveterately depraved the freedom to wander abroad, infect their fellows, prey upon society, and to multiply their kind. Whatever else society may do, and suffer to be done, this thing it ought not to allow, any more than it should allow the free perambulation of a mad dog. But before we come to this I would have every possible means tried to effect their reclamation. Let Justice punish them, and Mercy put her arms around them; let them be appealed to by penalty and by reason, and by every influence, human and divine, that can possibly be brought to bear upon them. Then, if all alike failed, their ability to further curse their fellows and themselves should be stayed.

"They will still remain objects worthy of infinite compassion. They should lead as human a life as is possible to those who have fallen under so terrible a judgment. They should have their own little cottages in their own little gardens, under the blue sky, and, if possible, amid the green fields. I would deny them none of the advantages, moral, mental and religious, which might minister to their diseased minds, and tend to restore them to a better state. Not until the breath leaves their bodies should we cease to labour and wrestle for their salvation. But when they have reached a certain point access to their fellow men should be forbidden. Between them and the wide world there should be reared an impassable barrier, which once passed should be recrossed no more forever. Such a course must be wiser than allowing them to go in and out among their fellows, carrying with them the contagion of moral leprosy, and multiplying a progeny doomed before its birth to inherit the vices and diseased cravings of their unhappy parents."

LABOR TESTS AND RELIEF IN WORK IN THE UNITED STATES.

ALFRED T. WHITE, PRESIDENT OF BUREAU OF CHARITIES, BROOKLYN, N. Y.

The scope of this paper is limited to a consideration of the organized efforts, now presented in the larger cities of this country, for the temporary employment of men and women out of work, where such employment is at once relief and labor test.

The sketch necessarily omits consideration of the individual work which is being done daily by the visitors of the charity organization societies and by others in finding employment for the poor in their care, although every such offer of work is a labor test in the mind of any observant helper. The field must be further narrowed by omitting consideration of the various institutions for special classes which give employment to their inmates by various industries, because these homes are not open to the poor at large. Nor can employment at sewing, as afforded by many churches and by some societies in our large cities, be considered as other than thinly disguised relief with little or none of the labor test idea in it.

The organized undertakings which remain within the province of this paper, seek (1) to provide immediate relief by employment for those able and willing to work, and (2) to prevent those who are able to work, but unwilling, from securing a livelihood by misrepresentations and beggary. In addition to these objects, many aim (3) to train those who lack work through incompetency into a fair ability to support themselves.

The provision of labor tests to relieve the country of able-bodied vagrants engaged the attention of our English ancestors three centuries ago, when the Elizabethan statute provided that every parish " should raise by a parochial tax, a convenient stock of flax, hemp, wool, thread, iron and other ware or stuff to set the poor to work." It is not a matter of record, I believe, that any parish performed the duty thus laid upon it, but the spirit of the statute that such of the poor as could work, must work, brought forth in time the English work-house system.

I have not searched to find the earliest application of the work test in this country; paupers were sometimes let out by the towns for service in early colonial days and in the annual election sermon before the legislature of Connecticut, in 1774, the preacher called the attention of the law-makers to "the multiplying of vagrant beggars and idle persons, well able to support themselves and to benefit the public, if put to labor, which it appears they have no disposition for, if they can find a support without it," and inquired "might not the civil fathers act to good purpose by ordering such vagrants to be taken up and put to service for their maintenance."

Passing immediately to the situation of to-day in this country, we find that consideration is being given everywhere in our larger cities, to the provision of temporary employment as relief, education and labor test combined. These schemes ordinarily take the form of woodyards for men and of laundries for women; variations in the kind of employment offered for women are more common than in that given to men, and the work afforded women generally has the nature of a training-school, an advantage which the wood-yard for men does not possess.

I give herewith a summary of the methods in use in the various cities of the United States which seem to me to fall within the limits of this paper. The cities are arranged in the order of population by the census of 1890. Those that do not appear in the list have either reported that no form of temporary employment exists or have failed to respond at all. The inquiry has been addressed in each instance to the secretary of the charity organization society of the place and but few have failed to respond. To some of the secretaries I am under special obligations.

NEW YORK.

The Charity Organization Society maintains a wood-yard, at which 3,959 days' work was given during the last year reported. This labor utilized 521 cords of wood. The wood-yard pays its expenses and a little more. Additional lots have been secured by the society, on which they propose to erect a building to accommodate 200 men on the lines of the Wayfarers' Lodge in Boston.

The state authorities some years since authorized the establishment of a municipal lodging house; but the city authorities have opposed its erection.

The Charity Organization Society also maintains a laundry "fully equipped and competent to do first class work; its object to teach women all kinds of laundry work."

New York city possesses, on Blackwell's Island, the only workhouse in the state under the care of public officials. I mention it here briefly, although outside of the scheme of the paper, because of its value as an index to the size of the work which needs doing. From the report of the superintendent for the year 1890, the last printed, the following extracts are made: "There has been a steady falling off in the census, being in 1890 a decrease of 23 per cent. from 1887, 16 per cent. from 1888 and 11 per cent. from 1889." The commitments during 1890 aggregated 22,340, of which 12,844 were men and 9,496 women. These commitments, however, represented only about 5,000 different men and about 1,500 different women, the men being committed not quite three times each in the average, and the women more than six times each. During the months from June to November inclusive the commitments are about one-third less than during the other half of the year. The men employed are as laborers, firemen, bakers, stone-breakers, etc., and the women at washing, ironing and scrubbing, but the work required does not suffice to deter applications for recommitment. The herding together of so many vagrants, &c., seems very objectionable.

CHICAGO.

The Chicago Relief and Aid Society maintains a wood-yard "to help able-bodied men through employment and to furnish a labor test. This is done by giving to any man who applies for it a meal or lodging after he has earned it by honest work, sawing wood. In exceptional cases, men with families are given work for cash." During 1892, work was given to 1,011 different men, who sawed and split wood to a value of $12,317, as appears from the sales reported.

There is also in Chicago, a laundry in connection with the "Home for Self-Supporting Women," where an average of 18 persons a day find employment, a large part of whom have become proficient enough to take permanent positions in families.

PHILADELPHIA.

The Philadelphia Society for Organizing Charity, maintains two wood-yards in connection with wayfarers' lodges which "as a labor test have proved invaluable, and in which the inmates earn from two-thirds to three-fourths of the cost of their maintenance, in spite of the fact that among their population are many disabled men and many women and children." During the 15 months covered by the last report, 865 cords of wood were sawed and split, realizing when sold $9,984. The Pennsylvania state treasury makes an annual appropriation to the Society to assist in maintaining the lodges. 14,336 men, 924 women and 216 children received in the lodges 60,062 meals and 31,956 lodgings, an average to each inmate of two lodgings and four meals. "Truly they are wayfarers."

BROOKLYN.

The Brooklyn Bureau of Charities maintains two wood-yards, two laundries and training-schools, and two work-rooms for unskilled women without recommendations, a more extensive equipment than appears to be furnished anywhere else. The two wood-yards pay their labor in cash, instead of in tickets for meals or lodgings, and their doors are open to any man whether coming through the Society or applying on his own impulse. In the two yards 827 different men were employed in the last year reported, to whom 11,265 days' work was furnished. For the weaker men the superintendents endeavor to provide lighter work, such as splitting and bundling in place of sawing. One of the yards is kept open until ten o'clock at night, so that men applying anywhere in the city for alms for a night's lodging, may be sent there to earn the cost. The aggregate sales were $12,920, of which just one-third was paid in wages to the men, and the balance for the material, rent, superintendence and delivery. Although the average pay earned by the men, does not quite reach forty cents, which is earned usually in five hours, some earn much more. At this rate of pay the yard regulates itself automatically. It will happen for a few weeks every year, perhaps, that the men who apply can be given work only every second day; but a newcomer always has a place made for him. It will also happen a few weeks in every year that the sales exceed to a considerable extent the amount which men can be found ready to saw and split, and this has to be covered by carrying some stock of prepared wood. Both wood-yards are self-sustaining.

The same society manages two laundry training-schools, with an excellent equipment of porcelain tubs, etc. One of these has been running since 1885, the other is comparatively new. In the older laundry, 8,266 days' work of nine hours each was performed by 191 different women, an average of 43 days to each. The number of women given work, varied from five up to forty-three daily. The cash received for laundry work was $8,152, of which $5,452 was paid to the women, and the balance for superintendence, materials, expenses of delivery, etc. This laundry is now nearly self-sustaining, and would be entirely so were it not also a training-school. The newer laundry accomplished about one-half the work of the older laundry in the year last reported.

The first work-room "for unskilled women without recommendations" was opened in Brooklyn in 1886, and a second one a few years later. These experiments when initiated were unique, and merit the comment of observers that "The essentials of Mr. Booth's plan were already in successful operation in Brooklyn before they were announced in London." (Report of Overseer of the Poor—Providence, R. I., 1892.) The women who come into these rooms are below the grade of those that can be taught to sew or to do laundry work; to be sent from the workroom to the laundry is in nature of a promotion. 680 different women were given 4,429 days' work, an average to each of seven days' work. The women are mostly employed in making rag carpets and rugs. The more helpless ones are given the task of cutting and tearing the rags to pieces or assorting them by colors. These women are paid exclusively in meals and lodgings, while those who work in the laundry are paid in cash. A lodging house for women is owned and managed by the society in connection with the work rooms and laundry, where 4,300 lodgings were furnished to women and children.

The City Mission and Tract Society maintains a "Home of Industry," at which 6,656 lodgings were earned last year in manufacturing brooms. Those employed are mostly ex-convicts; but others are admitted.

BOSTON.

The Overseers of the Poor maintain a wayfarers' lodge and woodyard, which were established together in 1879. This lodge receives all the men who formerly went to station houses for nights' lodgings. Before the lodge was established, the station houses averaged 60,000 lodgers annually, reaching sometimes 600 per night. The annual number is now about 37,000, and the largest number recorded in any one night by last report 200. 91,329 meals were furnished, also earned by work in the wood-yard. Of the lodgers not quite one-half were Americans, about one-third were Irish and one-sixth of other countries, mostly of British origin. The ordinary stint required of lodgers is to saw and split two feet of wood. Each man is obliged to take a bath; his clothes are taken care of, are cleaned, if necessary, and a clean nightgown is given him. "It rarely takes more than two hours for him to perform the task which secures the lodging and breakfast. It is not to be wondered at that the same men apply again and again." Lodge and wood-yard together are nearly, but not quite self-supporting. (References: Reports of the Overseers, and papers at Conference of Charities, 1885.)

The Overseers of the Poor also maintain a temporary home for women and children, to which any such in need of shelter have free admission on application and in which the cost of their care is largely repaid by the work which they do. Only one-fourth of the women are Americans.

The Roxbury Charitable Society maintains a wood-yard, and gave work in its last reported year to 179 men, more than one-half of whom applied in February. Sales of wood $5,928.

The Temporary Home for working women maintains a laundry and sewing room, and during 1892 admitted 281 women, furnishing 7,368 lodgings and 23,661 meals, almost the whole of which was paid for in work.

The Boston Industrial and Appleton Temporary Homes, maintains a wood-yard for able-bodied men out of work.

The Co-operative Society of Visitors among the Poor, which now forms a part of the Associated Charities work, published in 1890 a tract on employment for poor women in which the matter of "charity sewing" is treated with unusual discrimination.

BALTIMORE.

The Charity Organization Society established in May, 1891, an electric sewing machine room, concerning which the manager reports "The experiment has worked itself into an entirely different channel from the original plan, which was that the rooms were to be established for very delicate women, who were unable to use the foot-power machine. In most cases these women were fit only for hospitals; but in their stead came women who had no money, no friends, no work and often no machines. There have been only two women here with work of their own; we have had to furnish it for all the rest and teach them how to do it. As the greater part are no longer young, it takes several months before they can be made self-supporting. The younger women can find work in factories. Few lazy women come." The report further states that "the factories send the rooms as much work as can be handled" and that in six weeks women capable of learning to sew can learn to run a machine and make $4 to $5 a week.

There is a Friendly Inn, with a wood-yard in connection, with a capacity of 125 beds, under independent management. The average number of lodgers annually for eight years has been 15,000, of whom nine-tenths pay for their lodgings and meals by sawing and splitting wood. Lunch is paid for by sawing and splitting four sticks, and a lodging by ten sticks.

CINCINNATI.

A labor-yard for men has been recently established by the Associated Charities and, in connection therewith, lodgings, baths, dining room, etc. It is not yet self-supporting, but has come near it. There is also a work room for unskilled women on the Brooklyn plan.

BUFFALO.

The Charity Organization Society maintains a provident wood-yard, open during the winter months. In January, February and March, 1891, 70 men applied for work, of whom 44 came once only. Annual business about $2,000.

WASHINGTON.

A municipal lodging house and wood-yard has been recently established, which is to be supported by appropriations of Congress. Some account of it was given by Amos G. Warner in a recent number of the "Charities Review."

The Associated Charities maintains a small wood-yard.

NEWARK.

The Female Charity Society has a laundry and training-school.

LOUISVILLE.

The Charity Organization Society maintains a wayfarers' lodge and wood-yard in connection. It takes one and one-half hours' labor at sawing and splitting wood to earn a meal or lodging. 8,981 lodgings and 25,237 meals were furnished to 1,234 inmates last year. The experiment seems to be self-sustaining.

OMAHA.

The Associated Charities established a wood-yard last August and report that large numbers of men decline to work when the opportunity is offered. The county commissioners here send able-bodied applicants for relief to the yard, where their time is reckoned at 15 cents an hour, to be paid by the county in groceries and coal.

KANSAS CITY.

The Provident Association maintains a wood-yard, in which during the last year 553 men were employed for 6,240 hours and earned $634.

PROVIDENCE.

This city has maintained a municipal wood-yard for over fifteen years, thus antedating all others now existent, I believe. Its expenditures last year were $10,500, and receipts $8,384. There is no lodging house in connection with this municipal experiment and the men are paid in cash or in meals. It is recorded that 65 men applied 30 times each, which constituted about one-half the total employment given.

INDIANAPOLIS.

Has a friendly inn and a wood-yard near by in the care of the Indianapolis Benevolent Society.

DENVER.

The Charity Organization Society assists in maintaining a sewing room and laundry for the temporary employment of women, who are paid at 12½ cents per hour in orders on the grocer.

The above enumeration includes all cities which had over 100,000 population according to the census of 1890, and in which employment as a labor test is furnished, so far as I have been able to learn, being sixteen out of twenty-eight.

Of the smaller cities, the following have come to my notice; but doubtless some others have escaped my observation and inquiry. As a rule less attention is given to such agencies in the smaller cities than in larger ones.

NEW HAVEN.

Here employment as relief and test had early and broad development. The Organized Charities Association maintains a wood-yard for all who are ready to work for meals and lodgings, limiting employment to three days. They require one-twentieth of a cord of wood cut for each meal or lodging furnished. The yard also furnishes to recognized residents of the city employment for cash. The same society runs a laundry with an average of 65 weekly customers. The women do not stay long as the association places the competent ones outside.

The town furnishes employment on the roads and farm to able-bodied laborers who ask aid, and who are able to work for three days in every three weeks. Many men are said to wait their turn for this work, rather than accept regular employment elsewhere, as the town pays $1.50 per day. It would probably be better for the men if the town gave up this method and left these applicants to deal with the Organized Charities Association.

PAWTUCKET, R. I.

The Overseer of the Poor maintains a wood-yard at the city farm, in which also inmates of the asylum who are able to work are required to do something. To outsiders the overseer gives permits to work in the wood-yard. These people receive 50 cents per day and dinner, or 75 cents and bring their dinner. They are paid in orders on some grocer. No single men or tramps are employed, and the same person is rarely employed for more than two weeks. The yard is self-sustaining, though its business is small.

CAMBRIDGE, MASS.

The Overseer of the Poor has a stone ledge in connection with the almshouse, where the able-bodied poor, whether inmates of the almshouse or not, are employed. They are little troubled by tramps at present and have given up some wood-yards which they formerly had.

WILMINGTON, DELAWARE.

The Associated Charities co-operate with a private wood-yard, instead of running one themselves. They find men less willing than women to take work when it is offered.

TERRE HAUTE, INDIANA.

The Society for Organizing Charity is about to open a wood-yard for men and a laundry for women.

HARTFORD.

The Open Hearth Society maintains a wood-yard in connection with its lodging house, in which men are given employment but not for more than five days.

NEWBURGH.

In 1891, the Associated Charities succeeded in bringing together the Overseers of the Poor and the Street Commissioners in such a way that able-bodied applicants for assistance were set to work on the roads.

86 days of work were accomplished under direction of the street superintendent, for which the almshouse commissioners paid in relief tickets at the rate of one dollar per day. Then unfortunately the difference between the two boards caused the abandonment of this interesting and seemingly successful experiment.

PORTLAND, OREGON.

The City Board of Charities reports: "We have no surplus of women and find no difficulty in placing all who will do house-work. We have a considerable transient element of men, who drift along the coast from British Columbia to Southern California. Many of these are of a low order and never do voluntary work. At the time of our organization the city was overrun with the latter class, as well as by cripples, blind beggars, &c. Now we have none at all of the professionals. I have never found one who had not sufficient means to travel, when it was found that the law against beggary was enforced. The tramps who apply for aid are offered an hour's work for a meal or lodging, with the alternative of arrest and compulsory labor at the city park or wood pile. Any deserving man is given work at a wood-yard until permanent work can be secured. We have secured very full co-operation on the part of our people in this matter. We furnished work in 1889 to 258 persons, in 1890 to 396, in 1891 to 713, and in 1892 to 418."

As a work test for men, it will be seen that the wood-yard is in almost universal use; but this enterprise is managed quite differently in different cities. In its simplest form, the labor test is furnished by an arrangement made by the charity organization society of the place with the proprietor of any private wood-yard which handles kindling wood, so that employment may be given to any man sent with a card by the society.

In the larger cities, the society has its own wood-yard, either without a lodging house, as in Chicago, Brooklyn, etc.; or in connection with a wayfarers' lodge, as in Philadelphia, etc., and as is proposed for New York. In a few cases, the lodge and wood-yard may be found in the hands of others than the charity organization societies.

In Boston and Providence, the wood-yards are managed by the Overseers of the Poor, in the former city in connection with the wayfarers' lodge and in the latter without such connection.

Payment for the work done may be made to the men in meals and lodgings, or in tickets entitling the holder to such accommodation elsewhere, or in cash.

Municipal control of the lodge and wood-yard compels compliance with regulations which a private society finds it more difficult to enforce, as the city authorities can commit as a vagrant any refractory man. On the other hand, there is a manifest advantage in having the control of the wood-yard in the hands of a charity organization society, which will seek to promote the men from the wood-yard to some more useful and permanent employment.

Among the provisions for temporary employment with labor test suitable for women, the laundry holds the first place. The rooms for unskilled and unrecommended women in Brooklyn, and the electric sewing machine rooms in Baltimore, open up interesting fields not previously explored.

The amount of work which is being done in any of these cities by these agencies for temporary employment is so small that even were it multiplied many times, it would scarcely affect the work people regularly employed in the same industry. This is because the manufacture of kindling wood is mostly conducted in factories with steam power, where a single machine will do more work than an average hand labor wood-yard, and the same is true, though to a less extent, of laundry work. As economic experiments, however, none of these agents could be justified, but as furnishing a labor test with the temporary employment, they would be desirable even at serious cost in other directions. The rate of pay must necessarily be less than is to be had in other employment, or it could not be offered freely to all who may apply.

As a matter of fact, the number of people in any large city who are willing to work for just enough to earn meals and lodgings is very large, and if these should be steadily employed, any temporary employment agency might become clogged. It is not the business of a charity organization society to make people satisfied with this low order of living, but rather to stimulate them to self-support in home life. For this reason these employment agencies of whatever nature are most appropriately managed by, or in close co-operation with, the charity organization societies, which can and should do something more than use them to furnish employment or to expose frauds.

Except as their opportunities for employment afford the chance for further advance, the value of the employment offered is at best con-

fined to the money earned by the laborer, while it may be truthfully
said that the offer of work at the moment when the applicant most
sorely needs it may make a dollar worth more to the earner than $10.
would be at some other time. The value of these undertakings in
exposing those who are able to work but unwilling, is perhaps even
greater than their value in affording relief to those who are willing to
work. Yet this still misses the appreciation of the greatest value of
all in these temporary employment agencies, and that is the opportunity for any individual, who is willing to help another, to reach some
one who needs a friend at a critical moment when the service will be
most appreciated.

A vast amount of time is wasted in life in finding the right place and
the right time in which to grasp the man or woman who needs a helping hand. Both the time and the place are afforded to the visitors of
the charity organization societies by these industrial undertakings. It
is often a crisis in the life of the man or woman when the work place
is entered for the first time, and the friend who stands by and watches
at such a moment may control the future of the individual to an extent
not easily attainable at any other time or place. Thus these woodyards, laundries, work-rooms, etc., with the friendly visitor's assistance,
become the open doors to new lives of self-respect and self-support.

REGISTRATION OF CHARITABLE RELIEF.

BY MISS FRANCES R. MORSE OF BOSTON.

In speaking of registration I shall use the word in the somewhat arbitrary meaning which has become familiar to charity organization workers, as implying not only the recording of information on charitable matters, but also the constant exchange of such information between societies and individuals engaged in charitable work through a central office.

In examining the short history of registration of charitable relief in this country we wish to learn:

1st. What conditions led to a demand for it?
2ndly. With the expectation of what good results it was established?
3rdly. What objections have been urged against it?
4thly. What are the present methods of registration?
5thly. Whether the expectations of its projectors have been realized?

To determine the first two points let us turn back to the registration of relief by committees independent of any one charitable society, begun in New York in 1873 and in Boston in 1876, and in New York suspended for years, in Boston for months, until the Charity Organization Society in the one case, and the Associated Charities in the other, came into existence and made registration a part of their regular work.

I. *Conditions precedent to registration.*

In New York the conditions which called for registration are thus described:

"The wish of the public has been clearly expressed that adequate means of relief should be furnished in every worthy case of distress, it being understood that the law provided for the unworthy and criminal classes. It is evident that with the present want of system great individual suffering can exist; in fact, a family might starve before it could be relieved; and this arises from no want of public money or sympathy, but from want of information, from misdirected and ill-managed agencies of relief, or from the insufficiency of aid. It is evident that co-operation and organized division of labor among the societies would effect a great improvement in this respect."

"Want of system" and "want of information," therefore, are the conditions which in New York led to registration.

This statement is quoted from the valuable Report of the Bureau of Charities of New York (1874), and the objects proposed in the report are so closely connected with the subject of registration that I quote them here.

"*Objects.*"

"I. To obtain authoritative information regarding the objects and resources of the various benevolent societies of the city.

"II. To secure a system of registration of the persons receiving aid from the societies, and to arrange for such inter-communication of the officers as will prevent imposition.

"III. To ascertain whether existing organizations are adequate to meet existing wants, and whether special and extraordinary provision is required during the winter, and to report the same to the public.

"IV. To ascertain and report to the public the most simple methods of testing and verifying applications for aid, and of directing deserving claimants to the agency adapted to their respective cases.

"V. To ascertain and report to the public the state of the law regarding charitable societies, and also regarding street-begging and other forms of pauperism."

The experiment of registration in New York was given up after a year's trial because the co-operation of the largest relief-giving association in the city could not be secured; but Mr. H. F. Pellew, secretary of the committee which had organized the plan, says in his report, (October, 1874):

"Notwithstanding obstacles which have seriously impeded the efforts of the Bureau, a real and valuable field of work has been devloped. Important information has been obtained, many statistics tabulated, and others partly prepared, and a comprehensive and suggestive system introduced for recording and comparing the incidence of pauperism and of relief.

"After the successful trial which has now been made, it is impossible to doubt that some similar organization for the regulation of charity will be permanently established in the city."

Mr. Pellew's predictions were verified in 1882, when the Charity Organization Society was created, and made registration a part of its work from the outset.

The experiment abandoned in New York in 1874 was taken up in Boston in 1876 and successfully worked till 1878, when it was suspended for nine months until the Provisional Committee, subsequently the first Executive Committee of the Associated Charities made it an integral part of their work.

The conditions of Boston were somewhat different from those of New York; with a smaller population, and fewer nationalities to deal with, it was rather that some over-lapping of relief was seen, and a great deal more foreseen, than that the condition at the time was one of disastrous and disabling confusion.

A circular issued in 1876 says: "When we consider that at least twenty-five charitable societies, as well as numerous church benevolent societies, are now engaged in this city in distributing money and aid of various kinds, but that many of them are without exact knowledge of the specific objects, or the actual work of the rest, no further proof is needed to show that the very relief they aim to afford cannot be satisfactorily given, for they must more or less overlap one another, and waste of time, strength and money be the necessary result."

Thus, want of system and want of inter-communication between public and private agencies and individuals engaged in charitable work in the same field, were the conditions precedent to the establishment of registration in Boston as well as in New York.

Both cities gave public outdoor relief.

II. *What good results were expected to follow registration.*

We find that the New York committee say that it would be easy to make the office of the Bureau "the clearing-house of charities in New York."

More specifically, they believed that registration would afford positive information, would prevent the overlapping of relief, would detect imposture, would lead to improvement in methods of relief by showing where present methods failed of their ends, and through the street-directory would soon show, almost as on a map, the incidence of destitution and of relief.

In Boston the first published circular says: "This system of registration is in no way to supplant any existing society, nor to criticize its action; it is only to increase the power of each by adding to its means of information, and securing more unity of action."

A later circular says: "We believe that greater familiarity with each other's work would tend to diminish imposture and street-begging, which all are desirous to prevent, and thus greatly benefit the deserving poor." After describing the proposed methods of registration, the same circular goes on to say:

"It has been objected that such information would lessen the sense of responsibility of each society, and cut off assistance from many needing it.

"We urge that as the amount of help given in each case will be stated, it ought on the contrary to lead only to such communication between the persons interested as would make the relief more intelligent and efficient.

"There will undoubtedly be persons whose names it would be unwise and unnecessary to record; we trust that such will not be sent to us.

"No material aid will be given at this office, and no censorship assumed; its records will be open only to those to whom it will be of service in their work."

The first good result expected from registration, then, was a wiser, more efficient, and helpful administration of relief, both public and private.

The detection of imposture, important though that result might be, fell into the second place, and is not even mentioned in the first Boston circular.

The third result counted on was the localization of destitution and of relief.

III. *What objections have been urged against registration?*

The objections most strongly urged against registration when it was taking shape in Boston were three:

That it was *expensive—unnecessary—unjust.*

Let us examine these objections one by one.

1. That it is expensive.

This is true in a sense, as much clerical work is necessary: but that it is a wise expenditure has never been questioned by the successive boards of directors who have carried on the New York and Boston societies. On the contrary, they again and again, in their annual reports, speak of the money-saving power of registration, and money thus saved is money set free to be applied to better advantage than would be possible without its help.

In the report for 1891 of the Boston Associated Charities it is said, "Under the methods of co-operative charity, money from public and private sources which, under the old methods, would be worse than thrown away, amounting in the aggregate to large sums, is annually saved to the community."

2. That it is unnecessary.

This objection is now seldom made. The co-operating societies use registration, more rather than less, as time goes on and their work increases. As it undeniably adds to the daily clerical work, it is clear that these societies believe that in the end it is labor-saving.

3. That it is unjust.

It has been said that it is unjust to a family in misfortune to record their history, and thus make it public.

This objection wholly loses force through the fact that the histories recorded in the registration office are never made public, and can only be seen by those who can show that their interest is justifiable. But it is also said that there is injustice in giving, even to a person interested in a family, all the sad details of their previous history; that it is better that these should be gradually learned later, rather than a discouraging story should be heard beforehand. As well might we say that we unjustly prejudice a physician if we give him the previous record of a patient.

If something of the character and conditions of a family are known beforehand, there is less chance of sudden and utter discouragement on our part on learning that we have been deceived or mistaken.

We have brought this discouragement on ourselves, if we accept without verifying it the statement of a person in forlorn circumstances, who is very probably of weak character and weak health, and who may be under a strong temptation to exaggerate and misrepresent.

In such case there has been fault on both sides; there has been, perhaps, dishonesty on the one side, but we have gone half-way to meet it on the other, and are to blame for our want of imagination and intelligence.

Too often, after such discouragement, we fall back just when it is most important to keep on, leaving the person whom we undertook to help just so much the worse for seeing how lightly we pick up and drop human interests.

There is more serious injustice here than any that can be wrought by telling to a person already interested in a family the past events of their life.

IV. *Methods.*

The following extract from a circular of 1876 shows the method of work proposed by the Boston Committee; this was directly drawn from that of the New York Bureau of Charities of 1873.

"The committee charged with its management should receive from all societies, having persons regularly dependent on their assistance, a list of such regular beneficiaries, and should be notified of all changes made in this list.

"The committee of management should, moreover, receive from societies giving occasional relief among the poor, monthly reports of the names and addresses of the persons helped by them, and of the amount of relief given in each case.

"In return for this information, each society will be notified when any of its beneficiaries are found to receive assistance, whether in money, goods, or employment, from any other organization.

"The method of registration to be adopted is like that of the card-catalogue of a library.

"The name and address of each beneficiary are entered on a card, with a cypher representing the name of the relieving society; on the same card will be found the amount of relief given, and other statistics.

"When the same name is received from two, or more societies, an entry to that effect is made on the card of the person so assisted, and all such relieving societies are notified.

"In this way a compact catalogue is made, which of course can be indefinitely extended, and information as to the aid received by each person is procured."

The only changes since that time have been those of growth and development. More of the personal history of a family now appears on the card, so that it becomes quite a full record of character as well as of relief and the immediate cause of relief; also, the actual exchange of information takes place with a rapidity which was not supposed possible by the originators of the plan, the reports being now received, recorded, and sent out within a few hours.

Further than this, there have been only changes of detail.

The method is still that of the card-catalogue, the cards being about five by six inches in size. A separate card is added for each new society or individual helping a family, and all the cards relating to one family (or person,) are clamped together.

When a society or individual is ready to be responsible for the care of a family, undertaking to keep a friendly knowledge of them, and to find relief for them if relief be needed, there is a record made that they take charge to visit and relieve, and ask that no one else help without consulting them.

With regard to the superintendence of registration work, Miss Z. D. Smith, General Secretary of the Boston Associated Charities, permits me to quote a passage from a paper on registration, written by her in January, 1892.

"*First, the work must be secret and confidential.* The information must be entrusted to some one officer and the clerks necessary to accomplish the work.

"*Secondly, the work must be done promptly.* There must be enough helpers to make sure that, no matter how many reports come, in the morning, they will be recorded and sent out within twenty-four hours.

"*Thirdly, the work must be done without prejudice.* If the officer in charge does not believe in the way that the work of some agency is done, he must, nevertheless, report its action without saying so, exactly as he would report from some other source.

"While reports must often be abridged, it is important to avoid generalization, and to be careful to give information from the record and not the opinion that the officer may have formed from them.

"*Fourthly, the methods must be as elastic as possible.* There must be order to ensure promptness and simplicity in such a multitude of details, but if some society prefers that the reports should be sent on stiffer paper than usual to suit their methods of filing, we provide stiffer paper; if another wants the slips cut a little smaller, to fit their record-papers, we have them cut smaller.

"As to the way in which reports are received, we take them in any shape in which we can get them. We supply books or blanks where they are wanted, but we like best to borrow the records of the societies, returning them as promptly as possible."

V. *Have the expectations of the projectors of registration been realized?*

The permanence of registration as a part of the charity organization work of New York and Boston in a measure answers the question, but it may be answered more fully, point by point.

Registration has enabled us to improve the character of charitable work in the following ways :

A. It puts before a person interested in a family their previous history, so far as it is known, so that help or counsel may not be given merely to relieve the distress of the moment, but may at least be framed with a view to preventing the recurrence of the distress.

B. The knowledge that two societies are simultaneously trying to help a family frequently leads to the withdrawal of one society, while the other pledges itself that if the family need help they shall receive it. The number of families which each society is dealing with may be thereby lessened, and it may become easier to make the personal work for each family thorough, and the relief adequate.

C. Imposture is swiftly detected.

D. The street-registry makes the picture of social conditions clear before our eyes. It points out the places which are as it were, open sores,—houses, and groups of houses, where drink and poor-relief and improvidence all dwell together,—where the rents are high to leave a margin for bad debts,—where the landlord is slow to make repairs, and where the drainage is bad.

Thus we find registration justifying the belief of its projectors that it would afford positive information, would prevent the over-lapping of relief, would save waste of time and effort by enabling societies to narrow their field and thus make their work more thorough, would detect imposture, and would make it possible so to map out the city that one could see what neighbourhoods were most in need of improvement.

All these results of registration were foreseen.

One good result has followed it which, so far as I know, was unforeseen. *It spares many unnecessary questions.* This gain is greater than may at first appear. Not only is some unnecessary pain saved, not only is there less temptation to exaggerate and misrepresent, but there is lessened, also, the tendency to think one's self pre-eminently interesting and important, which is so disabling to those who most need that their attention should be drawn out of themselves and concentrated on the effort to regain a lost footing in the world.

This morbid state of mind is as easily recognized by any one familiar with pauperism as is the litigant's state of mind to the lawyer, or the hypochondriac's to the doctor, and we too often foster it by the questionings of misplaced sympathy—as dangerous a narcotic as we can give.

The registration of charitable societies may exist independent of the registration of individual charitable relief (with exchange of information,) as is the case in London where the Charity Organization Society publishes the Charities Register and Digest; but as it is sure to be carried on side by side with registration it is fair to count it as a coincident advantage.

This registration of charities (giving an account of their objects, method and scope) has a double value.

It is not only a means of direct information, but it shows to each association what others are working in the same field, and, if it is widely enough read, it may discourage the formation of unnecessary societies, and promote the combination of others. In London, during the last year, two associations occupying very nearly the same field, instead of longer crossing each other's paths have been joined into one.

Can we show sufficient reason why charity organization societies which have not yet made registration a part of their work should do so? I believe we can.

By the consent of those charity organization societies which now employ registration, and by the implied consent of their co-operating societies, it saves waste of effort and money.

It checks imposture and the "speculative spirit," which is too often led on by our easy indifference and pre-occupation.

It constructs for us a map of social conditions to which we should do well to take heed. We see that through certain houses, and sometimes through certain streets, moves a sad procession of people on the verge of pauperism, — drinking, thriftless, thoughtless, half-sick, which is more often the cause of the other conditions than is sometimes acknowledged.

We watch on this map also the drift of immigration, by which our methods must be shaped.

A generation which turns so eagerly to panaceas as does ours, needs registration as an element of order and organization. But, if thoughtfully used, it is by no means only an element of order, but becomes a strong incentive to personal service on behalf of those of our fellow-citizens who, for one or another reason, are at a disadvantage.

FRIENDLY VISITING.

BY MRS. ROGER WOLCOTT OF BOSTON.

The principles which underlie friendly visiting are steadily gaining ground among the many societies dealing with the problems of poverty and vice. More and more it is seen that it is individual work, personal love and thought which alone can help the weak and erring. In dealing with the subject of friendly visiting to-day, I am looking from the point of view of the Associated Charities, although the same qualities required for a visitor of this organization must necessarily belong to the visitors of other societies depending upon personal influence to help them in their work. In choosing a visitor for a new case of necessity, we try to provide the family with one, who by temperament and disposition is likely most easily to enter into helpful relations with them.

It sometimes happens that certain visitors make excellent advisers for people of one race, when they cannot adapt themselves to those of another. Oftentimes we find visitors by presenting to the members of a conference short synopses of the circumstances, characteristics and needs of various families, and these are assigned to such friends of the members, as are deemed to possess the necessary qualifications or peculiar fitness for each case. Under favorable circumstances, the relation of the friendly visitor to the family thus adopted, becomes very close and intimate.

What are the qualifications for a good visitor? And why is it that often we see a man or woman of high character and sincere purpose fail to enter into sympathetic relations with the poor they undertake to visit? A friend who had not thought herself successful in visiting once said to me, "I cannot enter into relations with the kind of persons dealt with by the Associated Charities, the chasm between us is too great." Another friend, also high-minded and conscientious, said that she could not feel at home with poor people and that they did not feel at ease with her. Of course under these circumstances, the very foundation of friendly visiting is lacking. There must be no chasm, there must be no sense of superiority, or condescension or difference. The heart must be full of love, the desire to help so ardent that all points of difference are eliminated from the consciousness, and what is common to humanity alone is recognized.

A visitor is generally introduced to a family during some great emergency, when it is his privilege to render important service, or to enter into such close and sympathetic relations with them, that he can be sure of a permanent vantage ground in their affection. And how responsive is their affection, how simply and naturally they accept the friendship offered, how touching is their trust, their gratitude and their patience.

The visitor must not allow the sympathy and confidence to be all on one side; he must communicate of his own joys and sorrows; of his own experience and interests. Let the poor feel the human touch in him, and let them see that he accepts their sympathy and interest. If he is a parent, let him talk of his children, perhaps occasionally take them with him on his visits. If it seem practicable, let the poor visit him in his own home and let them know the members of his family as he knows theirs. The poor like to hear even of the social pleasures of those whom they have come to regard as their friends. A young lady, who was visitor to one of the most needy of our families, was on one occasion chagrined and somewhat disturbed to find that the father of the family had read in the papers of her presence at some ball, where the magnificence of her dress was set forth in glowing terms. She showed her dismay in her face, and the quick reply came, "Bless your soul, Miss, don't you mind, you might be as rich as mud and covered with diamonds from head to foot, and I shouldn't mind, you ain't the kind I mind." Does not this last sentence hint at the fact, that if the poor are sometimes envious of those more fortunate than themselves, it is because the latter have been first guilty of emphasizing the difference in their conditions in an ostentatious or arrogant spirit. The plea for a sympathetic relation of the friendly visitor to the poor he visits, may seem superfluous sentimentality, but it provides a practical working plan; and without it the best principles and methods of the most enlightened thought cannot achieve the truest success. Add to this sympathy a never failing hope, which knows not discouragement, and a fertility of resource, which though often baffled, never despairs, and you have some of the most important characteristics of a good visitor. There is ample need of zeal, of wisdom, of self restraint in withholding temporary aid, when the suffering can be radically helped only by the slow upbuilding of character.

One of the first efforts of the friendly visitor must be to arouse the feeling of self-respect; the loss of which is so easy among the deadening influences of a life passed amid squalid surroundings, and is so long a step into the gulf of pauperism. One of the first encouraging signs in the upward struggle towards reformation of a difficult case, was the remark of a woman to her visitor; "Since I have known you, I feel disgusted with the old life."

With the re-awakened sense of self-respect, it is not impossible to arouse a proper pride and unwillingness to accept alms. Public alms seem almost more demoralizing than private giving; for, while in the second case, the recipients are at least aware that they are receiving charity, in the first, they seem to look upon the help given as almost an inherent right of citizenship. Once make the case clear to their minds, and they will oftentimes refuse to accept public aid. Two families within my knowledge have saved enough money to repay the sums given them by the Overseers of the Poor, and have asked to have their names erased from the official records of that body. One encouraging sign of restored self-respect in a family, which had come to the Associated Charities as one of the city's free soup applicants occurred after some years of friendly visiting. Their regular visitor, being unable for a time to visit, employed a substitute to take her place. Some months later, on resuming the charge herself, she visited the family one day, and found them in much trouble; two of the wage-earners being out of work, owing to a dull season, and the head of the family being ill. The substitute had sent in a bag of flour; but although the family were in real need, they asked their regular visitor if she thought it would be wrong to send it back, "because they did not wish to be paupers." The friendly visitor, by tact and delicate suggestion, must instil a desire for cleanliness, so necessary to self-respect. Mr. William D. Howells, who during his recent residence in Boston gave much of his valuable time as a visitor for the Associated Charities, was amused one day to be told, on knocking at the door of a house where he had studiously endeavored to inspire a sense of cleanliness, that he could not come in, as the floor had just been washed, and he might soil it again.

The visitor ought to be able to give practical advice as to the best and cheapest kinds of food, and the wholesome preparation of the same.

If a woman, the visitor ought to be able to give valuable hints for the making and mending of clothes and as to the proper materials therefor. The visitor's influence must be used to see that the children are being well trained in schools and in those clubs which furnish a stimulus to self-improvement. Through Mr. Charles W. Birtwell's scheme of Home Libraries, much may be done to make the home a centre of interest both to parents and children. I have recently read a report of the visitor of one of these home library clubs, which consists of thirteen boys from eleven to twelve years of age. In speaking of the most earnest of them, he says, "Their reading has been very wide and well selected, and they retain remarkably well what they read. They have learned almost by heart Young's histories, Abbott's biographies, besides a vast amount of collateral matter. One of them has read the Iliad and the Odyssey in some translation. They are very familiar with Scott and Cooper, and have read much of Longfellow, Dickens, Burns, and Gray. These boys address to me profound questions; for instance, on one occasion, Albert asked, 'What is the greatest poem in the English language?' 'That is hard to tell,' I replied, 'but I should say Paradise Lost.' 'There, I told you so,' exclaimed Albert to Henry, who said he had thought it was Gray's Elegy."

Provident and frugal habits are encouraged by the Stamp Saving Society, also by the Home Saving Society, whose agents call each week on a fixed day, in order to collect the penny savings, until the delighted contributor finds he has accumulated enough to enter upon the dignity of a separate bank account. To those who try to help the unfortunate, the problem of intemperance presents the greatest difficulties. Here, too, much may be accomplished by a faithful, loving spirit which hopeth all things. Very frequent visiting, and all the personal influence and power one can bring to bear, are necessary for the task. Between the visits, in extreme cases where the will power is much vitiated, it is a good plan to ask the sufferer to report daily, by a postal card, if all is well. By a victim of this habit, a promise of self-control from day to day, is more likely to be kept than a pledge which covers a longer period. When the habit is too strong to yield to these simple methods, we have taken advantage of the dypsomaniac law and have had our patients committed to the insane asylums. Now that the state of Massachusetts has built a separate institution for the treatment of these cases, better results are hoped for than were possible under the old system. In one instance, the superintendent of the insane asylum tried with considerable success the experiment of doubling the period of confinement on each recurring commitment.

I have imperfectly indicated some of the qualifications for friendly visiting, and tried to present a few of the practical questions which confront the visitor. The wiser the visitor, the richer the gifts he can bring to his work, the greater will be his usefulness, provided always that with his experience and judgment he brings to the service a hope not easily discouraged, and a spirit of sympathy and love. Often the fresh zeal and interest of an inexperienced visitor accomplish better results than the efforts of a trained worker who has allowed himself to lose hope because of previous discouragements.

Before leaving the subject of the relation existing between the visitor and the family committed to his charge, I wish to urge that even in the case of the family becoming self-supporting, the visitor must not altogether withdraw his watchful care. Friendship may not be thus lightly broken, and should an emergency arise in which there is opportunity of a friendly word of warning or advice, the poor family should not have lost their touch with the friend they have learned to consult and trust. If all were wise, all worthy of becoming their brother's keeper, the conference would not be so essential a part of the organization of the Associated Charities as it now is. The questions which the visitors individually have found too hard for them, have been answered before by some fellow-worker who imparts the benefit of his experience, and who, in return, receives new suggestions to help him in his work. The visitors find relief and help in confiding their difficulties to a band of interested hearers who are all working in the same cause and who can help by practical suggestions, as well as by sympathy.

No consideration of the work of the visitors of the Associated Charities would be complete without mention of the agent, a salaried official who keeps fixed hours at headquarters and who is the center of the group of visitors. She gives to one what she has received from another, and adds to it from her own experience and thought. She has a knowledge of new and important legislation bearing upon the work. She is in touch with other charitable societies of the city, and is often helped in suggesting new plans of work to be carried on by the conference. With the help of the conference and the agent, therefore, the visitor can enter upon his work without the necessity of previous training, other than that which has been afforded him by the circumstances of his own life.

In accordance with the present standard for friendly visiting, it will be seen that fully to perform the necessary duties of the position, it is wiser, in most cases, to confine one's care to not more than two families. It is therefore necessary that there be many workers in the field. The number is slowly increasing, but we need many more. In my judgment, the district plan of visiting is unsatisfactory in comparison with the system described above. In the former the method of assignment is one of locality and not that of peculiar fitness of the visitor to the family in need of aid. Secondly, it has been noticed in the work of our ward branch of the Associated Charities, that it is not well for a visitor to have under his care families who are acquainted with each other; and it has been proved difficult, even with the greatest tact, to avoid awakening suspicion and jealousy, which interfere much with one's opportunities for usefulness. We now try to assign to a visitor families who are not likely to have intercourse with each other. Therefore, whatever the district plan may appear to gain in simplicity and precision of method, it loses in the lesser degree of personality, and the greater friction involved in its operation. The element of personal and friendly interest, which lies at the very foundation of genuine and efficient aid of the poor, cannot be attained by statutory enactment or by town vote. I do not believe that the poor would enter into the same relations of intimacy and confidence with visitors so appointed; and the result seems inevitable that they would be regarded as officials performing an obligatory duty. I believe therefore, that there is a radical defect in the theory of the Elberfeld system of enforced municipal visiting of the poor, and I fear that in this country, under its present political conditions, the practice would be worse than the theory.

I feel that every visitor of the Associated Charities may do much in arousing interest among his friends in this most important work; and I would urge upon the members of conferences that they should use their influence to extend the work so far as it lies in their power. Much can be done by arousing and educating public sentiment, and I hope the time may not be far distant, when all those who are rich in this world's opportunities and see that their brethren have need, shall lend of their time and strength to help those unfortunate ones, so heavily conditioned in the school of life.

THE CO-OPERATION OF PUBLIC WITH PRIVATE CHARITABLE AGENCIES.

BY ALEXANDER JOHNSON, SECRETARY OF BOARD OF STATE CHARITIES, INDIANAPOLIS, IND.

As my friend and colleague, Professor Warner, is to discuss the subject of "Subsidizing of Private Charitable Agencies from the Public Purse," it is evident that the co-operation of public with private charitable agencies, of which I am to speak, does not include those most important forms which are exercised in institutions of miscellaneous support or control, most important when considered as to their immediate financial amount in cost to the public, or as to their ulterior effects.

The co-operation of which I propose to speak, is chiefly that of the overseers of the poor or relieving officers with the various charitable agencies, which together form the circle of charities in our towns and cities.

A few years ago the thought of such co-operation as we now make our aim would have been treated with neglect or derision. The intelligent, thoughtful agent of the public bounty looked upon private charitable work as either useless from its irregularity, its inefficiency and its insufficiency, or as mischievous from its tendency to pauperize. He regarded the occasional question from volunteer charity workers, as to what he would do or was doing for a given family, as perhaps well meaning, but certainly impertinent meddling, and his answers were not such as to encourage the question becoming frequent.

The public agent who was not thoughtful nor intelligent looked on the private charitable agents as a nuisance to be abated. Their questions being based on the theory that the object of his office was to relieve the destitute, especially the class sentimentally called the worthy poor, were alien to his views. He held his position because he had been and was expected to be active and successful in the political work of his precinct or ward. That was his *raison d'être*. Enquiries from so-called good people as to why he had not aided this, that or the other poor person, and still more why he had aided certain other persons whom not even the most gushing would class as worthy poor, were very naturally resented as childish and silly as well as vexatious.

But things have changed in this respect, especially during the last twelve or fifteen years, and the cause of the change has been the rise of the principle of charity organization. Like all other great principles that have been applied to human efforts, this has had an effect much wider than its immediate application. The leaven has spread beyond the bounds of the societies working under the name, and most forms of charity, even the most conservative, have felt its influence to some extent. A certain degree of co-operation, or at any rate, a thought that co-operation of this kind might be advisable may be noticed in many places, still it is only in the cities having charity organization societies, or other societies imbued with their principles, that it has taken definite and noticeable form.

For various reasons the public relief of the poor is one of the first departments of charity to receive attention from a new charity organization society. Its amount can be precisely known, and is often looked upon by economical public officers and taxpayers as excessive. Its methods of administration often appear open to criticism. It appears to be given without discrimination and in many places without proper investigation. It does not and cannot regard the moral worth of those upon whom it is bestowed, but chiefly, if not entirely, regards their physical condition, and so it is not satisfactory to the great bulk of charity workers, who still persist in dividing the poor into two great groups, the worthy and unworthy, the sheep and the goats of the charitable fold. The sheep, who are to be led into the green pastures and beside the quiet waters of plenteous material aid, and the goats, who are to be shut into the outer darkness of refusal, with the possible exception of those who will consent to go to the poorhouse.

Public relief usually appears insufficient in amount, especially to the minds of the recipients. It is not often designed as complete support, but as partial or temporary aid, and as those who apply for it usually imagine themselves entitled to complete support, or at any rate to all that they can get, they are generally found among the applicants at every other available source of relief. So that their names are sure to be among those detected in what we call duplication. Besides all these reasons is the fact, that many scientists in charity reprehend public outdoor relief altogether, and the young enthusiasm of the charity organization society is naturally turned to efforts to abolish or retrench a sufficiently condemned evil. Efforts of charity organization societies towards this form of co-operation have often been quite successful.

Several attempts have been made with greater or less success by the committee on charity organization of the National Conference, to estimate by means of percentages the degree of co-operation attained between the various charitable agencies and the agents of public relief. The most careful and successful of these attempts was made by the committee which reported to the fourteenth Conference at Omaha about six years ago. At that time several societies reported their co-operation with public relief agencies as complete, claiming a full 100 per cent. At many other times societies have reported better success in securing co-operation with such agencies than with any other kind. And the experience of most of us who have set about it in earnest has been that a formal co-operation is often more easily obtained with the public officers than with most of the other charitable agencies. This last remark must be taken with some qualification. It is a curious coincidence, if it is only a coincidence, that with one or two notable exceptions the charity organization society and the associated charities which have been most successful in securing the cordial sympathy and practical co-operation of the churches and their relief societies, have not been the most successful with public officials. I will not attempt to explain this fact, nor to find the ethical or social law underlying it, if there be one. I merely state a fact which I believe the charity organization society delegates from Philadelphia and New York will bear me out in. I confess that in my own experience in Cincinnati and Chicago I was always most successful with the churches.

In considering the question of co-operation between public and private agencies, it is essential to remember the great variance between the work of public relief in different states, a variance partly of law and partly of practice. In some states the laws are precise and the limits of legal relief clearly defined, in others they are very vague and the overseer of the poor is almost a law unto himself, and is only limited by the public opinion which is against lavish expenditure on the one hand, and against neglect of suffering on the other. In some states a settlement can be lost without another being gained elsewhere; in others no pauper can be left thus belonging nowhere, but retains his *old* belonging until he gains a new one. And in some states a law which allows of aid to strangers in urgent need, is stretched to cover all sorts of tramps and vagrants. In some States the laws appear purposely loose and are differently interpreted by each different officer.

The first essential of co-operation is mutual confidence, the next is clear mutual understanding. If you and I agree to work together for a common aim, we must have confidence in each other that each will do what he agrees to do, we must understand each other, so that each will not attempt to do the other's share.

Now it is often very hard for the public official to have confidence in the work of the benevolent society—because the average benevolent society neither can nor will accept much responsibility. This is in fact its usual greatest weakness, that its directors and officers do not feel sufficiently their responsibility to do all the work that their society is organized for doing. I have often heard an agent of a private benevolent society say, "We cannot help these cases for want of means." The assertion is usually false, or has been so in my experience, merely an excuse to get rid of the cases in point; but it shows the lack of the feeling of responsibility. A society organized for a certain work can no more refuse to do all the work for which it is organized that comes in its way, than a bank can refuse to cash its notes; in either case the result is practical bankruptcy and should result in suspension of the business; if it does not suspend, the bankruptcy becomes a fraudulent one.

This is one of the great hindrances to co-operation between public and private relief agencies, that the public agent cannot depend on the private society to keep its word and live up to its professions.

Another great obstacle in the way of co-operation between private and public benevolence is the hasty and inexperienced investigations with which private benevolence often contents itself. The private almoner discovers what is to her a new case in most urgent distress. She rushes off to the overseer to help her to give relief—for more is needed than she can supply alone—and he tells her it is an old chronic case of vice and beggary utterly unworthy, or criminal, and so forth. He naturally has little confidence in a report from the same person about a case of which he knows nothing, should such come in. Here comes in the great opportunity of the charity organization society. If it sees and accepts it, it is certain of successful establishment. A charity organization society does not agree to do relief work but to SEE it done, so that if one relief agency fails it can and will secure another. I know that the giving or securing of material relief is the smallest part of the function of a charity organition society. Still it is a function of a charity organization society, and an essential one; and much of the society's success depends upon its being properly performed. The charity organization society, feeling and accepting the responsibility, is able to propose plans of co-operation to the overseer of the poor which he can accept with confidence.

These plans are of four kinds, to which I must refer very briefly:— 1st. Co-operation in securing and imparting information, including registration. 2nd. Co-operation in giving relief. 3rd. Mutual delimitation of work. 4th. Co-operation in withholding.

The first of these kinds of co-working often depends at its beginning upon the second, though it naturally precedes the others in order. There are some relief societies and some public agents of charity who make very accurate and wise investigations, but they are the exceptions. The charity organization society agent who studies his work has available now such a mass of printed assistance, that his investigations with but little training soon become superior to the work of most public officers; especially is this true as soon as complete or even partial co-operative registration of the charity work of a city has been established.

The second, i. e., co-operation in giving relief, is usually the easiest way to begin. Many relief societies and some public agents establish queer limits for themselves, such as, that they will not give fuel and food to the same family—that they will not pay rent—that they will not give any money—OR—that they will not give anything in kind. In these cases, with the charity organization society as the medium, two or more relief agencies can often work together usefully as well as with those societies which exist for certain specific kinds of relief, like diet kitchens, flower missions, coal charities, &c.

3rd. The third form, mutual delimitation of work, is one of the most practical and useful. It often needs a high degree of confidence, as where, for instance, a charity organization society says to the overseer of the poor, "We will take the responsibility of all new cases, send them to us without investigation, you may still help those on the poor books; let us keep the new cases off them, for once on it is hard to get them off again."

A more usual form is when the charity organization society takes all the cases which only a strained construction of law allows the overseer to help, and yet whose necessity seems so great that he feels they need and must have aid. To this kind belong the frequent mutual agreements as to the placing of paupers in almshouses or hospitals, at the request of the private agency or charity organization society.

4th. Co-operation in withholding. This is the height of practical co-operation between the public and private agencies, and needs the highest confidence.

When a charity agent can say to the overseer with regard to a certain family—"They need to be thrown on their own resources; we will watch them and secure aid if it is best for them—you leave them to us." And when the overseer has confidence that the work will be done as planned and that only a KIND severity will be exercised, we have got near to success in co-operation.

I have not spoken about the form of co-operation by delimitation, which prevails in a few cities, where the overseer of the poor gives no out-door relief, but agrees to send to the poorhouse or city hospital all who should go, and leave everything else to the private society, because however good it may be, it is hardly to be called co-operative, and co-operation is what I had given me for a subject. I have sometimes felt that when charity organization societies have claimed full co-operation with public relief agencies, they are giving the term a different meaning from the one I give it. And the mutual delimitation such as our English friends develop between poor law and charity, is again very different from what we mean by co-operation, a co-operation which has something of the sentiment of brotherhood in it. It means more than an agreement as to how to do certain work or leave it undone. It means hearty, cordial sympathy, wise help, and true encouragement.

I have only time to say, that the place to effect co-operation, to win each other's confidence and keep it, is the weekly conference meeting. Get your overseer of the poor to attend; let him learn how you really feel and talk of your poor people, and he will soon say and feel that you help him and he wants to help you. He will soon feel that he is a part of the weekly conference and belongs there. You will find his point of view a little different from yours,—all the better that you shall see with a different pair of eyes. The more varied the point of view the truer the conclusions.

You will do him a great deal of good and he you. The profits of true co-operation are essentially mutual.

PUBLIC SUBSIDIES TO PRIVATE CHARITIES.

BY AMOS G. WARNER, PH. D., LATE OF WASHINGTON, D. C., AND NOW PROFESSOR IN THE STANFORD UNIVERSITY OF CALIFORNIA.

On the second of last February, while the Senate of the United States was sitting as town council for the city of Washington, a member moved to amend the appropriation bill by inserting a proviso that almshouse inmates and other paupers and destitute persons, who might be a charge upon the public, should be turned over to any private institution that would contract to provide for them at ten per cent. less than they were then costing the District. Senator Call, who introduced the amendment, explained that it was in lieu of one which had been rejected at the previous session of Congress, whereby he had sought to have forty thousand dollars of public money given to the Little Sisters of the Poor, to enable them to build an addition to their home for the aged. He defended the original proposal on the ground that this sisterhood cared for the aged poor better and more cheaply than the almshouse, and that the existence of their institution had saved to the tax-payers of the District, in the last twenty years, a sum believed to be not less than three hundred thousand dollars. It was not a novel plea, for Congress had already appropriated, since 1874, fifty-five thousand dollars to aid the Home for the Aged of the Little Sisters of the Poor; and each year the District appropriation bill has included subsidies for a large number of private charitable institutions, some of them avowedly under sectarian management and others not. How far the tendency to grant public subsidies to private charities has gone in the District of Columbia, is in some sort, indicated in the following table:

DISTRICT OF COLUMBIA APPROPRIATIONS FOR PUBLIC AS COMPARED
WITH PRIVATE CHARITIES DURING THIRTEEN YEARS.

	NO. OF INSTIT'NS		TOTALS FOR MAINTENANCE			TOTALS FOR WHOLE PERIOD—13 YEARS		
	1880	1892	1880	1892	% IN-CREASE	CONSTRUC-TION	MAINTENANCE	CONST. AND MAINTENANCE COMBINED
Public Institut'ns	7	6	$78,048.82	$119,475.30	160	$155,130.70	$1,296,125.95	$1,351,256.65
Private "	3	28	46,500.00	117,630.00	253	300,812.53	840,940.00	1,141,752.53
Totals . . .			$124,548.82	$237,105.30		$455,943.23	$2,137,065.95	$2,493,009.18

From this table it will be seen that the amount given annually for maintenance to private charitable institutions at the beginning of the period was a little less than one-third of the whole amount, while at the close of the period it is a little less than one-half. The most surprising fact, however, is that the District has given to private institutions nearly twice as much money to be used in acquiring real estate and erecting buildings, as it has granted to its own public institutions. Were we to deduct a sum of $66,900 charged to the workhouse, a purely correctional branch of the so-called Washington Asylum, it would appear that more than three-fourths of the money appropriated for permanent improvements in charitable institutions was given to private corporations to spend.

The government of the District of Columbia is, of course, in many respects unique, but this tendency to vote public money to private charities is by no means peculiar to it. The best known example of persistence in the policy of reckless subsidies to private institutions is that of New York. A single institution in this state, officered by a religious order, receives from city governments more than $260,000 per year. A list of over two hundred private institutions for orphan children and the friendless in New York state, shows that of their total revenue but $1,225,104.69 was derived from legacies, donations and private contributions, while more than twice as much, $2,664,614.40, came from the taxpayers of the state, the counties and the cities. A great part of the money handed over for disbursement to private institutions goes for the support of dependent children. The law provides for the placing of such children in institutions of the same religious faith as the parents of the child, and that the local authorities shall pay a certain weekly stipend for its maintenance. The managers of the institutions can admit children and have them charged to the public. If parents wish to have a child educated in the faith of a sect at the expense of the public, they have only to get it admitted to one of the institutions, and many well-to-do people are known to avail themselves of the privilege. As, at the rates paid, there is a slight profit to the institutions on each child admitted, they are none too careful about investigating the cases of applicants. The results of this system are indicated by the fact that New York city has a daily average of upwards of 15,000 dependent children, or about one in one hundred of the population. The proportion of dependent children to the population of the state is 1 to 251. In Michigan, under a system of state care and placing out, it is 1 to 10,000. California, which has practically the same system as New York state, has nearly the same high proportion of dependent children, viz: 1 to 290.

According to Mrs. Josephine Shaw Lowell, the administrative result of this policy in New York city has been to build up the private eleemosynary institutions at the expense of the public ones. She gives the following statement, covering a series of years, to show this:

YEAR	POPULATION	FOR PRISONERS AND PUBLIC PAUPERS	FOR PAUPERS IN PRIVATE INSTITUTIONS	TOTAL
1850	515,547	$421,882	$9,863	$431,745
1860	813,669	746,549	128,850	875,399
1870	942,292	1,355,615	334,828	1,690,443
1880	1,206,577	1,348,383	1,414,257	2,761,640
1890	1,600,000	1,949,100	1,845,872	3,794,972

The appropriations for 1890 to private institutions fall under three heads:

  For defective, sick and vicious, . . . $133,565
  For children admitted by managers, ... 1,081,746
  For board of children committed by magistrates, 630,561

     Total, ... $1,845,872

After showing how ruthlessly the estimates for the public charities were cut by the Board of Estimate and Control, she says:

"The point to which I wish to call attention is that the city continues, at the bidding of the legislature, to pay, without protest, year by year increasing sums for the support of public dependents under care of private persons in private institutions, many of whom, but for this provision, would probably not be dependent at all, while, at the same time, the public dependents under the care of public officers in public institutions are housed in buildings which are in danger of falling down and are a discredit to the city."

In 1889 the legislature of Pennsylvania appointed a special committee, which investigated very fully the management of the charitable and correctional institutions of the state, and especially the methods employed by such institutions in securing public appropriations. The constitution of Pennsylvania forbids the granting of public funds to "sectarian" institutions, but the word "sectarian" is not defined, and the report of the committee shows a strong tendency to increase the number and amount of the state subsidies granted to private charities. This tendency is characterized as an "insidious danger." The committee tabulated the expenditures during a series of years for charitable and correctional purposes, amounting to about $37,000,000, and found that nearly a third of it went to private institutions. The report says:

"The remarkable increase during the last few years in the number of institutions receiving aid from the state is confined, in great part, to the so-called private charities, or private hospitals, homes for the destitute and to miscellaneous charities. A proportionate increase will soon render the commonwealth a contributor to the funds of every charitable institution in the state."

The fact mentioned above, that there is no generally recognized definition of the word "sectarian," is noteworthy. There are few institutions that will admit its applicability to themselves, and there are few to which it is not applied by some one. I have been gravely assured that an institution administered entirely by the oath-bound members of a religious order, was not sectarian for two reasons; first, because it admitted beneficiaries without regard to religious faith, and second, because there was a Presbyterian minister on its board of trustees,—a purely ornamental body. On the other hand, an institution having among its managers representatives of all the religious denominations except one, is apt to be regarded as "sectarian" by that one. Many institutions having no trace of sectarianism in charter, constitution or by-laws, are yet administered in the interest of a sect. A willingness to admit beneficiaries of all denominations is frequently less an evidence of non-sectarianism, than of a tendency to make proselytes. Much might be said in favor of the idea that all private institutions are sectarian, when not in a religious, then in a medical or a social sense. Public aid to a hospital may help to build up a medical school or a school of medicine just as surely as aid to an infant asylum may be used to build up a church. Social rivalries may stimulate people in pushing charities just as much as inter-denominational competition.

In states where a constitutional limitation forbids the voting of public money to "sectarian" institutions, members of the Protestant denominations seek to have this clause so interpreted as to exclude the institutions officered by the Roman Catholic orders, while charitable enterprises in which they are themselves interested are nominally unsectarian. The Catholics try to evade the constitutional limitations by disingenuous and unfair subterfuges, usually successful, and the Protestants with characteristic short-sightedness, encourage such a course by their own eagerness to secure public money for the private institutions in which they are themselves interested. There is a logical and manifest distinction between public and private institutions. With the former, the Government owns the property and can modify or abolish the institution at will. In the case of the latter, the property is owned by a private corporation, usually self-perpetuating, its charter is a contract with the state that grants it, and the fact that it is a "private" institution protects it in a great measure from criticism. In Pennsylvania it is found that such institutions tend more and more to be managed by a few persons who really choose their successors, and the state which grants them millions has not even the membership vote of a private individual, who pays one, two, or three dollars annually as dues. Just before the advent of a Superintendent of Charities in the District of Columbia a congressional committeeman thus described the attitude of the subsidized institutions towards the Government:

"There is a universal feeling that while Congress must furnish the money, each society must have absolute control of the expenditures and none of them are willing to submit to any visitation or control of such expenditures, or even any auditing of the accounts. The beginning and end of their connection with Congress in their eyes, seems to be 'Give each one of us so much money and let us do what we please with it.'"

This fact, that there is a clear-cut distinction between public and private charities, but none between sectarian and non-sectarian charities is one that those who shudder at every symptom of public aid to sectarian schools would do well to recognize. Protestants are willing to tease legislators for public money on behalf of a hospital or orphan asylum in which they are interested, urging that it is "doing good" and that it is preventing crime and pauperism, and so saving money to the tax-payers. They do not see or will not acknowledge that the same could be said of a parochial school, and that the claim which they set up that their own institution is "non-sectarian" is equivocal and unfair, and one which in practice the courts have never been able to make definite.

A tendency could hardly have gone as far as has that to grant public subsidies to private charities, unless there were in favor of it many considerations of great force, either apparent or real. As favoring this policy the consideration which is first and foremost in the minds of practical people is the matter of economy. Especially where the number of dependents in a given class is small, it is cheaper to have them cared for than to establish an institution for them. This is the reason that in most small towns a private hospital is subsidized and one is not built at public expense; but, of course, when we find a great city, like Brooklyn, depending entirely on subsidized hospitals for the care of its sick poor, this argument is inapplicable. Economy, however, may result from other causes, as when the private institutions are administered by religious orders, the members of which receive no pay except their support. In almost every branch of philanthropic work, Roman Catholic institutions can underbid competitors, so to speak, because of the great organizations of teachers and nurses and administrators whose gratuitous services they can command, and if the state is to sub-let its relief on the contract system it is hard to see why those who can bid low should not get the contracts. In reformatory institutions, those under private management have an advantage over those managed by public officials, in that the former are able to keep the inmates busy at remunerative employment with less opposition from outside trade organizations. A public reformatory for girls that should keep its inmates busy with work from a great shirt factory, would be sure to be attacked on the ground of its competing with poor sewing women; but such employment in private institutions, even those receiving public subsidies, is quite common. Even in institutions not officered by members of a religious order, the salaries are apt to be lower, and all the items of expense to be more closely scrutinized than in a public institution. Add to all this the further fact, that frequently private contributors aid in the support of a private institution and we see how great may be its advantage on the side of economy. To the real economies, of this method of operation should be added the apparent economies, when a private institution is willing to make a very low bid, to make great temporary sacrifices, in order to get the subsidy system established—in order to establish connection between itself and the public treasury. "At first," said a United States Senator speaking of the charities of the District of Columbia, "at first they thrust in only the nose of the camel."

Secondly, it is urged that private institutions, especially those for dependent and delinquent children, have a better effect upon the inmates than can public institutions. For one thing, dogmatic religious instruction can be given. For another, the spirit of self-sacrifice that pervades a private institution has a good effect upon the inmates and is contrasted with the cold and officialized administration of the public institutions. Connected with this, as also with the matter of economy, is the fact that boards of trustees and of lady managers and visitors give freely of their time and energy and sympathy in aid of private undertakings.

Thirdly, it is urged that by subsidizing private institutions we free them from the blight of partisan politics and the spoils system. The miserable political jobbery connected with, so many almshouses and insane asylums, and other public charitable institutions, is pointed out and we are asked to shield as many as possible of the state's dependents from similar evils. In the matter of educating the blind and the deaf and the dumb, the private institutions managed by close corporations or corporations of contributing members, are thought to have been more successful than public institutions for similar purposes. The specialists needed to conduct them properly prefer to work for a private corporation, as their tenure is more secure, and it is more easy to map out and pursue a policy of steady development and improvement. At the same time it should be said that one of the institutions which the committee of the Pennsylvania legislature found most secretive and least well conducted was a private school for the blind, sustained by public subsidies.

A fourth consideration is that by means of subsidies we aid the poor without fixing upon them the stigma of pauperism. A home for the aged is more respectable than an almshouse, and a private protectory or industrial school is supposed not to discredit the inmates as much as does a public reform school.

But this last mentioned consideration brings us to a turning point, for it is urged against such subsidies, as well as in favor of them. It is urged that private institutions receiving public money, by disguising pauperism promote it. Children who would support aged parents rather than allow them to go to the almshouse, desert them promptly when some provision is made for them that is ostensibly more honorable. I have in mind the case of an abandoned woman, who supported her mother for years rather than permit her to go to the poorhouse, but who was trying all the while to get her admitted to a "private" home for the aged. Parents unload their children upon the community more recklessly when they know that such children will be provided for in private orphan asylums or protectories where the religious training that the parents prefer will be given them. And thus we reach the first great objection to granting public subsidies to private charities. While it may be cheaper to provide thus for each dependent during a year, yet the number of dependents increases so rapidly, that eventually the charge upon the public is greater than if the alternative policy were pursued.

The results are most astounding where, as in the case of dependent children in New York, the managers of each institution are free to admit the children and have them charged to the community. The so-called Children's Law was passed in 1875, and forbade the keeping of able-bodied children between the ages of three and thirteen in a poorhouse. On this, its negative side, it was beneficial; but in providing for the care of dependent children in private institutions at public charge, it led to results that have properly been called portentous. These results, so far as they relate to New York city, have been indicated. Commenting upon them, the Hon. Seth Low said at the National Conference of Charities and Correction in 1888:

"Nothing can be worse for the children than to be crowded in such numbers into large institutions; and nothing can be more unjust to the tax-payers of New York than to be obliged to assume the care of such armies of children."

On the same occasion, speaking of the effect of the "Children's Law" in Brooklyn, Mr. Low said:

"In August, 1875, there were about three hundred children in the Nursery, a branch of the almshouse. They were at that time transferred to sectarian institutions and the number of dependent children at once increased wonderfully. By 1883 the number had grown to 1,492. At the latter date the Commissioners of Charities and Correction, finding the number increasing again unduly, undertook a thorough inquiry into the antecedents of the children supported, which resulted in the discharge of two hundred and sixty-five who were not entitled to public support. Among those, the most flagrant case was that of three children who had been maintained at public expense for more than five years, though they owned $2,100, of which their mother drew the interest, while she also kept a shop in Jersey City."

Where public officials alone have the right to commit children or others to the subsidized institutions, a check is put upon reckless admissions. But even under this system there is danger that many will be charged to the public who would never have sought admission to a public institution. In Illinois the constitution forbids public grants to sectarian institutions, but a law was framed providing that a county court might adjudge a girl to be a dependent, commit her to an industrial school, and the school should then be entitled to receive ten dollars per month for her "tuition, care and maintenance" besides an allowance for clothing. After the passage of this act the Chicago Industrial School for Girls was incorporated. Of the nine incorporators and directors, seven were officers and managers of the House of the Good Shepherd; and all girls committed under the act to the Chicago Industrial School for Girls, were placed either in the House of the Good Shepherd or in the St. Joseph's Orphan Asylum, both Catholic institutions. Questions as to the legality of such arrangements brought the matter into court, and during the trial it transpired that about seventy-three girls who were committed to the Chicago Industrial School for Girls by the county court, were already in the House of the Good Shepherd and the St. Joseph's Orphan Asylum at the time of such commitments. "In other words being already inmates of the institutions, they were taken to the county court and adjudged to be dependent girls and at once returned to those institutions, and thereafter the county was charged with $10.00 per month for tuition for each of them and $15 or $20 or $25 for clothing for each of them."*

In Maryland the juvenile reformatories of rival faiths are so anxious to secure inmates that the courts are criticised by each side for com-

---

*The courts at first decided that the Chicago Industrial School was a "sectarian" institution and the payment of the money therefore illegal; but the institution has since found a way to evade the constitutional limitation. This is a very good example of the unsubstantial nature of the barrier which such a constitutional limitation forms.

mitting an unduly large number of children to the other institutions. A lobbyist opposing a bill before the New York legislature urged that it should not pass because it would reduce the number of inmates in an institution in which he was interested, and which was just building large extensions. The anxiety of a doctor to fill up any hospital in which he is interested is well known, and it has been openly charged in a leading medical journal that the managers of dispensaries and hospitals are the beneficiaries of the well intended philanthropy which supports them rather than the poor for whom they are intended. The average dispensary makes no attempt to determine the ability of an applicant to pay, and the most reckless competition for patients exists between them. When the new superintendent of charities for the District of Columbia called at dispensaries where he was unknown, offers were twice made to prescribe for him out of hand, although he made no attempt to appear especially unwell or impecunious. The success of the subsidy system as regards institutions for the education of the blind and the deaf and dumb seems to come from the fact, that in this particular work the number of possible beneficiaries is strictly and obviously limited.

In the second place, the argument from economy in support of the subsidy system is negatived by the fact that under this system there must be so many duplicate institutions. In Maryland, for instance, there are two reformatories for boys within a mile of each other, and two for girls, both in Baltimore. Catholics manage one pair of institutions and private Protestant corporations the other. Besides this inevitable line of cleavage between Protestants and Catholics, there are various causes of institutional fission resulting from medical or social sectarianism. Many charitable institutions have been established less from brotherly love than from a quarrel in a board of managers in an older institution. This, together with the influence of individual ambitions, has led especially to the establishment of a great number of charities. It has been estimated that one-fifth of the inhabitants of Philadelphia receive free medical treatment, and while public subsidies alone do not cause such a state of things, they help it. When the public begins to grant such favors it is hard to draw a line. As a United States senator once said, speaking of the situation in the District:

"The very fact that Congress makes these appropriations, has caused to a great degree, the multiplication of the organizations. A few people getting together who are desirous of doing charitable work, or who have discovered some special need, or who are dissatisfied with some feature of some existing institution, instead of adding to or modifying such an institution, will start a new one, because they can appeal directly to Congress for the money necessary to begin it, and can base their claim on the ground that they are just as good as some other association already on the list."

A third reason for objecting to the subsidies we are considering, is that when voting them the legislator must resist special pressure. He has not a clear cut question of a given service to be rendered balanced by a given expenditure, but it becomes partly a question of offending or favoring some sect or nationality. The contention that the subsidy system takes the charitable institutions out of politics seems to be unsound. On the other hand it drags them into politics in a new and unfortunate way,—in a way that is found in practice to give great scope to log-rolling and kindred expedients. Many who will not do anything else for a charitable institution are willing to bully a legislator on its behalf, though this is probably not common. Most of the lobbyists are sincere even to fanaticism, but their view of the situation is terribly one-sided. It had come to be, that when the District of Columbia appropriation bill was under consideration, and in the haste of the last days of the session, the congressional committee rooms would be full of the representatives of the various charities, both men and women, intent upon getting the largest share possible. There was neither time nor opportunity on the part of the committee to come to any intelligent conclusion. Often those applicants most skilled or most personally attractive were most successful, and sometimes the committees were obliged to average their gifts. After such a policy has been entered upon it cannot be altered without injury to great vested interests, and without giving offence to large and powerful constituencies.

A fourth objection to the public subsidy system of supporting charities is that it tends to dry up the sources of private benevolence. Individual contributors dislike to have their mites lost in the abundance of a public appropriation. Almost without exception, so far as my investigations have gone, those institutions that have received public aid the longest and most constantly, receive least from private contributors. In looking up the history of a considerable number of institutions I have found that, after the public became a contributor, private contributions fell off from year to year, not only relatively, but absolutely, and in some cases ceased altogether.

Commissioner Bolles, of Pennsylvania, says:

"The state by appropriating so generally is drying up the interest of individuals in organized charities. Our people have acquired great wealth, and their sympathies should be cultivated in every possible manner. * * * * The state can never do through its long perfunctory arm acts of mercy with the same degree of kindly interest as individuals, who live nearer the scene of relief, and who have a more distinct interest in the sufferers."

This brings us to a fifth reason for objecting to the granting of public subsidies to private charities. It frequently does positive harm to a charitable institution, and sometimes wholly destroys its usefulness, to receive public money. An institution that receives no public money is freer in all its operations and is more highly valued by those who sustain and manage it. The beneficiaries also feel differently toward their benefactors. When visiting one subsidized institution the request was made, that nothing should be said before the inmates that would inform them that the institution received any public money. I could understand the wish and presume that the inmates would work more faithfully, be more grateful for favors received, and finally "turn out better" because they were kept in ignorance of the fact. Yet I doubt the possibility or propriety of thus using public money and at the same time trying to conceal the fact of doing so. By no hocus-pocus of subsidy granting can we make taxation do the work of self-sacrifice.

It should be remarked that the several states and municipalities have entered upon this policy of subsidizing private charities without deciding to do so, and even without perceiving that a decision was called for. Each request for a subsidy has been treated as a matter of administrative detail, involving no principle, and not significant as a precedent. The resultant system, as it is applied to the care of dependent children in New York city, is about as business-like as though the city should try to get its streets paved by announcing that any regularly incorporated association that should pave a given number of square yards of street,—location, time and method to be decided by itself,— should receive a given amount from the public treasury. The Washington system is theoretically looser, but practically not so bad. It is as though private associations were allowed to do paving at their own discretion, and then, on coming to Congress and teasing with sufficient skill and pertinacity, they should be given subsidies, on the general theory that they were "doing good" and rendering "public service."

This is subsidy granting at its worst. At its best, the government must attend to three things. First, on behalf of the poor, as well as the taxpayers, it must provide for the thorough inspection of subsidized institutions and the systematic auditing of their accounts. This work cannot be done by grand juries or legislative committees, or *ex officio* inspectors, who may from time to time thrust their inexperienced noses into matters which they know nothing about. The work of inspection must be done by some thoroughly experienced and otherwise suitable administrative officer, who is definitely responsible for the thoroughness of his work. Secondly, the State must keep in the hands of its own officials the right of deciding what persons shall be admitted to the benefits for which it pays, and how long each person may continue to receive those benefits. If it pays for beds in a hospital, one of its own officials should have entire control of admitting and discharging the patients so cared for. This is necessary, in order that "there may be some gauge of indigency and some assurance that the gauge will be used." Third, subsidies should only be granted on the principle of specific payment for specific work.

But even at its best, and with these safeguards, the policy of granting public subsidies to private charities is one of doubtful expediency. There is ground for thinking that if the State is too big and awkward to do a given work, it is also too big and awkward to decide properly whom it shall subsidize, in order to get the work done. All that can be said against subsidies in general can be said against this form of subsidies, and more, because here we have to deal with religious, medical and social sectarianism. As a transition policy for growing communities and for new and developing varieties of benevolent work, it may have its place, but it should not be entered on inadvertently, for while all its advantages and economies are greatest at the beginning, the disadvantages and dangers of it increase as time goes on.

PAPERS

FROM

CONTINENTAL EUROPEAN STATES,

RESPECTING THE

Public and Private Relief of the Poor.

CHARITY IN FRANCE AND BELGIUM.

ITS HISTORY AND PRESENT CONDITION.

BY M. HERBERT VALLEROUX, DOCTEUR EN DROIT; AVOCAT À LA COUR D'APPEL DE PARIS; LAURÉAT DE L'ACADÉMIE DES SCIENCES MORALES ET POLITIQUES.

[TRANSLATION.]

INTRODUCTION.

Charity in France originated in private initiative and was at first practised only by individuals. This was its condition from the foundation of the French monarchy until 1789, with only occasional interference of the public authorities towards the end of that period. In 1789, it passed entirely into the hands of the government, which deprived individuals of the right of practising charity and reserved to itself its full control and management. This is the second epoch, which begins and ends with the Revolution. The third epoch begins with the Consulate, that is, with the present century, and continues to the present time. During this period charity has been exercised both by the public authorities and by individuals.

We have, then, three distinct epochs which it is our purpose to treat in their order.

I.

FIRST EPOCH: BEFORE 1789.

Sapiens non miseretur: "the sage pities not," says Seneca. But while the wisdom of the pagan wholly repelled the idea of charity, the Christian religion, on the other hand, placed the care of the poor and the sick among the first duties of the faithful. The early Christians also took great care to assist the unfortunate, the infirm, and even mere travelers and those who were persecuted. Nor did they limit themselves to giving aid to the aged, and the children and parents of martyrs who were killed during the persecutions; they gave aid also to pagans, and Julian the Apostate remarks with some bitterness, that Christians who gave to poor pagans, whom their co-religionists left without assistance, were hated and persecuted.

When Constantine gave to the Church external peace and a legal existence, he gave to charitable institutions the same right to hold property that was given to the Church. From that time endowments were made by Christian believers, either while living or by testament, for the purpose of endowing hospitals, almshouses, orphanages and asylums, which had before depended for their support upon daily offerings, and especially for establishing new ones.

These endowments were frequent during the time of the persecutions, for the Christians were always on the point of being put to death and did not wish to have any attachments to the world; and besides, they formed a sort of community after the example of the early Christians of Jerusalem, where the faithful brought to the Apostles not only their income, but also the price of their lands; *i. e.*, their capital, as we see in the case of Ananias and Sapphira. But when there was no longer any danger in being a Christian, such offerings became gradually less. In lieu of these constant, periodical endowments, on which the priests and the poor subsisted, there were only small offerings or, sometimes, large and valuable, but irregular and uncertain gifts. Was it not then the part of wisdom so to invest these large gifts that the subsistence of the poor or the sick might be assured without fear of any uncertainty in the supply of the daily alms? And, indeed, the endowments allowed this to be done. Where land, customs dues or certain seignorial revenues were given to a hospital, it was understood that these funds were in perpetuity, and that the revenue should be applied to its support. We have here the origin of those *foundations* or endowments which the Christian emperors authorized, and whose perpetuity was secured by their laws.

Charitable work extended through all parts of the vast Roman Empire as fast as they became Christian; and when the Franks conquered Gaul and received baptism, Christian charity began to flourish there, as is testified by its works. Clovis and his successors respected and admired these beautiful effects of the Christian spirit and took pleasure in increasing the patrimony of the poor.

But it is important to note that what was done by the kings, they did as individuals and as believers, and not with the view of having the government interfere with the exercise of charity. Charity was the outgrowth of the Christian spirit, and only those kings sustained, directed and exercised it, who were possessed of this spirit. It is true that private almsgiving was common; that alms were often given on certain days at the doors of great personages or of religious houses; but this form of charity was less efficacious and less commendable. The best system of charity was the founding of permanent establishments, such as hospitals, either for all classes of disease without distinction or for particular maladies, old people's homes, foundling hospitals, houses of refuge, travelers' inns *(maisons hospitalières pour les voyageurs)*—our night lodging-houses, which have existed from the beginning of the middle ages. In order to establish these foundations, the permission not of the public authorities, but of the Church, by which alone charity was encouraged, was necessary.

It was the ecclesiastical power, represented by the bishop of the diocese, which authorized these foundations and took charge of the execution of the work, or inspected it. The discussions that arose relative to the execution of the will of the founder or the management of the trustees, were taken before the ecclesiastical tribunals. The lay power —the civil government, as we say to-day—did not interfere except to assure the full execution of the will; that is, to protect this property like any other, and in case of need to defend the decisions of the ecclesiastical tribunals. But preliminary permission did not have to be asked of the lay power, nor did the latter exercise any control over these foundations.

We may take as an illustration the forms and methods of charity in the thirteenth century, the age of Saint Louis. We have no precise figures, for we have no statistics, but only a table of the results of Catholic charities, as exactly as they can be traced by the aid of charts of the times and of the chronicles and movements that have been handed down to us. At that time France was far from having the population that it has to-day. For if the rural population has remained about the same (a fact now well established by a number of excellent and erudite works), the urban population was then much less than it is now. Paris, which has now 2,500,000 inhabitants, had at that time only 300,000.

Towns with eight or ten thousand inhabitants were considered important, while to-day there are sub-prefectures with thirty or forty thousand. As to wealth, the two periods are not at all comparable. One-half of Paris was not even laid out into streets in the seventeenth century; the Queen of France, wife of Philip Augustus, made a triumphal entry into the capital of her kingdom riding behind her husband on the same horse; and not until the fourteenth century did the Queen possess a carriage, and then it was one which the women of our day would certainly consider very uncomfortable. The habits of life were simple in all respects and large fortunes were very rare.

But in spite of this, there were certainly more hospitals in France in the thirteenth century than there are to-day. There were many small hospitals on the country estates, which have now disappeared. In some departments there were thirty or forty rural hospitals, where now there is only one; they have survived only in the cities. Leprosy, then common in Europe, excited the pity of the faithful, and there were not less than two thousand lazar-houses (*léproseries*) in France wholly constructed and maintained by the liberality of these faithful believers; while in Christendom, that is to say in Occidental Europe, there were not less than nineteen thousand. Besides these hospitals for lepers, there were many others for various diseases, and almost all had a room for the reception of poor travelers at night.

We must not think that these hospitals and asylums were neglected or badly supported. This, indeed, might be true in the case of a few among a large number; but most of them were objects of the solicitude of the faithful, and were maintained as well as the simplicity, or, one might say in view of our modern ideas of comfort, as well as the poverty of the times would permit. Some, indeed, bore the marks of luxury, and though few of these still survive from those remote times, one may still visit the hospital of Beaune (a small village of Burgundy between Paris and Lyons), which was built in the fifteenth century by Nicholas Rolin, chancellor to the duke of Burgundy. The large ward has the aspect of a church, with its stained glass windows and frescoed arches; there is none of the depressing bareness too common in the wards of our hospitals. The patients' beds were arranged along the side walls and enclosed by variegated curtains, some specimens of the design of which have been preserved. At one end of the room a movable partition opened, which permitted a view of the resplendent and ornate altar, where mass was said every morning, so that the sick, even the most infirm, had the unusual consolation of being able to assist at the holy sacrifice on their beds. The same arrangement has been adopted in some modern hospitals, but there is surely no modern hospital covering so large an area or with such immense wards, nor any which has so cheerful and varied an atmosphere. The large ward in this hospital is vaster and more beautiful than any of the halls in the palace of Cluny, which was built at the same period, and still stands in Paris. It seemed to the pious Christians of that time that they could not do too much for the sick; and they always had at heart the words of Christ: "Verily I say unto you, inasmuch as ye have done it unto the least of these my brethren, ye have done it unto me." As the palaces of princes at that time partook of the nature of hotels, hospitals were called Hôtels-Dieu, and there may be still seen upon some this inscription, which was at one time not uncommon: *Christo in pauperibus;* that is "To Christ in the person of the poor."

There is a street in Paris called Geoffrey-Marie, named after a Parisian tailor, Geoffrey, and his wife, Marie, who owned the land where this street has since been made and who gave it in 1260 by a deed, which is still extant, to the Hôtel-Dieu of Paris. In this deed Geoffrey and Marie stipulate that both shall be received among the number of the *confrères*, or members, who take care of the sick, and that they shall remain there during their lives. Thus they gave not only their property, but also themselves, as was very common at that time. This calls to mind another charity by which a noble lady gave all of her property for a special purpose—the distribution of soup to the poor, (*bouillon des pauvres*). She also gave up her life to preparing and distributing this nourishment to the unfortunate.

In short, we must not think that these endowments had for their sole end the construction of hospitals and asylums. All sorts of charitable works were proposed. For instance, endowments were made for the purpose of giving yearly allowances to poor girls; others for the purpose of loaning grain without interest to needy farmers, either for seed or for food for their families. Many endowments (then called alms) were given for the purpose of distributing every year to the poor of a parish a certain quantity of wheat or bread, but rarely money. A very common form of endowment at that period was the building of a chapel, with a hospital and school attached. A small salary was sufficient to support a priest who officiated in the chapel, directed the small hospital and instructed the children, for establishments of this kind are usually found in the country. It was customary, indeed, at that time to combine three different objects: religion, education and charity.

Charitable associations were also numerous under the name of *guilds*, *brotherhoods* or *fraternities* (*confréries ou fréries,*) which included men and women of all conditions of life, and were usually co-extensive with a parish. Thus the King and Queen of France belonged to the guild or brotherhood of Our Lady at Paris, in which were also found citizens of the parish, both artisans and small merchants; for Christian charity effaced all distinctions of rank and class. The *confrères* or members of the brotherhoods were no longer nobles or peasants, lords or bourgeois; they were *confrères* united for the purpose of doing deeds of charity. They visited sick members, assisted at the obsequies of the dead, caused masses to be celebrated for the repose of their souls, and also gave aid to families that were left in need. They had not, as in our modern mutual aid societies, fixed assessments with relief provided for in advance at rates determined by circumstances. They made their contributions during the services, and in case of need an appeal was made to the charity of the *confrères*, which was always sure of a response.

Some of these associations were established for special objects: to watch with the sick, to bathe them, to dress their wounds, and to bury the dead and follow in funeral processions. They were recruited by persons from all ranks of life, and their members visited all the sick who were known to them. Every municipal corporation had its guilds,—associations for religion and piety. But ordinarily, though not always, they were confined to the masters and workmen of a trade, together with their families. Certain of these *confrèries* or guilds owned beds in the hospitals; the Parisian guild, for instance, had rooms in the guild hospital (*hôtel de la corporation*), the use of which they gave "to the aged poor of their craft who had not prospered." These poor people, being housed in this way by the members of their own profession, who saw that their colleagues had not succeeded, advised with their *confrères* on matters pertaining to their trade, and did not feel themselves despised or burdensome; they had always belonged to the guild and felt, so to speak, at home there. To those for whom a gratuitous lodging did not suffice some additional aid was given, and the giving of advice was a very delicate way of bestowing charity. At Paris the Guild of Cooks, on the festival of their patron saint, gave a grand dinner to the poor inmates of the Hôtel-Dieu, with the purpose of giving these unfortunates the pleasure of a good repast, and the master cooks themselves waited on the tables. The Bakers' Guild distributed to the indigent all bread that did not come up to the standard weight fixed by the guild.

There was, moreover, even outside of the guilds, an emulation in deeds of charity; in this way a number of hospitals and asylums have commenced on a small scale. Sometimes a person would take two or three poor invalids or orphans into his own home, and later the number would insensibly increase; but it was necessary to provide for their future maintenance; and so, when the charitable founder died, leaving for the purpose of carrying on his work all his personal property, or his house or some small revenue, he would find some good soul to guarantee the continuance of the work, and, as an old account reads, "the founder, as well as others, was eager to leave his property to it." In this way small gifts and many legacies were added to the endowment, which together not only assured the existence of the work, but even enabled it to be enlarged.

The management of charitable institutions, the distribution of alms and the care of the sick were more especially functions of religious communities. In the country these communities became centers of population, and to the very last continued to aid the inhabitants of the neighboring country; while in the convents medical advice and treatment were given, as is still done by our missionaries in countries where they desire to spread the gospel. When, in time of famine, recourse was had to the granaries and the reserves of the monasteries, grain and wood loaned to the tillers of the soil was a form of relief that would have been sought in vain elsewhere, because in many country districts there were no well-to-do inhabitants. When faith began to grow weaker, and it became difficult to find *confrères* to care for the sick, the Sisters of Charity, established by Saint Vincent de Paul, took charge of them, as well as of abandoned infants. That you may see how a new religious order was established, I will give an example from my native city of Paris.

In the second half of the seventeenth century, an epoch of distress and misery, due to wars with the league of Augsburg, a Parisian woman of a noble parliamentary family and a widow at the age of sixteen, Madame de Miramion, meeting a large number of unfortunates in the streets of Paris whom the city hospital was not able to accommodate, took them to her own home and gradually filled up her house until she had about seven hundred. When her own resources were exhausted, she went about soliciting contributions at the great houses to which her rank admitted her. She then dressed her numerous servants according to the fashion of the time and told them that she was no longer able to pay them. The good women requested their mistress to keep them without pay, that they might help her to take care of the sick and share with her in the eternal reward. Madame de Miramion then promised them food and clothing, and proposed that they should form a religious order, without waiting for the consecration of the church. With this consecration they received the name of *Daughters of St. Geneviève*, in memory of St. Geneviève, the patron saint of Paris, whose church was near the Hôtel de Miramion; but up to the time of the Revolution the people always called them the Miramionites; and during all this time they did not cease to care for poor invalids.

The number of charitable foundations diminished very fast in the sixteenth century on account of the religious wars, which put an end to many of them. In the following century Louis XIV conceived the idea of applying his method of administrative centralization to charity. In a certain number of towns he built large hospitals, which he called general hospitals, where all sorts of poor and sick people were received : sturdy beggars, the infirm, the aged, foundlings, and the insane,—a medley which could not but yield poor results. And further, in order to assure to these large houses sufficient resources, he transferred to them endowments given for the rural poor. This was violating the intention of the founders and changing the destination of their liberality. The rural poor, no longer receiving any, or receiving less aid, betook themselves to the towns, where they increased the indigent population already there.

By degrees also, the royal authority replaced the ecclesiastical in matters pertaining to charity. It had arrogated to itself the right to authorize foundations, to approve of the gifts and legacies left to them, and to interfere in the management of their patrimony. It also took advantage of some abuses to assume control over the entire system of charity, which had been established and administered with full freedom up to that time. This interference was not at all a happy one, for under the reign of Louis XVI a medical commission, charged with ascertaining the condition and needs of the Hôtel-Dieu of Paris, made a report upon the bad condition and inconvenient arrangement of the hospital, which created a great deal of excitement at the time, and led to numerous subscriptions for renovation of the buildings. The product of these subscriptions, which amounted to several millions, was put into the hands of the public administration, which used it for other purposes. Assuredly the Hôtel-Dieu of Paris was in a worse condition at the end of the eighteenth century under the management of the government, than in the thirteenth, when it was entrusted to notable ecclesiastics and citizens under the surveillance of the archbishop of Paris; at any rate, under the old *régime* the sums given for the poor in the hospital did not go into the public treasury, but reached the destination intended by the donors.

And yet the writers at the end of the eighteenth century—the philosophers and makers of systems—desired to see relief committed exclusively to the public authorities. By their extensive and much admired writings, which, unhappily for France, had a great influence over men and shaped public opinion, they gave rise to two parties or classes among their contemporaries. The dominant party (it matters little in what manner they had obtained supremacy) had all the ability and came to have the widest authority. Both the souls and the bodies of men became subject to their discretion. It was their purpose to shape the soul by an education imposed upon it from without; and by the system of government which they hoped to organize, they would be masters of the body, distributing relief and even labor. It only remained to them to follow, in the organization of education and of the government, the plans and ideas of the system-mongers (*faiseurs*), at that time all the fashion. As to the other class of citizens—those who were governed—they had neither the right of opinion nor of organization, nor indeed of finding out what such rights meant; they were regarded as incapable of doing good, and so were not allowed to practise charity.

The national assemblies of the Revolution were charged with putting into practice these dangerous and false ideas.

II.

Second Epoch: The Revolution.

The Constituent Assembly, which was the first of the revolutionary assemblies, had been in session only about a month, when it decreed the seizure of ecclesiastical property, that is to say, the foundations or endowments made for promoting religious worship and for giving a patrimony to convents, (November, 1789). This was a great blow to charity; for a part of the ecclesiastical patrimony was used for charitable purposes, and numerous charitable institutions found themselves without any, or with greatly diminished resources. A committee of the Assembly under the name of a committee on vagrancy, because this was one of its objects, charged with studying the question of charity, estimated that hospitals and asylums alone had thus lost, by a measure that was not indeed directed against them, but which nevertheless affected them, more than a third of their income—10,330,000 livres out of 29,074,000 ($1,911,050 out of $5,378,690). But they took account of only the money value of the loss, and were unable to estimate the damage done to the poor, especially those in the country, who were left without assistance by the suppression of the convents. A physician of Bourg, Doctor Ebrard, who not many years ago wrote a history of charity in Bourg, has told us that there are poor people still living, who recall with regret the time when they were permitted to gather fagots in the forests belonging to the Carthusian friars. These forests have been seized by the State and are no longer open; and the poor unfortunates, pursued by the state foresters for doing what was formerly permitted to their ancestors, exclaim: "Ah! the Carthusians were far better friends of the poor!"

And so the Assembly received a large number of petitions, emanating from the poor of different cantons, who protested against the confiscation of property to which they thought that they had some title. But transported by its own passion and love of theories, it refused to take any notice of them.

Another body, the National Convention, completed the ruin of charitable institutions by seizing what property still remained to them, that is, the hospitals, asylums, and other establishments for the benefit of the poor and sick. The numerous fraternities or guilds, even those composed of the laity, were dissolved.

"At Besançon," says M. Sauray, a historian of that town, "there were more than forty guilds, embracing all classes of society. In vain did they plead for liberty; one could wish it had been for their faith, and still more for their property. They were despoiled of their rents, their credits and the silver used in their religious services, though many guilds had nothing to surrender to the rapacity of the Revolution but the draperies used at the funerals of their dead members."

The guilds had all been dissolved and their property seized under Louis XVI through the efforts of Turgot, a writer and statesman of that period. The Convention proscribed even the religious orders which had for many centuries cared for the sick.

"Because," says the Decretal issued at that time, "in a truly free state no corporation ought to be allowed to exist, not even such as by the care of the sick and the education of children, deserve well of their country."

The state was now proprietor of all the patrimony of charitable institutions, which had been increasing for centuries through the liberality of devout Christians. In order to prevent the creation of new endowments and the exercise of private charity, it was forbidden to give alms; this was made a crime, and the laws of the Revolution punished those who gave their property to the poor, just as in a well regulated state the law punishes those who take the property of another. Charity became a monopoly, which the government meant to reserve to itself, and in doing so it exceeded its just rights and functions.

It is not possible, and it would be of little interest, to give an account here of the different schemes organized by the members of the various assemblies of that period for the purpose of having charity distributed by the State. Sometimes they would conceive some such idea as a "board of public relief," which would produce a uniform distribution of relief by departments or districts, according to the classes of unfortunates; sometimes they would invent new forms of organization. But it is worthy of note and remembrance that none of these beautiful conceptions were ever put into practice. Instead, they took away from the unfortunates the property whose revenues had served to give them relief, and in its place they gave them laws, decretals, and discourses. And they never received anything else from the revolutionary governments.

It had been repeatedly said that the property devoted to charitable purposes and administered by individuals was badly managed; that the revenues were poorly employed, and that the government would do better to take the administration of charity into its own hands. But when charity passed into the hands of the State, it almost entirely ceased; the poor were no longer helped, the sick were no longer cared for—everything was given over to pillage.

"At the hospital at Blain on the Lower Loire," writes M. Léon Maître, keeper of the records of the department, "the Sisters were driven out, their real estate sold, their furniture broken to pieces, the linen and medicines stolen, and the empty apartments were occupied by persons who live there without authority or opposition."

Of the thirty-four hospitals which existed in Paris in 1789, fourteen were obliged to close, and the others were in the most wretched condition. Their revenue, which before the Revolution was 7,100,000 livres, ($1,313,500), did not now amount to more than 900,000 livres, ($166,500). And with the government paying in assignats which no one would any longer receive, we can imagine the part played by the administrators of the hospitals which were still open, from the long-continued cries of distress, traces of which our archives reveal in letters filled with supplications and woe. The people of Bordeaux write that their resources are all gone, their food bills unpaid, and that being on the verge of bankruptcy, they are in despair.

"Laborers support themselves and share their bread with the poor; but this condition of things cannot long endure, and the people of Bordeaux are already inquiring how it is that asylums are no longer provided."

The municipality of Bayeux writes:

"The hospitals have in them only living skeletons, who are ready to succumb more from actual want than from natural infirmity."

The administrators of the hospital at Mauriac in the department of of Cantal, write to the Convention:

"Come quickly to the aid of our orphans; would you have us adopt them in the name of our country, only to leave them to perish from hunger and want? Allowances for the past thirty-five months are still due to them and their nurses."

Still others dared to write, even at a time when free speech was at the risk of death:

"The asylums of the Republic are no longer places of refuge opened by charity to the needy, but asylums for the dead."

Were these complaints exaggerated? The Directory, the last of the governments of the Revolutionary period, sent councillors of state into different parts of France to ascertain the real condition of the country. We have the reports made by them to the government on their return, and assuredly, as officers of the government, they were naturally disposed to present the situation in an advantageous light; but what they say of the condition of the hospitals is the severest that has been said.

Councillor Fourcroy, who visited the West of France, states that the wages of nurses were everywhere overdue, and the State did not pay them. In the department of Manche the arrears exceed 539,000 livres, ($99,550), which to-day would amount to three or four times that sum. In the department of Calvados, of 1,102,000 livres ($203,870) which were due, only 27,000 livres ($4,995) were paid.

As to the hospitals:

"They have become the abodes of the most frightful want; misery and sickness find in them but little relief. Everywhere, except at Rouen, the sick have no linen, or only torn and ragged pieces, and their beds have no coverings. The old people's and children's homes are in the same distressing condition."

Francis of Nantes traveled over the middle of France. He writes:

"The charitable institutions (*hospices*) continue to be in a pitiable state, and it is necessary that we should begin by giving them an assured income. At Toulon many invalids are put to bed without any coverings and without any straw in the mattresses. In the old people's home only a pound of bread is given per day, with some boiled beans, but without wine or meat."

He saw a woman on whom an operation had been performed, whose only restorative was a dozen beans.

"At Marseilles, out of six hundred and eighteen foundlings in the foundling hospital, only seventy-eight survived. At Toulon, of one hundred and four infants, only three survived; I have also seen in these hospitals four children in every cradle. They are wrinkled and present the appearance of premature decrepitude."

In the country the poor were wholly without aid; the institutions founded to give them assistance were seized and nothing else put in their place, and thus their misery was extreme. Councillor Redon, who was sent into the East of France, stated that "mendicity has increased very much on account of the troubles of the Revolution." and he might have added, because it had suppressed the means of giving relief. The administrator of the Department of the South complained loudly of the want of the inhabitants: "There is not a winter in which there is not death by starvation."

In the presence of so much destitution and suffering, many of the councillors who were sent on tours of inspection declared that, since the government was powerless, the remedy must be found in permitting individuals to practise charity, and even to establish foundations as formerly; and especially in allowing the Sisters of Charity to return to the hospitals, that they might care for the sick.

The Directory carried out only one part of these propositions. It gave back to the hospitals and other charitable institutions that part of their property which had been taken from them and had not yet been sold, that is, about two-fifths; and it promised further, that it would replace the property sold by other property of equal value which had been taken from churches, convents, exiles and emigrants, and those condemned to death by the Revolutionary tribunals. Singular justice which used one spoliation to compensate another, and which, in the end, never gave back to the hospitals what they had lost! The Directory, moreover, was overthrown on the second Brumaire (December 2, 1799) by General Bonaparte, who, first under the name of Consul and then under the name of Emperor, reorganized France and gave it the form in which we find it to-day. We thus come to the third and most important epoch—the present situation.

III.
Third Epoch: The Present Situation.

Napoleon I, exaggerating the tendency of the old royal government to interfere, took everything into his own hands, leaving as little as possible to individual initiative, and he did the same with charity as with everything else. The governments that have followed, although differing in name and representing different ideas, have all held to the same tradition. They have shown themselves strong partisans of the prerogative of the state and enemies of the liberty of the individual; so that the powers of the government have been increased and extended, with more or less readiness of application, according to the times. But it is worthy of note that the present government—that of the Republic —leaves far less personal liberty to its citizens than did the government of Louis XIV, who is still regarded as the model of absolute kings. The French of to-day have indeed the right, which they did not then enjoy, of electing a parliament. But the government, chosen in this way by a majority acting more or less under instructions, has more power than any of the old royal governments ever had; it penetrates more into the private life of citizens and, indeed, puts more constraint upon them. Proof of this may be found in that which forms the subject of this paper, *i. e.*, charity.

The ancient patrimony of charities, the gift of individuals, as we have seen, is now managed by the government, which, moreover, has organized different methods of rendering aid, its design being to make an administrative matter of charity; but on the other hand. as the provisions of the laws of the Revolution forbidding private charity have fallen into disuse, private associations have also been formed, so that we have in France to-day administrative charity, or *public assistance*, and private charity. (The official name *assistance* has been applied to the former because the term charity recalls a Christian virtue which is displeasing to a government composed of irreligious men). Of these two forms of charity we will now speak.

§ 1. PUBLIC ASSISTANCE.

The amount expended for this object does not form a separate item in the government's budget. There is no budget of "assistance" as there is of public instruction; in short the funds are supplied partly by the State, that is to say from the budget of France, and partly by the departments or communes, while still another part comes from the revenue derived from the capital belonging to the charitable institutions; and finally, the remainder is furnished by private alms. Thus the budget of "public assistance" is supplied from three sources: (1) taxation; (2) revenue derived from the property owned by charitable establishments and given by the liberality of individuals—a liberality in part recent, but chiefly ancient, some of the property having been given as early as the twelfth and thirteenth centuries; and (3) alms given annually by the faithful for public assistance, in order that they may be well employed.

The total budget for "public assistance" for 1889. according to a report made to the minister of the interior in 1888 by M. Monod, director of the Department of Public Assistance, (the latest figures received), was about 189,000,000 livres ($34,965,000). Of these 189 millions the State, that is, the central government, furnished seven and a half millions ($1,387,500). The remainder was furnished by the departments and communes, or by private charity, but in what proportion was not indicated. All that is shown is, that in 1889 the revenue from the institutions themselves increased to almost 47,000,000 francs ($9,400,000). There are no reliable and recent figures except for Paris, which on account of its importance has a separate administration. There the budget for "public assistance" for 1892, (for hospitals and asylums only), was 44,201,000 francs ($8,840,200), of which 19,339,000 francs ($3,867,800) were voted directly by the department or the municipality, and about 4,000,000 francs ($800,000) came from the collection of certain taxes given over to the hospitals; in other words, of the total amount, almost 23 millions and a half (nearly $4,700,000), or more than half of the whole, was furnished by the tax-payers, which represents a charge of more than ten francs on every inhabitant, including indigents. If we consider, further, that from this number should also be deducted children, domestics, etc., we find that every head of a Parisian family, excluding indigents, pays an average tax of fifty or sixty francs merely for obligatory public assistance. The burden on the inhabitants of the rest of France is, indeed, much less, being, according to M. Monod, only 1 fr. 60 centimes (35 cents) per inhabitant. We shall see below the reason for this enormous difference between the expenditure in Paris and that in the other departments for the same object.

It is important to bear in mind that in France relief is not obligatory on the public authorities. The right to ask and receive aid, which exists in other countries has no place in our legislation; no commune can be compelled to give relief to its poor. It relieves them according to the means at its disposal, and in many communes, especially those in the country, their means are extremely small or even *nil;* but no constraint can be put upon the commune. The law requires only that the departments shall maintain asylums for the insane and for abandoned infants. As to the insane, it is a measure of public order, for it would be dangerous to leave them at liberty. As to the foundlings, an ancient custom made them a charge on the lord of the place where they were found, and his duty has passed to the modern public authorities. But what are the means at the disposal of the Department of Public Assistance for giving aid to unfortunates?

We have hitherto spoken of hospitals and asylums (*hospices*). There is this difference between the two terms: hospitals are intended for the sick, and their inmates are continually changing; while asylums are intended for the aged, for foundlings, or for various kinds of infirm persons—the blind, the incurable, etc.—who, when once received into an asylum or home, remain there either for a very long time (as the foundlings) or for their whole life (as old persons and incurables). In small communities there are hospital-homes (*hôpitaux-hospices*) which receive the sick and foundlings, the aged and infirm, and sometimes the insane.

In large establishments the different classes of poor were carefully separated from one another; but in others not so much care was exercised. The legislators of the Revolution, who had strange ideas about everything, prescribed this confused rule: that "the old shall give the children lessons in civic duty (*civisme*) and virtue." As the homes contain vagabonds and beggars by profession, besides the honest people who have fallen into distress without any fault of their own, we cannot help thinking that they would give to the children very injurious lessons; that they would teach them to deceive the public and feign infirmity, so as to live without work, rather than to engage in labor and to practise virtue. In practice, however, separation between the different classes of the inmates of homes is the rule.

The number of hospitals and homes in 1889 (the last official figures) was 1,639—308 hospitals, 882 hospital-homes, and 449 homes. In 1789 the number was larger, for the *Committee on Vagrancy* reported 2,188 in 1799, and added that they had not been able to get a complete account. But although these establishments were more numerous than are those of to-day, their capacity was probably less. But we have no precise figures. There were then many small hospitals scattered about in many places; to-day the tendency is to build large hospitals, and these only in cities. It is said that at the end of the eighteenth century there were fewer hospitals and homes in the country than in the thirteenth, and that most of those that still existed in 1789 have now disappeared. We must not forget, however, that about one half of the hospitals and homes disappeared during the Revolution; those that have been erected since are almost all in cities. Indeed, of the many hundreds that have been built since that epoch, certainly not more than ten have been erected in the country. It is then quite correct to say that the sick in the country have less care than they had one hundred years ago, and, above all, less than they had in the middle ages. At present the sick in the country who must be cared for, either because they have no family or because of the gravity of their disease, contagious disease for example, have to be transported to the nearest city, which perchance is far away; and further, the administrators of the urban hospital often refuse them, because they are not obliged to receive invalids from outside of the city. Strictly they can receive only persons of means, unless the commune from which the patient comes pays for him; and in that case it is necessary, before transporting the sick, to call together the municipal council in order to vote the expense; and what becomes of the invalid in the meantime?

In 1889 there were in all the hospitals and homes together (*les établissements hospitaliers*) 180,473 beds, to wit: 78,497 beds for the sick, (of which, however, 13,293 were exclusively for the use of the army); 60,800 for the infirm, the aged and the incurable; 14,921 for assisted children; and finally 29,694 for the *personnel* of the hospitals and homes. The last figure may seem very high, but we must consider that the number of persons employed was 30,579, viz.: 2,976 physicians and surgeons, 2,931 employees, 11,199 nuns (*religieuses,*) and 13,199 servants. The cost of this service was more than eighteen per cent. of the total expenditure, and this proportion has a tendency to increase.

The hospitals and homes, however, are very unequally distributed and very unequally endowed. In some establishments there are empty beds; in others there are not enough. Some establishments are richly endowed; for example, the hospital at Vichy, which has the right, by an old royal ordinance, to collect a tax of five centimes (about one cent) for every bottle of mineral water obtained there, has a large income. On the other hand, there are hospitals whose only resources are the revenues from endowments made centuries ago, and, as the value of money has diminished, they are not able to maintain themselves except by subsidies from the communes.

In fine, it is remarkable, in view of the new establishments, to see the old hospitals and homes remain what they were. Thus at Paris, the Quinze-Vingts established by St. Louis in the thirteenth century for three hundred—fifteen (*quinze*) times twenty (*vingt*)—blind persons still exists, but having the same capacity as formerly, it never receives more than three hundred Parisians, though the population of France and the number of the blind have largely increased during six and a half centuries.

One reason for the largely increased cost of service in the hospitals of Paris is a measure adopted by the administration at the demand of the municipal council, which, in view of the large population of the capital and the great abundance of poor, who come there from all directions, was fatal—I mean the *laicisation* (exchanging nuns for lay service) of the personnel of the hospitals, homes and asylums.

The care of the sick in the hospitals had been assigned to the Sisters of St. Vincent de Paul, and physicians and patients alike were in accord in admiration of their zeal, their ability and their devotion. But the municipal council of Paris, by a very large majority, under the influence of the Masonic lodges, resolved to exclude from the hospitals all who had a religious vocation, as it had already done in the case of the schools.

It demanded of the government, on which the hospitals depend (for though the municipalities vote funds for these establishments, they have no control over them), that it should expel first the chaplains, then the sisters; and the government, desiring to please the municipality whose suffrages it sought, consented. The first to be expelled were the chaplains, or priests, who gave consolation to the sick at the moment of death, or during their illness, and then a very complicated rule of procedure was established for all the sick who should desire to have the consolations of religion,—a rule of such a nature that to-day a large number of the invalid poor die without having been able to reconcile themselves with God, and without hearing any one speak of Him or of their eternal salvation.

Finally the Department of Public Assistance, always ready to favor men who are without religion, drove out the sisters from the different hospitals and homes. The physicians of these hospitals, although beholden to a certain extent to the administration, complained loudly in the interests of the sick; they circulated a petition which was signed by doctors, both the religious and those of the most diverse opinions. All the signers, even Protestants, Jews and free-thinkers, said that the Sisters of Charity were invaluable on account of their experience, their absolute devotion and their disinterestedness, qualities rarely found among paid employees. Their complaint was no more listened to than was that of the sick, and to-day there are incompetent persons of both sexes paid for doing service in the hospitals.

One of the first results of this system is much slackness in the care and watching of the sick, and there are numerous complaints from the patients, who are well cared for only if they are able to fee their nurses. And the latter are sometimes even negligent and cruel. They have cost the lives of many patients and caused a greatly increased expenditure.

Doctor Despres, physician of the Charity Hospital and a free-thinker, wrote:

"A nun receives no pay; the government gives to the superior of the hospital 200 francs ($40) for every sister, which is called their clothing expense (*le vestiaire*,) and serves to supply them with shoes, underwear, stockings and clothing. A lay nurse, including her dress, costs 700 francs ($140) per year, and besides she is given food and a separate lodging." (He says elsewhere that they often get something from the parents and friends of those whom they nurse, at the expense of the hospital.) "You will get a better idea of the cost, when you learn that the *laicisation* of the Cochin hospital has cost 138,000 francs ($27,600) in capital and 18,000 francs ($3,600) in revenue; that is to say, a sum of money with which a hospital could be built and twenty patients supported. Yet this is not the whole of the expense."

"The *laicisation* of — has cost 300,000 francs ($60,000) in capital and 45,000 francs ($9,000) in revenue, sufficient to support one hundred or more old people in the old people's home. When beds are wanting for the unfortunate, it is no time to make such unnecessary use of the public resources. Every one knows that the sister's is the most reliable and the most useful service for hospitals; that no one can take her place, and that if she did not exist, it would be necessary to invent her. To whatever religion one may belong, it is impossible to deny this."

In spite of such conclusive testimony, different provincial municipalities have demanded and obtained from the government the removal of the Sisters of Charity. With the men who govern us the irreligious passion is everything; the care and interests of the sick count for nothing.

Besides the various kinds of hospitals it is necessary to say something of the institutions devoted to the aid of the healthy poor, such as the bureaus of relief (*bureaux de bienfaisance*.) This name dates from the beginning of this century and was taken from the writings of the Abbé de Saint Pierre, but the idea is an old one. There were at the end of the old monarchy a large number of *bureaus for the poor* (*bureaux des pauvres*) which originated, like all of the charitable institutions of that time, in private initiative, and were ordinarily made up of the leading men and some of the clergy of a parish. Their object was to receive the alms, either in money or in such things as might be entrusted to them, with the view of making a useful distribution of them among the poor after becoming acquainted with their needs. In 1789 they were numerous and had already received some endowments; the Revolution suppressed them and seized their property.

The present bureaus of relief are organized upon the model of the old bureaus for the poor, but they exist only by the authorization of the government, which establishes them by decree. They are administered by a commission chosen as follows: one-third of the members by the municipal council and two-thirds by the prefect; the mayor is president *ex officio*. There were in France on December 31, 1889, (the last public figures), 19,308 bureaus of relief. As there are but a little over 36,000 communes, and as certain communes have several bureaus (Paris for example, has twenty), the greater number of rural communes must have none.

The total receipts of these bureaus were in the year 1889 almost forty million francs (39,734,000 francs or $7,946,800); of these

19,747,000 francs ($3,949,800) came from the revenues of the property belonging to the bureaus. This property has come either from the old endowments, made before 1789 in favor of the bureaus for the poor or other analogous works and since given over to the bureaus of relief; or from donations that have been made since. It is thus that Mme. Boucicault, wife of the founder of the *Bon Marché* at Paris and proprietress of a large fortune, has left 500,000 francs ($100,000) to the poor of the little village where she was born. This sum is to be invested, and it will yield an annual revenue of 19 or 20,000 francs ($3,800 or $4,000). Few rural bureaus of relief have so large an income. 12,192,000 francs ($2,438,400) have been furnished by the communes, but chiefly by the city communes; 7,346,000 francs ($1,469,200) have been furnished by the poor tax, the name given to the tax upon the receipts of theaters and other places of amusement that existed prior to 1789. Gifts and legacies have amounted to 3,040,000 francs ($608,000); the remainder comes from different sources not specified.

The aid distributed in money or in kind (food, clothing and fuel) amounts to 30,879,000 francs ($6,175,800) and the number of individuals who have received aid to 1,616,481, which makes a little less than twenty francs ($4) for each person aided. But this implies that the distribution has been equally made; but in fact, in some places, where the bureaus of relief have only a small fund at their disposal, the poor enrolled in their books receive sometimes less than one franc (twenty cents) per year, that is to say, almost nothing. There are some bureaus which distribute nothing for want of funds.

Of this total of forty millions francs ($8,000,000) Paris contributes one-fourth, or about ten millions ($2,000,000), while the number of poor which it enrolls is from 110,000 to 120,000; upon which we may remark in passing that less than three hundred out of every thousand are native Parisians. Foreigners or people from the departments represent more than seventy per cent. of those who are aided. It is a matter of common experience that large numbers of people ruined, or upon the point of being so, press into Paris, either to conceal their misery in a place where they are not known, or with the hope of finding employment. Often the authorities of small towns send to Paris, paying their railroad fare, the infirm or habitual beggars who might otherwise become a charge upon them. To these must be added the immense number of persons of both sexes who come to Paris expecting to find work or employment, and who, not finding it, fall into distress.

It is certain also, though it is difficult to prove it definitely, that the relative abundance of the public relief is one of the motives that draws the country population into cities, especially into large cities.

Indeed from what we have said it is clear that relief must be inadequate, especially in the country. Louis XIV, touched by the condition of the rural sick, sent every year into all parts of his kingdom 932,000 bottles of medicine with instructions upon the labels. They were sent to the sisters who took care of the sick in the country at their own homes and also gave instruction to children. Louis XVI sent three times that number, but the Constituent Assembly in 1790 suppressed this distribution of medicines, giving assurance at the same time that it would establish a better and more complete system of relief. It established nothing, however, nor did the assemblies which followed; but in certain departments the general council have tried different means of aiding the sick of the country. The means most often employed consists in paying a small salary to the physicians practising in different cantons, for which they consent to visit gratuitously the poor where they live; though well intended, the system in practice yields but poor results. But what is most important to establish is that these results have been very variable; sometimes the system is praised, but more often criticised; sometimes opposite opinions are heard within the same department. Again, certain departments and communes, after having made use of this system, have renounced it.

We should also include with other forms of public relief the workhouses (*depôts de mendicité*), where vagabonds without a home (*sans asile*) are confined. Begging and vagabondage are crimes punishable by the laws of France, but the laws are imperfectly executed. If an attempt should be made to shut up the numerous vagrants, who wander through the country aided by the peasants who fear them, or encumber the streets of large cities, it would be necessary to build ten or fifteen times as many workhouses as there are now. Those which exist at present are so full, that many unfortunates solicit in vain the privilege of admission to them and for that purpose even submit to conviction and sentence by the courts: for these workhouses are prisons, as well as homes or asylums.

To get a true estimate of the *bureaux de bienfaisance*, which are the chief means of aid outside of the hospitals and homes, we should bear in mind that they are a source of hereditary pauperism.

"I have seen," wrote an inspector of public assistance, and a man who is largely occupied in questions of charity, M. de Watteville, "I have seen upon the registers of the bureaus of relief the names of the worst, even of the very worst, people among those who are registered there to-day."

In short, governmental assistance has always something formal, rigid and bureaucratic about it, which does not easily discriminate between the worthy and unworthy poor. As long as the bureaus of relief were under the charge of the Sisters of Charity, investigations and discriminations were made; to-day they have been put into the hands of the laity, and the result has been less discernment and more distress. The tendency, moreover, is to give aid in the form of public works, and as a function of the state for political and, above all, for electoral purposes. In many bureaus of Paris it is asked of the unfortunates who solicit aid: What school do your children attend? If they go to schools where religion is taught, and where prayers are said before and after recitations, aid is refused them. In order to receive any aid they must send their children to the communal schools, from which all religious instruction and ideas are absolutely banished. This, too, is done elsewhere than in Paris. And some years ago the sub-prefect of a city in Normandy replied to the inhabitants of a city destroyed by fire, who had come to solicit the aid voted annually for this purpose, (collective disasters: as inundations, conflagrations of a whole city, etc).

"You have no right to any aid, seeing that you did not at the last parliamentary election vote for the candidates who are agreeable to the government; relief is only for those who vote right."

It is indeed the tendency of the party at present in power to use charity as an instrument for perpetuating its power and realizing its plans.

§ 2. PRIVATE CHARITY.

It is not surprising that the power of the dominant party shows itself antagonistic to private charity; that everything which originates outside of itself is displeasing to it; and that everything that comes from the initiative and from the action of citizens is considered as hostile.

It is not that private charity is not well spoken of, for an official has said of it to the Superior Council of Assistance:

"A fair and unprejudiced opinion must admit that, when it gives with discretion, it furnishes both material and moral support. In certain kinds of work it brings a spirit of sacrifice, an ingenuity in its procedure, a tact in its application, that are looked for in vain from public assistance."

After this beautiful eulogy it would seem that this private charity which is so useful, should be encouraged; that, at least, it ought to be left to act freely, more especially as it fills up the *lacunae* and insufficiencies of public assistance. We shall see, on the contrary, that it is combatted without relaxation and shackled in every possible manner.

There is, however, one kind of charity that the Convention was no more able to hinder than the legislatures which prohibited almsgiving; that, namely, which consists not only in aiding neighbors and dependents, but in taking grandparents or children of relatives to live with one. We must call this charity, because too often do we see the kind of people who drive away their aged parents or send them to an old people's home, and who also show very little anxiety for their own children, for whom they incessantly demand supplies, allowances and gratuities of all sorts. On the other hand, in some provinces, where the religious spirit has been preserved, the people are anxious, even in the very poorest families, to take their grandparents into their homes, and even orphans whose parents are strangers. Thus we see that households burdened with children do not hesitate to take orphans whom they treat as their own children. Those who would abandon even their cousins would be poorly thought of by their fellow-citizens. Happy opinions and happy sentiments, which permit them to do without homes and bureaus of relief!

There are, however, some cases where one cannot perform acts of charity by single handed, as in building orphanages, free hospitals and people's homes, and in doing all sorts of works which are multiplied by Christian charity. Such establishments can very rarely be founded by individuals; ordinarily an association is necessary, since a fund must be raised, which will yield an assured income, and it is here that the hostility both of our legislation and our government manifests itself.

According to our laws, no association of more than twenty persons, founded for any purpose whatever, even a charitable one, can exist except by permission of the executive, and this authorization is given or refused at will, without justification and without giving any reasons for refusal. Even after permission has been given it is always revocable, arbitrarily and without cause. In fact, most of the existing charitable associations have been established without express authorization; they are tolerated, but always under the threat of persecution, which the government from time to time carries into effect where a society is displeasing to it.

In the same way a license is necessary in order to establish a hospital or a home, even in one's own house, which the government arbitrarily accords or refuses. Indeed, one cannot make use of his own house to receive poor sick people, or orphans, or old persons, except at the pleasure of the government. There exists full freedom for wine-shops; one can without a license open as many of them as he pleases. Their number is endless and constantly increasing. But liberty to do good does not exist; it depends upon the caprice of the authority in power. There is full liberty of debauchery in one's own house; it is the right of ownership. But one cannot practise charity there; the right of ownership then suffers a check.

In order that any charitable institution may be durable, it is necessary that it should possess some property—at least the building which serves as the home or orphanage—and a little revenue; but in order that any institution, even though it has been licensed as an association—a hospital or home—may own property, there is required another special license, and since it is an affair of favors and influence with public officials it is very difficult to get what is called the "grant of public utility," (*reconnaissance d'utilité publique*); and even a work thus recognized cannot receive gifts or legacies except by special authority in every given case, and this sanction depends absolutely upon the arbitrary will of the men in power. Further, the license may be withdrawn at any time, and the government then seizes the property of the establishment and distributes it as it pleases—for example, to the institutions of public assistance. This right is not conferred by any written law. But there is no remedy in France against abuse of power by the government,* and its will is law.

Another concession has been made by the government, which it sometimes uses according to its fancy, that is, permission to citizens to practise charity themselves—a great advance upon the principles of the Revolution. But if they desire to entrust the charge to others to

---

*Thus the Council of State, in a recent decision upon the appeal of a citizen, held that tax-payers are obliged to pay a tax even when destined to cover an illegal expense, simply because the administration desires to collect it.

do it for them, they must give it over to the charge of the Department of Assistance, and to it alone. Citizens are permitted to choose at will managers for their own affairs, to buy, sell and trade in their stead. But in the matter of charity they can choose only the Department of Public Assistance, even if it inspire but little confidence. This, also, is not in any written law, but the will of the men in office is as strong as the law and even stronger. Consequently certain functionaries seize the funds of such or such a private institution, on the plea that this money was intended for charity and is not expended directly by the benefactors. The administrative tribunals often distribute to the Department of Public Assistance legacies left either to ministers of religion or to certain designated persons for charitable uses, declaring that benefactors are interdicted from making other distributions of their alms than to the Department of Public Assistance, and, moreover, that they are well aware of this. We see from this that the French in 1893 have far less liberty to practise charity than they had in 1789. The word *liberty* is inscribed upon all of our public buildings, but in the matter of alms it exists neither in law nor in practice.

We have still to speak of the taxes imposed upon religious associations, even those which are solely occupied in works of charity, which fall on the buildings reserved for the infirm and sick, the beds on which they lie, the food which they eat, and the furniture which they use. These taxes are of recent origin. Formerly charitable establishments paid the same taxes as individuals; but for about eight years they have paid in addition special taxes levied for the purpose of ruining the religious communities, but which fell chiefly upon the sick and poor. For it is first of all necessary to satisfy the public treasury, and then there remains less for the benefit of unfortunates. They are therefore obliged either to restrict the number of those whom they assist or to retrench in the care and attendance they give to them. But the party which is in power at the present time would rather see the wretched without aid than to see them aided by private charity, and above all by Catholic charity.*

---

*I take the liberty to refer those who may be surprised at this allegation to a work that I have recently published, where many facts are cited which I cannot quote here, and which has been crowned by the Academy of Moral and Political Sciences, which shows its value and accuracy of statement: *Charity before and since* 1789. (*La Charité avant et depuis*, 1789. Paris: Guillaumin, éditeur: 435 pp.)

But in spite of this, private charity, so fettered and so combatted, produces a multitude of institutions and gives relief to an immense number of unfortunates. Zealous persons who are engaged in the work speak encouragingly, even in spite of the obstacles and risks which they have often to encounter. Their property is in the name of the president or treasurer of the work in hand, but as individuals, not as officers of an incorporated charity, for otherwise the property would be confiscated as belonging to an institution not recognized by the law. There is established, in fact, a sort of tolerance which is never very certain, which sometimes gives rise to prosecutions and convictions, but which never arouses the zeal inspired by the love of God and of one's neighbors.

There has also been formed in Paris a *Central Office of Charitable Works (Office central des oeuvres charitables: 3, rue Champagny)* which has for its object the giving information to those who seek to further the existence of the numerous private institutions that are unknown to the public, because they have but a modest existence, and are not known outside of their own locality. The bureau points out to what institution one may go who wishes to aid such or such classes of unfortunates; and one may also learn from it upon what conditions the poor, the infirm, orphans, etc., whom one may wish to help, are received and aided. On the other hand the bureau endeavors to find out who are considered generous persons, in order to request their aid.

To the charitable institutions it is fitting to add briefly an account of the provident institutions, which in their way also practise charity. First of all there are the *mutual aid societies (sociétés de secours mutuel)*, of which there were on December 31, 1890, (the last official figures) 9,144, with 1,436,000 members and possessing 173,432,000 francs ($34,686,400). They give aid to their sick members, and sometimes have old-age pensions *(pensions de retraite)*. We may note in passing that only those that have honorary members, *i. e.*, members who pay assessments without the right to benefits, are self-supporting; the others always have a deficit, due to the smallness of their assessments, which are always relatively low. Then there is the *National Old-Age Pension Fund (Caisse nationale de retraites pour la vieillesse)*, a state institution which receives deposits, however small, and in exchange guarantees pensions, proportioned to the sums received and to the time during which they have remained on deposit. Finally, we should mention the numerous charitable institutions created by employers in behalf of their employees, as the Fund for Insurance against Sickness (*Caisse de secours contre la maladie*), Pension Funds (*Caisses de retraite*), etc., by which about a million people are benefited, for the most part heads of families; but an account of these would transcend the limits of the present memoir.

And yet these useful institutions are menaced by several bills at present pending before our Parliament: bills for compulsory old age pensions organized, as in Germany, by the State; bills to compel employers to establish a fund or funds for insurance against sickness, also as in Germany. If such laws should be passed, they would be the ruin of institutions coming from private initiative. There is also before our Legislature a bill, under the modest title of "An Act for the Organization of free medical relief" (*Loi sur l'organisation de la médicine gratuite*), obliging the communes to organize bureaus of relief, so that every commune shall have its own bureau directed by men appointed by the national administration, and having in their hands the resources coming from the tax levied for the benefit of these bureaus. They are to occupy themselves first of all in giving aid to the sick, but one may well imagine that their rôle would soon be extended, and that under the name of aid they would give political subsidies.

It may not be useless in closing to note the constantly growing tendency of our legislators and administration to put everything into the hands of the government, and to replace the ancient form of charity, done by the faithful with their money and for the safety of their souls, by a charity done by the administration with the money of taxpayers and for electoral purposes.

IV.

CHARITY IN BELGIUM.

What has been said of charity in France before 1789 is applicable also to Belgium, with slight differences in details. As has been justly remarked by a profound thinker and great historian, M. Alexis de Tocqueville, the social situation of the different Christian nations of Western Europe was, in the thirteenth and fourteenth centuries, more nearly identical than it is to-day. The same ardent religious faith had everywhere created similar institutions of charity, which were obviously organized on the same plan. Everywhere, too, since the sixteenth century the lay power has interfered in the management of charitable endowments, and gradually drawn to itself powers, which at first belonged to the church alone.

The Low Countries of Austria—the provinces that constitute the present kingdom of Belgium—having been conquered by the French armies in 1792, were from that time treated as a part of France; that is to say, the property devoted to charitable works was seized by the state, and charitable associations abolished. Confiscation and destruction produced the same effects as we have seen in the case of the government of the Directory, which returned to the charitable establishments at least a part of their property.

Belgium remained a part of France until 1819, and during that time it accustomed itself so well to our civil and administrative methods that it has retained up to the present time not only our code, but many of our governmental practices. Charity there, as in France, is practised both by individuals and by public authority. There is, therefore, both private charity and public assistance.

Private charity is freer in Belgium than in France : first, because there the right of association exists, being recognized and guaranteed by the constitution; second, because the Belgian government (the Catholic party being in power) is favorable to private almsgiving, even though it has a religious origin, while in France it is looked upon in a bad light, and often persecuted by the irreligious government which at present is in power. As a result the number of private charities is large in Belgium, in spite of the small extent of the country (about six million inhabitants against thirty-eight millions in France). Belgium glories, and with reason, in being the classical land of charity, and the religious faith which animates the great majority of her population sustains and animates her in a noble course. And yet, in one respect, private charity is no better treated in Belgium than in France. I refer to the right of charitable institutions to possess property. In this respect the administrative rules and practices of France are found also in Belgium, and we have seen that these rules and practices are hostile to the existence of charitable foundations. In Belgium, as in France, most institutions do not hold property in their own name; what they have is in the name of a president, a treasurer, an administrator, or, indeed, of a society which has apparently some other interest of its own; for only to these does the law allow the right to openly possess property. This situation is full of uncertainty and there is danger from legislation in both countries alike, which does not recognize in individuals the right to dispose of their own property by will, but assures to children and relatives in the ascendant line a compulsory division of the succession. It is this which hinders charitable establishments due to private liberality from having the stability, security, and development which they would otherwise have, and which they still have in some foreign countries ruled by a more liberal legislation.

As to public assistance we may say that it is first of all given in hospitals, using the term in its broadest sense (*établissements hospitaliers*), hospitals, homes or asylums, orphanages, etc., whose legal position is very analogous to that of institutions of the same character in France. There are also some bureaus of relief,* but since Belgium has been separated from France she has had some peculiar laws of her own, which have given to administrative charity a different turn from what it has received in France.

The old canonical rule, which Charlemagne, even at that early period, recommended to be observed, would have every parish feed its own poor—*quisque civitas pauperes suos alito*. But this was a rule which had only a moral sanction and which did not give to the poor a right to demand help. The inhabitants of the parish might furnish it to them, but there was only an obligation of conscience; no human power could constrain them. There was nevertheless, in the northern part of France a greater tendency to regard this as imparting a sort of obligation, and it was the same in the countries which to-day form Belgium. Temporal sovereigns have at different times tried to give assurance of the maintenance of the poor by their own parishes. This gave rise to a dim idea of obligation, which, however, was not found in France. And even in Belgium it produced no serious results except in consequence of a law passed in 1818, while Belgium was under the rule of Holland—a rule lasting from 1815 to 1831, when Belgium became an independent kingdom.

This law made easier the acquisition of a domicile for purposes of receiving aid (*domicile de secours*,) and, gave a commune, which had relieved an indigent person found in its territory, the right to demand reimbursement from the commune in which he resided. But the communes could easily give aid in this manner, at the same time that they were harsh and even "inhuman" (the word is found in a

---

*Their revenue, according to the figures of 1889, amounts to about 10,500,000 francs ($2,100,000.)

recent report made by the Belgian Senate) in regard to the poor
whose support would finally fall upon themselves. The result was that
claims were made upon rural communes—often without resources—for
sums alleged to have been given for providing aid without their assent
and without their knowledge. It was the ruin of some. Legally, it
is true, the aid might be given by the commune where the indigent
person was living (*commune de la résidence*) in case of great necessity. But in fact this right was not observed. Says the preamble of
the law of 1891, of which I shall speak:

"We shall soon see the communes giving assistance without limit to
the poor who do not belong to them, and using all sorts of quibbles and
having recourse to all sorts of frauds in order to avoid their own obligations and to baffle the execution of a law, whose injustice would seem
to excuse all resistance."

A law of 1849, which was designed to improve the situation, is vicious,
because it retains the bad principle of the former law, which permitted
one commune to have recourse to another and even made it easy to do
so.

Further, while certain able-bodied paupers were aided with excessive
promptness, other unfortunates more in need of aid, but unable to
solicit it themselves—the demented, the blind and deaf-mutes—were
reduced to such a point that a special law was necessary in order to
secure them aid. In 1878 Parliament voted to create a *Common Fund*
in every province, to be furnished by a deposit made by the communes
in proportion to their population. The distribution was to be made
on the basis of need, that is to say, in proportion to the number of
unfortunates to be aided.

This law, which seemed sufficiently just, soon gave rise to the liveliest
complaints on the part of the rural communes, who declared that they
were sacrificed to the large centers of population. "We pay," they
said, "and we receive nothing; the Common Fund all goes to the
cities, and above all to the large cities." Thus in 1888, by the official figures, the city of Liège had contributed to the Common Fund of
the province 89,000 francs ($17,800); it had received from the same
fund 194,000 francs ($38,800); Ghent had contributed 149,000 francs
($29,800) and had received 268,000 francs ($53,600); Brussels, the
capital of the kingdom, had contributed 160,000 francs ($32,000) and
had received 330,000 francs ($66,000). The municipalities of the large
cities could allege with truth that they had received the poor and infirm

from all parts of the country; but one might reply to them that they had also the largest resources and the most wealth, and that a contribution to the Common Fund in proportion to population is at once onerous and unjust.

It was to satisfy these complaints that three acts were passed, November 27, 1891, which, though distinct, together form a whole which re-organized the public relief of Belgium.

One of these acts relates to the repression of begging and vagrancy: it provides for three kinds of institutions; workhouses for convicted beggars and vagabonds, which are already established, houses of refuge (*maisons de refuge*) for the same class of individuals, though not convicted, who may be sent there either by the courts after arrest, or by the communal authorities directly—and in this case the commune defrays the cost of their maintenance; and finally, the charity schools (*écoles de bienfaisance*) for individuals (always beggars and vagabonds) under eighteen years of age. In all these institutions labor is to be compulsory; and a part of the earnings is given to the inmates in money, part in clothing and tools, when they are discharged.

The other two acts relate to medical relief and public charity in general. Relief of the sick (*l'assistance des malades*) is obligatory. "The communes must provide medical treatment for the sick who are found within their territory." On the contrary, relief of able-bodied paupers is not compulsory. "Public relief will be furnished to paupers by the commune in which they are found." It will be noticed how the terms of the law differ in these two cases; there is in the second case only a kind of exhortation or, as it is called, a "moral obligation."

The commune which furnishes relief has a legal claim upon the commune where the pauper resides only in cases of sick persons, children under sixteen years of age, or persons over seventy; and yet no claim exists if it is a case "of a laborer, an apprentice or a domestic admitted into the hospital in consequence of an accident while at work." The expenses of strangers are met by the government.

The Common Fund is maintained because of the service which it renders in procuring relief for a class of unfortunates who would otherwise have nothing. But the province and the central government furnish only half; the other half is paid by the communes, in proportion both to their population and their resources, calculated according to the tax returns.

These new laws, then, alleviate the burdens of the communes, but increase that of the central government. This, indeed, is a popular tendency, since nobody then seems to pay anything. Besides, these laws are too recent, having been in force but one year, for one to be able to say what their practical operation will be, or whether they will satisfy the hopes aroused, and will do the good expected of them.

As to provident institutions, Belgium possesses numerous mutual aid societies (*sociétés de secours mutuel*). In 1889 there were 299 "recognized" societies, having 39,000 members and a capital of 7,641,000 francs ($1,528,000), and more than 90 societies not recognized. In addition to these, employers, especially the large corporations, as for example the *Vielle Montagne*, have organized for their employees numerous institutions for giving aid, which cannot be detailed here.

CHARITABLE ORGANIZATIONS AND CHARITABLE WORK IN ITALY.

BY EGISTO ROSSI.

In Italy, as in other civilized countries, benevolent institutions are of very ancient origin.

Although the *lex frumentaria* of Cornelius Gracchus* and the *congiaria*† of Julius Caesar, cannot be reasonably considered benevolent institutions in the sense in which we now use the words, nevertheless in those periodical distributions of grain and bread, we find, as it were, the very beginnings of the present system of legal taxation for the benefit of the poor, or the maintenance, to a certain extent, of the indigent classes at the expense of the town or city.

Under Trajan, public charity assumed a character somewhat more modern with the foundation of the "*Instituti Alimentari*," destined to provide the necessary food for the poor children of Rome as well as of the provinces. The many foreign wars undertaken by him had deprived thousands of families of their head, and it seemed only right to the Emperor to provide for the children until the latter should be able to live by their own labor. According to Pliny the younger, in his celebrated panegyric‡ upon the Emperor Trajan, these institutions were established about the year 853 of the foundation of Rome, and 100 of the Christian era. Under the Republic, as well as under the Empire,

---

*This tribune, as is well known, with the desire for popularity, proposed that a *modius* (8.64 litres) of wheat should be distributed to the poor every month at public expense, which custom afterwards became a law. (V. Appianus, *De Bello Civile*.)

†*Congiarium* from *congius*, a measure containing about 200 ounces. The *congiarum* is different from the *donativum*, which was a gift to the soldiers, while the former was given only to the people.

‡We find in Ch. 26 of this Panegyric the following words of Pliny, speaking of the children led by their parents into the presence of the Prince on the day of the distribution of the *congiaria*: '*Tu ne rogari quidem sustinuisti et, quamquam laetissimum oculis tuis esset, conspectu Romanae subolis impleri, omnes tamen, antequam te viderent, adirentve, recipi incidi jussisti, ut jam inde ab infantia parentem publicum munere educationis experirentur, crescerent de tuo qui crescerent tibi,* ALIMENTISQUE TUIS *ad stipendia tua pervenirent. Haec prima parvulorum civium vox aures tuas imbuit, quibus tu daturus* ALIMENTA *hoc maximum praestitisti, ne rogarent.*" Etc.

ancient Rome's conception of brotherly love was simply a natural instinct or philosophical sentiment, and even oftener a political and social expedient.

On the contrary, under Christianity this sentiment became a religious precept and the basis of the new social and religious life. And it is only in passing from pagan to Christian civilization that the foundations of modern benevolence were laid. Charities or donations ceased by-and-by to emanate from the government, especially for political aims as before, but became a moral duty. The *"panem et circenses"* was supplanted by private and voluntary charity. Government aid had produced corruption, whereas spontaneous help, the Christian *agapae*, tended to create a strong brotherly feeling.

The primitive church, with its large income, increased still more by the donations of the Christian Emperors, was able not only to decree in the Council of Nice the erection of a hospital (*xenodochium*) in almost every city, but also opened and rapidly multiplied public asylums of all kinds; as foundling homes (*brephotrophium*), orphanages (*orphanotrophium*), asylums for the aged poor (*gerontocomium*), and for invalid workingmen (*paramonari*), etc.

Although many of these institutions underwent great transformations in the middle ages, and not a few of them have ceased to exist, nevertheless a large part of the spirit which animated them has been transformed into the more modern institutions; as our present hospitals of various kinds, religious confraternities with charitable objects, poorhouses, foundling asylums, etc., of which we have now a large number, all testify.

In Italy the large majority of benevolent institutions have been founded by private means and are still supported to a great extent by perpetual endowments.

We have not a legal tax for the aid of the poor, although many municipalities make a yearly appropriation for that object in the form of subsidies for the charitable organizations already existing, as will be seen later.

The law prohibits absolutely all begging; but as the number of poorhouses is not everywhere sufficient for the need, in many cities and towns mendicity unfortunately is still tolerated.

With the object of removing this plague of begging, and also with the view of bringing about a much needed reform in the numerous institutions of benevolence, of which we shall speak later, various schemes have been brought before Parliament at different times, and with the new law (*Legge sulle Opere Pie*) recently put into execution, a great advance has been made in the way of repressing this shameful practice.

The charitable institutions having a perpetual endowment are many. Their total patrimony is very large and they have a great variety of objects, hardly exceeded perhaps in any other country.

There are, for example, institutions which are called "*Opere pie elemosiniere*," and which distribute to the poor money, clothes, or eatables; others which give a dowry to girls about to be married; others which provide for the nursing and care of foundlings; others for instruction in colleges or parochial schools.

Besides these, we have many hospitals, infant asylums, educational institutions, houses of rest and refuge, reform schools, houses of protection for recently liberated criminals, endowments for prison visiting, poorhouses, blind, deaf and dumb, and lunatic asylums, workhouses, homes for poor widows, house visiting among the poor, maternity hospitals, seaside hospitals for scrofulous or rachitic children, the furnishing of wheat and grain (*Monti frumentari*) to poor peasants for sowing, confraternities for the transportation of the sick to the hospitals, and for the burial of the dead belonging to poor families.

These and other similar institutions, which the piety and charity of our ancestors founded for the benefit of the needy classes in Italy, have usually been directed and governed according to the stipulations of the wills of their founders, although the origin of many of them is really lost in the distant obscurity of time. Many of much more recent date have been added to them, and their number is constantly increasing.

Before the constitution of the United Kingdom, the public charities in Italy were subject to no law of a general character, but each of the States into which the country was divided regulated its institutions according to its own ideas, especially where its interference was not contrary to the statutes of the same.

The first Italian law with regard to public benevolence was that of 1862, which had two objects: to systematize and give unity to the various Italian laws upon the subject, and to free them from injurious political interference, leaving the control mainly in their own hands. Italy had just escaped from a state of bitter despotism, whose effects had been felt even in the administration of charities, making them serve political or religious ends, which accounts for the very liberal character of the law of 1862; although according to its provisions, the administration of each institution was obliged to keep an exact account of all its property and documents, and to make an annual financial request to the proper authorities. Many neglected this, and the experience of about twenty-five years has demonstrated that the almost absolute autonomy then existing was not without its inconveniences, and that it might be necessary to strengthen the means of control and supervision.

The first investigating committee was appointed by Sig. Nicutera, at that time Minister of the Interior, but a change in the Ministry prevented their propositions from becoming law.

In the Congress held in Naples (1879), and in Milan (1880), this much needed reform was again discussed, resulting in the appointment by the Government in 1880 of a Royal Commission, who were to investigate minutely and prepare a report upon the conditions of the benevolent institutions throughout the Kingdom.

The commission, composed of persons most of whom belonged to the two houses of Parliament, went seriously and earnestly to work, receiving most valuable aid from the minute and carefully prepared statistics furnished them by Commendatore Luigi Bodio, the well known Director of the Bureau of Statistics in Rome, who had spared no pains to collect all information bearing upon the subject.*

After long and careful studies, occcupying a period of about nine years, the reforms proposed by the above commission assumed definite form in the new bill presented to Parliament in February, 1889, by Sig. Crispi,† at that time Premier, and an ardent supporter of the new reform. This bill, after long debate, was approved in July of the year 1890.

Before speaking in detail of this new law it seems desirable to give some statistics with regard to all such institutions, collected by the Statistical Bureau for the use of the commission, and also some of still later date.

In 1880 there were in Italy 21,769 institutions of charity. These were distributed among the different provinces, as indicated in the following table :

---

*These statistics are contained in ten large volumes, and constitute a most valuable monograph which reflects great credit upon our Statistical Bureau.

† Besides Sig. Crispi, among those who took an active and important part in the discussion of this bill, Senator P. Villari, whose writings upon this subject are well known, Senator G. Costa and Hon. O. Luchini, who were chairmen of their respective committees in the Senate and Chamber, are worthy of mention.

CLASSIFICATION OF CHARITIES ACCORDING TO THE PRINCIPAL

Enumeration.	KINDS OF CHARITIES.	Piedmont.	Lombardy.	Liguria.	Venetian Provinces.
	A. WITHOUT BOARD AND LODGING.				
1	Institutions for distributing alms	1,282	1,577	165	565
2	For instruction or educational purposes	151	124	26	55
3	For dowries to women about to be married	170	639	43	211
4	For subsidies for poor widows	......	24	......	5
5	For the nursing of infants	2	15	1	......
6	For orphans and deserted children	......	4	......	......
7	For helping the sick poor in their homes	148	784	39	224
8	For nursing mothers	4	76	......	1
9	For the aid of prisoners	3	......	1	......
10	For the help of criminals recently released	2	1	......	......
11	For the transportation of the sick poor to and from hospitals	......	......	......	......
12	For the burial of the dead	......	......	......	......
13	For the saying of masses for the dead and other religious objects combined with some charitable purpose.	71	172	24	37
14	For exclusively religious purposes	7	11	......	9
	Total number of institutions not offering shelter or refuge	1,840	3,427	299	1,107
	B. WITH BOARD AND LODGING.				
1	Hospitals, exclusive of chronic cases	170	149	58	73
2	Seaside hospitals for sick children	3	4	......	2
3	Institutions for the benefit of the rachitic	1	1	......	......
4	Lying-in hospitals	2	......	......	1
5	Foundling asylums	11	11	6	11
6	Asylums for nursing infants	3	4	1	1
7	Day nurseries or kindergartens (although not corresponding exactly to either)	284	126	53	23
8	Orphan asylums and boarding schools	91	79	18	43
9	Reform schools	3	6	......	3
10	Houses of industry	2	8	......	2
11	Homes for widows	4	1	......	2
12	Houses of refuge, poorhouses, hospitals for chronic cases	31	55	10	46
13	Insane asylums	2	3	1	2
14	Deaf and dumb asylums	1	6	4	......
15	Blind asylums	1	2	1	1
16	Other institutions combining several objects included above	13	72	5	33
	Total number, which offer refuge or shelter	622	527	157	243
	GENERAL TOTAL	2,462	3,954	456	1,350

OBJECT OF EACH, AT THE END OF THE YEAR 1880.

Emilia.	Marches.	Tuscany.	Umbria.	Rome.	Campania.	Other Neapolitan Provinces.	Sicily.	Sardinia.	Kingdom.
538	133	94	53	69	289	804	202	50	5,821
102	74	86	26	37	20	49	54	9	813
249	160	138	111	280	162	184	634	47	3,028
11	4	3	......	......	......	......	......	......	47
......	......	......	......	......	......	9	......	......	27
3	1	......	......	2	......	8	1	......	19
192	54	54	42	59	139	404	34	8	2,181
......	......	2	......	......	......	1	......	......	84
2	1	1	......	1	......	......	15	1	25
......	......	......	......	......	......	......	......	1	4
1	......	1	......	......	......	......	......	......	2
1	......	1	......	......	......	......	1	......	3
71	47	88	45	45	1,432	1,269	465	4	3,770
9	8	4	5	6	600	733	970	1	2,363
1,179	482	472	282	499	2,642	3,461	2,376	121	18,187
92	117	67	47	109	62	135	122	8	1,209
1	1	1	......	1	......	......	......	......	13
......	......	......	......	......	......	......	......	......	2
1	......	......	......	1	......	......	2	......	7
7	13	13	6	1	......	3	2	1	85
......	......	......	......	......	......	......	......	......	9
46	37	17	17	18	50	94	11	11	787
95	61	27	42	50	136	76	171	5	894
......	1	......	......	......	1	......	......	......	14
......	......	......	......	......	......	......	......	......	12
......	......	......	......	1	......	......	......	......	8
34	36	13	8	7	8	30	19	4	301
1	......	2	......	1	1	......	1	......	14
4	......	1	......	......	......	1	......	......	17
1	......	1	......	2	1	......	......	......	10
7	3	14	1	3	15	27	7	......	200
289	269	156	121	194	274	366	335	29	3,582
1,468	751	628	403	693	2,916	3,827	2,711	150	21,769

The entire patrimony possessed by all these charitable organizations amounted in the year 1880, to 1,890,617,124 francs; with an income from the same and from other sources, often including appropriations

GROSS CAPITAL, GROSS INCOME FROM THE SAME, AND GROSS INCOME FROM OTHER SOURCES.—EXPENSES INCURRED FOR CHARITABLE OBJECTS ACCORDING TO THE STATISTICS OF 1880.

	KINDS OF CHARITIES.	Number of Charities.	Gross Available Capital.	KINGDOM. INCOME. Gross Income from Capital.	Gross Income from Capital and from other sources.	Expenses Incurred for Charitable Objects.
			Francs.	Francs.	Francs.	Francs.
	A. WITHOUT BOARD AND LODGING.					
1	Institutions for distributing alms	5,821	267,343,116	13,087,381	14,880,137	7,668,454
2	For instruction or educational purposes	813	70,043,787	3,423,973	3,787,919	1,818,970
3	For dowries to women about to be married	3,028	61,989,092	2,874,026	3,015,055	1,477,714
4	For subsidies for poor widows	47	1,156,197	57,864	58,756	26,341
5	For the nursing of infants	27	1,235,591	60,064	108,191	80,907
6	For orphans and deserted children	19	1,074,662	60,098	95,950	63,129
7	For helping the sick poor in their homes	2,181	71,433,969	3,469,968	3,899,620	2,256,339
8	For nursing mothers	84	743,205	35,960	43,152	33,283
9	For the aid of prisoners	25	482,456	22,406	24,936	10,254
10	For the help of criminals recently released	4	376,482	17,651	22,630	11,678
11	For the transportation of the sick poor to and from hospitals	2	6,321	211	815	669
12	For the burial of the dead	3	92,001	4,522	8,401	4,823
13	For the saying of masses for the dead and other religious objects combined with some charitable purpose	3,770	105,218,896	5,319,280	6,782,591	3,708,025
14	For exclusively religious purposes	2,363	27,900,392	1,376,123	1,572,630	776,027
	Total number of Institutions not offering shelter or refuge	18,187	609,096,227	29,816,067	34,301,389	17,936,613

by the towns or provinces, of 135,133,850 francs; as indicated in the following table:

B. WITH BOARD AND LODGING.

1	Hospitals, exclusive of chronic cases	1,209	600,725,640	28,217,106	41,979,131	28,044,378
2	Seaside hospitals for sick children	13	1,168,269	39,969	326,171	236,118
3	Institutions for the benefit of the rachitic	2	211,236	5,771	33,280	26,309
4	Lying-in hospitals	7	3,985,399	185,208	230,658	141,677
5	Foundling asylums	85	47,075,044	2,027,642	7,777,268	6,720,982
6	Asylums for nursing infants	9	507,104	22,337	114,169	80,586
7	Day nurseries or kindergartens (although not corresponding exactly to either)	787	33,080,927	1,486,065	4,002,460	3,171,856
8	Orphan asylums and boarding schools	894	314,372,477	15,167,703	20,442,356	13,630,069
9	Reform schools	14	5,111,116	206,840	734,382	625,994
10	Houses of industry	12	3,949,030	167,951	283,617	197,773
11	Homes for widows	8	851,747	42,210	102,917	92,748
12	Houses of refuge, poorhouses, hospitals for chronic cases	301	134,341,573	6,349,959	10,735,236	7,780,782
13	Insane asylums	14	19,151,595	593,850	5,959,154	5,014,545
14	Deaf and dumb asylums	17	6,991,495	339,520	651,216	497,866
15	Blind asylums	10	3,897,652	168,081	377,214	291,364
16	Other institutions combining several objects included above	200	109,160,593	5,212,934	7,086,232	3,934,415
	Total number, which offer refuge or shelter	3,582	1,281,520,897	60,233,146	100,832,161	70,487,573
	GENERAL TOTAL	21,769	1,890,617,124	90,049,213	135,133,850	88,424,186

The patrimony of all benevolent institutions has considerably increased throughout the country from 1861 to 1880, as will be seen from the following table, which gives the precise amount of this patrimony in each region of the kingdom, at those dates.

GROSS PATRIMONY AND GROSS INCOME AT THE END OF THE YEARS 1861 AND 1880.

REGIONS.	Gross Patrimony or Capital. 1861. Francs.	Gross Patrimony or Capital. 1880. Francs.	Gross Income. 1861. Francs.	Gross Income. 1880. Francs.	Percentage of Increase from 1861 to 1880. Of the Capital.	Percentage of Increase from 1861 to 1880. Of the Gross Income.
Piedmont	149,730,412	272,240,552	11,692,725	19,405,016	81.82	65.96
Liguria	51,234,827	86,191,398	3,433,947	6,386,116	68.23	85.97
Lombardy	276,743,001	424,956,075	17,812,068	26,768,210	53.56	50.28
Venetian Provinces	*69,687,329	134,951,068	*7,994,686	12,081,311	92.36	51.12
Emilia	109,098,394	208,972,981	8,829,133	15,136,373	91.55	71.44
Tuscany	109,680,884	126,813,364	6,518,683	10,534,639	15.62	61.61
Marches	26,953,270	55,233,530	2,181,281	4,013,435	104.92	83.99
Umbria	22,340,969	34,241,499	1,510,524	2,441,498	53.27	61.63
Rome and Province		124,642,179		8,701,670		
Campania	137,904,711	190,904,303	9,698,234	13,760,480	38.43	41.89
Other Neapolitan Provinces	55,056,376	87,626,388	3,559,770	6,503,940	59.15	82.70
Sicily	89,976,807	136,193,457	5,658,964	8,768,522	51.37	54.95
Sardinia	3,886,406	8,550,330	285,455	632,640	120.01	121.63
Kingdom	1,102,293,392	1,890,617,124	79,175,470	135,133,850	†60.20	†59.68

*The figures for the Venetian Provinces refer to 1867.
†This proportion is calculated exclusive of the Roman Province.

This patrimony in 1880 was composed of real estate and buildings to the value of 888,794,891 francs; and of government bonds and notes of credit, amounting to 1,001,825,233 francs.

The real estate and buildings in 1880 represented an average throughout the kingdom of 50.32 per cent. of the whole patrimony; ranging from a maximum of 71.86 per cent. in the Marches to a minimum of 15.60 per cent. in Tuscany.

In 1861 the proportion of real estate was 50.91 per cent. of the whole, as shown by the following table:

Regions.	Value of Real Estate and Buildings. 1861 Francs.	Value of Real Estate and Buildings. 1880 Francs.	Percentage of Gross Capital in Real Estate and Buildings. 1861	Percentage of Gross Capital in Real Estate and Buildings. 1880	Population 1881
Piedmont	86,125,582	115,754,096	57.52	42.32	3,070,250
Liguria	14,804,207	31,289,677	28.89	36.39	892,373
Lombardy	172,118,266	241,548,714	62.19	50.84	3,680,615
Venetian Provinces	*26,522,858	58,107,783	38.06	43.35	2,814,173
Emilia	65,315,463	131,881,132	59.87	63.11	2,183,391
Tuscany	24,652,483	19,777,594	22.48	15.60	2,208,869
Marches	18,540,207	39,357,850	68.79	71.26	939,279
Umbria	16,296,915	21,300,606	72.95	62.21	572,060
Rome and Provinces	......	63,119,460	......	50.64	903,472
Campania	77,048,790	96,215,891	55.87	50.40	2,896,577
Other Neapolitan Provinces	34,090,703	41,145,204	61.92	46.85	4,688,666
Sicily	24,037,497	26,329,975	26.72	19.33	2,927,901
Sardinia	1,621,691	2,963,912	41.73	34.06	682,002
Kingdom	†561,174,662	888,791,894	†50.91	‡50.32	28,459,628

* For the Venetian Provinces the above figures refer to 1867.
† Not including the Province of Rome.
‡ This proportion is calculated exclusive of the Roman Province.

The amount of capital invested in government bonds (placing them at their nominal value), increased from 132,798,521 francs in 1861, to 454,929,798 francs in 1880; the latter including, however, the province of Rome, whose charitable organizations in the latter year held bonds to the amount of 27,920,261 francs.

The increase of this kind of investment between 1861 and 1880 has been 322 millions of francs. The largest increase took place in Lombardy, Sardinia, Piedmont and Emilia.

AMOUNT OF CAPITAL INVESTED IN GOVERNMENT BONDS.

Regions.	1861. Francs.	1880. Francs.
Piedmont	25,014,910	108,466,201
Lombardy	17,094,389	79,902,420
Venetian Provinces	12,883,920	31,258,201
Liguria	9,370,474	27,743,949
Emilia	5,228,431	21,050,935
Marches	932,806	3,284,718
Tuscany	15,775,946	44,211,915
Umbria	922,245	2,682,633
Rome and Provinces	......	27,920,261
Campania	22,556,855	44,674,927
Other Neapolitan Provinces	5,656,555	17,733,295
Sicily	16,928,077	44,128,513
Sardinia	413,913	1,871,830
Kingdom	132,778,521	454,929,798

One of the things most criticized by the commission, and one for which a new law seemed especially necessary, was with regard to the excessive expense of administration, the heavy taxation, and other burdens.

The total amount of these, in some cases, represented a conspicuous part of the income. In 1880 these three items alone amounted to 38,985,393 francs (43.29 per cent. of the total), which, deducted from the whole income (135,133,850), leaves 96,148,455 francs, to be disposed of for charities.

Of this sum, only 84,516,283 francs are available for actual charitable purposes; 3,907,903 francs being for religious purposes in connection with the institutions of benevolence, and 6,296,425 for exclusively religious objects (*spese di culto*), the latter representing 7.45 per cent. of the entire sum expended for charities. This proportion varies greatly in the different provinces. Out of every 100 francs expended for benevolence in Piedmont, 2.93 per cent. is for religious objects solely; in Lombardy, 4.42 per cent.; in Tuscany, 5.19 per cent.; in Rome and provinces, 6.26 per cent. The greatest proportion is in Southern Italy, being 36.16 per cent. in Campania, and 18.01 per cent. in Sicily.

With regard to the institutions for the distribution of alms, we are in position to give with accuracy the number of persons benefited by them, which in 1887 amounted to 769,809 for the entire kingdom, out of a population estimated December 31st, 1886, at 29,942,142 inhabitants.

The amount distributed by the same institutions for charitable purposes in the same year reached the sum of 10,995,425 francs. The greater part of this amount was furnished by the larger cities and towns, as would be naturally supposed. The number of persons aided by them averages 26 for every 1,000 inhabitants throughout the kingdom. If we make comparison with other countries of Europe, we find in Germany,[*] in 1885, an average of 34 individuals for every 1,000 inhabitants, who received aid in the same way.

In France,[†] in 1886, the *bureaux de bienfaisance* gave help to 1,440,746 persons, in a total population (according to the census of 1886,) of 38,218,903 inhabitants, which would make an average of 38 for every 1,000.

In England and Wales, this proportion is represented by 22 for every 1,000 in the year 1886, 594,522 poor people having received aid, out of a population of 27,499,044 inhabitants. These comparisons, however, have only a limited value, as it is impossible to know in all cases whether there were duplications in the persons aided by the same institution, or by others, during the same year.

If then we make a comparison with regard to the average amount distributed per individual, we have in Italy an average of 15 francs for every person aided. In France this same average, in 1886, was about 20 francs, the *bureaux de bienfaisance* having distributed the sum of 30,375,219 francs among 1,440,744 persons. This comparison we cannot extend to Germany and England, because in the institutions of

---

[*] V. *Statistische Jahrbuch für das Deutsche Reich für* 1888.

[†] V. *Annuaire Statistique*, 1886.

these countries, the amounts distributed by this kind of institutions are not given separately, but are included in the general sum of charities dispensed by various benevolent institutions.

As we have indicated above, the towns and provinces, by making a yearly appropriation, contribute more or less to the support of the hospitals, insane asylums, orphanages, and other benevolent institutions of which we have already spoken. These appropriations by the towns and provinces, for the year 1889, amounted to 20,273,500 francs for the latter, and to 42,683,917 for the former, making a total of 62,957,414 francs.*

EXPENDITURES FOR CHARITIES BY THE PROVINCES AND TOWNS DURING THE YEAR 1889.

Regions.	Expenditures by the Provinces. Francs.	Expenditures by the Towns. Francs.	Total. Francs.
Piedmont	2,294,226	2,472,662	4,766,888
Liguria	877,710	1,276,863	2,154,573
Lombardy	3,190,696	6,626,627	9,817,323
Venetian Provinces	2,241,851	5,969,444	8,211,295
Emilia	2,122,339	4,165,424	6,287,763
Tuscany	1,752,111	4,669,275	6,421,386
Marches	682,680	1,993,109	2,675,789
Perugia—Umbria	382,630	1,208,556	1,591,186
Rome and Provinces	845,018	3,609,055	4,454,073
Campania	1,605,924	2,582,714	4,188,638
Other Neapolitan Provinces	2,345,162	4,313,858	6,659,020
Sicily	1,846,103	3,159,622	5,005,725
Sardinia	87,050	636,708	723,758
Kingdom	20,273,500	42,683,917	62,957,417

About half of the above total amount is for the maintenance of the sick, insane, and foundlings, as will be seen by the following statistics:

* In the year 1891 the provinces alone contributed 20,724,960 francs.

APPROPRIATIONS BY THE TOWNS IN 1889.

Francs.
For salaries for physicians, surgeons and midwives 12,851,542
For general sanitary service... 7,755,984
For the maintenance of foundlings.............................. 4,834,178
For contributions to hospitals..................................... 4,758,164
To homes for the poor and infirm................................ 2,768,127
Subsidies to the poor in general.................................. 3,071,471

APPROPRIATIONS BY THE PROVINCES IN 1889.

Francs.
For the maintenance of insane poor........................... 10,730,766
For the maintenance of foundlings............................. 6,592,093
For contributions to the poorhouses, to colleges, hospitals, deaf and dumb asylums, and other benevolent institutions 2,076,435

These appropriations are for the greater part* included in the gross income of all the charitable institutions, as already given, and do not constitute an addition to the amount of that income, as above referred to.

Of late years the number of legacies and of new institutions for charitable purposes has considerably increased, as will be seen by the following statistics, published by the Bureau of Statistics in Rome.

From 1881 to 1891, inclusive, the new foundations and legacies amounted to 11,715 with a total patrimony or capital of 186,751,696 francs, of which 84,543,103 is represented by real estate and buildings, and 102,206,593 by other property.

The average increase in the eleven years, 1881-1891, of the patrimony has been about 17 millions per year.

The new institutions founded during this period were 940, representing altogether a capital of 75,184,934 francs, the remaining amount being represented by legacies or donations to institutions already existing.

The largest sums were given in Lombardy (42 millions), Piedmont (42 millions) and Liguria (36 millions).

Next come the Emilian provinces with about 12 millions, the Venetian provinces with 10 millions, and Campania with about 9 millions, etc., etc.

*The salaries of district physicians would not, for example, be included.

With regard to the kinds of institutions, the hospitals received the largest amount of donations (62,030,545 francs) and next came the poorhouses with new donations amounting to 21,078,972 francs; day nurseries and kindergartens with 19,709,167 francs; orphanages and colleges with 18,233,507, institutions for distributing alms with 27,782,194 francs.

Having examined the various institutions of the kingdom somewhat in detail, with their respective patrimonies, let us now consider the new law of 1890 in its relation to them.

The institutions of charity coming under this new law, are best defined by quoting from the law itself.

Art. I. All institutions which render assistance to the poor, both in the state of health and sickness.

II. Those which provide for their education, or instruction in some profession, art or trade, or which tend to better their moral or economical condition.

III. Savings banks and co-operative institutions.

One of the most important changes introduced by the new law was with reference to the so-called "*Congregations of Charity*" (*Congregazione di Carità.*) These existed under the old law and were to be found in every city or town, being a sort of associated charities under which were included all small local charities derived from bequests, which had been left to the care of the town instead of to separate executors or trustees. Besides these, there was still a large number of charitable organizations, which were managed independently, resulting in much unnecessary expense, a large part of their incomes being consumed in their administration. On the contrary, under the new law, all such institutions, whose income did not exceed 5,000 francs each per annum, became included in the Congregation of Charity. By thus simplifying the administration, the expenses are greatly reduced, leaving a much larger available income for the purpose for which it was destined. Not only these, but other institutions of charity were included, the terms of whose bequests could no longer be fulfilled owing to the changed conditions of society; for instance, those for the liberation of captives taken by pirates in the middle ages; those established for shelter of pilgrims coming to Rome, rendered now quite unnecessary by hotels and other places of accommodation. Funds left for the outfit of poor nuns on entering a convent also found a place here, *i. e.* before 1870, after which date convents and other religious organizations underwent a complete change; also money left to minister to those condemned to death, capital punishment being now abolished.

The administrators of these associated charities* are appointed by the city council, one-fourth of them being changed every year, and are responsible to it; thus many of the abuses which existed under the old *régime*, when they were controlled largely by priests, especially in the small towns, are avoided.

Under the new law, all institutions of chartiy, whether included in the *Congregazione di Carita*, or not, are obliged to keep an exact account or inventory of everything pertaining to them, and render a financial report each year to the proper governmental authorities. The trustees or administrators who neglect to fulfil this duty cannot be re-elected for a second term, and no one can be appointed as director or superintendent of an institution of benevolence, whose position or office is incompatible with its best interests.

Under the new law an opportunity is also given for observation and criticism by the general public, the government authorities offering to try any case at their own expense on the deposit of security by the plaintiff.

Upon the Minister of the Interior devolves the general oversight of the work as to the general condition of each institution, and as to whether it is conducted in accordance with its own statutes and regulations, and in accordance with the law.

For one to receive the benefits of charitable work, he must have lived more than five years in the town where he is asking help, or have been born in the town, without regard to legitimacy of birth.

The above are the main points of interest in the new law regulating charities, which was heartily welcomed by all serious minded people, as abuses had become very great under the former system. Thousands of institutions of very small income allowed themselves a very large number of managers, with high salaries and a right to pension their widows and children; while many hospitals, worth millions, employed the larger part of their income in the same extravagant and expensive administration, instead of for the needy sick or poor.

We can easily see how, by all this mismanagement, begging and indiscriminate almsgiving were increased and encouraged, especially as no effort was made to educate the poor to a sense of self-dependence.

---

* Women too may be elected to this office.

If the ancient benevolence of the middle ages was the giving of alms, modern charity is work and education. The latter, however, is no less prompted by the heart, but rather the heart is guided by a greater intelligence and deeper appreciation of the needs of the poor man, who should not be encouraged in idleness and improvidence, thus rendering him an object of envy to the man who works; but true charity should be preventive and should help him to help himself.

The new law of public charities is imbued with this spirit and we may sanguinely expect great and lasting results from its execution, results which will be felt more and more as the years go by, and will help to raise the poor and degraded classes into a state of greater self-dependence and usefulness.

Vide: "Atti della Commissione d'Inchiesta delle Opere Pie." *Roma*, 1889-90. Tipografia Nazionale. (9 Volumes.)

"Statistica delle Opere Pie of 31 Dicembre, 1880, e dei lasciti di beneficenza fatti negli Anni 1881-91." *Roma*. Tipografia Nazionale (10 Volumes.)

"La Beneficenza Romana dagli antichi tempi fino ad oggi." Studio storico critico dell'Avvocato Quirino Querini. *Roma*, 1892. Tipografia Tiberina. (1 Volume.)

Rivista di Beneficenza, edita in Roma e diretta dal Comre. G. Scotti.

"La Riforma della Beneficenza," an article by P. Villari, published in the *Nuova Antologia* of May, 1890.

THE INTERNATIONAL TREATMENT OF CHARITY QUESTIONS.

BY BARON VON REITZENSTEIN, FREIBURG, GERMANY.

[AN ABSTRACT OF THE PAPER SUBMITTED TO THE FIRST SECTION OF THE CONGRESS.]

The growth of internationalism as a theory and an ideal force in the treatment of charity problems is first contrasted with the limitations of nationalism, as shown in legislation having in view the circumstances of a single country, in the narrowing sphere of questions to be discussed, in the larger number of men of practice chosen into the commissions as opposed to men of theory, and finally in the waiting attitude assumed by the Paris Congress of 1889 towards the question of the systematic organization of charities on an international basis. The International Congress of Charities now to assemble in Chicago will find this open question awaiting its consideration. A solution can be reached only through a study of the systems prevailing in single countries together with their conditions and limitations. The further question, whether such existing systems may be transplanted to other countries, or universally applied, forms a second stage of the general inquiry.

The French, Italian, English, American and German systems are then compared. The test to each system is applied in the question: What has been done to counteract and overcome the defects and limitations of national and local administration of public charities? Very high praise is awarded to the English-American charity organization societies as a corrective from the point of view of charities privately organized, but the German (Elberfeld) system is given the highest place among existing methods, as a successful development along the line of public (State) charities, but also as placing the administration of charity where it properly belongs, in the hands of the township, while making the freest use of the unpaid services of responsible private citizens. The charity organization societies represent a healthy reaction among private circles, and have shown that they are able to organize and centralize already existing private efforts, and to extend and individualize the benefits of charity; but they by no means supply the place of the Elberfeld system, nor does their existence preclude the possibility that the Elberfeld system may be found available for other countries than Germany, Austria and German Switzerland. In the first place, a public administration of charities (*i. e.* one controlled by State and local authority) offers a better guarantee of stability than the fluctuating views of private associations; but it is particularly in the open country, away from the large cities, that the greater organic usefulness of the Elberfeld system is seen, fixed as it is upon the basis of local administration and with responsible citizens called in as aids.

America is peculiarly fortunate in possessing the township system, and were it not for the fear of political corruption a system similar to the German could be applied. The author recommends the point of view of Professor Peabody, in approaching this part of the question.

The educating influence of the charity organization societies upon the circles of society engaged in the work is rated very high. Here the powers are to be schooled which may afterwards be used in the administration of public charities, and the charity organization societies may from this point of view be regarded as a movement of transition towards a system similar to the German.

The author, in closing, admits Germany's urgent need of a systematic organization of private charities, as supplementing the system of state charities, and recommends to his countrymen the study of the charity organization movement in England and America.

THE ELBERFELD SYSTEM OF POOR RELIEF.

BY DR. THEODORE MÜNSTERBERG, OF HAMBURG.

[TRANSLATION.]

I.

In Germany, except in Alsace and Lorraine, the care of the poor is recognized as a duty devolving upon the public authorities. This was felt to be a public duty in the various German states even before the foundation of the Empire. At that time, however, each state was entirely independent of the others in the matter of charities; so that the same kind of poor relief was not given to persons coming from another state as to the inhabitants of the state itself. When the German Empire was founded, the principle was laid down that the inhabitants of all the states which belonged to the Empire, were citizens of the Empire and were entitled to the same privileges in all the different states. The origin of this relation was the recognition at that time of the general right of free domicile for all citizens of the German Empire, and it is of the greatest economic importance. Its effect upon the poor laws was also considerable, inasmuch as it not only permitted a man to change his residence and practise his trade in his new home, but it compelled the state in which he had settled to undertake his support should he in any way become a pauper.

This duty of taking care of the poor (*Armenpflege*) was not, however, imposed directly upon the states or the state officials. It was committed in the course of its historical development entirely to the civil communes (*Gemeinden*). The old principle, that each commune must take care of its own poor, was extended, so that help must be given to any German who has lived for two consecutive years within the limits of a commune. But in order that communes, with which indigent persons have not established close relations by a residence of over two years, may not be unjustly burdened, the State, or a large district determined by it, assumes the care of those who have not been residents of any commune for a period of at least two years.

A pauper has no legal claim corresponding to the duty of relief, a duty which, indeed, is imposed by the arbitrary action of the individual citizen himself in his voluntary choice of residence. Only state officials, appointed to supervise the affairs of the communes, are authorized to use forcible measures to hold a commune to the performance of this duty. A cardinal principle of the German poor laws is that no citizen of the German Empire, who is in distress, no matter to what state or commune he may belong, shall remain without such help as may be necessary to maintain him. For this reason it is provided that the commune in which a pauper is residing must in case of need at once furnish temporary relief, without regard to the question whether the responsibility rests on it alone.

The principle of law in regard to the duty of the commune with reference to the care of the poor, which rests on the fact of residence, is purely a financial one. Its object is to equalize and distribute accruing expenses as much as possible among the different communes. The extent and nature of the relief is, however, entirely independent of any financial question, and must be bestowed impartially upon every person in every part of every commune.

Nevertheless this principle is rather an ideal general principle of law, than one which can be universally put into practice. For the law rests on an assumption which is not in fact true, namely, that the communes of the German Empire are in all respects alike. But in reality they are alike only in their political position and by no means so in their extent and resources. The realization of the principle of giving the same sort of relief to the poor everywhere is essentially dependent upon the extent and resources of the communes. It is quite evident that a little village with two or three hundred inhabitants must have a system of poor relief entirely different from those of great cities like Berlin and Hamburg. So poor relief must be very different in purely agricultural regions from what it is in municipal communes, and a poor commune must maintain a different system from that of a rich one.

It is important to make these brief remarks in the beginning, because only with them in mind is it possible to understand how efforts in the sphere of poor relief, not only in Germany, but throughout the world, have been guided not so much by prescribed laws as by the force of circumstances.

So that, without regard to the law, there is a much greater resemblance between the efforts in New York and Berlin for the solution of the pauper question than between those of a small German village and those of Berlin. For, with or without law, no great city can suffer a part of its population to remain in a state of pauperism; and, with or without law, it will look for the same kinds of remedies to meet the existing distress. Of course national customs and political events alter the situation; yet the tendency remains essentially the same.

The chief characteristic of this tendency is the effort which is made to relieve the helpless person in such a manner that his bodily need— lack of food, clothing, shelter, etc.—may be supplied. In order to insure such relief, it is necessary first of all to have societies which will consider the necessities of different cases as they arise, and will select the most appropriate methods for relieving distress. The larger the community, the greater is the need for such societies; the greater the number of societies, the greater is the difficulty experienced in the methodical and practical direction of their efforts. This is illustrated by the contrast between a large city and a rural community. In the latter every one knows every one else, and knows exactly to what extent they need relief. But it frequently happens in small communities that the means are lacking for the relief of distress. There may be, for example, a lack of proper hospitals, practised surgeons, etc. In a large city, on the other hand, one citizen knows practically nothing in regard to the affairs of others, while the means for alleviating suffering are numerous. A bad system of charities often exists in a small community, therefore, because of the lack of suitable appliances; in a large city, because of a lack of organization which prevents a proper use of existing resources. So it is comparatively easy to help a small community, because it is only a matter of money. But in a great city, one dare not be too hopeful, because there the chief question is "Organization."

II.

Organization! This is the magic word which alone can solve the difficult problems of poor relief. Without proper organization every charitable movement must remain incomplete and unsatisfactory, and will be often hurtful rather than helpful. For the financial, moral and economic results of poor relief do not depend solely upon the laying down of certain universal principles, but quite as much upon the consideration and treatment of each individual case which may come to light. Not only is it a question of finding out the extent and nature of the needs of individual cases, but it is much more important that the manifold causes which bring about their unhealthy condition be studied and determined.

The variety of unfortunate and painful mental and bodily conditions through which a man must pass to reach the level of a pauper is simply without limit. And as every individual differs from every other in his manner of life, and in his capacity for making a living according to his moral, mental and physical endowments, so a man requires such treatment as will correspond exactly to his wants, and to the particular circumstances which give rise to his need. It is not sufficient to recognize this as applicable to any one particular case or occasion, or to bestow a single gift only. There must be a continuing acquaintance with and study of the cases, and a continuous prosecution of the work among the poor. For relief must neither stop arbitrarily nor be kept up through caprice or carelessness longer than is really necessary.

But to keep up study and oversight of this kind in a really effective way is possible only by securing a large body of persons who are willing and capable of doing this kind of work. In other words, there must always be two classes, those who receive and those who give; and the latter must be perfectly familiar with their work and with the conditions which surround the poorer classes, so that they may know how to direct their gifts in such a manner that they may do most good.

Such are the true functions of systematic poor relief. To regulate its activity, to establish co-operation of the right sort on correct principles, this is the task of organization.

The numerous systems which underlie charity organization in no way recognize this universal and fundamental requirement. For a demand for individualization is everywhere heard. It is found in the charities of the old Christian societies and in those of the medieval church, no less than in the schemes of the end of the last century, which were due to the rise of the spirit of enlightenment. Still we are met with the complaint now, as formerly, that poor relief is both inadequate and expensive that the claims of the poor are on the increase, and that in many cases deserving persons are not properly cared for. And when these complaints become too loud and the traces of mismanagement too evident, an attempt is always made to improve the condition of things.

It is not possible to consider the history of such attempts at this point. Only let it be borne in mind that everywhere this striking fact appears, that in small communities there is usually a lack of means, and occasionally also a lack of inclination to employ them; while in the larger communities, as a rule, the lack of system is what is chiefly to be deplored. Thus every attempt at improvement leads immediately back to the question of proper organization, of an organization which will correspond to the cardinal principle of good, healthy poor relief, namely, the principle of *individualization*.

To the German city of Elberfeld belongs the honor of bringing this principle again to life, and of having carried it out in a model manner. The Elberfeld system, which was established by an ordinance passed on the ninth of July, 1852, and has therefore been in use for forty years, has met with universal approval, and now stands as the type of a good and appropriate system of poor relief.

The following are its most essential principles:

(*a*) The whole city is so divided into precincts (*Quartiere*) that usually there are not more than four paupers within the limits of any precinct. When one precinct is overburdened, relief is obtained by distributing a number of paupers among those less heavily burdened. An overseer of the poor is appointed for each district. The overseer is the most important agent in the relief of the poor. He has to visit the poor in his district at least once in fourteen days, to acquaint himself with their circumstances, especially as to the existence of property or income from other sources, from labor, etc., to record the results of his investigations, and to act as an educator to the needy and the members of their families. He must be the friend and adviser of the poor, but must strictly require good behavior and order; and it is especially his duty to bring vicious and idle persons before the police courts.

(*b*) The precincts are united into districts (*Bezirke*), and each district is put under the direction of a district chairman (*Bezirksvorsteher*). The executive body of a district is the district board (*Bezirksversammlung*), which consists of the district chairman and all the active overseers of the district. One of the essential points of the system is, that all the overseers participate in the deliberations concerning what aid shall be given, and only such aid is given as is decided upon in joint consultation.

This is an important step in advance of the older systems. Formerly wherever the plan was adopted of having districts and overseers, the latter were merely reporters, while the final decision remained entirely with an executive board to which they reported. In the Elberfeld system they constitute the executive body; thus their interest in the cases which present themselves in the districts is considerably strengthened, and the feeling of personal responsibility heightened. They learn to appreciate more fully the varied nature of the work, because they are not limited to an acquaintance with their own cases, but also learn from every case in the district which is brought up for discussion. The meetings foster a spirit of neighborly harmony and give rise to varied personal relations among the members, who otherwise might remain unknown to one another. And the meetings are of direct benefit to the work itself, for frequently more than one of the overseers know the circumstances and reputation of a pensioner; and, at any rate, the general discussion of the various domestic and social relations which come up for consideration is more thorough than it otherwise would be. Evidently these regular gatherings enlarge and increase the sum total of knowledge on the subject of poor relief, which is obtained step by step from many different kinds of cases.

The district chairman presides over the meetings of the district boards, while the overseers bring before the meeting the different cases to be acted upon, about which they have collected information. Even when one of the overseers is compelled, in a case of extreme necessity, to grant temporary assistance without having obtained the consent of the district board, he is expected afterwards to bring the matter up for approval at a later meeting.

(*c*) The keystone of the system is the central administrative board (*Hauptverwaltung*). Its more important offices are filled by representatives of the municipal government. This body exercises a general oversight of the districts, and considers complaints and such cases as naturally come before such a body. It must study the conditions of the poorer classes and determine the most appropriate means for relieving them. It must see that the funds contributed for the relief of the poor are expended in the most advantageous manner, and, in short, it must do everything of a general or more important character that may be of service in the advancement of this branch of government.

The connecting link between this board and the overseers is the district chairman. He is responsible for the carrying out of the poor ordinances, and must see that all cases are treated on uniform principles. He also receives the communications, decisions and directions of the central board, and is expected to make them known to his overseers and his district board. On the other hand, he receives reports from the overseers and transmits them, as well as the decisions of the district board, to the central board.

It is evident that under the Elberfeld system the heavy burden is borne in the best way by many shoulders, and that a livelier and more active interest and co-operation are secured from a large number of citizens in the economic, as well as in the financial workings of poor relief. Besides, it is possible for the directors, because of the small size of the board, to survey the whole field and thereby insure uniformity in the administration of poor relief.

(*d*) The offices of overseer, district chairman and members of the central board are to be distinguished from the honorary offices (*Ehrenämter*) of the business department, which will be mentioned below under (*g*). The persons holding these latter positions are selected from the citizens and receive no remuneration for their services. This is not peculiar to the system, for the principle of honorary office exists in all forms of municipal administration, and in all other branches of government. Only the highest positions, in which undivided attention to the duties of the office is required, and which are to be held for a considerable length of time, are filled by paid officials. The law makes the acceptance of these honorary positions obligatory. As a rule however, no compulsion is necessary.

Still, these honorary positions are of peculiar importance in poor relief, because no other branch of government shows such bad results when left to paid officials only. For in the care of the poor there is one thing which cannot be secured by even the truest devotion to one's office, and which can never be obtained under a bureaucracy, namely, the fostering of neighborly relations between man and man, the practical exercise of what we express by the charming word "Charity." For poor relief relates not to one side only of civil and business life, but to human life as a whole, which only true charity can succeed in reaching. It has, therefore, been laid down as a settled principle that, in the administration of poor relief, the paid official should be kept in the background, and the chief responsibility should rest on the honorary officers.

(*e*) One of the cardinal principles of the Elberfeld system is that no grants can be made for an unlimited space of time. It is prescribed that relief may be given for only fourteen days at a time, and permission for its continuance can be obtained only from the district boards. So it is possible for a needy person, by means of successive renewals of grants, to remain a pensioner for a long time, possibly for life. Continuance of the relief is, however, never assured. Hence arises the necessity of continually making new examinations into the circumstances of the pensioners, in order to look after them properly, and to prevent their thinking that their support is guaranteed. From a practical and financial point of view this is very important, since by a change in a person's circumstances, as, for example, the death of a member of the family, the inheritance of money, the remarriage of a widow, the finding work, etc., the need of help may entirely cease or at least be lessened. On the other hand, the allowance may for similar reasons—such as an increase or sickness in the family, loss of work, etc.—be for a while increased and a greater though temporary want may be taken into consideration.

(*f*) There is a difference between the management of indoor and outdoor relief. Of course in both cases it is the duty of the overseer to make the first investigation of the case. But it is only in the case of outdoor relief that the district board decides as to the nature and extent of the relief to be given, while in cases of indoor relief, it can only express an opinion as to whether relief should be given. The central board decides, upon the recommendation of the district board, whether indoor relief shall be given and what its nature shall be, as, for instance, permanent assignment to asylums for the infirm, the blind or the deaf and dumb, orphans' homes and similar institutions. Another exception is made in the case of indoor relief with reference to the time for which relief may be given, namely, that persons may at once be placed in an institution for a long period of time or even for life.

(*g*) In addition to the methods of administration already mentioned, there is a well managed business department. This department is not independent like the tax and police department. It keeps, so to speak, the ledger of charitable work, and furnishes to agents proper forms for making uniform reports of their observations. It performs the clerical work of the central board, places before it the resolutions of the district boards and records its decisions. It collects complete information regarding the various persons relieved and makes abstracts of the facts, so that they may be easily accessible to the overseers when necessary. Finally, it manages the finances of the organization. It pays out all money as directed by the district boards, and delivers all orders necessary to enable the overseers to give relief in money or to buy supplies, such as clothing, shoes, beds, etc., for the persons to be relieved.

It is not possible to go into all the details of the work of this department, yet it is necessary to emphasize the fact, that the importance of the functions of the business management must not be underestimated. The wider the scope of the department, the more important it is that its system of bookkeeping and of collecting information should be clear and intelligible.

Should a larger community desire to remodel its system of charities after that of Elberfeld, it would be well for it to thoroughly acquaint itself with the work of the business department of a city of its own size, where the Elberfeld system has been introduced. It may be mentioned that Cologne and Frankfort, cities of 200,000 and 300,000 inhabitants, have each in operation a model and satisfactory business department, patterned after that of the Elberfeld system. Hamburg reformed its system of charities on April 1st of the present year, and at the same time recognized the necessity of making a complete change in its business department.

III. *Application of the Elberfeld system to conditions prevailing in larger cities.*

The Elberfeld system has run a victorious course through Germany, and we are told that it has also attracted attention in England and France. The Rhenish cities of Germany, such as Cologne, Duisburg, Crefeld, Mulheim, etc., for reasons similar to those which existed in Elberfeld, recognized the need of reform in their systems of charities, and their attention was directed towards the success of the system adopted in Elberfeld. Among other large cities adopting the system, may be mentioned Leipzig, Dresden, Magdeburg, Konigsberg and Frankfort-on-the-Main. It is remakable that nearly all of these cities were induced to reorganize their systems by the same causes, and that they have had almost the same experiences as Elberfeld in adopting its system. Almost everywhere complaints had been made regarding the increase of begging, the disorderly conduct of the indigent, lack of method and insufficient relief. Wherever greater attention was given, a better administration adopted, and, above all, where the number of overseers was increased and they were permitted to take part and vote in the meetings, there was a very marked improvement in the condition of the poor, while at the same time the expenditures for poor relief decreased. No doubt, in the beginning there was a noticeable increase in expenditure, because, by increased attention to relief work, many indigent persons were brought to light, who until then had been languishing in misery.

It would, however, be unwise to adopt the Elberfeld system in all its details without careful revision, or to introduce exactly the same system of administration everywhere. In the first place, there exists a considerable difference in the character of the population of various cities. While Elberfeld has a rather settled population, composed mostly of skilled workmen, the towns in the German coal region, the large seaports, and especially the metropolis, have a very unsettled population coming from all parts of the Empire and composed to a large extent of unskilled laborers. Under such circumstances it is more difficult to understand the general social situation or to become thoroughly acquainted with the special needs of the poorer classes. Besides, one does not find such neighborly relations among the inhabitants of larger cities, and therefore many of the propositions upon which the Elberfeld system is based do not apply there. It must also be remembered, that in the cities there are certain districts in which the poorer classes predominate, while there are others which are occupied almost entirely by the wealthier classes. It is, therefore, almost impossible to divide the whole city into definite precincts, and assign each one to an overseer, because in some districts the overseers would be overburdened with work, while in others there would be nothing to do. Sometimes a single house contains more paupers than the overseer of the precinct in which it is situated can attend to. Thus the principle of granting relief only for short periods, which is a most important provision, cannot always be carried out under such conditions, because an examination of all the cases every two weeks would require more time and energy than the board could give to it. Finally, we must consider that in larger cities close relations between the district and central boards cannot be maintained, on account of the great number of the former, and that the intervention of a decentralizing body is necessary. It is probable that Berlin will not be able to continue its system of poor relief much longer—especially when its numerous suburbs are incorporated and the population is thereby increased by two millions—unless it inaugurates a strong decentralization by administrative circuits presided over by paid officials.

In accordance with the views above expressed, the city of Hamburg, having a population in round numbers of 600,000, has recently effected a change in its system of poor relief. Hamburg also regards the overseer as an essential agent in relief work. Each overseer is not, however, assigned to a fixed territory, bounded by certain streets and house numbers. Instead of each district being divided into definite precincts, the number of districts is increased—to ninety for the present—and each district placed in charge of a chairman. The latter has a corps of fifteen or twenty overseers at his command, to each of whom he assigns such cases as he thinks best. It is evident that there cannot be as close a relation between the overseer and the paupers as in Elberfeld, because the former is not limited to a small fixed territory, but is assigned to individual cases which may be scattered over a moderately large area. Of course, for practical reasons, the field of work of each visitor is generally near his own home. As a consequence of this arrangement, there are greater demands made upon the chairman of a district, because it is only through him that the overseer comes in contact with the person requiring relief. In Hamburg, as a rule, an overseer must take charge of a larger number of cases than in Elberfeld. About six to eight cases are assigned to each overseer in Hamburg. In order that overseers may not be too severely taxed, a plan has been adopted which is not very desirable, namely, that in certain cases relief may be given for a longer period of time than two weeks—even as long as six months—without a re-investigation. This is permitted in all cases where the persons relieved are old or maimed, or whenever it is safe to assume that they are likely to be in need of relief for a considerable time. In other respects there has been a strict enforcement of the rules requiring a careful investigation of each case, visits to the homes, and examination into the circumstances of the families and their capacity for earning money.

The district board is likewise the body by which the individual allowances are made. All the overseers take part in its deliberations. All suggestions for the granting of relief must be brought before this body. Only such allowances as are approved by it are regarded as legal.

The large number of districts has made it necessary that a new body should be created to hold an intermediate position between the central board and the districts. Such are the circuits (*Kreise*), each of which comprises a certain number of districts. Like the districts, they meet every month. The members of each circuit are the chairmen of the districts composing it. The presiding officer of each circuit is a member of the central board, specially appointed for this purpose. The circuit boards at their meetings discuss matters in which the districts have a common interest, and act upon the recommendations of the districts in regard to the granting of indoor relief. This must be regarded as a happy arrangement. As the districts are represented in the circuit by their chairmen and the circuits in the central board by their presiding officers, the highest body is brought directly in touch with the lowest, the work can be distributed according to the peculiar characteristics of each body, and the central board is relieved from the necessity of acting upon individual cases. The central board has charge of the general administration of poor relief, the supervision over the circuits and districts, the administration of the various asylums coming under its jurisdiction, and above all it keeps a careful watch over the economic and social developments of the system of poor relief, so that further improvements may be made as occasion demands.

For the same reasons the business department has been correspondingly extended. It keeps all the accounts and is the connecting link between the individual overseers, the chairmen and the central board. It keeps a systematic record of all relief given and examines all reports of workers regarding the persons relieved. The object of this examination is not so much for the purpose of seeing whether the relief in each case has been given judiciously, as to make sure that the matter in hand has been treated strictly in accordance with the business regulations, and to call attention to any errors that may have been made. For instance, whenever relief has been given in any district in violation of the regulations, and of such a nature that only the circuit board should pass upon it, the error is reproved and brought to the attention of the latter body. The more extensive the system of poor relief, the more important it is to remember what has been said above in regard to the value of a business department, with paid officials in charge, who can follow up the work done by the overseers and the district boards. It is indispensable for preventing partiality and arbitrary action. The systematic collection of reports about all persons relieved makes it possible to trace any individual case of want. This is especially useful in the case of a pauper moving from one section of the city to another, where his circumstances are entirely unknown. Another useful feature of the business department is that it can examine into the family relations of a pauper with a view to discovering relatives who may be in a position to maintain him, or at least to contribute towards his support. Finally, it has charge of negotiations with the systems of other places, and looks after the settlement of claims arising under the laws as to the right of domicile of paupers.

In this form the re-organized system of poor relief entered upon its course April 1, 1893. On its active force of workers it has nine circuit chairmen, ninety district chairmen, and about fifteen hundred overseers. The central board of charities has twenty members, and in the business department there are about sixty officials and twenty other employees. From all appearances this organization is likely to be maintained. Its success is partly assured by the fact that Hamburg has been longer accustomed to self-government than any other place in Germany. Its strength lies in the zeal with which the citizens of Hamburg enter upon the duties of public office, and in their great practical aptitude for self-government, due to an experience of centuries of independence. Besides, Hamburg has always been a fruitful field for charitable and philanthropic effort.

In this place and connection we have had to deal only with the organization of relief as an institution which aims to secure the most complete and practical method of providing for those in want. This, in itself, is a worthy task so long as we realize the fact that destitute and helpless persons will continue to exist in spite of all efforts. But we cannot dismiss the subject without remarking that all poor relief is only a makeshift. To prevent poverty, to remove its causes and thereby make relief superfluous, is the higher and more important problem, which can be only partially solved by relief.

THE ELBERFELD SYSTEM OF POOR RELIEF, AND ITS PRACTICAL APPLICATION.

BY DR. THOMA, BURGOMASTER OF FREIBURG IN BREISGAU, BADEN.

[TRANSLATION.]

I.

The sixth section of the International Congress of Charities, etc., in Chicago, in choosing for the subject of its second session, "the visiting of the poor in their homes by volunteer helpers," and in wishing to discuss the question of the utility of such visits to the poor under the direction of organized charity, as well as the question of selecting efficient friendly visitors (*Armenbesucher*), whether for single cases of poverty or locally for defined districts, has proposed as a theme for deliberation precisely the system well known throughout Germany as the "Elberfeld System," so called after its home, the city of Elberfeld in the Prussian Rhine-province.

With a few exceptions, which are without interest here because of their purely local nature, there are at present only two systems of public poor relief in Germany: the old system of *Centralization*, also called the bureaucratic system, and the new system of *Decentralization*, which is the Elberfeld system. The former, as indicated by its name, is characterized by the fact that the whole system of poor relief of a city or community is governed from one centre, where the need of help is looked into, and relief is allowed and given. The duty of investigation is assigned to a few salaried commissioners. At the first glance it becomes apparent that this method is applicable only to villages and smaller towns, where it has great advantages. It is found now in hardly more than three or four of the larger cities of Germany.

Under the Elberfeld system, the system of decentralization and volunteer members, a town or community is divided into several administrative circles or districts, (*Bezirke*) and for each district an independent administrative centre of poor relief is established. The general connection between the several districts is maintained by a supervising board. Under its direction the district boards (*Bezirksvorstände*), which meet periodically, preserve a certain uniformity in the general administration of poor relief. In the year 1853 the city of Elberfeld inaugurated this system of individualization of poor relief. Since then the system has spread victoriously over all Germany, so that now its title has gained a thoroughly typical significance.

Under the principle of decentralization every district manages its poor relief as independently as possible. Under the district chairmen (*Bezirksvorsteher*) are a number of overseers, (*Armenpfleger*) (friendly visitors, helpers). It is a rule following the principle of individualization, that one overseer ought to give his attention permanently to not more than four poor individuals or families. To that end the different districts are subdivided into precincts (*Unterbezirke*) or subdistricts, each of which is administered by one overseer. To accept the office of overseer of the poor is in Germany a civic duty, as it is to accept any other office in the community. As soon as a poor person needs relief he must first of all bring his case before the overseer of his precinct, who inquires into his personal affairs, his family circumstances, occupation, cause of need, etc., and enters the results of his investigation on an examination or information blank. If convinced that relief is unnecessary, he simply rejects the application, but has to report the case and the cause of the rejection at the next meeting of the district board (*Bezirksversammlung*). The poor person, on his part, may address a complaint to the district chairman. But if the overseer is convinced that relief is proper, he has the power, in conjunction with the district chairman, to grant the necessary relief at once in urgent cases; in other cases he must make his report to the meeting of overseers (district board), which meets every fortnight under the presidency of the district chairman, when the matter is decided by a majority vote.

Above these district boards is the central board (*Centralverwaltung*), the council, commission or directory of poor relief (*Armenrath, Armencommission, Armendirection*), which has the right of annulling or modifying the decisions or orders of the lower boards, provided relief has not been already given. Here appears a difference, inasmuch as some cities nominate to this supreme body only men who have nothing to do with poor relief proper, and, therefore, have neither seat nor voice in the district boards. Other cities try to establish a connection between the central and the district boards by making the chairmen of district boards members of the central board, which is then called poor council or commission of poor relief. The latter method is decidedly to be preferred; for under it the members of the central board, who are occupied in their own professions and not acquainted with the condition of the poor by personal contact, get more graphic and certain information; while, on the other hand, the volunteer chairmen of the district boards become familiar with the views of the central board by their participation in the revision of grants, the formulation of principles, tariffs, etc., and in the discussion of legal questions which arise, and put these views into practice in the district boards. By this means the uniformity of the general administration is essentially promoted.

Another notable contrast exists in connection with the powers of the district boards or district committees (*Bezirkskommissione*), as they are termed more frequently. Under the Elberfeld system proper, the district boards pay out directly, *i. e.*, without authority from a higher board, all amounts allowed by them. Many cities, however, question the propriety of allowing a council of more or less inexperienced persons, who act only as honorary officials, to dispense city funds directly; they require either the consent of the central board in addition to the decision of the district board, or they treat the proposals of these boards merely as expressions of opinion and in every case refer the final decision to the central board. The latter arrangement guarantees by its double examination greater thoroughness, but could scarcely be employed in a large city of 100,000 to 150,000 inhabitants. For in the latter case the approval of the central board, which could not possibly obtain sufficient knowledge as to every case of relief, would degenerate to an empty formality and unnecessarily relieve the overseers and district chairmen of part of their responsibility.

As emphasized above, the Elberfeld system proper assigns to the overseers as their sphere of work precincts containing four cases at most.

Some few German cities have deviated from this rule. They make no division into precincts, but leave it to the district chairmen to assign any case of poverty occurring in their districts to one of their overseers, and not over four at one time to one overseer. This way of choosing visitors or overseers for particular cases is less commendable. In view of the scattered condition and the frequent change of residence among the poor, the continual watchfulness and care, which are indispensable, become in many cases impossible. Besides, an overseer gets into a habit of attending only to the cases assigned to him, having neither eyes nor ears for the rest of the pauper population. Just those considerations which are most important in the economic movements of the people, the variations in the prosperity of the poorer classes, changes of occupation, of residence, and of sanitary conditions are thus utterly lost. So the local delimitation of the sphere of relief is without doubt preferable. The visitor ought to live within his district and try to obtain a full knowledge of all interesting events that happen there. It is of the very greatest importance to make visits at all times of the day in those quarters where the poor—whether being assisted or not—reside, and thus to form one's opinion from personal investigation.

II.

Concerning the practical operation of the Elberfeld system and the success to be attained under it, I must here refer to my personal experience as head of the department of poor relief in the city of Freiburg in Breisgau. The system is without doubt a very good one; if we can draw any conclusion from the splendid results attained since 1853, it will hold its position in the future not only in this city, but in all Germany. But it has here and there its weak points, which come to light only in practice; they may, however, be certainly and thoroughly corrected by the adoption of proper measures borrowed from the old system of centralization.

The Elberfeld system has been in operation in Freiburg since 1879. The whole city is divided into ten districts and these again into eighty-two precincts. At first glance it is clear to everybody, that the good results of this system depend chiefly on the personal fitness of the chairmen and overseers. But just in this respect the experience of this city has not been very happy. It was often very difficult to fill the places of retiring chairmen and overseers. The most incredible excuses were sometimes offered and women played a rôle which must not be underestimated. The more rich, refined and independent the person applied to, the greater were the difficulties encountered. The acceptance of the office of overseer is, indeed, a public duty which can be legally enforced. But of what use is a man who only yields to force, who has no zeal and love for his work, especially where the whole success depends on willingness and personal sacrifice! Constraint was, therefore, never actually employed with us. In this way it happened that in this city the offices of chairman and overseer fell mostly into the hands of people from the middle classes, small tradesmen and mechanics. who do not lack willingness, but very often lack the necessary discernment and, because of their business, the necessary time for energetic treatment of individual cases. I have, for instance, proved that in the case of one overseer not he, but his wife had for years distributed relief, and that only in response to direct appeals by the poor. Under such circumstances we must not wonder, that when the work is reviewed by the central board bad abuses appear. A widow, for instance, continued to draw a sum once allowed, although she had found a sufficient support by marriage with a healthy, strong man; in order to conceal the real state of affairs she signed the receipts with her old name. This fact remained undetected for some time, because the overseer did not make regular visits, on account of business, as he stated. On the other hand it must be admitted that there are localities in large cities, which many people dislike to visit, and that there is work to be done now and then in the course of administering poor relief, which cannot be reasonably expected from an overseer who holds an honorary office.

In order to alter this condition of affairs two official and paid chairmen were placed in two districts containing a large population of laborers and people of the lower classes, where no volunteers fit for the position could be found, while the remaining features of the Elberfeld standard were fully maintained. Besides these, there were appointed paid official inspectors (*Armenaufseher*) or comptrollers (*Armencontroleure*) for the poor throughout the whole city. The task of the latter is a double one. First they must, like the comptrollers of the sick benefit associations, exercise a continual and watchful vigilance over all who obtain relief; then they must, when directed by the central authority, make the investigations necessary for the re-examination of individual cases of need. In the latter case they not only exercise a control over less conscientious chairmen and visitors, but they also gather such information as the latter cannot be reasonably expected to get. For three years the best results have followed these new arrangements. Moreover, regarding the comptrollers the conclusion has been reached that they are a necessary supplement to the Elberfeld system, since they keep up a stable and active connection between the central board and the districts. The comptroller of the poor is just as indispensable as is the comptroller of the sick in the sick benefit associations. The comptroller renders very important service in caring for the children of the poor, who must be closely watched not only in regard to relief, but in regard to their education.

Another material innovation, which was introduced in 1889, is the adoption of the fundamental principle that relief shall be granted for a fortnight only, that is from one session of the district board to the next. This had already been the rule elsewhere. On the one hand, a new investigation of the case every two weeks is assured and abuses are excluded as far as possible. On the other hand, the interest of the overseers in their districts is kept alive. New life is infused into the whole administration and with increased work comes an increase of interest, because every one feels that his activity is recognized as very important and useful to the community.

Good results have also been obtained by the co-operation of public charity with church charities, relief giving associations and private persons, by reason of which the destructive results of overlapping charity are becoming more and more rare.

Finally, the overseers as well as the comptrollers in their rounds and visits are obliged to exercise a constant oversight of the sanitary condition of the tenements of the poorer classes. At times such defects as cannot be remedied at once by kindly intervention are reported through the poor-counsellor to the police department with a view to employing coërcive measures against the landlord.

The re-organization of public poor relief in Freiburg described above, which is not an alteration of the principles of the Elberfeld system, but only a necessary completion and perfecting of it, has had good results in every direction. The expenses of administration have diminished by one-third, or even by one-half, in comparison with former years; other factors however, as, for instance, the enactment of compulsory insurance of laborers, have contributed to this result. But to avoid possible mistakes, it must be distinctly stated here that the principle of critical investigation as to the necessity for relief, as well as the rules about the kind and amount of relief, have remained exactly as before. The sole intention was to stamp out thoroughly all abuses in poor relief. On the other hand, the moral gain must not be underestimated. All help for the poor that goes too far has the bad result, that the poor completely lose the sense of the duty to be fulfilled toward themselves and their families. They leave the care of themselves and their families to the public, become lazy and afraid of work, and live under the mistaken idea that it ought to be so, that they should be supported at public expense. The poor relief of this city is managed on this principle: real want must be relieved generously and in a manner worthy of humanity; but where with some assistance a pauper is able to improve his condition, but shows no inclination to do so, even a penny is denied him.

It is possible that in some other German cities better conditions prevail for practising the Elberfeld system unchanged than in our city. But I am firmly convinced, that the same defects may be found elsewhere in a greater or less degree, if we only take pains to investigate. The numerous letters that have come to me from other cities since I published my first observations about the re-organization of poor relief in our city, corroborate this statement.

THE ELBERFELD SYSTEM OF POOR RELIEF.

BY L. F. SEYFFARDT, PRESIDING OFFICER OF THE CHARITY ADMINISTRATION IN CREFELD AND MEMBER OF THE HOUSE OF DELEGATES FOR MAGDEBURG.

[TRANSLATION RECEIVED FROM THE AUTHOR.]

At the meeting of the committee of the German Association for Relief of the Poor and Charity last spring, Mr. John Graham Brooks addressed to me various questions about the working of the so-called Elberfeld system of poor relief, which during the last generation has won its victorious way into the administration of most German cities. Mr. Brooks had been told that year by year new cities were introducing the system, with alterations, however, differing in various details, and particularly in one highly important point, from the old model of the Elberfeld organization. This point consists in the limitation of the powers of the local overseer and the local district regarding the final decision about what relief is necessary in favor of the central board, and in the latter being authorized to engage paid officers of control. Mr. Brooks wished to know whether these facts were correct, whether they indicate that in the most important respects the Elberfeld system has proved insufficient, and that the necessity of returning to the old system of relief through paid officers appears as a matter of course. I did not hesitate to answer the question of Mr. Brooks to the best of my knowledge, whereupon he asked me to give a written account of the matter for the proceedings of this section of the Chicago Congress of Charities, etc.

In doing this I must say that, as far as I know, the matter in dispute has never been spoken of in the special literature of the subject, though wherever the Elberfeld system has been adopted, it has never disappeared from the order of the day. No time is left before the time of meeting in Chicago to send a sheet of inquiry to a number of cities in order to get a proper basis for a scientific report. I am therefore limited to my own experience obtained during thirty years of practical work with the Elberfeld organization.

Mr. Brooks in his question has indeed found out the weakest point of the Elberfeld system, which occasionally has cost some headache to its friends. The new system has transferred the provident care of the poor and weak from the hands of paid officers, who had to care for a large number, and therefore were obliged to work according to fixed rules, into those of unpaid citizens, who have to provide for a very limited number of poor people only, and are in consequence able to treat every case individually. Theoretically this is undoubtedly right and has led to wonderful success in the average of cases in practice. Whenever the three factors, overseer, director of district and central board do their duty fully, it all goes of itself. But if one of them does not come up to the mark, errors and false decisions will occur which must be contested one way or another. The principal means made use of to control the giving of relief consists in revisions of the districts, arranged by the central board, and taking place at regular intervals, when the overseers have to give an account of every case entrusted to them, while members of the central board and directors of various districts are in attendance. This means of control however has proved unreliable, because people who are adroit in talking will always know how to veil that which is dubious, as long as an inspection of the place of living and working is out of the question. From the experience of different towns, in which the Elberfeld system has been long in existence, another means of control seems to be preferable. The central board itself inquires into the details of the family circumstances and money earnings. Its members reserve the decision for themselves, while they make use of the services of paid officers to collect the facts of the case. However discreetly such measures may be carried out, they may occasionally offend the overseers, jealous of their right of decision. They cannot object to the control of the central board, that being an honorary body, but are very displeased by any real or apparent control by paid officers. To avoid such occurrences, the statutes of different organizations of modern date stipulate for the appointment of special paid officers to investigate every new case or cases already assumed, which appear to be doubtful and suspicious. For the same reason the appointment of such officers has been inserted in different statutes of older date. It will entirely depend on the selection of these officers, on their education and capability, whether the sensibility and jealousy of honorary overseers is sufficiently spared.

What has been said will undoubtedly prove, that the measures in question do not constitute an alteration of the fundamental principles of the Elberfeld system, but only the filling up of a gap in the statutes of a former period, statutes composed at a time when no experience about the methods of control were at hand. All these statutes contain a paragraph of about the following tenor:

The central board shall keep close acquaintance with the decisions of each poor district, by the study of its resolutions or in any other suitable way. It is authorized to annul such decisions, whenever they do not correspond with the circumstances stated or the prescriptions given, and to decide differently.

Wise practice will make use of this paragraph in very rare cases only, in order not to weaken the very vital nerve of the Elberfeld system, the moral responsibility of the overseer for the poor whom he has to take care of. The necessity for such consideration is at the present time even more generally acknowledged than at the time when the system was introduced. In any case, in which measures adopted to strengthen the control are at variance with this admission, they are disadvantageous and prejudice the efficiency of the Elberfeld system of poor-relief.

CO-OPERATION BETWEEN PUBLIC AND PRIVATE POOR RELIEF.

BY DR. VICTOR BÖHMERT, CHIEF OF ROYAL SAXON STATISTICAL BUREAU, DRESDEN.

[TRANSLATION.]

1. *General remarks regarding the Pauper Question as distinguished from the Labor Question.*

The benevolent efforts of the present day are by no means confined to the care of the poor and needy, but have in view the welfare of the great mass of the population, especially the wage earning class, which in most civilized communities represents about two-thirds of the population, and is placed at a far greater disadvantage than the other third, which includes the rich and the middle classes.

Aided by scientific and technical improvements and inventions, agriculture, manufactures and commerce have materially facilitated the production and accumulation of wealth and greatly raised the social position of all classes of the population. The laboring-classes especially take a greater interest than formerly in the intellectual and political life of the nation; though at the same time, through the increase of the great industries, many new sources of danger to the health, morals, and economic condition of the laborer have arisen and necessitated legislative and administrative measures of social reform. Most of these are intended to protect minors and female laborers, but others to protect adult male laborers from injury to their physical, economic, intellectual and moral interests; for example, laws regulating the observance of Sunday, hours of labor, labor contracts, factory regulations, inspection of factories, laborers' insurance, etc.

The efforts to advance social reform and the welfare of the laborer, seek principally justice for the laborer and differ entirely from the care of the poor, which requires practical sympathy and busies itself with the needy, the weak, the destitute, the widow, the orphan, the sick, the infirm, the neglected, and the fallen, striving to lift them up again and lead them on the right road.

A sharp distinction must be drawn between the pauper question and the labor question. Laborers want neither alms nor relief, which would deprive them of important civil rights, such as the right of suffrage. In many places their attitude is one of opposition to a patronizing guardianship, or the bestowal of favors which are distributed after all only to a few individuals. On the contrary, they wish to be regarded as co-laborers of equal birth with their employers and superiors, and desire, after attaining political equality, to elevate their class by their own efforts to a better economic and social position. But at least a portion of the poor, either through their own fault or the fault of those who should support them, or through infirmity or extraordinary mishaps, have been brought to a precarious condition, from which they cannot lift themselves by their own efforts.

The following discussion is not intended to dwell upon the labor question, but considers only one branch of the care of the poor, namely, that which relates to the co-operation of public and private poor relief, (*armenpflege*).

The author of these lines was led to the discussion of this subject by an invitation to participate personally, as well as by papers, in the International Congress of Charities, Correction and Philanthropy. In the sixth section of this Congress, the organization and practice of charity in states, cities and rural communities, and preventive poor relief are to be discussed; also the sphere and duties of voluntary societies, churches and private charities and their mutual relations to organized charity.

Efforts are being made to fix the limits of public as well as private poor relief, and to practically unite and organize them.

2. *The necessity for organizing public poor relief and supervising private charity.*

In nearly all departments of public, professional and business life, proper organization is a pre-requisite to success. The wealth of the great modern industries is due chiefly to the division of labor. Many a manager of an industrial enterprise, who has properly organized his employees and rightly distributed their efficiency, can accomplish more with two hundred laborers than his incompetent competitor with three hundred. The same rule holds in the government of states and communities, the command of armies, and the superintendence of institutions. The bravest soldiers will be defeated when they have a bad leader. But a united force, inspired by the right spirit and properly led in the right direction towards a common goal can accomplish much, even though it has little or no strength. This is especially true of ideal philanthropic efforts. All who are interested in this work must put aside every selfish motive, every capricious impulse, everything of secondary importance, and must keep in view only the great object of promoting the permanent welfare of their fellow man.

Regulations concerning poor relief can produce no lasting results without organization of the forces which are necessary for the alleviation of the wants of the poor. Such organization cannot be entirely of a non-official character, because the State and the community confer rights and impose duties upon the poor, and because, without police regulations and measures of restraint, justice could not be upheld nor public order be maintained. For instance, no government, whether of a state or a community, can leave only to chance or to benevolent societies the care of the poor, the sick, the insane, or of women or children deserted by those who should support them. The necessary police regulation of contagious diseases and a proper consideration for the welfare of the community forbid the authorities to maintain a passive position. But the community must not only consider those who are infected with contagion, but also deserted children, discharged prisoners, beggars and vagrants who are suffering from alcoholism, and in general all the poor, native or foreign, and must ward off anything that may threaten or harm the body politic.

In large communities workhouses cannot be dispensed with for men and women, who by intemperance, gambling, vagrancy, vice, licentiousness or indiscretion have brought those dependent on them to a condition requiring public support. Boards of charity must therefore be established everywhere and entrusted with the supervision and management of poor relief. These boards, like every other authority, can require private persons and societies which wish to help the poor to accommodate themselves to general regulations, and not prevent the attainment of the main object nor make it difficult. The Saxon poor law of 1840, which is in many respects still regarded as a model, had already provided for the co-operation of public and private poor relief to the extent of requiring that private societies must not refuse to give information to the board of charities about persons relieved by them. The duty of giving this information, and the keeping of a statistical record of the number, age, standing of the family, nationality and other circumstances of the poor, were the first steps towards co-operation of public and private relief.

It is not only to the interest of every community to become better acquainted with its destitute inhabitants, but it is also its duty to observe the work and results of its benevolent societies.

Benevolence may become a plague and a curse for the poor, as well as for the benevolent and for whole communities, when anarchy rules in their charities, and individuals, societies, churches and institutions scatter their gifts regardless of one another. All benevolence requires not only sympathy, but wisdom, discretion and prudence, and regard for the general welfare. If at the time of an epidemic any one wishes to erect a hospital at his own expense for the purpose of having the sick taken care of, he cannot be permitted to do so in any locality he may select, but must submit to the public health regulations. Whoever would check the spread of mendicancy or the destitution of whole families and communities, must not scatter money without system among unknown persons and lead them astray into idleness, but must act in the general interest of the poor and of the inhabitants of the community which is threatened.

Begging is carried on in many places as a business which is fraudulent and dangerous to the community. Young or adult persons unwilling to work appeal to societies or good natured individuals who like to give relief, and by applications, either verbal or written, succeed in getting help under false pretences in many places. By this means they lead a far easier life than those who live by the work of their hands. Their bad example and the consequences of an idle life of mendicancy spread contagion and encourage discontent far and wide. The impulse to advance by one's own exertions is weakened, and by such misdirected charity proper relief is really withheld from persons in need, who deserve to be helped. For these reasons, under the imperial penal law of January 1, 1872, § 361, begging in Germany is threatened with punishment, and in many parts of Germany—in Saxony, for instance, where the relief of penniless vagrants is regulated by special relief stations, (*verpflegungsstationen*)—the police ordinances even go so far as to punish the giving of money to beggars. For the unsystematic relief of unknown persons exerts a corrupting influence and greatly endangers the safety and order of communities. It is a public duty of benevolent societies which control funds and often acquire the rights of enrolled corporations, and corresponds to their public legal standing, not to interfere with the activity of officials, but to come into closer touch with public relief as well as with kindred benevolent societies.

Whoever has a sincere desire to stem the tide of distress must foster efforts similar to his own, and take note of societies which are working in the same direction. Mutual ignorance prejudices the work of the agents of general benevolence, who unconsciously compete in matters of charity, and unnecessarily incur double expense. On the other hand, many schemes for the public welfare go by the board, which through united action could have been carried to success. A recent circular of the Board of Charities of Paris addressed to the public sums up the consequences of unsystematic charity in a few words, as follows:

"The same persons are relieved twice and oftener; much money and labor is squandered; the capital is overwhelmed with the destitute from the provinces and abroad, who can neither be properly relieved nor sent back to their homes."

In Germany the public authorities have another reason which compels them to assume control of the organization of benevolent societies and private charities.

The imperial German law of June 6, 1870, in reference to the right of settlement, imposes the duty of continuous support of a pauper upon the community in which before becoming a pauper he has been uninterruptedly a resident for two years after the completion of his twenty-fourth year. This right of settlement is forfeited if public relief is given to a pauper before the expiration of the prescribed two years, but not if he is relieved by societies or by private charity. So it frequently happens that persons who are afraid of work or destitute or incapable of earning a livelihood, move to large cities and manage to live on private charity for two years, at the end of which time they present themselves to the city authorities as paupers entitled to public relief. This surreptitious acquisition of the right of settlement, means a heavy charge upon the finances of cities, where poor relief offers many more attractions than in smaller and especially in rural communities, and withdraws from many smaller communities labor which they require.

3. *Attempts to regulate private benevolence in Germany.*

To combat injudicious relief, as well as to prevent private relief of persons who hope by its help to be able to reside for two years in a large city and so acquire the right of settlement, steps have been taken in several German cities, within the last two decades, to bring about harmonious and united action between public and private relief. This is regulated by the size of the cities.* In the cities of Elbing, (having in 1890 a population 41,576), Colberg (16,999), Coburg (17,106), and Bremerhaven (16,414), a co-operation of public and private relief was attained by having representatives of the benevolent societies take part in the meetings of the department of the poor.

In Elbing a member of a society was assigned to each overseer's district. In Colberg a representative of each society has a seat on the city board of charities. In Coburg the secretaries of the two principal societies take part in the sessions of the city board of public charities with a right to vote; while in Bremerhaven the representatives of churches and benevolent societies are invited to the sessions of the city board.

In the cities of Halberstadt, (having a population of 36,786, December 1, 1890), Hagen (35,428), Landsberg (28,065), and Greifswald (21,624), the reverse is true. Representatives of the public poor relief take part in the business management of the private benevolent societies.

In Halberstadt and Greifswald the presidents of the public poor relief are members of the boards of private benevolent societies; in Hagen and Landsberg several members of the city boards of charities are members of the boards of societies.

In the cities of Zwickau (population 44,198, December 1, 1890), Brandenburg (37,817), Hildesheim (33,481), Reichenbach (21,496), Ludwigsburg (17,418,) and Coburg (17,106), a co-operation was likewise established between public and private relief, which consisted partly in the giving of information by the societies, and partly in the mutual intercourse between the city boards of charities and private societies.

The plan of the Saxon provincial town of Mittweida (population 11,298, December 1, 1890), is peculiar. During the last eight years the directors of its five benevolent societies which give out door relief have been in the habit of holding general conferences in which they exchange experiences. These general conferences and the mutual exchange of information have had two notable results. The directors have learned to know the "beggars by inclination," and were soon able to put a stop to their trade. They have learned also to unite for general

* A fuller description will be found in a compilation made at the request of "The German Society for Poor Relief and Charity," (Deutschen Verein für Armenpflege und Wohlthätigkeit) by Dr. Victor Böhmert, " Poor Relief in 77 German Cities," Dresden, published by the Bureau of Charitable Statistics of the German Society for Poor Relief and Charity.

support in matters where only large gifts could be of service and the resources of a single society would not suffice.

In April, 1889, further progress was made in Mittweida. They decided to found a "Central Bureau of Information for Poor Relief" for the use of the public. This central bureau is not a part of the municipal department of the poor, but is a private undertaking. The office of manager is an honorary one and is bestowed on some distinguished citizen, after mature deliberation by the conference of directors of the five benevolent societies. He himself cannot be president of any of the interested societies. The purpose of this central bureau is "to effect a concentration of all private poor relief in Mittweida." They try to attain this object by regularly making out for the benefit of the boards of the several societies at the central bureau, lists of persons relieved by individual societies and of persons not relieved, though they have applied for aid.

The manager, after comparison of these lists, calls the attention of the directors to such persons as make a business of begging, and from his records and experience keeps the boards of the societies and benevolent individuals informed about applicants and special cases of destitution. All the interested societies have the right to call the manager into any board or committee meeting to advise with them, and at the suggestion of the several societies, the City Council has accorded to him the privilege of having a voice in the regular sessions of the city board of charities, and of keeping a record of applications for relief which are accepted and rejected at these sessions, with such memoranda as are necessary to make this record complete.

The features of the system in operation in Mittweida are that a competent person carries in his head and on his books all the facts connected with local poor relief, and that he is designated to act as adviser to all visitors to the poor, official or voluntary. This system evidently applies only to communities of limited extent, and requires a supply of competent persons. The verbal interchange of information among members of a properly constituted board, is much preferable to a mere exchange of recorded memoranda.

While in the small and medium sized cities of Germany mentioned above, a variety of regulations have been developed to guard against the harm resulting from capricious and irregular charity, in Berlin an attempt has been made to combine the regulations described above for the use of the various poor districts of the great city. The famous

"Society for the Prevention of Poverty in Berlin," which was founded in 1869 by Dr. Strassmann, president of the lower house of the City Council, (also founder of the "German Society for Poor Relief and Charity") and which to-day has members scattered over every part of Berlin, permits its representatives to take part in the sessions of the district boards or poor commissions, which are the centers of poor relief in Berlin. On the other hand, the representatives of public poor relief take part in the sessions of the district committees of the society. In every poor district of the city the public charity commission co-operates harmoniously with the private district committee of the society. By this means an exchange of experiences is secured, and an uninterrupted co-operation of public and private charity is established.

Besides this, in Berlin a mutual exchange of information is maintained between the different societies, as well as between them and the public boards. By a series of well tried regulations made by the poor department, efforts have been made to prevent the imposition which is so easily practised on boards of charities and benevolent societies. It is prescribed, for instance, in the instructions for the conduct of business for the public charity commissions of Berlin of June 7, 1884, in paragraph 85: "that, as a rule, applications for an increase of current relief within the first two months after a change of residence of a pauper should not be considered;" for it has often happened that paupers of a district, where their application for an increase has been refused, have removed to another in the hope of gaining their object more easily. By paragraph 13 of the same instructions, the chairman of a charity commission must superintend the affairs of the poor in his district, and keep himself informed as to the work of all benevolent societies and individuals in the district, so that he may know how the poor who apply to his commission are already taken care of. It is his special duty to attend the sessions of the district committee of the Society for the Prevention of Poverty, either in person, or by his substitute, or by another member.

The Society for the Prevention of Poverty in Berlin has since its foundation exerted itself unceasingly to establish an organic co-operation between the benevolent societies of Berlin and the agents of public poor relief. Dr. Strassmann, who was for many years president of the society, did not succeed in having the mutual relations between public and private poor relief regulated by statute; but at his suggestion, and shortly before his death in 1886, the establishment of a common central office on the model of the Bureau of Information for Poor Relief and Charity of Dresden, to which all benevolent societies should report, was decided upon, and its establishment guaranteed by the Berlin board of charities. This plan has not yet been put into practice in Berlin and the organization of poor relief in Berlin is still in an incomplete condition.

Before the Dresden regulations above referred to are described, the attempts to regulate private benevolence in Austria, should be briefly noticed.

4. *Efforts to regulate private benevolence in Austria.*

According to Professor Mischler's book, "Poor Relief in Austrian Cities," attempts were made in Austria previous to those in Germany to prevent the injurious effects of relief giving by private societies. As early as 1882 (really in 1864), an attempt was made in Vienna to secure co-operation between the benevolent societies of Vienna and public poor relief by statute. But it was a complete failure. A start in the same direction was made in Graz (population in 1890, 97,791), where the plan was adopted of giving a seat and voice in the municipal administrative board to representatives of such societies as had applied for and been given the privilege by the local government. Also in Trent (1890, 19,585), where at regular intervals consultations are held between the executive committees of the charitable institutions, (*Congregazione di Carita*) and the municipal board of charities; also in Brünn (1890, 147,842), where poor relief was left entirely to a private society from 1816 to 1866. The "Men's Benevolent Society to Abolish Begging and Relieve the Really Poor" of that place, to which a "Woman's Benevolent Society" was attached, was absorbed in 1840 by the old Parochial Institute for the Poor. On the executive committee of this society, representatives of the state, city, and church have seats beside members of the society. The eight parochial districts were placed under the central board of this society, and this board administered the funds of the charitable institutions with the help of contributions from the city and state. This condition of affairs continued until 1866, when poor relief passed under the control of the local government.

Finally, in the manufacturing city of Gablonz a. N. in Northern Bohemia (1890, 14,653), according to Professor Mischler, the municipal poor relief was actually transferred to the "Society for the Prevention of House and Street Begging." The Gablonz system proposes to commit the management of poor relief entirely to the society, *i. e.*, to the co-operation of honorary officers taken from the most widely different classes of society, and to raise the material means for the relief of the poor by levying a poor tax on the community. The burgomaster of Gablonz is president of the society.

The business and financial management is assigned to members of the municipal poor districts, while the remaining official positions are generally assigned to members of the upper and lower houses of the Common Council and other capable citizens. As far as the voluntary contributions of the members of the society do not suffice, they are supplemented from the public treasury; and legal provision is made for an appropriation to cover all the expenses of the society.

5. *The Municipal Bureau of Information for Poor Relief and Charity in Dresden.*

The city of Dresden, which in 1880 had a population of 220,818, and in 1890, 276,522, about April 1, 1880, re-organized its poor relief after the model of the Elberfeld system. Before the introduction of the Elberfeld system there were in Dresden in 1877, with its population of over 200,000, only 33 poor directors and 41 overseers for 1583 paupers. On the 23rd of March, 1880, a peaceable army of 400 official overseers was formally installed into the new offices. And it was provided in the new regulations that as a rule not more than five persons or families should be assigned to one overseer at once. At the same time a large private "Society for the Prevention of Pauperism and Mendicancy" was founded, which, on March 10, 1880, sent out an appeal to the citizens of Dresden to join, and in a few weeks received more than 4,000 members and yearly contributions of over 22,000 marks. This society next established a central office to which local and transient paupers were referred for relief, and where every one could receive information regarding destitute persons.

It also erected an institute for voluntary helpers of both sexes and in this way attracted a large body of women to the work, a matter which up to that time had not been thought of by the public relief department. The Society for the Prevention of Pauperism directed its activity more and more towards the prevention of destitution. For this purpose, it established among other things a rent savings bank, workshops for residents and transients out of work, and an employment bureau. Recently, it has undertaken to build small dwellings for families without means. As early as 1881 a desire was awakened in this society to form closer relations with the other benevolent societies, more than fifty in number, and to make a combination with them that would secure a proper distribution of private charity work in Dresden. The great object of this arrangement was to advance the moral and material welfare of the entire community.

The outlines of such a combination were given more in detail by the author of these lines in an essay: "The Organization and Co-operation of Public and Private Charity in Dresden," in 1881, in part two of the *Arbeiterfreund*, (Laborers' Friend).

In the discussions on the co-operation of all the benevolent societies of Dresden, it soon became apparent that to establish a closer co-operation among the voluntary societies would be peculiarly difficult, because each individual society would have to put itself on an equal footing with all the others and must avoid all self assertion or criticism of undertakings related to its own. It was also evident that the organization of so many societies in a large city would not in itself be sufficient, but that the combination must depend upon and eventually be subordinated to the public relief. The committee of the poor board, which was taken into the counsels of the society, was forced to conclude that it was its duty to proceed independently and establish a central bureau of information as a public municipal institution, and to call upon the different societies to join in the officially prepared plans, and enter into closer relations with one another, as well as with the public relief. Out of these deliberations grew in 1883 the "Central Bureau of Poor Relief and Charity" of Dresden, which has proved a help to all societies and private citizens of the city in the administration of their charity and an excellent centre of information. And it has been imitated in several large German cities.

From this central bureau the societies are informed whether applicants appear by the records to be worthy or unworthy; whether they have ever been punished for violation of law; whether and to what extent they have previously received relief: whether they have acquired the right of settlement in Dresden, or have emigrated recently; whether they have presented applications to the city board of charities and to other societies at the same time, etc. It is customary in Dresden for the benevolent societies generally to hand over incoming applications for relief to the central bureau of the city board of charities for information.

The central bureau distributes to the different benevolent societies special forms for this purpose. It also sends question blanks containing special headings for such questions as can be filled out only by the central bureau, on which the several societies enter particulars as to each applicant. The central bureau is accustomed to return the applications and blanks or forms as soon as possible to the societies; and it is their duty to make a careful investigation of the condition of the applicant or his family, in case the information received does not necessitate a refusal of relief. The action of Bern, does not however, tally with this view. There the committee of the Charities Aid Society dismissed the proposition to establish a central bureau of information for poor relief and charity on the ground that

"A thorough knowledge of the special circumstances of the poor cannot be obtained at all through the medium of a central bureau, but only through the precinct officer; and, for the present, decentralization alone can solve the problem both for official and voluntary poor relief."

The central bureau gives no special information, but answers only certain very important general questions; for instance, whether the applicant has been punished at any time by either the law or police courts, his time of residence, and other points to which answers can be obtained only from an official source.

This official information does not deprive a society of the right of making a special investigation of the personal affairs of the applicant, and in no way limits its power of deciding upon the application; of course, any suggestions from the poor board, as to refusing relief to persons who are afraid of work, drunkards, or such as wish to acquire the right of settlement by fraud, are as a rule gratefully received.

Not only for societies, but for private persons who are applied to for help, such information regarding unknown persons is important. It is therefore advisable from time to time to direct the attention of a community to the bureau of information for poor relief and charity and to encourage them to make use of it.

Every poor board, by establishing a bureau of information, can little by little make itself acquainted with all relief given in the community, whether public or private, and can have the relief entered in a special register, under the name of the person relieved or in a card catalogue containing a special card for each case. In this way the poor board keeps a continual oversight of the condition of poor relief; of the increase and decrease of applications; of the coming and going of applicants. The board is placed in a position to readily detect professional beggars, to guard against superfluous relief in single instances, to watch over the acquisition of the right of settlement, and to render valuable service to societies and private persons by means of its register and card catalogue.

Individual applications for relief coming from what we may term the uncomplaining poor, or rather the relief itself may occasionally present special difficulties. It may at times appear impracticable to hand in these applications to the bureau of information for discussion beforehand. On the other hand it is impossible to deny to the board of charities a special interest in informing themselves as to the condition of such persons and their families, since the management of special funds for the support of the uncomplaining poor is often committed to it. In Dresden the chairman of the poor department himself keeps a special register of the uncomplaining poor. The fundamental principles of the Dresden central bureau for poor relief and charity were thoroughly discussed in a meeting of the representatives of public and private poor relief held in November, 1882, and having been accepted in every essential particular, were put into effect March 1st, 1883. During an active existence of ten years the Dresden central bureau has materially reduced professional mendicancy, and successfully prevented excessive giving to either individuals or families. Many undeserving persons have in these ten years been cut off from charitable relief, and many newcomers in needy circumstances have been prevented from obtaining the right of settlement. From published statistics covering the years from 1883 to 1891 inclusive it appears that during that period 23,235 applications for relief were passed upon. Of these, however, only 13,112 obtained relief from societies or individuals and to the rest it was denied.

In the latter year fifty-two societies co-operated in this work. The fact that more than 10,000 applications, concerning which the central bureau had given information, were refused, is a proof of the practical utility of and necessity for this whole organization. From the statistics given farther on in this paper it appears that, especially of late years, more than half of all the applications were not deemed proper cases for relief.

In a conference of the boards of the charitable societies of Dresden called together by the chairman of the city board of charities, on the 23d of November, 1889, the opinion was unanimously expressed that the co-operation of charitable organizations inaugurated by the establishment of the central bureau, had proved an excellent policy, and that any further progress should be made along the lines of this union. Although previously some of the Dresden societies had worked together in isolated instances to relieve cases of exceptionally pressing need, in future this joint relief was to be regulated by the official central bureau, which was to co-operate with the societies. The representatives of the various societies further expressed the desire that conferences of the boards of the different societies should be called at regular intervals, in which technical and legal questions relating to the poor might be discussed, and an exchange of experiences and a closer affiliation rendered possible.

To facilitate the imitation of this Dresden system it may be well to introduce here a few official data.

(A) *The principal grounds of association in Dresden between charitable societies and public poor relief.*

1. In Dresden all private societies and institutions of a charitable nature or for the care of the sick or poor co-operate with the official system.

2. The objects of this co-operation are: (*a*) The entire abolition, or at least the greatest possible limitation of professional mendicancy. (*b*) The prevention of excessive gifts to individuals or families. (*c*) The rejection of unworthy persons. (*d*) The cutting off of indigent newcomers from private relief. (*e*) Uniformity of action in procuring relief in times of general distress.

3. For the attainment of the objects named above in 2, (*a*) to (*d*), each association pledges itself: (*a*) To submit to the bureau of poor relief for preliminary discussion all applications for relief laid before it or directly presented to it, except applications for sick relief. *Vide* 4. (*b*) To report monthly to the bureau every case of relief granted, whether in money, in kind, or in meal tickets, or sick or medical relief, or even when it takes the form of temporary or permanent consignment to homes, asylums or educational institutions. (*c*) To follow the suggestions of the bureau respecting the unworthiness of certain persons, absolutely in so far as concerns their right of settlement, and in other respects so far as practicable.

4. The preliminary discussions mentioned above in 3, (*a*), cover the right of settlement, the character of the applicant, as disclosed by the records, the public or private relief previously received by him, and the propriety of admitting outside or state paupers to participation in the enjoyment of the funds of the associations.

5. The result of the discusions upon any of the above points, which follow as promptly as possible the receipt of the applications, are officially noted on each application and it is then returned to the society from which it came.

6. The relief reported as mentioned above, 3, (*b*), must be entered upon the records of the respective cases or where there is no such record, in a register provided for the purpose.

7. A special officer is appointed for the central bureau by the Council of Dresden, who has charge of the preliminary discussions mentioned above and whose duty it is to keep a register, to make for each of the associations a list of their applications for relief, to make proper entries of these upon the general record, and to send reports to the registration officers of the respective societies for entry upon their records of cases.

(*B.*) *An appeal to the citizens of Dresden to make use of the municipal bureau of information.*

With the advent of the cold weather and stimulated by the approach of the Christmas season, increased demands are made upon private charity. It is certainly the wish of every giver to bestow his charity only upon those who are really worthy and in need of it. In this connection the systematic co-operation of private charitable societies with public relief, now of some years standing, has proved most effective and been blessed with the happiest results. Public relief would, however, have a far better and wider scope, if the charitable instincts of individuals were better instructed. Many well known and habitual beggars, who dread publicity, know how to work skillfully several sources of relief at the same time, and live by begging better than many of their fellows who have to earn their bread by hard labor. The necessity for caution cannot, therefore, be too strongly urged, and it is fervently to be wished that before granting relief individuals would satisfy themselves, as do the societies, of the worthiness and need of the beggar. Opportunity for discussion on these points is afforded by the local bureau of poor relief. As it has often declared publicly, all persons may obtain at its central bureau, Landhaustrasse, No. 7, I, prompt and, of course, free information in reply to all written or verbal questions as to applicants for relief. The use made of this bureau of information is deserving of all the more consideration, from the fact that its object is not to restrict private charity, but only to guide it.

(C.) Statistics of the Dresden Municipal Bureau of Information for Poor Relief and Charity.

	Charitable societies and institutions reporting the relief granted to the Bureau of Information.	Applications for relief reported to the Bureau of Information by societies, institutions and individuals for the purpose of obtaining written information.	Number of applications for relief granted by the several societies in accordance with information given by the Bureau of Information.	Propositions of the Bureau of Poor Relief to the Royal Police Department as to the definition and punishment of mendicancy.
1883 (March to December)	49	1875	1137	—
1884	52	2198	1618	6
1885	50	2456	1495	2
1886	50	2130	1537	4
1887	47	2418	1358	—
1888	51	2755	1283	—
1889	53	2979	1552	—
1890	53	3062	1506	—
1891	52	3362	1626	—
		23,235	13,112	

6. Concluding Remarks.

From what has been said above this lesson may be drawn, that the co-operation of public and private poor relief works no harm, but rather profit. All who are ready and feel called to share in the work of relief must bring their freedom of action in the matter of benevolence into harmony with the oneness of the object in view and with their duty to the community.

The charitable societies will gradually place themselves more and more at the service of the community, or actually become absorbed into the public relief administration, as is already the case in Elberfeld and to a certain extent in Crefeld, two model cities in the line of the organization of poor relief. Of course the care of the poor cannot be everywhere organized on one and the same plan, but different systems for effecting the co-operation of the various societies and public boards must be employed according as the community is a large, moderate sized or small one. Only experience can decide whether the end to be aimed at is not rather a common co-operation of societies and communities working together as a united whole, than an organization of various bodies working on parallel lines.

The attainment of this end can be accelerated by collecting the experiences of many communities, states and peoples, comparing them with each other and carefully testing their value, as is contemplated at this International Congress. The various civilized nations exhibit great differences in their systems and methods of poor relief, and can learn much of each other as to the use of the proper appliances for relief and the means of alleviating human suffering. It is especially advisable to strive for unity of purpose. The chief aim of poor relief must be to combat the causes of bodily, spiritual and moral need. These causes lie partly in the circumstances of the individual, very often in the fault of the person in need of relief, but partly also in conditions which are general, and in the lack of love, sympathy, justice and compassion, which is so common a fault in social life and international intercourse. Not only individuals and different classes of society, but whole nations injure each other by inconsiderate self-seeking, envy, hatred, enmity and war; whereas it is their duty to live together in peace and unity, and by joint labor and free exchange of the fruits of that labor, to contribute to the advancement of their material welfare, and to prevent the mutual destruction of each other's property.

Of still greater importance is it that the nations should exchange with each other their spiritual goods, their inner experiences, and learn of each other better manners, useful methods, profounder wisdom and virtue.

International Exhibitions and World's Congresses are intended for the special purpose of bringing nations together, and causing them to see the spiritual and moral unity of man, and his community of purpose. In the sphere of poor relief and charity every nation must strive to combat not only the physical but also the spiritual and moral wretchedness of humanity. Since poverty results in many instances only from the pursuit of self, pleasure or drink, from dissipation or immorality, the roots of the evil must be extirpated, and the human soul purified and refined. The chief object to be pursued and the chief means to be used in the care of the poor is the care of the soul. Not only must the souls of the poor and the alms receiving class be cared for, enlightened and disciplined, but the souls of the rich and alms-giving class as well, in fact the souls of all classes of society. The number of those who help and care for the poor can never be large enough in any community; and beside every one who needs help should stand some one ready to help him as a true friend. "Not alms but a friend" must be the watchword. Through our care for the poor we will come to learn to look upon all our fellow beings as our brothers and sisters and lovingly to serve them according to our strength. Side by side with the weal of the individual we should ever keep clearly in view the common welfare of the community and the State and the lasting advancement of the well being of mankind.

THE PEOPLE'S CLUB, "VOLKSWOHL," OF DRESDEN. ITS EVENING ENTERTAINMENTS AND HOMES FOR THE PEOPLE.

BY DR. VICTOR BÖHMERT.

[TRANSLATION.]

I. *General Remarks on Efforts for the Welfare of Mankind and of the People.*

We are living in an age of labor agitation and efforts for the welfare of the laborer. A generation ago Mr. Gladstone, the English Prime Minister, spoke of the present as "the workingman's century." The changes taking place in the views and opinions of men seem to point to the consummation of a great movement toward social improvement before the end of the century. On one of the most frequented thoroughfares in the East end of London, where the population of the city of five million souls is densest, and where, too, the greatest misery exists, a grand palace was erected some eight years ago, surrounded by gardens, play grounds and public baths. The interior contains one of the largest halls in the world, besides many smaller annexes in which may be found a library, class-rooms, entertainment and sitting rooms, a small museum, etc. All of these arrangements are intended chiefly for the benefit of the laboring people of the East End and are the results of public spirit. The name People's Palace was given to it, instead of Working People's Palace, and its object is to further the well-being of the people generally. In nearly all languages and countries the term "working people" (*arbeiter, classe ouvrière*) is often interpreted in a very narrow sense. It has generally been applied only to wage workers in factories and larger industries, whose condition it was sought to improve by means of labor legislation and labor insurance. It was, found, however, that this class of wage workers is by no means the poorest paid or the most unfortunately situated. For side by side with them are the small mechanics, the helpers and apprentices in smaller work-shops, the clerks, packers and porters in mercantile houses, the farm hands and the daily increasing number of office employees in the larger cities, all of whom deserve as much attention and protection as the workmen in the larger industrial establishments. The masses of either sex, whether occupied in manual or mental, indoor or outdoor labor, have as great a claim to the protection of the authorities and to the public spirited services of their more fortunate fellow men as the factory operatives. It is therefore high time that we recognize by our acts and public expressions the fact that future efforts for the general welfare must be called by another name than "work for the laborer's welfare." The efforts for social improvement of the present day are directed towards lifting the masses out of misery and ignorance to a loftier cultivation and a higher moral standard. Their object is the general welfare and they begin with the care of our nearest neighbors. Following this line of development, societies have been founded in a number of German cities, during the past decade, known as "societies for general welfare," (*Vereine für Volkswohl*). They seek to advance the well-being of mankind without distinction of class, age, religion, politics or nativity.

What follows is an account of only one of these societies, the People's Club (*Volksklub*) of Dresden, called *Volkswohl* (*public welfare*). It will serve as an illustration of the growth of this very recent movement for the improvement of humanity.

II. *Origin and Development of Popular Evening Entertainments* (*Volksunterhaltungsabende*).

The People's Club is an off-shoot from the District Society for the Prevention of the Abuse of Spirituous Drinks (*Bezirksverein gegen den Missbrauch geistiger Getränke*), and a step in advance of the popular evening entertainments arranged by the latter society. The object of this temperance organization, founded in 1884, was from the very beginning not only to work against the intemperate use of alcohol, but while doing so to establish places where higher enjoyments and recreation could be had. It adopted in its programme, among other things, (1) series of popular lectures on hygiene and nutrition, (2) the institution of evening entertainments and higher forms of amusement for the people.

A committee on public welfare appointed from among the members of the temperance society undertook the entire management of this part of the programme. The first large evening entertainment was held on Sunday, November 28, 1886, and the committee extended a general invitation to people of all classes in Dresden to attend. As a large hall was not available for a Sunday evening, the Turnhall in

Neustadt-Dresden, with a seating capacity of about 2000 persons, was converted into an entertainment hall. A platform was constructed for the performers, and chairs and tables arranged in the hall for the audience. Cards of admission had been placed with manufacturers and other employers of labor, as well as with labor organizations, so that they might be distributed among the laboring classes, for whom the entertainments were chiefly intended. The services of working people's singing societies were also secured as a feature of the entertainment. The first entertainment was fittingly opened with Uhland's beautiful German hymn "*Das ist der Tag des Herrn!*" (This is the Lord's Day!), set to music by Kreutzer, and rendered by the singing section of the Neustadt-Dresden Turn-association, with organ accompaniment. After the opening hymn the chairman of the committee on public welfare made an address of welcome. In his speech he dwelt upon the fact that the public evening entertainments were intended to give an opportunity for mental and moral refreshment to all classes without regard to rank or station, religious or political convictions. He said, that all men and women present depended upon the same source of subsistence, namely, labor, and that it mattered not what the nature of that labor might be, whether in the workshop, in the factory, in the counting room, in the study, in the office or in the open fields, and he advised every one to be energetic in his own sphere, be it great or small. When the day's or week's work is over we should aim to encourage a generous sociability and a proper enjoyment of life, partly for the general good, partly for the special good of persons in single life, and as a consequence serve ourselves. This fundamental idea, and the aims of the committee as expressed at the opening meeting, have continued to be the standard of development of this project in Dresden, and have also been adopted and even extended in other German and foreign cities. Wherever the example of Dresden has been followed, it has soon been demonstrated that the club evenings, instituted for members of workingmen's city and town clubs, and the parochial evenings of church societies, which have existed for years in Germany, were not sufficient for the masses. There was still a need in all large cities of some kind of association, where opportunities for unrestricted social intercourse and entertainment might be given to all adult persons regardless of club affiliations, religious beliefs, occupation or rank, and where all might find intellectual and artistic enjoyment of a high order, to replace the public houses and dance halls where they would be forced to drink. In these public evenings an instructive lecture ought always to be the main feature, accompanied by musical exercises, recitations and other features of a sober, but cheerful character. Choral singing, dramatic and historical representations, tales of travel, popular classic poetry, stereopticon illustrations, and other proper amusements may well be given. In the selection of subjects for instructive lectures, the efforts of the Dresden society have thus far been confined to the sphere of public education, public welfare, public health, popular art and poetry, and to biographies of persons of merit. Unsolved scientific problems and doubtful questions have been avoided, attention being given rather to completed results of scientific research which are little doubted, and to expressing in popular terms such conclusions as are generally accepted and have become public property.

In arranging the entertainments, what is simple and beautiful, pure and noble, and truly harmonious in art and poetry was selected, rather than what is speculative, fashionable and showy. Most of the lectures were delivered gratuitously by professors of the Dresden technical high school and physicians. For the other features of the entertainments special efforts were made to secure the assistance of those classes for whom the amusement was chiefly intended, for example, working people's singing societies and amateur talent from amongst the poorer people. Nevertheless, prominent artists and the first singing societies of Dresden frequently took part in the entertainments. There is a real absence of class distinction, all participants cheerfully offering their services for the common good. During the six years of the existence of these public evening entertainments there has never been the slightest discord—in fact they were so popular that additional space was required. During the first five winters, entertainments were held once every month, on Sundays or holidays, in the large hall of the Turn-association in Neustadt-Dresden. Last winter, however, ten additional entertainments were held in Dresden, four of which took place in the largest hall in Altstadt-Dresden, which could be obtained only on Saturday evenings. It was found that Saturday was not a bad day for entertainments of this kind, provided that in the interest of the working classes the performances did not begin until 8 P. M. The result of this was that many men and single women after a hard day's work closed the week peacefully in the enjoyment of high intellectual and artistic amusements and were better prepared for the Sunday rest than by frequenting public houses. On the occasion of the first entertainment in the Tivoli Hall in Dresden, on Saturday, October 26, 1892, the hall, which holds 3,000 persons, was completely filled, and the number of adherents and friends of the People's Club was greatly increased.

It is worthy of special mention that great pains are taken to remove all political and sectarian feeling from the evening entertainments. Shortly before the third entertainment of the society was held in February, 1887, and when at the national elections all the candidates of the social democratic party in Saxony had suffered defeat, a rumor was spread in the factories that this entertainment was to be made an occasion for celebrating a political victory. In view of this rumor, the chairman in opening the entertainment took occasion to declare that the public evening entertainments had nothing whatever to do with political affairs, but that, on the contrary, it was hoped by their means to bridge over the gulf which separates classes and parties. He also said that the society desired to win over persons of social democratic views to this movement for the public good.

The committee on public welfare considered it equally important to avoid, in these public entertainments, all religious questions which related only to particular sects. There are, of course, thousands in every large city who like to associate only with people who agree with them in politics or religion. This is a perfectly legitimate view, but it is also right and proper that associations of men and women should exist whose primary object is to bring about a friendly understanding amongst the various classes and creeds, and whose members gladly associate with persons of different views and from other stations of life. At any rate, experience has shown that in many small as well as large communities in all countries a desire prevails seriously to encourage the exercise of a brotherly spirit towards all one's fellows. This movement for popular evening entertainments has spread very rapidly during the past six years, and not only has it taken root in the larger German cities, such as Berlin, Hamburg, Bremen, Lübeck, Leipzig, Halle and Düsseldorf, but also in the medium sized and smaller towns, such as Kiel, Bremerhaven, Lüneburg, Görlitz, Flensberg, Zittau, Guben, Bromberg, Elmshorn, Husum, etc. In many rural communities, and even on islands in the North Sea, popular Sunday evening entertainments are held once every four weeks when the roads are lit by the full moon. And in some cities of Austria and Switzerland these institutions have been imitated, and about three years ago popular evening entertainments were started in Christiania, Norway, modelled entirely after those in Germany. Last winter the rural community of Norik, near Christiania, followed the example of the Norwegian capital. The weekly organ *Volkswohl* which appears in Dresden contained a very complete description of this Norwegian rural institution.

On the occasion of the first entertainment the invitations were distributed by the joint action of an employer, a workingman, a farmer, a government official and the communal administration of the locality. Entertainments of this character cannot always be modelled after the same pattern. In a rural community, for instance, where religious differences rarely exist, it is advisable for the clergyman, the school teacher, the physician and perhaps a prominent employer to take the initiative. These persons should secure the co-operation of local societies or individual workingmen and farmers, not omitting the women, and all should unite in distributing the invitations and arranging and developing the scheme in accordance with the needs of the particular locality. Officers of the State or locality should not take part in their official capacity, but should, nevertheless, as private citizens use every effort to further the success of schemes for public recreation and the intellectual development of the adult population.

III. *Origin and Development of the People's Homes* (Volksheime) *in Dresden.*

In consequence of the success, which the public evening entertainments inaugurated in Dresden in 1886, met with everywhere, the executive board of the District Society for the Prevention of the Abuse of Spirituous Drinks, and its committee on public welfare appointed in 1888, resolved to go one step farther in fostering sociability among persons of all ranks and creeds. This new scheme consisted of the establishment of social centres where persons might meet, not only once a month, but at all times, for friendly intercourse and mutual education and improvement. These centres were called "People's Homes," (*Volksheime.*) They are not public kitchens nor philanthropic institutions, but really people's club houses managed by the members themselves, and are intended to be self-supporting. Plain food and refreshments are furnished to guests at low fixed prices, schedules of the latter being posted in the rooms. The essential differences between them and ordinary taverns and restaurants are that members have access to them at all times without being required to spend any money; that they contain reading and sitting rooms, libraries, gardens for recreation, and playgrounds and gymnasiums for young people, that fresh drinking water is always on hand in the rooms and gardens, that the attendants are not permitted to accept fees for their services, and no partiality is allowed in serving guests. In fact, most of the guests help themselves to food and drink at the buffet.

For the purpose of establishing homes of this kind the People's Club was founded December 7, 1888. By the end of December, 1892, three homes had been established. The founders of this society were, with few exceptions, the same persons who originated the Society for the Prevention of the Abuse of Spirituous Drinks in 1884. There might not have been any necessity for creating a new society, as the old one could as well have undertaken the establishment of people's homes. It was done, however, because many persons, though they approved of the object of the parent society, objected to its name, which had been contracted in common parlance into Drinking Society (*Trunksuchtsverein*) and feared that by joining a society of that name they might be taken for drunkards or at least for friends of alcoholism. Many members had expressly asked that the monthly journal of the society, which bore the name *Mitteilungen gegen Trunksucht* (Information in relation to Drunkenness), should not be delivered at their homes, because they did not wish to arouse a suspicion among their servants that they were in need of a monthly paper to warn them against alcohol. It is at times advisable to take the prejudices of the masses into account in order to overcome an obstacle in the way of a useful institution. For this reason the executive board of the Dresden society publicly appointed the "Committee on Public Welfare" to inaugurate evening entertainments instead of doing so itself, and afterwards changed the name of the monthly organ of the society to *Volksgesundheit, Blätter für Mässigkeit und gemeinützige Gesundheitspflege* (Public Health, a Journal of Temperance and Public Hygiene.)

As another means of avoiding the creation of a new society it was proposed to convert the parent society into the new People's Club. This suggestion was not received with favor. The old society already counted a membership of nearly two thousand persons contributing annual dues to the amount of about 4,000 marks ($1,000) and had a small sum in its treasury, and many persons objected to turning over these resources to the new society. Then again, there were many persons who were willing to contribute towards maintaining a society having the specific object of combatting drunkenness, but were averse to aiding an organization bearing the more comprehensive name of *Volkswohl*, behind which they suspected a doubtful social or possibly social democratic scheme was lurking. Only recently, a Dresden physician gave 5,000 marks ($1,250) to the District Society for the Prevention of the Abuse of Spirituous Drinks, because in his daily practice he observed the undisguised ravages of drink. This physician was not a member of the People's Club and would probably not have made the donation had the new society superseded the old. It must also be remarked in this connection that in the Dresden Society for the Prevention of the Abuse of Spirituous Drinks, the small annual fee of 50 pfennigs (12½ cents) entitles members to all the privileges of the society, including admission to the popular evening entertainments, while in the People's Club an annual membership fee of at least 2 marks (50 cents) is required.

The executive board of the club did not hesitate to require a higher annual membership fee than the old society, because experience had shown that in the latter organization there were many persons, even with small means, who voluntarily contributed more than was asked of them. A good illustration of such a case was that of a servant girl, who joined the society shortly after the first of the evening entertainments, and agreed to pay 2 marks (50 cents) a year for membership. The officers of the society, knowing that the girl was a servant in a rather modest household, gave her to understand that only 50 pfennigs (12½ cents) were required and that this would entitle her not only to attend the entertainments, but to receive the publications and reports of the society. She insisted, however, upon paying the 2 marks, because, as she said, for so good an object as the popular evening entertainments she would gladly give that much of her wages. This readiness to contribute on the part of the members of the old society has shown itself to a still greater extent in the club, because the aim of the latter is higher and its field of work greater.

An experience of four years has demonstrated that they were in the right, who had claimed that two distinct societies were not too many, though their aims were so similar. There are, especially in large cities, many public spirited men and women who are quite willing to be doubly taxed for a good object. Many members of the society whose annual contributions are quite considerable, pay at the same time still higher annual dues into the treasury of the club. Some time ago the society erected at great cost a people's home of its own, which it afterwards turned over to the People's Club.

In the preceding pages we have endeavored to show that experience justifies the founding of new societies of general benefit, because there are many otherwise worthy men, who strongly oppose the tendency to private organization of our time without discrimination, and without considering that there are certain new problems relating to the improvement of mankind, which can never be solved without the creation of new societies. The State and the community should not be burdened with everything when private beneficence is quite as effective. Had it not been for the creation of the new People's Club one of the most beautiful garden sites in Dresden would have fallen into the hands of building speculators. This was the estate of the late Princess Pauline of Schleswig-Holstein, which now serves as a people's home and garden, a refreshing resting place for thousands of adults, and a healthy playground for many more children. Upon the death of the Princess Pauline in 1888, the president of the District Society for the Prevention of the Abuse of Spirituous Drinks obtained an option for several months on the estate at a price of 188,000 marks ($47,000). In the meantime he called for subscriptions and donations from citizens of Dresden to cover the first payment. In response to his call one prominent manufacturer gave 20,000 marks ($5,000), another 5,000 marks ($1,250), a third promised an annuity of 2,000 marks, and many others promised annual contributions of from 100 to 300 marks ($25 to $75). The executive board of the newly created club hesitated, however, about undertaking the purchase of this expensive piece of property, and so the option at the same figures was transferred to the city, which acquired the property and leased it to the club for a people's home.

This people's home and grounds are in Neustadt-Dresden at No. 7, Wasserstrasse. The estate was named *Paulinengarten*, after the late owner. Since its opening it has become a great centre of public sociability. In the building there are on the ground floor two rooms for social entertainment with buffet and kitchen adjoining, and a spacious reading room, in which also dinner is served to the numerous boarders who come there at midday. A fourth room contains the staircase to the second floor. Here there are two rooms set aside as business offices for the club and the society. Two other rooms on this floor are used during the winter months as class rooms and for society meetings. There are also a library and a large hall, in which lectures, meetings and smaller evening entertainments are conducted.

The chief attraction of this people's home is the large garden, which is one of the most beautiful ornaments of Dresden. It has large lawns and magnificent old trees. While in the foreground under a splendid group of plane-trees a grand view is spread out of the Elbe, covered with life, and the first hills of Saxon Switzerland, at whose entrance the towns of Loschwitz and Blasewitz offer a friendly greeting. Here under the shady trees hundreds of working people and others, who like a well prepared dinner at 25 pfennigs (6¼ cents), come to take their meals in summer time. Many women with their children may be seen here in the afternoon, while in the evening and on Sundays men and women of all classes congregate. The garden is divided into two parts, one for adults, the other for children. That for adults is laid out as a park, with shady walks and quiet nooks, beautiful lawns, trees and shrubbery. The other and more important section of the garden belongs to the children and is subdivided into five or six separate parts. There are several sand piles for the very small children, an enclosure for swings which are constantly in motion, a space set aside for such games as require the direction of an adult, another ground for other games, and an enclosure containing both gymnastic apparatus and games. Partly by this subdivision of the play-grounds and partly by the presence of an overseer, it has always been possible to maintain strict order in the garden, notwithstanding the fact that hundreds of children are often present at the same time. The games are under the guidance of specially employed teachers and assistants. There is also a large covered room in the playground for protection in case of rain. Benches are placed in the midst of this children's paradise, where mothers sit knitting or mending and enjoying the mirth of their little ones. And when the day's work is done, the fathers, too, find their way to the garden, and often with their wives and children sit down to a simple evening meal under the trees. Or they may bring their food with them from home and refresh themselves with a glass of light beer or a drink of fresh water, which is always to be had in the rooms and in the garden.

The grounds and home are also used at times by other societies for children's picnics, and as a place of rest and refreshment for school children of the surrounding country making excursions to the city. In the summer of 1892 several Dresden singing societies for the first time gave concerts in the garden, which were attended by hundreds of members and others. By this means the noble art of music becomes more and more the common property of all classes of the people.

Besides the above described people's home of Neustadt-Dresden, which is the most important one, there is a second in Altstadt-Dresden and a third in the Bischofsweg. In outward appearance these homes do not differ from respectable restaurants. But the difference is very marked, when one finds water on all the tables, and plain notices on the walls informing the guests that no one is compelled to spend anything and that fees will not be accepted by the waiters, and there is no card playing with its accompanying noise and disputes. Many of the guests occupy themselves with books and newspapers or games of chess, draughts and billiards. A midday meal is served at the people's homes for 25 pfennigs (6¼ cents). Light beer is drunk by about one-third of the guests. The visitors to the people's homes are mostly ambitious young men anxious for improvement, and of the older men mechanics and factory operatives. There are also many office employees and wealthier and better educated people among them. A plain man visiting one of these club houses for the first time is at once made to feel that he is welcome and that he is under no constraint, as long as he conducts himself properly. Although non-members are, as a rule, cheerfully admitted as guests, only members have a right to stay at the homes and to expect a hearing for any complaints or wishes regarding the management. When we consider that wine and brandy are not kept in stock, and that the only beverages served are light beer, coffee, "warm beer", cocoa, tea and fresh water, we must realize that these people's homes have little in common with bar-rooms. Ample provision is made in Dresden for those who prefer the attractions of a bar-room, and they require no assistance from public spirited citizens to satisfy their tastes, but there exists a need for many more places where, away from a barroom atmosphere, all classes may meet for a higher social intercourse without being expected to constantly spend money in drink. Two of the people's homes are more than self-supporting, the surplus being devoted to the payment of the original expenses. The third still requires some assistance from the society to cover expenses.

IV. *Other Institutions of the People's Club.*

Lectures and Class Instruction. Besides promoting sociability among all classes, another aim of the People's Club has been, from its very beginning, the intellectual cultivation of the masses. With this end in view various courses of study were arranged during the past four years, including among other things, bookkeeping, penmanship, German,

English, French and Italian, modern history, the chemistry of daily life, stenography and singing. There were also lectures by physicians on first aid to the injured, medical lectures for women, lectures on botany with botanical excursions, and lectures on art supplemented by visits to the Dresden Art Museum. In the arrangement of the course of study many branches were undoubtedly omitted, which would have been more useful than some of those selected. Nor can it be denied that there is still a lack of proper system in this respect, and that the selection of subjects depends greatly upon chance. In arranging the courses the management acts only as a medium between members who are anxious to learn, and such persons as are willing to impart knowledge gratuitously. Besides, the object of this instruction is not only to impart knowledge to the people, but to create in them a taste for nobler pastimes and higher aspirations, and to give them a harmonious view of the world. Novel and especially attractive were the botanical excursions to the environs of Dresden, and the rambles of the art classes in the city. The participants in the former saw before their eyes the spring flowers and the foliage and pines of the German forest, as well as the exquisite plant life of the environs. For the latter, Dresden is specially adapted by its wealth of art treasures. It was clearly seen in the very beginning of these new experiments that not only professional men, but the masses have a desire, and in no small degree a capacity to receive mentally and morally the lessons taught by the treasures of art and nature.

In connection with this organization, there have also been started two singing societies, one in Neustadt-Dresden for a mixed choir, the other in Altstadt-Dresden for male voices only. The former frequently assists at the popular evening entertainments. A dramatic club has also been formed, which devotes one evening a week to the reading of classic drama. The library of the society is a potent means of encouraging education. It is made up almost entirely of donations from the wealthier members, and already contains about 1400 volumes, which were given out 5000 times during the year 1892. Many parents, whose work prevents them from visiting the people's homes, avail themselves of their benefits by sending their children or half grown members of the family to the gardens in summer time, and to the classes or the library in winter, in order that the latter may bring home information or entertaining books. Many an afternoon the library is filled with persons, especially children, waiting their turn to get good books, or more often illustrated periodicals to take home, either for themselves or for other members of their families, so as to pleasantly pass away the long winter nights in reading at home.

Finally, as another means of education, a monthly paper is issued by the society, called *Volkswohl,* which is delivered gratuitously to all members at their homes. This paper contains a review of general matters relating to the society, together with articles and communications on public improvements, popular education, public health and social life. Reports of lectures delivered at the public evening entertainments, also appear occasionally in this journal. It also serves to keep the members more in touch with the executive board and with each other.

Women's Meetings. Among the many minor divisions of the present organization, the People's Club, the women's meetings instituted at the people's home in Wasserstrasse, October 28, 1890, have been especially successful. This association meets every Tuesday evening from 8 to 10 P. M. It has a membership of 130, and a regular attendance of about 80, consisting of women and girls over 12 years of age, who come there for instruction, cheering society, and contact with companions of their own age and sentiments. The time for social intercourse is from 7 to 8 P. M. Then follows an instructive lecture or reading, and after that comes a lively discussion of the letter-box, which contains all sorts of inquiries by members, relating chiefly to subjects of domestic economy. Portfolios containing patterns for cutting and crocheting, and ladies journals are placed on the tables to assist in educating the members in all branches of domestic economy. On the evenings set aside for them, the women have the exclusive use of the large hall and adjoining room on the second floor of the home. Two special courses were given during the past winter, one in cutting, and the other in darning and mending. A course in measuring and drawing patterns is to be added. Great tact and earnestness is displayed by the woman under whose guidance the meetings are conducted. She is a teacher in one of the public schools, and in her work at the meetings she seems to have succeeded in securing a united hearty effort on the part of all the members, to strive after definite aims and to foster a feeling of sociability among themselves regardless of rank. Often the women's meetings are enlivened by some of their members playing on the piano or singing. The aim is to make them sociable and instructive, and to remove all restraint. Members often bring needle work with them, with which they employ themselves while pleasantly chatting or listening to lectures on domestic affairs and other matters of interest to women, or they exercise their wits with riddles and games. It is not to be denied that many women and girls without family homes have as much need of such harmless associations as men.

Home for Girls. This institution, also conducted by the People's Club since July 1, 1889, was originally intended to accommodate working girls whose means were so small as to compel them to live in bad lodgings. It was designed to take in women employed in factories, and by means of the regulation of a well-ordered home managed for the common benefit, to educate them in good manners and domestic duties. The cost for lodging, breakfast and dinner was fixed at 70 pfennigs (17½ cents) per day or 3 marks 70 pfennigs (92½ cents) per week. The factory girl, however, did not take kindly to this idea, and seemed to prefer the dangerous surroundings, in which she was free, to a home where rules must be observed. So it came to be used chiefly by servant girls who boarded there while temporarily out of employment. From July 1, 1889 to December 31, 1892, 1550 out of a total of 2005 girls accommodated, were servants. It was quite natural that efforts should be made by the management of this home, to secure employment for these girls, and therefore, on July 1, 1890, an employment bureau was opened at the home. A fee of 25 pfennigs (6¼ cents) was charged for securing a situation, and the employer was charged 50 pfennigs (12½ cents). 3200 girls have secured situations through this bureau since its creation, the number in 1892 being over 1500. Employment is not only secured for inmates of the home, but for all who wish to patronize the bureau. As there are always many applications for servants on file, nearly every girl applying can obtain employment. The business of the employment bureau increased so much recently that the quarters were enlarged on April 1, 1893. The income from board and lodging and from fees of the employment bureau is sufficient to cover all expenses.

Home for Apprentices. Youths of from 14 to 18 years of age are also exposed to many dangers when forced to seek support away from home. The dangers arising from the indiscretions of youth are at least partially guarded against by the establishment of homes and educational institutions where apprentices, who are removed from the care and guidance of the parents, may be protected from the temptations of a great city. The establishment of such homes is daily becoming more urgent, in view of the fact that fewer employers board their apprentices, and that the hours of recreation are constantly being increased by legislation and custom.

Two years ago the People's Club obtained a donation of 10,000 marks ($2,500) from a person interested in the welfare of young men, for the purpose of providing an apprentices' home. Several rooms in the People's Club were specially devoted to Dresden apprentices, and provided with games, books and illustrated papers. A young teacher was employed during one winter to look after the entertainment and instruction of the boys on Sunday afternoons and week-day evenings. Sunday walks were added in summer. All this, however, is not sufficient and it only leads to the conclusion that larger apartments and better attractions must be offered to Dresden apprentices and that board and lodging and permanent supervision must be procured for apprentices who are strangers in Dresden—in short, a real apprentices' home must be founded. The home should be at the same time a place where the master, the manufacturer, the merchant and the teacher may co-operate in the systematic education of young men whose school days are over. A general call for subscriptions for this purpose was made to the citizens of Dresden at the close of the year 1892, and as this has met with a hearty response, the plan will in all probability be carried into execution during the current year.

5. *Conclusion.*

The various institutions described above are not the result of a previously conceived plan, but grew up from time to time as the members found them necessary for the encouragement of sociability and intellectual improvement, and were developed from within. Without much help from the executive board, which rarely finds it necessary to meet, men and women, youths and girls, from all classes of society, earnestly co-operate for the good of the society, so that after their day's work they may have opportunities of refreshing their minds and strengthening their bodies. And they learn by personally managing their own affairs, that peace and harmony are always more agreeable than quarrels and dissensions. Notwithstanding the present unfavorable economic conditions, the membership in this society increased during the year 1892 from 2161 to 2274. All classes and occupations are represented in the membership, but especially small mechanics, laborers and government employees, who lead a temperate life, enjoying the visits to the garden with their wives and families in summer, and in winter gladly availing themselves of the reading room, library and courses of study. A skating rink is another attraction where young and old can amuse themselves at small cost. The income from membership fees amounted to 9,536 marks ($2,384,) in 1892. Since its creation, the society, unhampered by political, social and religious differences, has by its various institutions worked its way deeper and deeper into the hearts of the people. And while it cannot remove all or even many social troubles, its promoters cherish the hope that through the cheerful service and sacrifice of all classes of society, it may overcome at least some of the difficulties of the social life of the masses.

THE ORGANIZATION OF CHARITY IN RUSSIA.

BY DR. H. GEORGIEVSKY, ST. PETERSBURG.

[TRANSLATION.]

In Russia, until the end of the seventeenth century, works of charity were regarded as a means of saving one's soul. So the centre of beneficence was the Church and into her hands were turned the offerings both of sovereigns and of private persons. From the beginning of the 18th century the State recognized the need of interposing in this work and of regulating charity, by adopting measures in regard to various kinds of needs, namely, caring for the sick, helping those unfit for work, and making those persons work who were able to do so. In order to check the growth of beggary the government forbade the giving of alms, under penalty of the law; it obliged each parish as well as each landlord, to help its own poor and not to let them become vagabonds; and it strictly enjoined upon all local authorities of the State to see that these laws were carried out. At the end of the 18th century committees of public charity were founded, having for their duty the organizing of all necessary establishments (schools, hospitals, orphanages, workhouses, penitentiaries, etc.) In 1825 these committees possessed a capital amounting to 24,000,000 roubles.

If the organization for helping the poor bore until the end of the 17th century an ecclesiastical character, it bore during the 18th century rather that of police. At the beginning of the 19th century this work of aiding the poor became a task, in which not only the organizations of the Church and the State were joined, but to which private individuals and free associations readily and voluntarily gave their aid. It was in 1802 that the first organization of this kind was formed.

During the 19th century, up to the present time, questions concerning the relations which should subsist between the work of government organizations, private societies and individuals, in order to establish perfect harmony of action, have been studied in theory as well as in practice. At the end of 1892, by a supreme order of his Majesty the Emperor, a special commission was formed with Grott, a member of the Imperial Council, as president, to revise all laws concerning the relief of the poor; the work of this commission is already somewhat advanced.

At the moment there is not any general organization, that is, there is no central ministerial administration for charity. In each province the responsibility of giving assistance rests (since 1864) with the General Council, or where such a council is not established, with the Committees of Public Charity. There is no general report given of work done throughout the Empire, and even in St. Petersburg the Municipal Council was not able to collect any complete or precise information concerning the work of the beneficent institutions of the capital. There is still less information concerning the cities of the interior.

Besides the organizations of the government and private societies, there are beneficent institutions of a semi-official character—for example, the Imperial Society of Philanthropy, which spends a considerable amount of money. As to official organizations mention must be made of the establishments of the Empress Marie, the expenditures of which in 1888 greatly exceeded 11,000,000 roubles, but of which no printed account is given.

The parochial associations, instituted in 1864 in connection with the orthodox churches, merit special attention. Besides their other duties, these organizations must engage in helping the indigent of their parishes. As they give help without religious distinction and as they are brought into immediate contact with the people, these should be the most valuable forces for regulating the organization of private as well as of public charity. Unfortunately it has not as yet been possible to establish even in St. Petersburg any bond between these various parochial societies; so that the money at the disposition of each one, and in consequence the amount of aid given, varies according to the wealth of the inhabitants of each parish.

If information is lacking concerning whole departments, whose special work is the aid of the poor, information in respect to the charitable work of individuals or of private societies is still less to be expected. With the information that I have received from various points in this vast country, I can assert that even the smallest cities have their charitable societies; but the task of collecting information from all Russia is recognized as an impossibility even by the commission established to supervise the actual work of helping the poor and prepared to help in its re-organization. Therefore, I limit myself to the statistics of St. Petersburg for 1889, which were obtained with great care by the municipal administration. These statistics enumerate 757 establishments, among which are 326 schools, 146 asylums for children, 90 asylums for the unfortunate, 70 ambulances, 55 hospitals, 40 lodging houses (either free or very reasonable in price), 13 boarding houses (either free or moderate in terms), 8 workrooms, 4 night refuges, 4 establishments for sewing, and 2 workhouses.

The expenditures of all these establishments (governmental, public and private) rose in 1889 to 8,350,000 roubles; the schools and hospitals received 3,540,000 roubles, and the 4,810,000 roubles remaining were used in other charitable works. Nearly ninety-five per cent. of the sum total was spent in the institutions and only five per cent., namely, 430,000 roubles, was spent in outdoor relief, that is to say, 335,000 roubles by private societies and 95,000 by various agencies.

It is impossible to give statistics concerning the number of persons helped on account of the lack of unity of action among the charitable societies. A person helped by one institution is perhaps also helped by several others; a person having received help during the course of the year from one or more institutions might be received as an inmate of an institution; so that the same person might be counted several times and we should evidently have a very inaccurate result if we added together the number registered by each society. The lack of connection between the societies being observed, it is evident that the number given in the records, 846,000, is that of *cases aided* not of *persons aided*. It is also quite impossible to estimate the considerable amount of aid given directly by private individuals. Unfortunately it is still quite customary in Russia to give alms in the street or at the church door to persons who pass as beggars, although in the few cases where it has been possible to find out their true condition it was discovered that some among them owned houses or other capital.

In order to give the charities of St. Petersburg a more regular organization, I have elaborated a scheme for a special bureau of information about the poor modelled after one in Dresden, although differing from it essentially. The Imperial Philanthropic Society has organized a bureau (in part without me and in part with my non-official concurrence) where persons who are willing to work without remuneration collect information about those who seek aid from the Philanthropic Society or from two or three other societies. The principal part of this staff of workers is composed of women, teachers of the city schools, who have thrown themselves with ardor into this useful work. The information collected is written on special sheets of paper which are arranged like a card catalogue in alphabetical order, and these statistics are constantly added to and verified. Although this bureau has existed but a short time (three years at the most) it has already about 9,000 cards giving quite detailed information respecting the poor living alone or supporting families. So that they have on the register the names of probably twenty-five or thirty thousand individuals.

PAPERS

ON THE

WORK AND PROBLEMS

OF

CHARITY ORGANIZATION

IN

GREAT BRITAIN.

INTRODUCTORY NOTE.

BY C. S. LOCH, SECRETARY OF LONDON CHARITY ORGANIZATION SOCIETY.

I was asked by the Committee of Arrangements for the Sixth Section of the Congress of Charities, Correction and Philanthropy, to procure a full and careful statement of charity organization work and problems covering the field of Great Britain. This was a large task. I could only fulfil it within the time at my disposal by asking members of charity organization societies and others to write papers on the subject with special reference to the town or district which they best knew. No exhaustive statement was possible. The work and problems could only be tested by samples; and these samples, it appeared to me, would be of special value, if they disclosed the opinions and hopes of persons engaged in the daily work of the society, who would be likely to outline clearly and sharply what lay before them, and were, in the spirit of practical men and women, likely to minimise, rather than exaggerate, what they might accomplish in the future.

Of the general work and problems of the societies the fullest particulars may be learnt from the books and papers on the subject, which form part of the English Exhibits of the Bureau of Charities and Correction. (See page 31 of the Introduction of these Exhibits, especially No. 161: Annual Reports of the London Society 1885 to 1892, No. 172: the Register of Charity Organization Societies 1891, and No. 366: Annual Reports of Charity Organization Societies in the United Kingdom, 1891.) I will not repeat in epitome what may there be found at first hand. I will make only one or two remarks on the papers to which these few words serve as a preface.

I have endeavored, as the Table of Contents shows, to obtain first a fair representation of the opinions of men and women who are engaged in the work of charity organization in the metropolis, and then a similar representation of opinions from industrial and other centres in the country. Two general papers head the London list. One is written by Rev. B. H. Alford, the Vicar of St. Luke's, Nutford Place, S. Marylebone, who has for many years been a member of the S. Marylebone Committee and a Guardian of the Poor. It describes the close proximity of rich and poor in a west end district, the lodging of beggars and the overlapping of benefactors, and the great changes for the better that have been made in the administration of poor law relief and charity in the last twenty years. The other is written by Rev. Dr. Bradby, a member of the Whitechapel Committee and Chairman of the Administration Committee of the London Society. He knows the East of London well and has drawn a picture of the industrial and charitable characteristics of that part of the metropolis. It is a plain unembellished tale, and for that reason may be appreciated by those into whose ears have been dinned so many accounts of the romance of distress and degradation to which the East of London has given rise. Then follow four other London papers. That from Shoreditch describes the problem of Charity Organization and the Poor Law in a civil parish, usually classed as part of the East of London, but very distinctive in the character of its population and its industries—an old parish with many endowed charities and a strong local feeling. S. Olave's comes next, another old parish and well endowed, south of the river. In the account of it but little is said of the actual work of the local committee of the society, but the problem stands out clearly, and might be summed up by the words "Reform public administration: purify social politics." And in this direction there are, we hope, the beginnings of a salutary change. A short account of Islington as a fairly typical North London district follows. And the section concludes with a paper by Mr. T. Mackay on co-operation between the Poor Law and charity, with special reference to the improved administration of the Poor Law in S. George in the East and elsewhere. In this paper the problem of the Poor Law reform from the point of view of charity organization is discussed, and the main objects which it is the policy of the society to accomplish in this field, are definitely stated.

The next group of papers deals with the provinces.

Mr. McDougall, who has a long and accurate acquaintance with the conditions of the poor in Manchester, is to describe the great reform in the administration of poor relief which has been accomplished by the Guardians of the Poor in Manchester, in concert with himself and other charitable persons there. At Manchester there is no Charity Organization Society but a District Provident Society, which was instituted before charity organization societies came into existence. Bristol takes the next place, interesting for two reasons amongst others. It has a quite abnormal supply of charitable endowments, and many of its citizens are now bent on introducing judiciously and gradually into their administration of its poor relief changes which will make the charitable resources of the town of more real service to its poor. Mr. Leach, the Clerk to the Board of Guardians at Rochdale, has kindly sent an account of the administration there—a typical north country industrial town known all the world over as the pioneer of co-operation. Mr. Milne's account of Aberdeen describes some phases of charity organization which are to be found only in Scotland, where no Poor Law relief is given to able-bodied persons. And there, too, are associations for the improvement of the condition of the poor—an older form of charity organization society now working in alliance with the general movement. Lastly comes Mr. Willink's detailed and most interesting account of Bradfield, a rural union, where outdoor relief has almost reached the vanishing point, and where some principles of charity organization which were formulated by the Poor Law Commissioners of 1834 and their predecessors are applied, but there is no charity organization society.

In addition to these other towns and districts might have been chosen. But the reports of provincial charity organization societies, to which already reference has been made, and the papers furnished from Birmingham, Oxford, Leeds and elsewhere for the charity organization conferences held in Oxford in 1890, will give the reader information, should he desire it. (See No. 162 of the Exhibits Charity Organization Review.)

On special departments of the society's work, the care of the feeble-minded, the epileptic, etc., I do not add any remarks. Reports and papers in regard to them will also be found in the Exhibit.

THE WEST OF LONDON: S. MARYLEBONE.

BY REV. B. H. ALFORD, POOR LAW GUARDIAN AND MEMBER OF THE S. MARYLEBONE COMMITTEE OF THE C. O. S.

I am asked to contribute a paper for the International Congress of Charities which shall deal with that small portion of the field of enquiry which has fallen under my own personal observation; that field is the parish of Marylebone, lying in the West of London and containing a very mixed population of over 142,000. Throughout this parish the extremes of want and of wealth lie near one another. In Lisson Grove between 50 and 60 per cent. of the inhabitants are returned in Mr. Charles Booth's statistical tables as living in poverty, while in the neighborhood of Baker Street 100 per cent. of the inhabitants live in comfort. Occasionally the juxtaposition of the extremes is very close; for it takes only three minutes to walk from Bryanston Square, colored "gold" in Mr. Booth's reference maps, to Horace Street, colored "black." The direct consequence of this interstratification of opposed classes is to intensify distress, emotionally first of all, because bitterness is naturally engendered through a contrast so glaring; and also practically, for the services required by the rich are to a great extent casual, lasting for the season, and no longer; while the rent of rooms rises considerably higher than where land is less valuable. The consequence is that in no part of London are the operations of the Charity Organization Society more necessary or, if I may say so without local partiality, better carried out.

1. *It is desirable to curb the impetuosity of the well-to-do.* Moved by the distress and squalor of their neighborhood they are anxious to apply the speedy remedy of giving. Those that appear with a whining tale at the back door get broken meat or a dole; those who occupy themselves in letter writing find a fair harvest. There has lately established herself a few doors off from me an impecunious beggar, whose trade it is steadily to go through the list of inhabitants in the adjacent squares, and send an appeal varying in particulars with those addressed to every householder. But perhaps the most fatal form of corruption is when a soft hearted lady undertakes on her own impulse to

visit and relieve the poor at their own homes. I have known an instance of a request for a trifle to buy rice acceded to by a gift of a sovereign. In such personal intercourse with neighbors there is indeed "the promise and potency" of valuable help, but only on the condition that the hand does not go ordinarily to the pocket. Until antecedents be known, temptations recognized, and the whole field of circumstances reviewed, there should be no money-giving attempted, if even then. The Society is ready to step foward and advise such as have no patience or capacity for the process of sifting facts, of considering alternatives, of deciding upon that which will best aid effort and least hinder energy.

2. *It is desirable to methodize the works of charity, which are already afoot in Marylebone.* It follows without saying that a parish of the kind I have described teems with charities. I have a list by me of 39 churches, 27 chapels, and about 15 missions within our boundaries. Each of these will certainly have a machinery of its own for the assistance of the poor. The societies of the different churches may be expected to keep within their respective districts. Some of the chapels also, being for special forms of worship, will have only a limited *clientèle*, but the remainder will spread their work indiscriminately, and some of the least deserving characters in Marylebone may easily be getting help with both hands from more sources than one. When I add a number of institutions not directly religious, such as dispensaries with their supplies of medicine and sick food, hospitals with their indoor, outdoor and convalescent treatment, almshouses, orphanages, homes—you will perceive the imperative need of interchange of knowledge and partition of labor. This the society has undertaken to promote; but its efforts are hampered by lack of co-operation. Some smaller communities do not think it worth while to give information as to work done. Some larger communities seem jealous of interference, and would rather act rashly than act openly. It is to be hoped that time and good humor may smooth away difficulties. Those who take counsel in common about their cases find individual judgment strengthened and corrected by the general judgment, and (I speak for myself) leave the committee room thankful for the sympathy of other minds, the sidelights of other experience.

3. *It is desirable to repress the endeavors of the unscrupulous to prey upon the unwary.* Our streets in winter time are a constant haunt of tramps; they sing sometimes popular ditties, sometimes popular

hymns, and always badly; but their voices seem to affect the emotional, and I occasionally listen to a rain of half-pence pattering in the street from the front windows. The Society offers an alternative to this practice so discouraging both "to him that gives and him that takes." It accepts the task, difficult and generally thankless, of investigating the alleged want, of supplying honorable forms of help, of endeavoring to obtain work for those who plead that they have no employment. The result frequently is to discover that the last thing desired is employment, and that the life of the pavement is the present equivalent of the life of Sherwood forest among a certain set of "merry men," whom it is scarcely wise to encourage in their outlawry from order and work. Those, again, whose profession is more sedentary and whose pen is their organ of appeal, are taken to task by the Society; if they cannot be won from their mistaken industry, and especially if this industry borders (as it frequently does) upon fraud, their names are printed on a "cautionary card," which invites any one around to communicate with the office before rendering help.

4. *It is desirable to co-operate with the Guardians of the Parish*, so that charity and State relief, may each find its proper object—neither interfering with the other. If the Society were able wholly to realize its intention, and brought into a focus all the voluntary forces of the neighborhood, it would then be able to address the State with entire confidence, and arrange a full concordat. As it is, it is entitled to speak with a certain force of authority as an accredited mouth-piece of several agencies, and the only one so accredited. At present there is a change passing over the administration of the Poor Law in London. The process began in the East; it is gradually spreading to the West. Instead of money being promiscuously bestowed on a pauper family in the home, there are distinctions made. In the case of sickness, admission is offered to the infirmary; in the case of a destitute widow, maintenance for some of her children in the parish schools; in the case of ordinary want, admission to the workhouse. But this sifting discloses necessitous cases which are either partial, or exceptional, or temporary. Under the first category come those who still retain a certain power to earn, but whose earnings are by reason of age or ailment inadequate to their support; or those who have relatives able to supply some, but not able to supply all their maintenance. Here the Guardians—and I write as chairman of the Relief Committee of the Marylebone Board— do not desire to throw aside the amount coming in to the applicant,

and yet do not wish to initiate fresh out-relief. Again a not unfrequent occurrence is the case of a respectable man or woman or couple entirely devoid of means; they have worked themselves out, or they have failed without fault, or some sickness has overtaken them, with which their club is unable to cope. Here, were the workhouse to be pressed, we should insist on a remedy incommensurable with the disease, we should needlessly wrong

"that feeling of decent pride," (I quote from the last Report of the Marylebone Charity Organization Committee) "which is worth preserving, if only as a shadow and ghost of the true independence of character which the working classes have now such multiplied temptations to lose utterly out of sight."

In this dilemma the Society aids the Guardians; it accepts the special case for special investigation; it traces out its past history; it examines its present surroundings; it weighs the evidence for thrift and uprightness and, if the case endure the ordeal successfully, the Society organizes a pension, working in such earnings as are possible, and such help from relatives as is forthcoming. And of all pieces of work this is to my judgment the most satisfactory. Character finds its reward in exemption from the stigma which must fall—and righteously fall—upon State aid; while the public sees that the recent rule of refusing outdoor aid, though strictly applied by the trustees of the State, has yet its way of escape through careful voluntary aid, and they are not thereby encouraged to rush into almsgiving of their own through false compassion. The Marylebone Committee of the C. O. S. was one of the first, if not the very first among the committees, to arrange a special Pension Fund: it thus expends upwards of £700 yearly in allowances to old men and women, while the parish authorities are able to reduce their out-relief correspondingly to a minimum,* feeling that no hardship is likely to result while this concerted action lasts.

I note two illustrations from the Committee's Report of last year's work in this direction.

"14,146, A. R., a thrifty, industrious woman, formerly a domestic servant. She had saved £150, which she lost through a bad investment, but she struggled bravely on, supporting herself until she was seventy-six, notwithstanding bad health and extreme deafness. It would have been a terrible hardship for this woman to go into the workhouse,

*There are now only 323 recipients in a population of 142,381, whereas in Dec. 1886, there were 1043.

and ultimately a pension was successfully organized." "13,916. A. B., a respectable housemaid most highly spoken of by her mistress as a good servant and a devoted daughter. She left her place to nurse her old father, who was very ill, but refused to go into the infirmary. She was able to earn so little while attending on him, that they were half starved and were rapidly sinking into pauperism. Some help was given and influence brought to bear upon the father to induce him to enter the workhouse. This he finally did, and a loan was then made to the daughter to enable her to re-enter service respectably. She repaid the money as soon as possible, expressing much gratitude for all that had been done for her, and she is now doing well."

It is evident to those who watch the social signs that some radical alteration in the rules of the Poor Law is approaching: such alteration will doubtless take the form of exempting certain classes of the destitute from its stricter requirements, and providing them with exceptional aid in old age. The Local Government Board would be well advised to make use of the machinery existent in the Charity Organization Society—if only it could be duly extended to the provinces—in order to bring every source of relief to a focus for the provision of pensions. If relatives are overlooked, if the kindness of old employers and present friends is not invoked, if the Christian pity of church or chapel is excluded from its share in the national object, and only compulsory rates and taxes are drawn upon—then we shall have a purely mechanical scheme, unrelieved by any human element. It would be within the desire and the power of the C. O. S. to supply this leaven of humanity and redeem officialism from waste and disrepute. Every year by calm persistent work the Society is more and more mastering details, extending knowledge, fixing principles. Its collection of facts as to the needy of the metropolis written in thousands of volumes of papers and hundreds of volumes of indices, is an invaluable gift to enquirers; its discussions of method have dealt with fallacies which fettered thought and encumbered action twenty years ago, but now are discountenanced things of the past. The ground is open for a forward movement, and while to prophesy its details would be presumptuous, to affirm its near occurrence is permitted to the sanguine.

THE EAST OF LONDON.

BY REV. DR. E. H. BRADBY, MEMBER OF THE WHITECHAPEL COMMITTEE OF THE C. O. S.

SYNOPSIS.

I. Brief descriptive sketch of the whole area covered. Characteristics of the several districts in which the Society has Committees. These are conterminous with the Poor Law Unions. Whitechapel. St. George's in the East. Stepney. Mile End Old Town. Poplar and S. Bromley. Bow and N. Bromley. Unoccupied territory beyond.

II. Enumeration of the chief difficulties in the way of Charity Organization in East London. 1. The absence of a leisured class and the consequences of that absence throughout the vast area that has to be dealt with. Enumeration of really available resources. 2. The multitude of competing agencies which have to be organized and refuse organization. 3. The shifting character of the population. 4. "The unemployed." Distinction between those who do and those who do not really belong to this class. 5. The large foreign element in certain districts. Concluding observations on the work and position of the Society.

I. The stranger who for the first time visits the East End,—the workshop of London as it has been styled—will probably be agreeably disappointed. He will encounter few outward signs of the want and squalor with which he has probably been taught to associate the name. Broad airy thoroughfares, traversed by tramcars, omnibuses, and every description of vehicle except the gentleman's carriage, stretch far away into the suburban regions of "London over the border." The principal streets are alive all day with a motley crowd of more or less shabby passengers. The houses which flank the thoroughfares are chiefly shops, commonplace buildings enough, when looked at individually, but at least having the merit of being low, so that the air can circulate freely, and presenting a vast variety of outline.

A glance down the side streets will show that the characteristic of most of them is a dull respectability. House succeeds house, and street succeeds street, built after the same pattern, and only distinguished from one another by their numbers or their names. And if one penetrates behind these streets to the courts and alleys which, not unfrequently, lie between and behind them, though the spaces will be narrower the general features of the scene will not be changed. Only here and there will a really dark spot be found, and their number is being yearly reduced. It is only when he penetrates inside the fairly prosperous looking houses that the stranger will discover that very many of them are not the homes of a single family, but of several families, and that where this is not the case lodgers are common. Thus the population is often much more closely packed than would appear to the outside observer. What will strike a visitor more than the signs of anything like squalor is the general plainness and monotony, not to say ugliness of the region: the absence of striking and important buildings, the lack of all those suggestions of stateliness and antiquity and refinement, which we are apt to associate with the idea of city life. To complete the general picture, it should be stated that the East is bounded by somewhat similar districts on the North; that to the eastward it melts indefinitely or by slow degrees into the country, embracing whole districts to which the society has not yet extended its operations, though it is now contemplating an advance; whilst on the southern side the Thames, with its long stretch of wharves and docks, and all the concomitants of a vast mercantile port visited by ships from every quarter of the globe, affords a welcome variety to the general sameness of this portion of the far-spreading metropolis of London.

But in order to understand its character, and the kind of problems which it presents to the organizers of charity, it is necessary to break up the wide area just described into smaller portions. Each of these will be found to possess its own distinctive marks. Our task will be rendered easy by following the grouping of the C. O. committees, which are, as a rule, conterminous with the Poor Law Unions. The first of these as one passes eastward from the city proper is Whitechapel, (Population 71,363.)* On the broad pavement of its High Street people of all nations jostle against one another, but they are the poor, the shabby and the toiling of all nations, not the rich and well-to-do. Half of the inhabitants are foreigners, mostly Jews. These congregate chiefly in this Union, and there are whole streets and districts in which they have gradually supplanted the native, and whole Board Schools, in addition

---

* The numbers given here and below are those of the census of 1881.

to the excellent Jewish Free School, where their children occupy all the benches. Their ways are foreign, and they mix but little with the English. As a rule, they are a peaceable and industrious population, and in such virtues as thrift and sobriety they excel their neighbors; but they crowd unwholesomely together, and their standard of comfort being low, they tend to lower the wages of the trades in which they compete. From their practical isolation it is very difficult for any of our native agencies to come into real contact with them. Happily the Jewish poor are looked after with increasing judiciousness by the Jewish Board of Guardians, a splendid voluntary charity; while the Friends of Foreigners in Distress vindicates its name by an assistance which would be more effective if it were less frequently dissipated in doles. Of these two societies, the former is in active co-operation with our committees, while the latter frequently refers cases to them for investigation and advice. Another feature of Whitechapel is to be found in the large number of shelters and common lodging houses which are crowded into this district. The shelters especially form a serious and increasing evil, by attracting into this centre the tramps and ne'er-do-wells from all parts of the country. More particularly during the winter months, when relief of some kind is to be had for the asking, is this attraction potent and mischievous. The result is that while a wise policy of *dispersion* is being actively followed, on the one hand, by sanitary and moral reformers, their work is being as actively counteracted, on the other, by the efforts of a misguided philanthropy. When we add that Whitechapel has the misfortune to contain two or three streets which are notorious for the bad character of their inhabitants, it will be seen that there are many obstacles to contend with in this district. Besides this foreign and this floating population, there remains that of the regular residents. Many of them are Irish by birth or descent. They get their living by labor of all kinds, much of it casual, or by working at small trades. It is among these that the Charity Organization Committee finds its chief field of work. The two most satisfactory branches of that work are aid in sickness and convalescence, and pensions for the aged and deserving poor. In both branches co-operation and organization are needed and are obtained. Beyond this, in spite of much active co-operation on the part of many of the clergy, who in no place are more friendly than here, the committee is more successful in preaching the true principles of charity than in securing their practical acceptance by the host of independent agencies that are at work around them.

We pass on to St. George's in the East (46,747). As this is more fully described elsewhere, it may here be briefly dismissed. It has a less mixed multitude than Whitechapel, and it is plagued with fewer shelters. It is the home of the docker, the riverside laborer, and the very poor. As their work fluctuates with the seasons and with trade, so fluctuates the prosperity of the district. There are times of much want and depression, especially in a hard winter. The bulk of the upper part of the population is made up of artisans and small storekeepers. The district, poor as it is, seems to be gradually becoming poorer, from the removal of some large undertakings. Meanwhile the foreign element in the population is increasing.

Beyond St. George's on the East lies Stepney (58,500). Stepney was once a favorite suburban residence—Mr. Pepys sent his goods there for safe custody to a friend's country house during the great fire of London in 1666—but the strong tide of population setting eastward has long covered and flowed far beyond it. With its arrival the more wealthy residents have disappeared. Those who make their fortunes in the district live apart from it. Clerks and small business men, whose work lies chiefly in the city, occupy the better neighborhoods. There is also a large number of artisans scattered throughout the district, but the bulk of the population find their living on the waterside in one way or another, and suffer with the ups and downs of trade. There are few large manufactories to furnish centres of life and industry. The foreign element is absent. Stepney has not the busy varied life of Whitechapel, nor the poverty of St. George's. It is poor but respectable, orderly but dull.

Mile End Old Town (105,573), which lies north of both the two districts last described, covers an area almost equal to them both. There are in this district two or three big manufactories; there are also a brewery, a distillery and large confectionery works; whilst one of the great London Gas Companies has it headquarters here. These, of course, give employment, much of it regular employment, to many. Hence there are large spaces in this wide-spreading district from which few, if any, applications come to the office of the society. By the side of these more fortunate persons lives a multitude of dockers, carmen, hawkers, and unskilled laborers. Add to this that the Jews have flowed over from Whitechapel, and occupy one quarter to the extreme west of the district. There is no rich resident class to take the lead in charitable work, or in organizing public life. Here, as elsewhere in the East End, those who thrive by the district live away from the district, and the region is given over to trade and labor.

Very different from the Unions already described is that of Poplar (156,525) to which we now pass. The area of this huge Union is divided by the Society between two committees, one for the north, the other for the south. The district cared for by the southern committee, called that of Poplar and S. Bromley, lies still further east down by the river side, and contains within it the Isle of Dogs. The Thames here makes a large semi-circular sweep or loop, washing the island on three sides, whilst its fourth side is formed by the great East and West India Docks. North of this lies the more thickly peopled quarter of S. Bromley where the bulk of the workers live. Poplar is the seat of a great iron industry. The banks of the Thames are studded with iron works, girder works, wire rope works, iron bridge works and lead works. The shipbuilding trade, which was once flourishing here, has fallen into almost complete decay. There is more independence, more hope, stir and resource among the men of Poplar than are to be found nearer the city. It is the headquarters of trades unionism and clubs; whilst the large seafaring population contributes its energy and its knowledge of the world. Of course, times of depression come, but they are encountered with more vigor and pluck. Owing to the nature of the industries followed, there is a considerable connection with the North of England, and, as a body, the workmen of the North are ahead of those of the South in intelligence and organization. To give an idea of the distance of Poplar from the centre of things, it takes about an hour to get from the Committee's office to Charing Cross, the headquarters of the Society, by tramcar and railway.

Immediately north of this region lies the twin district of Bow and North Bromley, which is the last that we have to describe. There are some works here for the making of jam, chemicals, paper, and colors, and there is also a large brewery, but Bow is not a manufacturing centre in the sense in which Poplar is. The factories lie mostly in the north corner of the district, round about Old Ford. They employ with fair regularity a large number of people; in one quarter reside a good many clerks, whose business lies elsewhere. The rest of the inhabitants are artisans, such as carpenters, painters and plumbers, and below them are laborers of various kinds. There is just a sprinkling of dockers. Few Jews are to be found in Bow: The foreign element, which is not conspicuous, is formed chiefly of Germans, many of them old residents. There are plenty of poor, some very poor, in the district, and in one locality is gathered a criminal or semi-criminal population—one of those black spots scattered over Mr. Charles Booth's famous Map of East London—which the operations of the Society do not touch. In Bow there are no wealthy residents, but a certain amount of local help in money and service is forthcoming. Much as it is to be welcomed, it is but a trifle when compared with the wants of the district and the opportunities for service which it offers.

Though we have reached the end of our committees, we have not reached the end of East London. There are large densely peopled regions beyond, notably at Canning Town, and around the works of the Great Eastern Railway at Stratford. Into some of these the society is already meditating an advance, but its progress is slow and its resources few, and the day is yet distant when it will be in the happy position of being able to sigh for still more worlds to conquer.

II. What are the chief difficulties which confront the Charity Organization Society in the vast thickly peopled area which has now been briefly described? To name these is to state the problems which it has to consider, and, if possible, to solve. First and foremost must be placed the general absence of a leisured and cultivated class—men who have time and intelligence to devote to local matters. Consider the wide areas, the swarming numbers that have to be dealt with, and what are half a dozen centres for such a work? And yet even these poor half dozen are manned chiefly by workers who come from distant parts of London, and have a long journey by train and cars to encounter, coming and going. The richer tradesmen used to live over their shops; now they leave them after business hours for a suburban home, which is the real centre of their affections and interests. They cannot, at any rate they do not help us. Of the clergy we shall speak presently. There remains the great class of well to do artisans. They are always on the spot. Their aid would be invaluable, for they form the upper class of the really resident population, but hitherto we have failed to enlist their support. And there are great obstacles in the way. Not the least of these is the fact that their leisure time is in the evening, while much of the work of our committees must be done in the daytime. But there is more than this. Partly they do not understand, partly they do not sympathize with our methods. With our *aims* they would in theory agree, but they do not see the close connection that exists between our aims and our methods, for, much as they study social questions, they do not study them from the side of charity. Hence there is much ill-founded prejudice against us, and those who would agree with us in private will not speak up for us in public. Intercourse alone can break down prejudice, and intercourse is hard to achieve. One of the chief problems set us is how to make the Society more popular without sacrificing principle. One important source of aid has yet to be mentioned. The parochial clergy are distributed throughout the region, and their organization for charitable purposes is the most complete and the most universal. Could we capture them, we should have made a great stride forward, for they are the only cultivated residents whom you are sure to find on the spot in every district. The only way to capture them is to convince them, and this is a long and difficult process. Perhaps our best hope in the near future lies in the acceleration of that process. At present the amount of their co-operation varies much in different centres. In Whitechapel it is hearty and pretty general; in most districts a few work with us genuinely, more are half convinced, and many stand aloof; the actively hostile are becoming fewer, and it is very possible that the next few years may see a great change for the better.

2. Next comes the multitude of competing agencies that have to be organized. A few great societies, notably the Society for Relief of Distress and the Metropolitan District Visiting Association, work in hearty co-operation with us, but the smaller and more or less local societies form the *crux*. Their name is legion. As a rule, they fight each for his own hand, and they despise or mistrust, at any rate they neglect, scientific charity. They are all heart and no head. The consequence of no concert is much overlapping; the consequence of much overlapping is the degradation of the poor. The poor are being diligently trained by them to dependence and a hand to mouth existence, instead of to manliness and self-reliance. This is the great national curse of charity as now administered by too many. Not those who need most get the most help, but those who know best how to exploit existing institutions. The wily applicant has many strings to his bow. No doubt this thoughtless but well meaning charity often mitigates much present distress, but it does it at the cost of character, and it helps to perpetuate it. Were all the money and personal service thus lavished given on wise principles and in concert with others, it would

go much further, and would do more good and much less mischief. Problem, to convince the charitable public of this.

3. The shifting character of the population. The East Londoner is not much given to taking root in one spot. Why should he be? One street is very like another, one house is very like another. There are few of those charms of locality and association which make a man cling to his home at any cost. Hence he shifts his quarters very readily to suit his work, or his convenience. Now the essence of charity organization is friendliness and personal contact, and the unit on which it works is the family. But how can you get to know families who are here to-day and may be off to-morrow? How can you get a hold on them, and be helpful in the long laborious process of aiding to build up self-help, self-respect, frugality? Of course, there remain many fixed residents; but so far as the population fluctuates hither and thither, so far the work of charity must be imperfect. The only soluble problem here is how to make the best of a bad bargain.

4. The difficulty of the unemployed, of which so much has been heard of late. Now here there is need of much discrimination. Who are the unemployed? It is a term somewhat vague, as generally used. No trade gives unbroken employment to all who follow it; most trades have their busy and their slack time; some can only be pursued at all at certain seasons. It would be unreasonable to constitute the hands which from these various causes, from time to time, are short of work into a class, and call them "the unemployed." And yet this is frequently done. The lack of employment of these persons is not chronic, but temporary, and for the most part can be foreseen and provided against. In the long run it is taken into account in the wages paid them. The genuine "unemployed" consist of two classes. It sometimes happens that a trade leaves a district altogether, or almost entirely. This happened a few years ago with the sugar-bakers in Whitechapel and St. George's; it is happening now with the ship-builders in Poplar. In that case a large body of steady workmen may be thrown out of work altogether, and may have great difficulty in migrating or getting absorbed in other trades. This is the first class, and theirs is a case very hard for charity to deal with effectually; for charity cannot invent work, which is what they want. But besides these there are in East London a vast number of men who know no trade, and are too poor, too ignorant, and too shiftless to learn one. They live solely by manual labor. They seldom have regular employ-

ment. When trade is in the flood-tide of prosperity, they pick up a living; when it ebbs, their fortune ebbs with it. Then the half employed become the unemployed, and suffer much privation. Especially is this the case with the "casual" dockers and other riverside laborers, who are not enrolled on any organized staff. In dealing with these two classes, charity organization may possibly meet the special crisis of the one by a special effort, but the condition of the other is chronic, and all temporary expedients are at best but palliatives, and can never effect a cure. Many of the plans at present advocated, tend only to perpetuate and aggravate the disease. Time, patience, the spread of education, the spread of organization, the elevation of the standard of comfort, and, above all, a recognition of the truth that underlies the much abused and much misunderstood law of Malthus, appear to the present writer to be the chief remedies.

5. It will have been observed that a large foreign population is quartered in Whitechapel and the parts contiguous to it. They are principally Jews. Their numbers have been a good deal increased during the past few years, but not to the extent which alarmists have reported, by refugees from Russia. These people live by trade and traffic of one kind or another, not by manual labor. They present a special difficulty to charity organization: they live in the midst of the native population without mixing with it, they speak and understand our language imperfectly. The result of these facts is that it is very hard to get to know much about their real condition and their real wants. Our best hope of success seems to lie in a closer co-operation with the two great societies already mentioned, which make them their special care and have better means of knowing and dealing with them.

It is time to draw this brief sketch to a close. It will be evident to those who have followed it that the Charity Organization Society has much as yet to do, and few men to do it with, in the vast field of East London. It cannot be said, at present, to have effectively occupied that field, but in every Union it has, at any rate, one active centre, from which its influence may radiate. Nor is that influence to be fairly judged by the number of cases in which co-operation has been established, or distress relieved, through its direct intervention. Its widest influence is that which is exercised on the minds and opinions of men, and there are not wanting signs that that influence is beginning to tell. A juster estimate is abroad of the problems and the responsibilities of charity. Bad ways of relief are more readily discredited than they were. The absolute need of inquiry before relief is becoming more widely recognized. Overlapping is admitted to be mischievous. The methods of the society are sometimes partially adopted even by those who profess no sympathy with it. The society is essentially a missionary and propagandist society, and in proportion as the principles which it preaches come to be accepted and acted on by others, whether they join its ranks or stand aloof, it may claim to be achieving success.

SHOREDITCH.

BY MR. C. N. NICHOLSON, POOR LAW GUARDIAN AND CHAIRMAN OF THE SHOREDITCH COMMITTEE, C. O. S.

The Union of which I am asked to write is that of Shoreditch, situated about twenty minutes walk north of the Bank of England. Its population is rather over 120,000 and almost the whole of them belong to the working classes, the remainder being small shopkeepers and a few factory owners, who of course reside outside the district. The principal trade carried on is the cabinet-maker's. In Curtain Road, Great Eastern Street and that part of Old Street that runs through the Union more than half the shops are furniture shops, wholesale and retail, the goods being made in the houses in the streets adjoining where the workmen live. A considerable part if not half of this furniture is thus made in the workmen's own home and not in the factory. The work is also very much split up, a chair, for instance, having to go through a large number of hands before it is turned out. There is also a considerable number of timber merchants in the district and many people are employed at the sawmills which supply the small workmen who make for the furniture dealers. The boot trade also employs a certain number, but very small in comparison with the furniture trade. There is also a zinc works and a white lead factory, and the inevitable box-making business which exists over a great part of London. The district is very fairly open and airy, the streets as a rule being wide and the number of courts and alleys small. The houses also are all low and the streets are consequently lighter than in many parts of London.

At the time at which I am writing, the cabinet trade and the boot trade are very much depressed, the warehouses being full of goods for which there are no purchasers, and consequently employment is slack to such an extent that the small workmen can frequently be seen in the streets trying to sell the goods which ought properly to go to the warehouses.

One would naturally think that this would increase the number of people who have to be supported by poor law relief, but somehow the numbers in the house are very little above the average while the out-relief has been coming down steadily through the year.

It will be perhaps right to explain at this point the rules for the giving of State relief in accordance with which the guardians of the poor of each Union are bound to act. In the first place no person is entitled to receive relief unless he can plead destitution. Now this particular term has never been defined and is probably incapable of definition. In practice its meaning is fairly well shown by a remark which I have heard a relieving officer make to his board of guardians, when asked by the chairman why he had given relief to a particular individual. He said, "The man told me he was destitute and I saw no signs of food in the house." It was evident therefore that the term is an elastic one and that probably a certain number of people get assistance who are not at all within measurable distance of starvation.

Dividing up these cases who are taken as destitute they are sorted into two classes, the able-bodied and the not able-bodied.

As to the able-bodied, out-relief is not allowed to be given unless there is sickness in the family; in all other cases the house must be offered. This exception of cases of sickness leads however to many difficulties. For instance, suppose a family consisting of a man and woman and three children to apply to the relieving office for assistance, the woman being ill and the man out of work. In such a case the medical officer will of course attend; but medicine is not much good without food, and therefore out-relief will be given—with the result that the pressure on the man to get back to his work is slackened and malingering, from which the friendly societies suffer so much, is encouraged. Of course if the woman had not been ill the house would have been offered in the first instance for the whole family.

As to the not able-bodied, who form the greater number of the applicants for relief in the Union of which I am writing, the position is very different. They can be given out-relief or can be offered the house.

Now if a board of guardians could be trusted to discriminate carefully between those people who would be likely to make a proper use of the money or food given in out-relief and those who would probably make a bad use of it, and offer only the house to the latter, no difficulty would arise. But this is precisely the point at which the arrangements break down.

In the Shoreditch Union the number of cases brought up before the ordinary weekly board varies, according to the time of year, between

250 and 350. These cases are disposed of at an average of rather over three to the minute. It is therefore evident that the guardians themselves cannot possibly be aware of the position or circumstances of the cases brought before them, and except in very glaring instances, or when a particular applicant is well known through his frequent appearance, they must rest entirely on the judgment of the relieving officer.

The position of this officer is by no means satisfactory, he is paid about £130 to £160 a year, and before he actually comes into contact with the poor he passes through no course of training in his duties but picks up his experience as he goes along. He has a heavy amount of responsibility thrust upon him. He naturally wishes to keep his list as small as possible, for the board then considers that he is doing his work well; but, on the other hand, if anything goes wrong with one of his cases, the whole blame is cast upon him; and how serious the consequences to him may be can be imagined from the fact that I have known the guardians express the wish to discharge an officer on the spot for an imagined breach of discipline, which further investigation showed had never occurred.

The length of a relieving officer's list depends a good deal on his power of sifting his cases quickly and accurately, but on the whole he is more likely to assist a doubtful case than to refuse.

As mentioned above the relieving officer when bringing his cases before the board can only recommend certain things. He can offer to take the applicant into the house or the infirmary, or if he wishes to treat the case outside, he can recommend the board to give the applicant so much a week either in money or in kind; or, if the applicant is in want of medical treatment, he can send the parish doctor to his house, or he can, in case of certain infectious diseases send him off to one of the rate-supported hospitals.

Now these powers enable him to deal with the immediate necessities of the moment, but in no way to prevent their recurrence. He may provide a family with sufficient food to drive away the spectre of starvation for twenty-four hours, but he can do no more.

The necessity of the existence of voluntary charitable institutions working side by side with the state institution for relief is therefore tolerably evident, as a good example of the powerlessness of state relief to put a man on his legs. I may give the following instance which occurred under my own observation. A. B. a painter by trade had a wife and three children. His wife died about two winters ago, and he was so seriously ill with bronchitis and rheumatism that having spent all he had put by, he was obliged to come into the poor law infirmary, and his children, having no home, were taken into the workhouse. When he recovered he was transferred to the workhouse from the infirmary, and there he is still. The Board very properly refused to let him go out, unless he took his three children with him.* and, as he had not got a penny and would not be paid until he had been out at work for a week, he had no choice but to stay where he was.

The case was brought to the notice of private charity a few days ago, and arrangements are being made for the man to go out to work, while he and his children will be supported for a week or ten days, until the man gets his first earnings.

This family has been living at the expense of the ratepayers of the Union for a year or fifteen months, and must have cost at least £60. The actual cost to the charity concerned will be about £2.10.0.

In a case of this nature owing to the necessarily narrow powers of State relief, the man might have remained in the house, a charge upon the ratepayers for the remainder of his life, or until his children had grown up and started work on their own account.

Another example of this and one which is frequently occurring is that of widows. A young woman marries and frequently gives up the work which she has been doing to attend to her new home. If she does not do this at once, the necessity is more or less forced upon her if she has children.

If then her husband dies without making sufficient provision for her and the children are young, there is nothing for her to do except to take State relief, and this relief can do nothing more than keep her and the children alive. On the other hand, voluntary charity can assist her to get back to her old work, or, if that is impossible, have her trained to some occupation which will render her self-supporting.

Now if a widow is once put upon the out-relief list, it is exceedingly difficult to have her name removed. She will get to depend upon it, and will not be likely to look out for work, or, if she does take work, she is, by the receipt of the relief, able to sell her labor at a price below that which would be paid to a woman not in receipt of relief. I have known of two women who applied for out-relief, stating at the time that, if it was granted, they would be able to take tailoring work at the

---

* This rule is very necessary, as if a man is allowed to go out on the plea of looking for work, he not infrequently deserts his family.

starvation wages at which it was offered. The disastrous results from following such a policy in lowering the rate of wages is sufficiently obvious.

I have known a case of a widow to be on the out-relief list for four years; and the relieving officer stated that at the end of that time she was no better off.

Again, the State is only able to provide such maintenance for blind and crippled people as will provide them with food, clothing and lodging; voluntary charity being unfettered, can go much further, and by careful training, can teach these unfortunate people certain trades which will not only enable them to earn at any rate something towards their own maintenance, but which will preserve them from the misery of enforced idleness in a workhouse.

Further examples of this nature can of course be easily given, but enough has been said to show that, while it is the duty of the State to see that none of its members starve, there is a still higher duty which is imposed on the individual and one which the State cannot fulfil, namely, as far as possible, to prevent any member of the State being degraded to this position of dependence.

Now I am quite aware that it will be suggested that the proper course to remedy these defects should be a reform of our present poor law, and that the boards of guardians should be instructed to exercise a greater amount of discrimination in treating the applicants for relief; and if this could be done, it would probably be the most satisfactory solution of the difficulty. But unfortunately the boards of guardians, at any rate in the poorer parts of London, are not composed of people who are likely to exercise this discrimination, even if they were able to do so. The Shoreditch board consists of eighteen members. Of these, last year, two were clergymen whose time was quite enough occupied with looking after their parishes. One was a large timber merchant, who was also a member of the London County Council, and rarely found time to attend the meetings. Four were retired men of business, and about the best members. The remaining ten were small shopkeepers, each engaged in business from which they drew incomes varying from £200 to £400 per annum. These men, too, though they attend with fair regularity, have quite enough to do to look after their own affairs. In these circumstances there is always a tendency to get through the business as fast as possible; and that part of the work which gets the greatest amount of attention is the contracting for supplies or building, the appointment of officers, and the correspondence with the Local Government Board, the central authority which superintends all the unions through the country. But the visitation of the workhouse and the infirmary is not to my mind satisfactorily done, and, considering that these two institutions shelter a daily average of over 1000 people, I do not think that it is right that this should be left, as much as it is, in the hands of subordinate officers.

The out-relief list, as I have stated above, is got through at the rate of three cases a minute. It should be added that the cases of old people who have been in receipt of relief for some years, are passed every two months simply on the word of the relieving officer. No questions are even asked about them. Can it then be wondered at that there are cases receiving assistance who do not deserve it, and also cases that are not being assisted in a proper way.

If then the powers of the Guardians were enlarged, the probability is that they would not be used advantageously, but that greater waste and greater pauperization would follow.

The ideal Board of Guardians while paying proper attention to the ordinary business of maintaining the institutions under its care, would use its best endeavors so to give relief that it would not pauperize, but give the deserving applicant the power to rise again to a position of independence, and at the same time force the undeserving to maintain himself. Unfortunately we are a long way off from this. The ratepayers of the poorer districts are far too apathetic; and consequently voluntary charity is the only agent that can rescue the deserving applicant from the mire of pauperism.

I pass now to charity and charity organization. The different methods in which is administered the charity of the churches whose parishes make up this union, show probably more clearly than anything else the enormous differences of opinion which exist on this important subject. The high churchman will not work closely with the low churchman, and both, though unwilling to admit the fact, would, as a rule, decline to recognize the dissenter or the Roman Catholic minister. The latter say, "we look after our own congregations;" the Church of England vicar says, "I have the care of all the poor in my parish." Hence, as these parishes cover the whole ground, overlapping abounds, and a poor person is sorely tempted to attend the church services of two or more denominations so as to qualify for the charity that is too readily given for purposes of propagandism. Women frequently attend the mothers' meetings of two churches so as to be able to draw on both sources of supply in case of need. Here is indeed an extraordinary state of affairs. All these bodies have at any rate one common bond, respect for Christ's teaching, all profess to recognize the charitable duties which He laid down, and yet they cannot agree to meet to discuss the best methods of dealing with the funds entrusted to them and are apparently careless how their administration may affect adjoining parishes. The injury that can and does occur through this want of co-operation and absence of definite rules in the giving of relief is considerable as the following instance will show.

There exists in London a society formed for the purpose of sending for a few weeks to the country certain sick and ailing children in the hope that fresh air and good exercise may improve their physical condition. One of the rules of this society is that the parents of any child sent away must contribute one-third of the cost, this representing the approximate cost of the child in its own home. Another society more or less opposed to this, but professedly working on the same lines, sends away the children in a particular parish in this union, but does not call upon the parents to contribute anything. The effect of this upon the adjoining parishes where the second society does not work is that the parents decline to contribute the one-third demanded by the first society, and the children who would be benefitted are in danger of being left alone. Now quite apart from the question whether the rule is right or wrong, is it not absurd on the face of it that these parishes cannot meet and agree upon some *modus vivendi* which will enable them to work in harmony?

The first thing that is necessary, if we are ever to get to a solution of the question, what to do with the poor of our great cities, is to sink all these differences of opinion. Each vicar, Roman Catholic priest and dissenting minister should consent to carry out loyally such a system of relief as is agreed to by all. And it should be recognized that the grant or refusal of charitable relief ought not to depend upon the question whether the applicant has or has not attended so many services—is or is not a member of a particular congregation, but upon the question whether he can be assisted in such a manner as will be of permanent benefit to himself and to the community.

Will this idea ever be realized? It must be confessed that at present the signs are not hopeful. So long as the clergy are content to leave the relief of the poor of their parish in the hands of sisterhoods or like institutions, careless whether the assistance given is suitable to the particular case, or whether it is likely to be of any benefit at all; so long as by their express or tacit sanction they allow children, who ought to be maintained by the parents who brought them into the world, to be fed and clothed by charitable societies so long as they are willing to prevent an individual from experiencing the punishment of his own folly and wickedness—so long shall we have distress and pauperization.

The above remarks apply though in a slighter degree, for the responsibility is less, to each individual. He, too, is bound to take care that what he gives in charity is given wisely, for he may feel sure that to deprive a man of the wholesome feeling that he is under a necessity to maintain himself, is the most certain way of making him a permanent pauper. But, subject to this, the sphere of the charity of an individual is bounded only by his own powers. He can place his sympathy and experience at the disposal of all those who are in trouble, and a kind thought or a gentle word is often worth more than so much weight of gold and silver.

The troubles of the deserving poor arise more from ignorance than anything else. How is the workingman to know which is the best market for his labor? The rich man when he invests his capital has various schemes placed before him, and chooses among them those which are most likely to bring him a safe return. No such opportunity is open to his poorer brother. How is the poor woman nursing her sick child at home to know what is the right treatment to adopt? How is a workingman to know which is the safest friendly society for him to join? Here is a field where individual beneficence can exercise itself to the full, and with the certainty that the work is useful and that it is helping others to help themselves. How simple it all seems and yet how difficult it is to do.

But this is by no means all that the individual can do. There is a common idea, which seems to exist among almost all classes of society, that they have only to pay their poor rate, and to subscribe to voluntary charities, and that these institutions will then work themselves. I believe that if the funds contributed for charitable institutions were doubled and the existing management continued, so far from relieving distress and bringing us all to a happy Arcadia, the result would be infinitely worse. A fairly good instance of this is, the use that is made of what are called endowed charities in certain parts of London. The management of these is allowed to remain in the hands of the local tradespeople and of the vicar of the parish, and very often they are given in very small sums to a large number of people, totally regardless of what the recipients may really need, or of what would be the best way of helping them out of their trouble. It never seems to occur to the managers, that it is infinitely better to raise one person to a position of independence than to keep ninety and nine in a state of idleness, in expectation of a shilling or two to tide them over the next week. Here then is another piece of work for the individual who will seriously interest himself in the welfare of the poor. Let him serve as a charity trustee, with the resolve that he will not attempt to do anything for a case, unless he can see his way to benefit it permanently, and that at all hazards he will refuse to let the money be squandered where no lasting good can be produced.

A striking instance of the neglect of these principles came under my notice a week or two ago. What is known as a "midwifery letter" was given to a certain woman, and by her passed on to the wife of the vicar of the parish whose duty it was to "cash" it. The vicar's wife called and found a large family living in one room without a particle of furniture. The woman had recently been confined, and her rags and her husband's coat were her only covering. Both husband and wife were known to be habitual drunkards. To give them money was absolutely useless, for it would have gone at once to the public house; to give them clothing was just as bad, for it would only have been pawned for drink. The nurse employed by the vicar attended the case and kept the room as clean as she could, and had the other children looked after. But have these people been taught in any way that they must suffer for their own neglect, and that if they choose to spend their earnings in drink, they must accept the degradation and restraint imposed by poor law relief? Surely not. But in reply it will be said, what is the remedy? The answer is, that if people wish to see their money do good and not harm, they must study the problems of poverty, and if they cannot afford the time for visiting the poor themselves, at any rate they can take the trouble to see that those in whose hands they place their money do make a proper use of it. For those who can give the time, the organization of charity is a most important duty. Here in London the income of our charities amounts to about £4,000,000 a year, exclusive of what is collected at the ordinary church offertories or given away in the streets. From the latter source I have known a beggar to state, that he could make 30 shillings a week. Our charitable income then is enough and more than enough. Our business is to see that it is not wasted, but properly applied.

To prevent waste every one can do something. As a ratepayer he can take care that only those are elected to serve as Guardians of the poor, who will administer the poor rate so that the old and feeble may be properly maintained, and that the able-bodied may be encouraged and forced, if need be, to maintain themselves. As an administrator of charitable funds he can assist in those cases where the Poor Law can do nothing, always bearing in mind this main purpose—the restitution of independence.

ST. OLAVE'S.

BY C. P. LARNER, DISTRICT SECRETARY TO THE ST. OLAVE'S COMMITTEE, C. O. S.

On the south side of the Thames, opposite the Tower, lie the parishes of Bermondsey and Rotherhithe, which, with three smaller parishes near London Bridge, comprise the poor law union of St. Olave. The whole district stretches from the Borough on the west, to Deptford on the east, the semi-suburban parish of Camberwell constituting, roughly speaking, its southern boundary. With a population in 1891 of 136,000, St. Olave's offers many features of interest, and also of difficulty, in discussing the question of social reform. Like many other metropolitan districts, it has changed much during the last fifty years, both in the character of its population and in their manner of living. Bermondsey was one of the centres of the leather trade; Rotherhithe partook of the nature of a port outside the metropolitan boundary; South Bermondsey, as it now is, was left to the tiller of allotments, and to the market gardener. Now a great part of the leather trade has gone either to the North of England or to America, and one would have to walk a long time about Rotherhithe before meeting a sea-captain. Employers of labor generally, with the exception of shopkeepers, live away from the district; the educated classes are represented by clergymen and doctors; the people themselves belong to the working classes, with a sprinkling of clerks and board school teachers. In fact its proximity to the city has made the district almost a residential one for the weekly-paid wage earner, who finds that ten minutes spent on the railway at an expenditure of 1½d. takes him from his home in Bermondsey to the heart of the city.

In a community of this kind relief whether private, endowed, or from the State, has ample opportunities for good or for evil; it is to be feared that the latter influence has not been altogether absent. For if the demand is great the supply is no less so. First in the district in the ranks of public assistance stand the medical charities, and at the head of these is the famous Guy's Hospital. Established by the old city bookseller in 1725, it has undergone numerous alterations and has been greatly enlarged, so that now it has accomodations for 695 inpatients. The out-patients are counted by the ten thousand. That it is a great boon to the poor of south-east London cannot be doubted; that it is a great and permanent block to the development of provident dispensaries is equally certain. Attached to the hospital is a lying-in charity limited to the district situated within a mile of Guy's. Two other medical charities exist—the Surrey Dispensary founded in 1777, with its 14,000 patients in 1892, and the Lady Gomm Hospital in Rotherhithe. The latter is a small foundation. In addition to these there is a District Nursing Association maintained by annual subscriptions, and the district, as a working class one, shares largely in such metropolitan institutions as the Hospital Saturday and Sunday Funds, and the Surgical Aid Society, the latter with their highly objectionable many letter system. The chief endowed charities are found in the old parishes of St. Olave and St. John, near to London Bridge. Up to quite recently these charities presented many of the abuses so often associated with ancient foundations. With an income of over £10,000 a year, there was ample room for unwise and extravagant expenditure. About two-thirds of this sum went for the support of a free grammar school for boys and a similar school for girls. The remainder was spent in pensions to persons, some over fifty and some over sixty, in apprenticeship fees, in training poor girls as servants, in bread, and in temporary relief to residents. The trustees were chosen from the principal inhabitants of the two parishes, or from gentlemen carrying on business there, and it will readily be seen that with an elastic fund for such delightfully vague purposes as temporary relief, a trustee's position carried with it many opportunities for jobbery and corrupt patronage. Individually the trustees could give help in the form of tickets and bring the case forward for money grants at the monthly board meetings, where it would be pretty sure to receive help. Under these conditions to have lived for a number of years in these parishes was no small advantage to a poor person, while to have been born there was pretty sure to meet with substantial recognition. A very simple instance of the sense of injustice which may be produced in the minds of the poor by a careless though well-meaning administering of charitable funds may be seen in the action of the trustees with respect to country holidays for school children.

There is in London a society called the Children's Country Holiday Fund, which collects subscriptions for the purpose of helping poor children to have a fortnight's stay in the country. The society has local committees distributed through the metropolis, which work through the elementary schools in their respective districts. The parents contribute according to their means, and the average sum paid by them is between 3s. 6d. and 4s. for the two week's stay. But in the parishes of St. Olave and St. John, the trustees have been in the habit of taking children for the sum of one shilling, and it is a difficult thing for the poor people of Bermondsey proper to understand why they should be called upon to pay 4s. for their children when their neighbors on the other side of the street, and possibly in a better position, pay only a quarter of the amount.

Attached to both Bermondsey and Rotherhithe are a number of old-fashioned parochial charities for the supply of food and clothing to poor folk. They are, almost without exception, in the gift of the rectors, church wardens and overseers, and the suggestion that regularity in attending the parish church may bring about material gain is more direct than pleasing. Rotherhithe has two pension funds, dealing with about fifty pensioners. One, the Gomm Charity, provides pensions of £10 each to fifteen old men and women. The other, the Bayly Charity, grants £5 a year to thirty-four widows, aged fifty and upwards, and not receiving parish relief. This sum is obviously absurdly inadequate, and one of two results follows: either it serves as a nucleus to which other sums will be attracted, thus enabling the recipient to live—and assuming that proper discretion is used, to this there is no objection; or it is given to widows who are able to work, and becomes merely a grant in aid of wages and is little removed in this respect from ordinary out-relief. And this is exactly what very often occurs, for it is well known that the ordinary working woman does not stop work at fifty; she goes on with her employment to sixty-five or seventy, sometimes later, and the £5 thus enable her to live on a correspondingly smaller amount of wages than her less fortunate neighbor. Beside these fixed charities, there are attached to all the churches and chapels in the district various funds for the relief of the sick and the poor. Those belonging to the established church are helped largely by the Metropolitan District Visiting Association, and are used for parish purposes generally; those belonging to the non-conformist places of worship are more commonly confined to members of the respective denominations. There is a goodly number of friendly societies in the locality, the Odd Fellows and Foresters being the most numerous. Some of the lodges and courts have supplementary funds attached to them, formed by extra voluntary subscriptions of the members, for the purpose of paying the regular subscriptions of such members as, through lack of work or some other exceptional reason, cannot keep up their dues. Several of the trade societies have sick funds attached to them, but this is not usual, and does not of course in any way affect the riverside and unskilled laborers who form so large a proportion of the population. In winters of exceptional severity there is the usual tendency to form relief funds, but the unsatisfactory nature of working them has become more apparent each time they have been formed.

From what has been said it will be inferred that the St. Olave's Union is more generously supplied than many with the means of assisting and permanently benefiting such of its population as may be in need of help. And when added to these sources of relief, there is the charity organization committee prepared to deal with any applications which may come from the district, one might not unreasonably suppose that the work of the poor law authorities would lie in a very restricted province. Unfortunately this is not the case. St. Olave's has the reputation, and a very just reputation, of being one of the worst administered unions in the country. Out-relief is rampant and has for the last few years been on the increase. The results are the usual ones, demoralization of the poor and high rates. The latter is an important point, but not to be compared with the former. It is positively painful to be continually coming across apparently decent respectable people, who have lost their self-respect and seem to have no sense of degradation in becoming paupers. A visitor at the parish offices is told by an official when discussing the increase in the number of applicants, that "lots come up on the chance of getting something." The vice-chairman of the Board of Guardians expresses surprise that the numbers of in-paupers should have gone up when they are giving more out-relief, as if the two were not bound up together. Similar instances of demoralization and ignorance might be added galore. Financially the result is to send the rates up in Bermondsey to 7s. 6d. in the pound, and this has had the effect of at any rate making people think about what they are doing, and the recent elections show a tendency towards improvement. This condition of things has been aggravated greatly by the elections being fought on political lines. The two parties have issued their tickets and their programmes. The candidates have been chosen, not because they were likely to be wise administrators, but because they were staunch Radicals or good Tories. The union has accordingly been in the hands of men who could do almost anything except administer the Poor Law. With a wise poor law policy there would be difficulties enough; with a policy that scarcely deserves the name, the situation is much more serious. It is impossible to have an intimate knowledge of the district without a profound feeling that at the bottom of every charitable effort must lie a reform of the public administration. When this is effected, and not before, those responsible for the dispensing of charitable funds, both private and public, may feel that there is some hope of their work producing results not altogether out of proportion to their efforts.

CHARITY ORGANIZATION IN ISLINGTON.

BY MISS L. SHARPE, HONORARY SECRETARY TO THE ISLINGTON COMMITTEE, C. O. S.

No present stands without its foundation in the past, and the future, as has been aptly said, "does not come from before to meet us, but comes streaming up from behind over our heads;" so no statement of charity organization in Islington can be complete, without some consideration of the local history and the special characteristics of the district in which the society here works.

Islington seems to have been distinguished from very early days for its piety and its pastimes. On the one hand we have the records in old times of numerous monastic and ecclesiastical foundations, while in later days the parish has been a remarkable stronghold for Evangelical Protestantism in church and dissent, and on the other hand the citizens of London seem to have looked on Islington from time immemorial as a place for pleasuring and entertainment. While Goldsmith selects Islington as the abode of the man who ran "a godly race," John Gilpin's "merrie Islington" is equally characteristic.

The pious founders of the many parochial charities of Islington, in the same way bear in mind in their bequests the spiritual and material interests of the parish. There are many endowments for the saying of masses, the distribution of Bibles and prayer books, the preaching of sermons and the catechising of children, side by side with perpetual gifts of coal and bread and clothing to the poor, legacies for the maintenance of the testator's tomb and, in one case, for an annual dinner to the trustees.

It would seem as if the mantle of their predecessors had in some degree fallen on the shoulders of the present inhabitants, for never was there a district where flourished so many concerts and dramatic entertainments for charitable objects, so many bazaars and sales of work for churches, chapels and missions. We have heard of the Shetland Islanders who "earned a scanty living by taking in one another's washing," and it appears as if charities in Islington maintained their existence by the mutual exchange of fancy needle work and the musical and dramatic talents of the charitable.

Another notable feature in the history of Islington is its recent extraordinary growth of population. In the 17th century Cowley speaks of "a village fair as Islington," "a solitude almost." In 1793, the population was estimated at 6,600. The census of 1801, gave it as 10,212, and the census of 1891, as 319,433. During the last 50 years it has increased at the rate of 5,000 per annum, though the increase has been less in the last decade than in the two preceding ones. The little rural village once stood in the midst of its 3,000 acres of fields and farmland. The 3,000 acres still remain one ecclesiastical parish and one union as far as Vestry and Guardians are concerned, but the fields and gardens and lanes have given place to streets of houses and blocks of industrial dwellings; the mother church is supported by forty district churches, while one Vestry and Board of Guardians are still responsible for its local government. The parish is in some respects like an overgrown family, where the children have increased out of all proportion to the strength and resources of parental government. We have in the centre the parochial traditions and institutions of a small village linked with the huge proportions and all the indifference to local interests of one of the largest of metropolitan suburbs.

This sudden rapid growth may account in part, for an incapacity to keep pace with the times, in some directions. It is typical of the mind of Islington that it has steadily resisted a free public library, though canvassed for it several times. The administration of the Poor Law, which is so intimately connected with charity organization work, is distinguished in Islington by a lax system of outdoor relief. The pauperism, especially the outdoor pauperism, shows of late years a steady increase. Although the population made far greater strides between 1871 and 1881, than between 1881 and 1891, the increase of pauperism has been more than twice as great in the latter decade. The official records for the half years ending Lady-day and Michaelmas, 1892, show 19,127 and 17,440 paupers relieved in the respective half years in Islington and of these numbers more than half received outdoor relief. Between £15,000 and £16,000 per annum is being spent on money and food given to the poor at their homes. Those who have any experience of the matter know the degradation of the poor of the district which this state of things represents. The impossibility of discriminating between good and bad applicants—since destitution is the only claim for assistance—makes poor law relief without the workhouse check a constant encouragement to idleness and want of thrift; and the Charity Organization Society whose aim is the increase of thrift and independence, and the elevation of moral character among the poor, has up-hill work in such a district. Not only the poor themselves, but their charitable helpers are entirely confused as to when there is "a right to relief," and the energy of self-helpfulness and mutual helpfulness is gradually sapped.

There has been no systematic co-operation between the Board of Guardians and the Islington Charity Organization Committee in Islington, as in many other districts, but a better feeling of understanding has been slowly growing and it is hoped that in time an established plan of mutual assistance may result.

The Charity Organization Committee like other agencies in Islington suffers from too large a constituency, and while attempting to bring itself into touch with very many people and to bring them into touch with each other, is in danger of having no thorough co-operation with any. The Society has been at work in the district some twenty-one years, at first taking the whole parish. But about ten years ago the Committee wisely determined it was useless to try to cover 3000 acres, and deal with a population of 300,000, and they cut off from their operations about half the area of the parish. It is a melancholy fact, indicative of the want of appreciation of the charity organization idea, that in these ten years no serious attempt has been made by charitable workers or the inhabitants of the district cut adrift, to establish any committee of organization and many of its streets remain the happy hunting ground of beggars and impostors, while churches and institutions for assisting the people rapidly increase.

Spite of many drawbacks charity organization in southern Islington has made slow but sure progress. The first records of cases dealt with by this committee in 1871 are curious and interesting as showing how methods and aims have changed since then. At the second committee meeting a man was apparently given into custody of the police at the office for persisting in false statements and thus attempting to obtain money on false pretences. This experiment of repressing mendicity does not appear to have been repeated, although in the first 21 months 103 prosecutions for begging were undertaken. A very large number of false addresses and otherwise "undeserving" cases shows that the system of thorough inquiry had hardly yet been realized by the impostors and the unworthy who now to a great extent avoid charity organization offices or "object to inquiry" when they come, thus reducing the proportion of unhelpable cases dismissed by committee. Let us hope also that growing experience and increased resources have developed better means and methods of helping.

The original Islington Committee set out, like the rest of the Society, with the idea of repressing mendicity and inquiring into and reporting on cases of distress for charitable people and agencies. And it is very probable that bad or doubtful cases were most often sent to them. Now it is notable that the clergy of Islington send cases almost exclusively with a view to assistance and hardly ever for information as to character.

In the first three months of the committee's existence it appears that out of about 200 cases, 82 were not recommended for help, 90 were recommended and referred to private individuals and charitable agencies, though whether they were assisted is not shown. 5 received hospital and convalescent letters and 1 remarkable person a grant of money. About 30 tramps were given bread to eat at the office, and it is not wonderful that a number of homeless people continued to apply for this privilege until the system was modified and the number of people with "no home" rapidly diminished.

It was really not consistent with the human nature of committees to continue this plan of inquiry and reporting only, and it was soon given up, and grants and loans of money and other gifts through the committee increased and "adequate relief" became the watchword.

But record books show little of the good work that may be done by committees and their allies, and it would be unfair even to judge them by their annual reports, though these, with occasional waves of depression, show in Islington an advancing tide of life and zeal, with higher and wider aspirations and greater courage in attempting their realization.

The present Islington Committee has the advantage of being composed entirely of local members, people who live in the district and care for the district they live in, and who are all, moreover, earnest workers and assist beyond the committee meetings in carrying out the work of the society. Linked with them is an always increasing number of local workers, who give valuable aid in various ways by visiting and talking with applicants, collecting loans and savings, befriending sick and old people, assisting in spreading the Society's views, and in the necessary business routine of the office. Each one does far more for charity organization in its widest sense than the special piece of work they take up. For once introduced to the ideal of a higher charity and trained, however unconsciously and inadequately, in some of its methods, there is no going back to a lower standard, and the influence of each person so initiated must surely spread in time to a wider circle, and must make itself felt in whatever sphere of work they choose. Some of our allied workers have formed a band of visitors to collect the savings of the poor, others have taken up rent collecting and the superintendence of neglected blocks of buildings on Miss Octavia Hill's plan; others are superintending a library, and some are visiting for the Children's Country Holiday Fund, or the Society for Befriending Young Servants; while others again have been called to posts of responsibility in other parts of London, and in religious or social work are putting into practice, we hope and believe, the lessons learnt with our committee. As a proof nearer home that the idea of thorough help hand in hand with the promotion of thrift and character is spreading, we note that one clergyman at least has abolished the ticket dole system, and established a committee for inquiry and consideration of cases in his own district. Another is substituting substantial help in the way of convalescent aid for smaller gifts, and two or three are encouraging "provident visiting" for collecting savings, a plan almost incompatible with dole giving.

But such influence and results are slow to show themselves, and the committee's work is still far too isolated from the rest of the community.

All charitable work in Islington centres round some church or chapel or religious movement, and while this brings into the field many earnest workers, their point of view in dealing with poor people in need remains still very different from that of the Charity Organization Society. Religious instruction, combined with intermittent attempts to *alleviate* suffering and distress, the weekly visit, the weekly ticket, the Bible reading and invitation to church or chapel or prayer meeting, these are the methods most in vogue; while soup kitchens, free breakfasts, halfpenny dinners, and wholesale Christmas beef and plum pudding distributions are largely supported by the richest inhabitants, and administered from churches and chapels, with little or no co-operation between the various agencies, rather it would seem a rivalry as to which can attract the most applicants for relief, and the largest potential numbers of attendants at their services.

The great problem of charity organization in Islington is how are we to bring these good people into sympathy with each other and with ourselves, and how are we to persuade them to act on those convictions which thoughtful experience must bring home to all minds. All will be ready to admit that character is the basis of any real improvement, moral or spiritual, that truthfulness of word, deed and thought can be the only real foundation of religion, and that small, irregular gifts without inquiry of circumstances or knowledge of other givers lead to concealment, hypocrisy and untruthfulness; but few are ready to take the trouble and the time which action consistent with this belief entails. All will agree with Emerson's words: "It is a low benefit to give me anything, it is a high benefit to enable me to do something for myself;" but how are we to set to work in combination—for in selfish isolation we can do nothing—to help to enable the poorer inhabitants of Islington to do better things for themselves? What is the most effective way to work for character? That should be the question before all religious and charitable workers, and pity it is that all cannot combine thought and wisdom, heart and head to answer it.

There is another large section of the population that charity organization has practically left untouched in Islington, but which must be captured before any real progress has been made. The parish has the advantage of being, for the most part, neither very rich nor very poor. On Mr. Booth's map of London, Islington shows but few golden, or wealthy spots, and very few blue and black resorts of criminals and the lowest class. Shades of pink and red prevail and the best houses are often quite near to the poorest.

The majority of the population is composed of respectable artizans, railway servants, warehousemen and clerks, who hate the very name of charity in connection with themselves or their families, but believe in charitable gifts and outdoor relief for those poorer than themselves, and object to the Charity Organization Society, if they know anything about it, because they have heard that it protests against this kind of relief. From their ranks come the men and women who are active in political associations, who are leaders at dissenting chapels and among trades unions, benefit clubs and co-operative societies, and many of whom are beginning to take part in local government. Their experience of hard work, industry and economy ought to be most helpful to charity organizers in keeping before their eyes the healthy side of working class life, in contradistinction to the diseased and decrepit aspects which are brought most often to the front.

The power of these people in lifting "the next below" them ought to be immeasurably greater than that of those who have to come down a step or two to reach the position of the unfortunate; their influence in social and political movements is undoubtedly great. For all these reasons we ought to be in sympathy with them, to be learning from them and at work with them. But so far the Islington Charity Organization Committee know almost nothing of these neighbors and it is to be feared that what they know. or fancy they know of us they dislike.

Such are some of the problems of charity organization with the local color of Islington. The aims and ideals which we share in common with the whole society will be better dealt with elsewhere and need not be diminished in brightness and force by the prentice hand of the local artist.

Briefly stated here is the Islington position with the problems and work that lie before the Charity Organization Committee:

Granted, that we have made some progress in twenty-one years and that many who formerly turned their back on us and spoke evil of us, now look on us with friendliness and occasionally lend us a helping hand;

Granted, that we have extended our power of usefulness and have brought up the level of our "case work," so that we have gained a character for thorough help;

Granted, that we have trained to a certain extent a number of workers whose influence spreads abroad;

How are we to bring about a better administration of the Poor Law which is so absolutely essential to the improvement of the district?

How are we to subdivide our district so as to get to know the charitable workers and persuade them to *act* on the principles they will often admit in argument to be right?

How are we to learn to understand the upper working class and how bring them to know the truths we are striving for, so as to have their sympathy and influence with us in social reform?

For all these things we need evangelists, united by a common enthusiasm for the gospel of charity, patient with its slow progress and its humble details, strong with the "undying hope" which is "the secret of vision."

CO-OPERATION OF CHARITABLE AGENCIES WITH THE POOR LAW, WITH SPECIAL REFERENCE TO ST. GEORGE IN THE EAST.

BY T. MACKAY, HONORARY SECRETARY TO THE ST. GEORGE IN THE EAST COMMITTEE, C. O. S.

All agencies for the relief of the poor should have two objects in view : (1) The relief of distress ; (2) The removal of the causes of distress. It is sometimes said that the Charity Organization Society concerns itself too exclusively with the prevention of pauperism, and that it is indifferent to the cause of abundant and adequate relief. On this criticism I will only remark that the bitterest element in the distress of the poor arises, not from mere poverty, but from the feeling of dependence which must of necessity be an ingredient in every measure of public relief. This feeling cannot be removed, but is rather intensified by liberal measures of public relief. This fact might in itself be justification for those who would say, "The object of our efforts is not only the relief of the poor, but their independence." There is a section of the well-to-do classes of society who, unfortunately, limit their conception of their duty to their poorer neighbors to relief, and plenty of it, from legal or from voluntary sources. It is in their view the ransom due from those who are well-to-do in this world's goods. There is a section also among the poorer classes who have a vague feeling of some injustice which depresses them. It is foreign to the purpose of this paper to discuss how far this feeling of resentment is justified. It is mentioned only to remark that this feeling sometimes makes itself felt by demands on the Poor Law for forms of relief which have been already tried and condemned in the experience of the past. It is worth notice that such demands, as a rule, take the form of "work," not "charity," and that among the poor themselves little or no support has been given to a mere policy of extensive relief, such as making the old age maintenance of the community a charge on the rates. What the poor want, they say, is better wages and better conditions of life. Controversy, of course, rages as to what is the best course for the poor to follow in this quest. The Society, unpopular though it may be with the working class, can yet distinctly claim to have them on its side in this matter.

Its business is to insist, in the hearing of all men, that independence is a nobler ideal than any form of dependence, however adequately and abundantly relieved.

As a further justification of the practical wisdom of its attitude in aiming at the independence, as well as the relief of the poor, it may point to the fact that during the fifteen years covered by the last report of the Statistical Abstract, 1877–91, the invested savings of the working class have risen from 111 millions to 220 millions.* Here is a new creation of wealth, not arising out of the confiscation of other men's

---

* This assertion is based on the following calculation from the Statistical Abstract, 39th number, and other available sources, as to the more obvious institutions where working class savings are deposited:—

Present Time, say 1891.

*Post-office Savings Bank, 1891	£71,608,000	
*Trustee Savings Bank, 1891	42,875,000	
*Government stock standing in name of depositors at Post-office, 1891	5,087,000	
*Government stock standing in name of depositors at Trustee Banks, 1891	1,282,000	
		£120,832,000
*Building Societies, 1890		52,482,000
*Industrial and Provident (Co-operative) Societies, 1890		15,621,000
*Industrial Insurance Companies, 1890	8,873,000	
†Friendly Societies	20,167,000	
‡Collecting Friendly Societies, 1889	2,565,000	
		31,605,000
		£220,180,000

Fifteen Years ago, say 1877.

*Post-office Savings Bank, 1877	£28,740,000	
*Trustee Savings Bank, 1877	44,238,000	
*Government stock standing in name of depositors at Post-office, 1881, (no earlier figures given)	738,000	
*Government stock standing in name of depositors at Trustee Banks, 1881, (no earlier dates given)	124,000	
		£73,840,000
*Building Societies, 1876		20,854,000
*Industrial and Provident (Co-operative) Societies, 1876		6,224,000
*Industrial Insurance Companies, 1880, (no earlier figures given)		1,476,000
†Friendly Societies, 1876, (as estimated by Mr. Ludlow, "Chief Registrar's Report," 1890, Part A, p. 9,)		9,336,000
		£111,730,000

*Statistical Abstract, 1877 to 1891, 39th number.
†Rev. T. Frome Wilkinson, "Mutual Thrift." Estimated, p. 101.
‡Rev. T. Frome Wilkinson, "Mutual Thrift," p. 104.

goods, but owned and acquired in accordance with the laws of our country and the principles of private property. Surely a process is here disclosed from which we can justly hope for the spread of the blessing of independence among our laboring class. Contrast this with the vague hopes held out that some species of common property will yet be devised which will make the acquisition of private property by the poor an unnecessary thing. I will not carry this controversy into other fields, but in the province which it has made its own the Society protests against the futile assumption that the progress of the poor can be advanced by inducing them to rely on the common property which can be derived from the voluntary benefactions of the rich, or from the enforced contributions of the taxpayer.

The Society has, however, taken up no doctrinaire position; its subject-matter is the charitable effort of the community at large, and if it can be shown that there is no adequate provision made for a certain class, the Society, as in the recent report on the condition of the feeble-minded and epileptic, is ready to advocate an extension of charitable effort. In the case cited a certain form of co-operation between the Poor Law and voluntary effort is recommended. It is suggested that charitable agencies shall establish and manage the necessary institutions for these unfortunates, and that the Guardians shall be permitted to send patients there and pay for them out of the rates. Under certain restrictions this form of co-operation already exists, but I think I am right in saying, that in every instance the persons in whose favor this exceptional provision is made are, so to speak, marked out and separated from the rest of the community automatically by what in another connection is spoken of as the "act of God or the malice of the Queen's enemies."

By reason of this condition, it is obvious that we get rid of some very familiar difficulties in poor law administration; the capricious discrimination of Guardians and the rankling feeling of injustice to which it gives rise; and, secondly, that deterioration of character which results when the poor are tempted, as they are by outdoor relief, to qualify themselves for pauperism by presenting themselves in a real or feigned condition of destitution. It is the absence of these dangers that warrants our committee in urging that from one source or another ample provision should be made for this class.

Let us go a step further, and use this principle as a dividing line between two classes of pauperism:—

(1) Those who become paupers by fulfilling or accepting an automatic test. (*a*) Those afflicted by some congenital disabling disease, *e. g.* epilepsy, deficient intellect; (*b*) those who accept in some shape or another the workhouse test.

(2) Those who are selected arbitrarily by Guardians for outdoor relief, and who in many cases (it is impossible to say how many) have been brought to their present condition by the attraction of a maintenance to be obtained without effort.

With regard to the first class of paupers—those determined by an automatic test—there is a very large field for the work of charitable volunteers. As recommended, charitable bodies may establish and manage institutions to which paupers may be sent. Volunteers may with great advantage visit the poor law institutions, schools, infirmaries, workhouses; may organize employment for the old and infirm on the lines of the Brabazon experiment; may take steps to help inmates of the workhouse to make a new start in life; may by judicious interposition save young people from lives of pauperism; and do a variety of kindly actions which it is impossible to enumerate.

Here the Poor Law and charitable agencies combine to assist the same person, and for the sake of clearness, I will term this form of action *co-operation proper*.

A totally different account, and a totally different recommendation, is to be given in regard to the second class of paupers.

Those who have paid most attention to the question condemn the state of the law which permits a man to receive from the rates an addition to his income to be used in exactly the same way as a similar sum derived from wages or savings, on the sole condition that he can succeed in persuading Guardians that he is destitute. It has been shown over and over again that relief given under these conditions is rarely adequate and is always demoralizing.

Those, therefore, who wish well to the poor are anxious to reduce the evil results of the present law to the smallest dimensions. Their recommendation is simple. They say to Guardians, cease to give this demoralizing form of relief, and allow such relief as may be required by people at their own homes to be administered by voluntary agencies.

By this division of labor there will result, they argue, a great diminution in the burden borne by the Poor Law, and a great diminution also in the burden borne by charitable institutions, for a third agency will be called into existence, viz: the successful effort of the poor themselves.

If these expectations are realized, if by this policy sickness, old age, premature death, and the ordinary risks of life are more and more provided against by the provident associations of the poor, it is obvious that the demand both on compulsory and voluntary funds will be a diminishing quantity.

For this reason there is a disposition to argue by those who hold this view that we should not commit ourselves irrevocably to the proposition that the feeble-minded and the imbecile should be relegated to the care of the law and made a burden on ratepayers; for it is maintained that in the future—in the not very distant future, let us hope—the ordinary risks of life will be so fully provided for by the thrift associations of the poor that the contributions of the charitable will be set free for extraordinary occasions of distress such as arise from epilepsy and deficient intellect.

This condition of affairs has not arrived. It is my task to show that this prospect of reformation is not Utopian. I will endeavor to do this by a brief reference to the past and present history of the subject. And at the outset let me insist on one point which I believe to be *the governing truth* in all this controversy. Reformation will not come from any gerrymandering of the Poor Law or charitable funds, but from the development of the poor man's capacity for a life of independence. All our administration of legal and voluntary relief should be made subservient to this idea, provided always that adequate relief is not thereby withheld.

The most serious crisis of poor law administration which this country has ever experienced was that previous to the Poor Law Amendment Act of 1834. The idea that an able-bodied working man could support himself and his family was regarded as chimerical. Every man received an allowance from the rates in proportion to the number of his children, and the employer obtained his services at a nominal wage. The single man or the man without a family was not employed, because the farmer or manufacturer had to pay his wages in full. The poorer classes of the country lived in a state of discontent and open rebellion; land went out of cultivation because its produce was not sufficient to pay the rate. The country was brought to the verge of ruin. The Poor Law Commissioners inquired and reported on this state of affairs. Now what was their recommendation? It was simple enough. Stop, they said, all outdoor relief to the able-bodied. Throw the poor man absolutely on his own resources, and do not fear for the result. Their advice was carried into legislation, and, as all now admit, with the happiest results. It is hardly an exaggeration to say that we have got rid of the able-bodied pauper—or to be more correct, and the distinction is important, we have got rid of those economic conditions which condemned the able-bodied man of that day to pauperism and dependence. Poor law reform does not war against the person of the pauper, but against the economic conditions which arise when the poor are encouraged to look to rates rather than to wages and savings for their maintenance, and against the formation of the parasitic habits of dependence, the necessary correlatives to this economic condition.

But to return. We have got rid of able-bodied pauperism, but we are still struggling with a pauperism that is not able-bodied.

Let us review the situation briefly. Throughout a great part of the country, more especially in the rural districts, there is still a perfectly unbroken tradition of pauperism handed on from generation to generation. It is assumed that the laborer must become a pauper in his old age, in his time of temporary sickness; that his widow and children must at his death become pensioners on the rates.

Is it possible for us, without inflicting undue hardship, to break this tradition? And if so, how is it to be done? Time does not permit me to elaborate all the detail of the argument. I will state, however, in baldest outline the policy which I think has now become an integral part of the theory of those who support the Charity Organization Society.

In the first place, we rely with absolute confidence on the precedent of the abolition of able-bodied pauperism. The only way in which the legislator or the administrator can promote the reduction of pauperism is by abolishing or restricting the legal endowments provided for pauperism. The country can have, there is no doubt of it, exactly as many paupers as it chooses to pay for. Abolish or restrict that endowment, or the more acceptable form of that endowment—I mean, of course, outdoor relief—and new agencies are called into activity, man's natural capacity for independence, the natural ties of relationship and friendship; and under this head I would include private as distinguished from public charity, for private charity in any real sense of the word is not a virtue practised toward a stranger, but arises out of the natural affection of neighbors, and proceeds on the Gospel rule of seventy times seven rather than on any pedantic weighing of merit and demerit. By the action of these forces pauperism, so to speak, evaporates.

I insist on this aspect of the question, for I think it is apt to be overlooked. The abolition or limitation of outdoor relief is urged not merely because outdoor relief can be best administered by voluntary agencies, but because its abolition restores men to their independence.

There are many subsidiary reasons why it is desirable that the Poor Law should confine itself to giving relief within the walls of some one of its institutions, and leave the relief to be given at people's homes to voluntary agencies; but I venture to think that the reason I have given is the paramount reason, viz., that this policy more than any other calls out the successful effort of the poor themselves. Every other consideration, though some of them are of great force, is relatively trivial.

Now let me meet the objection which is at once raised to this. It is often said, but I think only by persons who have no practical experience of such matters, that there is no difference brought about by transferring the duty of giving outdoor relief from a legal to a voluntary agency. Others ask what is the necessity for this. If we could secure really good Boards of Guardians, Mr. Marshall has argued, they would administer out-relief with quite as much discrimination as any charity organization society. This argument evades the whole point of our contention. We do not rely on the greater discrimination used by a voluntary agency. We rely on a much more efficacious protection, viz., the greater moderation of the poor in making claim on a charitable fund.

Legal relief seems to be, indeed is, the right of all the poor equally. All are "poor," that is, have an insufficient income; application for relief, therefore, is made by all, or at all events by many more than will apply to a charitable fund.

The success which has attended the administration of the Poor Law in Bradfield and Whitechapel is often, and no doubt with justice, ascribed to administration, but it can never sufficiently be insisted on that the action of the Poor Law is purely negative—it is restriction, abolition; the positive element in the reform is the quickened development of the spirit of independence among the poor themselves. This quickened development again rests on the fact (too often ignored by the mere theorist) that the moderation of the poor is such that they will not apply for indoor relief, or for relief from the funds of a charitable society, if those funds are protected by a very slight exercise of discrimination and inquiry.

I am not merely theorizing as to the existence of this moderation of the poor in pressing demands on charitable funds, as the following facts will show. In St. George's East the outdoor relief in 1871 was £8,916; in 1874, £4,391. It is now a merely nominal sum, and the local Charity Organization Society is giving relief at the rate of about £600 per annum. The clergy of the union are firm supporters of the Society, and the indiscriminate almsgiving is probably less now than in the old out-relief days. As a matter of fact, moreover, the committee does not refuse many cases. The trade of the union is, on the whole, less prosperous than in old days, owing to the decline of the shipbuilding and sugar industries. To what, then, are we to attribute the fact that the Society (which I may add, has never refused a case for lack of funds) has had to meet a demand so comparatively slight? They have never been so absurd as to pretend that the diminution is due solely to their greater industry in investigation and discrimination. Far from it. It is due much more to what I have termed the moderation of the poor.

It has frequently been pointed out that it is necessary to restrain the acceptance of poor law relief by deterrent conditions. There is something repugnant to our feelings in this. I would have you observe, therefore, that by relegating the duty of giving relief to people *at their homes* to voluntary agencies, the condition of deterrence is replaced effectually by a much more honorable and salutary safeguard. I mean the moderation of the poor themselves.

The offer of institutional relief, to which legal relief is by our proposal confined, will be said by some to be inhumanly deterrent. Such an opinion requires some qualification. It is urged by the Poor Law Commissioners, and ratified by common sense, that the condition of the pauper ought to be inferior to that of the poorest independent laborer. Now, the condition of the poorest independent laborer is poor indeed, and attempts to maintain the pauper at his own home in a still inferior condition result inevitably in inadequacy of relief. Juries occasionally find verdicts of starvation at inquests on the death of persons in receipt of outdoor relief. Such a state of things cannot be thought satisfactory, and it is aggravated by the feeling of injustice which arises because all are not treated alike. There is no union where everyone gets outdoor relief. Some are everywhere refused. The inferiority of the pauper's condition ought not, on grounds of humanity, to be brought about by inadequacy of relief. What is the alternative? Nothing more than this, that the same measure should be given to all, namely, carefully managed and adequate relief within the walls of some poor law establishment. When the Irish Poor Law was created it was feared that the scale of maintenance in the workhouse, which, relatively to the standard of living of the Irish peasant, was ample, even luxurious, would attract too many applicants. Those who understood the question insisted that there was no fear of that. The result proved that they were right. The dilemma is a simple enough one. It is desirable that the condition of the pauper shall be inferior to that of the poorest independent laborer. Will you effect this by giving inadequate relief and half starving the pauper at his own home? Or will you not rather import the necessary element of inferiority into the lot of the pauper by attaching conditions of restraint and discipline to an adequate and, on the whole, comfortable maintenance? On grounds of humanity, quite apart from the fatal influence of outdoor relief on the thrifty habits of the people, can we have any doubt as to the best choice in this dilemma?

There is no wish to pursue the pauper with penalties. His destitution arises from the fact that from one reason or another he has failed to fit himself into the framework of free economic society. If there are causes which have brought him to this pass, removable without injustice to others by legislation, by all means let them be removed. In the meantime his condition is a *misfortune;* no legislation can reverse this verdict and convert failure into success. Remedies are only a choice of evils. Civilized society will not permit the unfit to perish, nor will it ruin itself by permanently fostering failure by giving it all the rewards of success. In a sound administration of the Poor Law it takes a third course. It gives a maintenance to failure more adequate than that which can be won by those who live on the border line between success and failure; but in order that this shall not be a premium on failure, it imposes conditions of discipline and restraint.

To return, however, to our proposed division of labor. Although it is true that the moderation of the poor and their latent capacity for independence will contribute largely to the success of this policy, still it is necessary that schemes of public charity should be conducted with care and discrimination. I can best explain my meaning by an illustration.

The heaviest year our Society ever had in St. George's was 1886, the year of the Mansion House Fund. This fund was raised amid great excitement and boundless advertisement. The idea of relief was in the air, and though some £2.000 was expended in the district by the Mansion House Relief Committee the only result was that a larger demand was made on other agencies. The moderation of the poor was in this instance, and by the means above mentioned, broken down. The fund was happily only temporary, but its influence while it lasted was very similar to the state of things brought about by a permanent system of lavish out-relief. The poor were kept in a state of speculative ferment, and during the sittings of the Mansion House Relief Committee application for relief was made to it on behalf of about one-third of the whole population.

Public charities of a permanent character managed in this manner would, without doubt, be very nearly as mischievous as outdoor relief. Public charity, therefore, should be administered without ostentation, and under the safeguard of full and deliberate investigation. In this way, and in this way only, can the whole benefit of the policy now advocated be secured. I use the term *public* charity advisedly, for the action of *private* charity, as already indicated, is not a matter to be controlled by organization societies, whose work lies mainly with funds arising from endowments and subscriptions, and from the donations of the rich for persons unknown to them. Private charity, in the strict sense in which I use the term, is liable to error. A father may be over-indulgent to a son, and a friend, by misplaced liberality, may confirm a friend in unprofitable habits; but this is a form of error not to be dealt with *ex cathedrâ* by any organ of public criticism.

The co-operation of the Poor Law with charitable agencies, as carried out in three of the poorest unions of London—Stepney, Whitechapel, and St. George's—was commended in the report of the Select Committee of the House of Lords, and the experiment is often quoted in poor law discussions. There is, however, one misapprehension on the subject which I should like to correct. The reform of the Poor Law in these three unions was begun and carried out before our system of organized charity had taken root in the soil. The poor law reform in Whitechapel and Stepney began in 1870-71. The first report of the Tower Hamlets Pension Committee is dated 1878. When I first became a member of the Charity Organization Society in 1879 the Whitechapel and St. George's committees had a common office, and at an earlier date there was only one committee for the whole of the Tower Hamlets, which used to meet in a little room in Philpot Street*. We have been enabled

---

*The following note has been supplied to me by Mr. Loch with reference to the early history of the society in the East End:—

The East End Inquiry Committee was opened in February, 1871, and continued to be the only office for five of the East London poor law divisions (viz., White-to extend and consolidate our operations because the Poor Law Guardians have taken the first step and confined themselves to giving indoor relief only.

It is impossible to make any subdivision of labor till the more powerful party to the agreement has become satisfied of its necessity. I argue, therefore, that Poor Law Guardians must take the first step, under a profound conviction that whether there be an organization of charitable agencies, or whether there be none, they have no right to withhold from their union the benefit of sound administration. As matter of fact there can be no doubt that, if Guardians have the courage and disinterestedness to face this reform, there will also be found among them men of sufficient position and energy to organize the charitable agencies; but I confess there seems to me to be very little to be done till the policy of Guardians is animated by a profound conviction of the necessity for reform.

At the same time, though I must insist that the initiative lies with the poor law authorities, I think that our organization of charity has been of service in strengthening the party of reform on the various boards. Guardians are able to say that provision has been made to deal with exceptional cases, and they have not been deterred from continuing to the union the enormous benefit of a sound administration. They have never (and this is the danger to which I desire to draw attention) asserted a right to choose our applicants for us, or to override our decisions. The two bodies are entirely distinct, and there is no publicly ratified compact between us. The only bond between us is that we both believe that by the tactics pursued the poor are learning to do without the help of either of us.

The proposal of Professor Marshall, that we should be recognized as a part of the legal machinery of the Poor Law, would, therefore, be fatal to our usefulness. The co-operation which we advocate is, therefore, more a division of labor than co-operation pure and simple. It consists in this, that the Poor Law should confine itself to institutional relief; as a result the greater part of the outdoor legal relief now given

chapel, St.George-in-the-East, Poplar, Stepney, Mile End Old Town), till February, 1873, when the joint Whitechapel and St.George-in-the-East Committee and the Poplar Committee were formed. The East End Inquiry Committee became in April, 1873, the Stepney and Mile End Old Town Inquiry Committee. In March, 1875, separate committees were formed at Whitechapel and St.George-in-the-East, and they continued to make use of only one office. In April, 1875, separate committees were formed in Stepney and Mile End Old Town. The East End Finance Committee was formed early in 1874.

will be rendered unnecessary by reason of the increased independence of the poor, and the remainder is so small in amount that it can be dealt with by voluntary charity.

The administration of the Poor Law and of voluntary relief should go hand in hand, animated by the common purpose not only to relieve adequately, but, as it has been well put, to make the influence of our relief system centrifugal, and not centripetal. When this purpose is not present in the minds of administrators, the most senseless and disastrous competition between the Poor Law and charity is set up.

The City of London is a contiguous union to Whitechapel. At the time of the Lords Select Committee the pauperism of Whitechapel was 16 per 1,000. In the City it was 62 per 1,000. Some years ago I made some remarks on this contrast, and I was taken to task by an influential city paper. This gentlemen, it was said, is very badly informed about the City Union. "Many poor persons have come into the city for the small charities which have hitherto been obtainable in different parishes, and it is hardly fair to compare the City" with other places. How far this is an exculpation of the City Guardians I do not stop to inquire, but it does confirm my view that where no definite division of labor exists, the larger and more numerous the charitable institutions, the greater the burden on the Poor Law. In the chaos here delineated both legal and voluntary relief act with an overpowering centripetal force, so much so that their warmest defenders can only excuse the authorities by saying, "What can they do? The place is a nursery for paupers."

Let me say a few words on the experience of those country unions which have reformed their Poor Law administration. In none of them, as far as I know, has there been established any charity organization society. The contrary is often asserted, but without foundation. A charity organization is very desirable, nay, even necessary, where there are a number of public charities and a large mass of population, but there is much less necessity for it in a sparsely populated rural district. The squire and the parson and the ladies bountiful of the neighborhood ought to exercise their common sense, and if there be many of them, there is no reason why, if they choose, they should not meet in a committee, but neither at Bradfield nor at Brixworth has this been found practicable or desirable. The late Mr. Bland-Garland told a friend of mine, who has repeated it to me, that when he became responsible for the administration at Bradfield he put aside a certain annual sum—£100 I think—which he was prepared to give away, in order to make the transition to a stricter system more easy. He added that in the first year the demand on his purse did not reach half that sum, and that in subsequent years it became gradually less.

Very similar is the information given to me by Mr. Bury, Chairman of the Brixworth Board. He has from his own resources, and from moneys entrusted to him, a small fund which he has used much in the way described by Mr. Bland-Garland. He is definitely of opinion that he would much rather not have any organization society. It is not—there, at all events—necessary. I do not think I misinterpret Mr. Bury's opinion if I say that he does not regard the reform of administration at Brixworth as a mere transition from dependence on poor law relief to a dependence on charitable funds, but rather that under the administration for which he is responsible the poor are successfully learning to achieve an absolute independence for themselves. This desirable result would be endangered if a charitable committee were established permanently and prominently before the eyes of the people. I mention Mr. Bury's opinion and experience—even though it may seem to show that co-operation with charity is not necessary—because it emphasizes what I have already stated, viz., that the *positive element* of reform in all this matter is neither charity nor the Poor Law, but the spirit of independence in the people themselves.

In the foregoing remarks I have advisedly avoided going into detail. The first step in reform is to convince the majority of a board of guardians of the necessity of reform. The details of the methods taken to give effect to the principle must differ widely in each district and with each board. It would be very desirable, I think, that the Society should publish one or two statements similar to the late Mr. Bland-Garland's paper, "From Pauperism to Manliness." It would be interesting to have an account of the success of the cross-visiting system pursued in Manchester; of the method of reducing pauperism by rigid investigation, as in Paddington; of the successful establishment of a provident medical society covering the whole union, as at Milton in Kent; of the history of efforts to affiliate provident societies to hospitals, with a view of making our hospital system the auxiliary, and not the hostile competitor, of friendly societies and doctors' clubs; of the efforts for the improvement and better management of the indoor establishments in Whitechapel and elsewhere, and a thousand other matters which will readily occur to you all. I hope this meeting may encourage both the London and the provincial societies in collecting and circulating in a readable form information on such points.

If time had permitted, I should have liked to say a good deal on these matters of detail, but I hope I shall not be blamed for confining myself on this occasion to the larger aspect of the question. I have presented to you an ambitious programme—the reformation of public opinion on this whole question.

I do not disguise from you the difficulties, but to some minds its attractiveness is its difficulty, the splendid opportunity that it offers for being unpopular in a good cause. My reading of poor law literature has discovered to me one little bit of sentiment. It is where Sir G. Nicholls, to whom as much as to any man the country owes the reform of 1834, relates how, on his return to his old home at Southwell, he was met in the market place by a party of laborers, who shook him warmly by the hand and thanked him for having been their best friend. In a momentary lapse from the dry, unemotional language of a public official, he bids us imagine how "gratifying" the incident must have been to one whose conscientious discharge of his duty had for years made him one of the best abused men in England.

There is one element of encouragement which I think worth mention, there is no subject in which there is a more complete unanimity of opinion among persons who have made any intelligent study of the question. Among the recognized authorities there is absolute conformity. The enemy in this case is ignorance and inexperience. There has been a disposition in the past to relegate this matter to the "loose ends" of society—to the unemployed busybody of the leisure class. But the question is becoming urgent—it is becoming a question for statesmen—and with the hour let us hope there will come the men of courage and insight. Hitherto the politician has not helped us much, but rather the reverse. Legislation of various kinds is proposed, most of it of a mischievous character; but the debate is only just begun, and those who have for years made study of this question must not be silent. I confidently believe that we shall be able to defeat the pessimism of those who assume that inadequacy of wages and spendthrift habits are ineradicable incidents in the life of the laborer. We, at all events, cannot admit that the only solution of this question is to be found in conferring easy terms of pauperism on those who were born for independence and freedom.

MANCHESTER.

POOR LAW RELIEF AND CHARITY ORGANIZATION IN AN INDUSTRIAL TOWN.

BY ALEXANDER McDOUGALL, J. P., VICE-CHAIRMAN OF THE MANCHESTER BOARD OF GUARDIANS.

The consideration of the development of charity organization in a town or district must be based upon knowledge of what is being done within it by the poor law authorities and by voluntary associations for the relief and mitigation of distress.

The city of Manchester has a population of about 505,000; the Poor Law administration is carried out by three separate Boards of Guardians, but as two of them (the Chorlton Union and the Prestwich Union) extend also over rural districts outside the city, it will suffice to describe briefly the methods of the board whose district lies entirely within the boundaries and includes the older portion of the town. It is officially known as the Manchester Board of Guardians, and acts for the township of Manchester containing a population of about 145,000, with a density of 91 persons to the acre. Within the township are the chief portions of the commercial buildings—the warehouses and offices and also some of the manufacturing establishments. The majority of the population are of the operative class, living in streets of cottages, and there are many instances of streets formerly occupied by middle class tenants, now inhabited by persons of the laboring class—the houses being subdivided into tenements. The better houses of the township are chiefly occupied by the lower middle class and artisans. Manchester stands in close relation to several large towns within a radius of 12 miles, the high roads leading to them running through populous places containing factories and works surrounded by the cottages of the operatives. Throughout these surrounding districts a considerable number of hawkers of small articles, casual laborers and others pick up precarious livings. The great majority of these "travellers" as they are called have their homes in the township—many of them using the lodging houses, of which there are some with as many as 400 beds. It is the portion of the city in which the largest amount of poverty may be expected.

The Guardians have for the last twenty years devoted very much time and consideration to methods of administration of both indoor and outdoor relief, striving as far as possible to meet the real needs of all suitable applicants, and yet not to attract from labor and habits of self-support any of the large numbers on the borders of pauperism. Whilst they have not abolished out-relief, they have reduced it to narrow limits without adding materially to the number of indoor paupers. The change has been brought about by the adoption of the following standing order.

STANDING ORDER.

"Outdoor Relief shall not be granted or allowed by the Relief Committees (except in case of sickness) to applicants of any of the following classes:—

"(*a*). Single Able-bodied Men.
"(*b*). Single Able-bodied Women.
"(*c*). Able-bodied Widows without children, or having only one child to support.
"(*d*). Married Women (with or without families) whose husbands, having been convicted of crime, are undergoing a term of imprisonment.
"(*e*). Married Women (with or without families) deserted by their husbands.
"(*f*). Married Women (with or without families) left destitute through their husbands having joined the militia and being called up for training.
"(*g*). Persons residing with relatives, where the united income of the family is sufficient for the support of all its members, whether such relatives are liable by law to support the applicant or not."

The effect of strictness with regard to outdoor relief may be seen by comparing the average number receiving relief on one day for 1873 and the average number on one day for the year 1893.

OUTDOOR RELIEF.

For the year ending March 29th, 1873, average number of persons receiving relief on one day was.................. 3,198
For the year ending March 25th, 1893, average number of persons receiving relief on one day was.................. 594

Being a *decrease* of................................. 2,604

INDOOR RELIEF.

For the year ending March 29th, 1873, average number of persons receiving relief on one day was.................. 2,298
For the year ending March 25th, 1893, average number of persons receiving relief on one day was.................. 2,718

Being an increase of................................ 420

There have been other remedial causes at work to reduce pauperism, and also some decrease of population owing to public improvements and erections of large railway stations and warehouses, but these have been counterbalanced by the change during the same period which has taken place in the township from the removal of well-to-do tenants to the suburbs—the houses becoming occupied by the wage-earning class.

This large reduction in the number of persons granted out-relief has not been at the cost of hardship and suffering. Careful enquiry has failed to discover any cases of necessity unrelieved because of strict adherence to the regulations. On the other hand, it has raised the respectability of out-relief and made really worthy persons less disinclined to apply. The collateral results have been most beneficial; the character of notoriously pauperized localities has been changed. Out-relief readily granted causes groups of improvident persons to localize. These nests of pauperism were soon broken up when out-relief became restricted to exceptional cases only.

For indoor relief purposes the workhouses are well arranged. The Guardians have, within the last twenty years, built a very commodious infirmary and abolished all nursing of the sick by paupers. Medical oversight is fully provided for, and the nursing is in charge of a lady superintendent and highly trained nurses. There is but little unwillingness on the part of the sick poor to go into the infirmary; it has become popular even to an extent not desired by the Guardians, as it is a fact that sick persons from a distance are attracted.

In the workhouses every effort is made to keep the inmates employed, but not to raise the impression that the work done is something for which the Guardians have any desire to retain the workers in the house.

The children of parents in the workhouses, deserted children, and some children of widows receiving out-relief are maintained and educated in schools at long distances from the workhouses, no pauper labor being employed at the schools, so dissociating the children as much as possible from pauper influences.

There is very general provision made for sickness and burial by joining friendly societies and also sick and burial clubs. The operatives largely avail themselves of such facilities, especially for burial, many of the very poorest managing in some way to keep up club payments for burial. A considerable number of those dying at the workhouse are buried not at the cost of the Guardians, but by means of money due from clubs.

Medical charities place the very best medical aid within reach of the poorest. The local infirmaries and hospitals are readily available for necessitous sick persons, but on convalescence, though perhaps still unable to work, they must leave, and the supply of food and nourishment ceases. The medical charities as a rule endeavor to obtain payment from patients who may be able to afford it, and for some years have striven to make the generous aid to the sick as slightly pauperizing as possible.

Manchester has some municipal charities, but they provide chiefly gifts of blankets, calico, shawls and counterpanes once in the year, and only occasional doles of money.

There are active and successful societies for the rescue of children from the streets, penitentiaries, preventive homes, prison gate missions. A considerable amount of aid is given in money, food and clothing by the churches, chapels and missions of the city acting independently of each other.

The operations of the Manchester and Salford District Provident Society are based upon some of the chief aims of charity organization. Its first rule describes its object. "The encouragement of industry and frugality, the suppression of mendicity and imposture, and the occasional relief of sickness and unavoidable misfortune."

The methods of the Society are:—

1. *A thorough system of inquiry into all cases brought under the Society's notice.*

By the inquiries made by the experienced officers in response to requests for information by benevolently disposed persons much imposture is exposed, and frequently the intending donor turns his charity into useful channels. The society not only seeks to expose imposture, but to guide assistance to real service.

2. *A fund for the relief of sickness and unavoidable misfortune.*

The distribution of this fund is most carefully conducted. A large number of respectable persons and families are assisted during periods of sickness. Grants are made to widows of money, sewing machines and mangles to enable them to become self-supporting; and for men in distress, when investigation has shown there is good probability of a livelihood being earned, tools, donkeys and carts, and other capital outlay is provided.

3. *Provident Dispensaries.*

The system of weekly payments by persons of small incomes, ensuring medical advice and medicine when sickness arises, has been successfully developed. The majority of the dispensaries established have become self-supporting. The effect is most beneficial to the members subscribing, habits of thrift are induced. But for membership in a dispensary, many of them would be compelled to apply to the Guardians for medical relief when sick and be thus brought into at least temporary pauperism. There are nine provident dispensaries in Manchester and Salford. The number of members on the books on December 31st, 1892, was 21,581. The amount paid by members during the year ending on that date amounted to £4,340 17s. 6d.

The Society undertakes investigations for the hospitals of the city into the circumstances of patients receiving aid, who may be considered able to pay for the hospital service rendered to them. The following figures show the percentages from year to year, of those applicants to the medical charities co-operating with this association who were found on investigation to be ineligible for *gratuitous* medical relief, and who were in consequence referred to the branch provident dispensaries:—

1875	42.32	per cent.	1884	14.19 per cent.
1876	24.50	"	1885	13.57 "
1877	24.00	"	1886	11.15 "
1878	19.74	"	1887	9.29 "
1879	13.61	"	1888	6.53 "
1880	14.76	"	1889	6.89 "
1881	14.48	"	1890	6.49 "
1882	13.51	"	1891	7.49 "
1883	12.12	"		

4. *Convalescent Home at the Sea Side.*

This home is of great value in enabling wage-earners to quickly regain strength for work. There is a fixed charge per week for maintenance there, paid either by subscribers, or by patients and their friends, or in necessitous cases by the Society, which debits its relief fund with the charge.

5. *Penny Banks.*

The Society led the way in the city in the establishment of these useful encouragements to thrift. Since then increased facilities for small savings have been provided by the Government and the School Board. Opportunity for the lodgment of small savings is regarded by the Society as of great service to poor persons.

Though the Society does not make money grants from its funds except for temporary assistance, yet there are some cases of aged persons of good character aided for longer periods by private gifts of some of its members, which are placed in the hands of the secretary for small weekly payments to the recipients.

This rapid glance into the chief agencies in operation in Manchester for the relief of distress and assistance towards self-support makes apparent some developments still needing to be undertaken. There is no provision for permanently aiding enfeebled and weary aged women and men who are failing in the struggle of life, who dread the workhouse and who shrink even from out-relief by the Guardians because of repugnance to becoming paupers.

Nothing appeals more to the sympathy of the benevolent than the deep poverty of an old woman or man of good character, who growing past work and without any or only partial support from children, holds aloof from poor law relief, and dreads coming days with still lessened earnings. The number of such persons even in a large population is not great, because the majority of aged persons have children able to contribute to their support; and though this duty is often neglected, it can be no function of charity organization to relieve children, who are able, from proper contribution to their parents. They are principally women. Old men do not live so long in necessitous circumstances as old women do; they much more readily seek the food and shelter of the workhouse.

A member of the Manchester Board of Guardians, who has interested himself specially in the administration of out-relief and is fully alive to its dangers and advantages, having the impression that there were in the city a number of elderly women and men of excellent character, living in great poverty, who instead of regarding poor law relief as an available provision, feared it with such intensity that the probability of its becoming inevitable became the sharpest trial of their lives, began seven years ago to search for them. They are not readily found, they make no noise and give little sign of their deep want. His experience has been that regular small gifts of money, which can be relied upon, make all the difference between anxiety and contentment, and brighten to a wonderful extent lives otherwise darkened by daily fear of want. Relieving officers, district nurses, clergymen and city missionaries have assisted him in finding the right persons. A friend having joined in the cost, it has been possible for him to continue his visitations and provide weekly grants. He is, in fact, taking small pensions—of from 2s. 6d. to 3s. 6d. per week—to respectable old persons who have some slight source of income or house-room, but are without relations who can support them, and who can be relied upon to expend the money beneficially.

The development of organized charity to meet this work would require the society undertaking it to add to its present system of investigation inquiry for aged persons of good character who are without children able to support them, and in satisfactory cases to make grants of weekly sums of money, which will not be discontinued, except on change of circumstances, for at least six months. The fact of some degree of permanence is of great comfort to the recipients.

The society should also see that removal to a hospital or to the workhouse took place in cases where sickness or incapacity might make it necessary. But these cases are few. Decent old people have almost always friends and neighbors who come to their help for nursing and attendance at the last. The warmest expressions of thankfulness that have been made by old persons assisted by such weekly grants have been from persons who have thus been enabled to meet the expected last illness at home and among friends. It is noteworthy that, during the seven years the gentleman named has been assisting aged persons, in every instance of death provision had been made by the recipient for the funeral by payments to a burial club, often commenced early in life.

Poor Law Guardians are becoming disposed to make special provision for aged persons of good character in homes outside the workhouse proper. This will remove some of the causes of unwillingness on the part of such persons to avail themselves of Poor Law relief. But there will remain scope for the operation of organized charity on behalf of some, who through no fault of their own "have waxen poor and fallen into decay."

There are some aged persons of good character in worse circumstances than those who are without children capable of aiding them, namely, those who have children able to contribute, but who are neglected by them, receiving nothing or only occasional sums. The fact of the ability of their children puts them out of reach of aid from organized charity. They can only obtain magistrates' orders to compel children to support them by first becoming chargeable to the Guardians. There is a bill before Parliament to give power to parents to apply directly to the magistrates. When this bill becomes law it may prove to be one of the functions of organized charity to assist poor and feeble parents to obtain orders for maintenance against capable sons and daughters.

THE CHARITIES OF BRISTOL.

BY MISS ELIZABETH STURGE, A MEMBER OF THE BRISTOL C. O. S.

Bristol is an ancient city whose municipal life dates from Saxon, if not from Roman times. It is not an easy task through the chequered history of a thousand years to trace the growth of its institutions for dealing with the poor and destitute.

Before the Reformation it possessed its Abbey and other religious houses whence, doubtless, alms were dispensed according to the usage of the middle ages; but with the dissolution of the monasteries this form of relief to the poor ceased. The deplorable destitution throughout the country which followed this and other changes, and led to the passing of the great Act known as the "Forty-third of Elizabeth," doubtless moved the hearts of the charitable to deeds of mercy; and after this period religious activity took the form of endowments for the relief of the indigent rather than, as in former times, of noble works of church architecture.

In Bristol henceforth a long succession of benefactors sought by larger or smaller bequests to provide for the bodily wants of the poor of the several parishes. Thus St. Mary Redcliff draws from its endowments £345 for the uses of the poor; St. James has gradually acquired an income of about £640; while St. Nicholas possessed, until they were recently diverted under a scheme of the charity commissioners to general educational purposes, revenues amounting to about £1,000.

The vicars and church wardens of twenty parishes still distribute yearly from their endowed charities a total of about £2,500; of which between £500 and £600 appears to be given away in bread; £500 in clothing and fuel; and £650 in doles of money, which range in amount from £10 to a few shillings.

Beside the founders of the parochial charities, Bristol has been rich in benefactors whose generosity has extended over a wider area. Thus Alderman Whitson, about 1629, left large bequests to be distributed in the form of doles to the needy in any part of the then existing town; and Edward Colston, about 1690, founded numerous schools and almshouses on so liberal a scale, that his name has ever since been representative for Bristol citizens of large-hearted charity. Three societies, established during the last century and called after him the Colston Societies, are still in active operation, subscriptions to the amount of £3,000 being raised annually by them and dispensed as annuities and doles.

The non-parochial endowed charities are in the hands of trustees, of which the most important board is responsible for the administration of those formerly in the gift of the corporation. These consist, besides schools on which an income of £12,000 is expended, of annuities, almshouses, gifts of money &c., and amount to a yearly value of £8,000. In addition a large number of almshouses and annuities are in the bestowal of more private bodies. Almshouses provide for a total of 526 persons; annuities, which range in amount from £35 to £5 5s. for 439; while about £2,144 is expended annually by parochial and other charities in doles.

This large provision for the poor would be a subject for local congratulation if good intentions could ensure good results; but unfortunately this is not so; and it is not too much to assert that while temporary comfort and satisfaction have doubtless been given in many individual instances, the effect of the action of the charities on the wellbeing of the poorer citizens has been on the whole for evil, because of the weakening effect on character resulting from encouragement to rely for the future on the help of others.

The law guards jealously, and no doubt wisely, the sacredness of testators' rights. Property of more than a small yearly value which has been left for a particular purpose cannot be diverted to any other, except under special legal powers, even when it is obvious that its present use is doing harm.

In Bristol, as elsewhere, the lapse of centuries has wrought great changes. Parishes which were formerly populous have become comparatively deserted. The inhabitants of the ancient city, who alone share in the benefits of many of the charities, form now but a small proportion of the total population, and since the passing of the first Reform Act the freemen of the city, for whom and whose families many benefactions are reserved, have much diminished in numbers, so that the charities limited to this class have become far less generally applicable than was the intention of their founders.

The operation of the system of doles must be regarded as productive of harm rather than good to the classes affected by them. In general the church wardens and vestries are not guided in their choice of recipients by considerations as to thrift and permanent benefit; and even if they were, they would be unable under the rigid terms of their foundations to vary either the amount or the time of bestowing their gifts. These are not as a rule therefore available for cases of temporary difficulty, while at the same time they are too small and too irregular to be of permanent benefit as pensions.

The methods pursued by the municipal trustees for apportioning the charities in their gift cannot be regarded as adequate. There is a very large number of applicants for every vacancy, and there is no other means of judging between them than such as is afforded by the enquiries which the time and opportunity of individual trustees—generally men honorably occupied in other important duties—may allow of their making. As no candidate can obtain a hearing who has not such personal support, it inevitably results that the provision thus existing is unavailable except for the few who are known to or have access to one of the trustees.

There is no reason to believe that the case stands differently in regard to the almshouses and annuities controlled by other trustees; but as to the methods of these more private bodies it is less easy to obtain information.

As regards the action of the Colston Societies, the main object of two of these is political, and their annual dinners are made the occasions of speeches by members of the Government and others, so that they are involved with matters unconnected with the relief of the poor.

The distribution of their annuities and doles is managed as in the case of other voting charities. One or more known citizens having granted their names as recommending a case, details are generally neither asked nor given, and the voting is determined in the usual way by canvassing and personal pressure. By the action of the three societies about £1,872 is annually distributed in annuities of the value of £13, and £1,200 in doles.

In addition to the gifts thus bestowed, Bristol is not behind other places in supporting liberally the many societies and charitable institutions which modern benevolence has called into existence. According to the report of the commission of enquiry of 1885, about £38,000 is annually raised for these purposes. A very large sum is also given away privately; much of it in the form of that true charity which silently provides for the needs of neighbors and dependents, but much also of that unwise charity which gives without enquiry, and enables the importunate and idle to live on the credulity of the careless rich.

Side by side with the great charities we have of course the Poor Law.

For poor law purposes Bristol is divided into three unions of which the parishes comprising the ancient city form the central one, wholly urban in its character, and containing now 55,500 inhabitants; while Barton Regis (193,000) and Bedminster (77,500) include different parts of newer districts and suburbs, as well as portions of the outlying country districts, and involve the difficulties of administration incident to a mixed urban and rural population.

In Bristol as a whole, but more especially in the ancient city, there has long been an exceptionally high rate of pauperism as compared with other large towns; and this undesirable distinction still continues, although the last twenty years show a steady decline in all three unions, corresponding with the decrease throughout the country.

Causes connected with the industrial condition of the city may have had something to do with this state of things. A century ago the port of Bristol was one of the most important in the kingdom. It has entirely lost that position now, and ranks far behind many newer towns; partly in consequence of the ruin of its sugar industry brought about by the results of emancipation in the West Indies, followed by the French bounty system; partly owing to the difficulty and danger attending the navigation of its narrow tidal river by large modern steamers; partly, too, owing to the short-sighted policy of the authorities, who in the early part of the century exacted exorbitant dues, and long neglected to supply dock accommodation at the mouth of the river. Trade thus left the port, and Liverpool and other towns prospered at its expense.

Another cause of pauperism must be noted in the low rate of wages, which have not risen in Bristol to an extent commensurate with the general rise throughout the country. It may be open to question, however, whether this may not be an effect as well as a cause of the large amount of out-relief which has always been given; for, making allowance for the drawbacks to prosperity alluded to, we should, we believe, ignore a commonplace of experience if we did not recognize the vital connection between a free administration of out-relief and the existence of large charities on the one hand, and low wages and a high rate of pauperism on the other.

It will be seen that there is thus no lack of aid to the poor from many sources. The real difficulty has been the want of method and intelligence shown in bestowing it. No attempt has been made by any centre of relief to work with reference to any other. Overlapping has gone on unchecked. Guardians and dispensers of charity of all kinds have relieved the same people, none of them having any knowledge of what others were doing. The idle and improvident have thus flourished at the expense of the industrious and thrifty; for under such conditions it is those who ask most who receive most.

No serious effort was made to improve this state of things until about 1870, when the interest aroused in the subject of wise methods of charity, which had led to the issue of Mr. Goschen's Poor Law Minute of 1869 and the subsequent establishment of the London Charity Organization Society, extended itself to Bristol, and a Charity Organization Society for that city was formed. Before that time a Mendicity Society did useful work for nearly a quarter of a century; but it seems to have limited its operations to efforts for the prevention of begging, and not to have attempted to deal with the larger and more complex aspects of the subject.

The difficulties in the way of the pioneers in this work in such a city as Bristol cannot be exaggerated. The complexity of the questions involved; the difficulty of learning the truth; the vested interests to be disturbed; and, not least, the impossibility of arousing public sympathy; all this made the work seem for many years well nigh hopeless. Warm friends of the cause, disappointed and disheartened, withdrew one after another to more hopeful fields of labor. Nevertheless the Society continued to do useful work. Its main office through all changes remained open, although branches which were tried from time to time had to be closed. At present it is not claiming too much for it to say, that at its table case-work, as careful and sound as that of any of the London committees, is done weekly. Still the amount accomplished remained small when compared with the needs of so large a town, and the committee failed to bring about any system of co-operation between the poor law authorities and the dispensers of the endowed and other charities.

Most of the influential inhabitants of Bristol and Clifton have held aloof from giving the Society the advantage of their personal support' and guidance, and perhaps the unpopularity attaching to such work has not invariably been lessened by tact in its dealings. It was impossible, too, that one office should really do the work involved, and that dispatch and thoroughness should not suffer while such long distances had to be covered by a limited staff.

The appearance in 1885 of the valuable report of the "committee of enquiry into the condition of the Bristol poor" threw a flood of light upon these subjects, and suggestions as to wise methods of improvement were made. It did not succeed in arresting public attention, however, and the efforts which followed to bring about co-operation consequently failed.

But during the past three or four years prospects have brightened. Bristol has shared in the revival of interest in questions affecting the welfare of the poor which has everywhere shown itself. In 1889 at the annual meeting of the Society many valuable speeches were made by representative local men, who from different points of view had come to see the need for action on its lines. These were published in permanent form, and the pamphlet was widely circulated in the city with an appeal for co-operation. As a result consultations took place between members of the Society and some of the Guardians of the ancient city. An influential council has been formed in order to establish a committee to work within that union, which shall act as a medium between the charitable agencies and the Guardians, and much local interest has been aroused among the clergy and others who are in contact with the poor. It is hoped that this committee, acting in co-operation with the Charity Organization Society, will begin work before long.

What is needed is that the Guardians and different charitable agencies should arrive at an understanding as to the class of cases coming within the sphere of labor of each; so that cases of temporary distress, which may be saved from a condition of permanent dependence, may be helped adequately and at the right time by the action of charity. As regards permanent cases, the pensions and almshouses should be reserved for the most thrifty and deserving, apart from accidents of acquaintance and personal favor; the bodies which dispense these gifts bearing in mind that they are intended for the good of the citizens as a whole, and not of any special individuals accidentally more fortunate than the rest in their opportunities for pressing their case. The system of election to the Colston charities by voting should be abolished, and the choice of applicants should rest with a wise committee. In addition to consideration as to general good character, thrift and forethought on the part of all candidates for almshouses or annuities should count as important factors. In such a large city and among many hundreds of applicants the task of decision must involve the expenditure of much time and trouble. The trustees and others, therefore, should obtain assistance in the necessary labor of enquiry.

Could such changes as these be brought about, Bristol might well be proud of her noble institutions for the aged poor.

In order to facilitate co-operation between the various charities and the Poor Law, it has been proposed to form a central council, on which Guardians, trustees and all relieving agencies should be represented, and which by subdivision of work should furnish the needful means for enquiry and render each agency more effective within its sphere of action. Of such a general council, that which has been established for the central union may be regarded as a foreshadowing. Its work must necessarily be extremely difficult, but when it is realized how important is such common action, surely the Guardians and others will not shrink from the trouble involved.

The enterprise of Bristol citizens is not yet extinct. At immense cost they are about to build large additional docks at the mouth of the Avon, and the city will once more be abreast with other great ports in its provision for the shipping requirements of the day. Should this undertaking succeed, the future may see a large extension in the trade and prosperity of the city.

The labor agitations, though they have been accompanied by much that is deplorable, may have the ultimate effect of somewhat raising the rate of wages, and it is earnestly to be desired that, should an opportunity thus be afforded to the working classes of Bristol of sharing in an increased general prosperity and advancing to a position more favorable to permanent well-being and independence, the improvement will not be hindered, so far as the unskilled and the less able are concerned, because the dispensers of poor law relief and charity refuse to co-operate, and continue to uphold a policy which is inimical to the best interests of the poor.

Rate of pauperism in Bristol: Ancient City 1 in 20. Bedminster 1 in 25. Barton Regis 1 in 42.

Number of places in almshouses, 526. Number of annuities (£35 to £5 5*s.*), 439. This may not be quite all.

Amount given yearly in doles about £2,144 to about 1,746 persons.

ROCHDALE.

INDUSTRIAL AND GENERAL CHARACTERISTICS, POOR LAW ADMINISTRATION, AND CHARITIES.

BY R. A. LEACH, CLERK TO THE ROCHDALE BOARD OF GUARDIANS.

I. *Industrial and General Characteristics.*

Rochdale, in the County of Lancaster, is a manufacturing town which is typical of many others to be found in the county and in the West Riding of the adjoining County of York. So long ago as 1680, William, Lord Byron (Baron of Rochdale, and Lord of the Manor) described it as "an ancient market town of great resort." Flannel, which was the staple trade of its inhabitants for centuries, was manufactured in the town so far back as the year 1322. Notwithstanding its great age as a market and manufacturing town, it is said to be poor "in historic fact and antiquarian memento," but the fact that it was the birthplace and home of John Bright, that it could claim Richard Cobden as its member in Parliament, and that a few of its working men (the "Equitable Pioneers") gave the breath of life to the co-operative stores movement, which has yielded results inestimable and far-reaching, is alone sufficient to make any Rochdalian proud of the place of his origin.

The area of the town is 4,180 statute acres, and the population 71,458 (Census 1891). The area of the poor law union, which covers the town and stretches out to the surrounding district, is 34,822 statute acres, and the population 123,910 (Census 1891). The annual rental of the town is £281,135, which permits of a net valuation for local rates of £229,492. The annual rental and net valuation for rating purposes of the union are £625,639 and £511,227 respectively. At present the chief industries of the town are flannel, cotton, and engine and machine making. Among the minor industries are manufactories of silks, velvets, carpets and paper, dye works and corn milling, and, as may be supposed, there are several building contractors. In the surrounding district, besides the industries mentioned, there is stone-quarrying and also coal-mining, but coal-mining is not carried on to any large extent. There is farming, too, though it is not of a kind that enables us to speak of any part of the poor law union area as "agricultural" in the popularly accepted sense of the term.

The population of the town and district may be truly characterized as a working-class population; and though there may be nooks and corners in and about the town and district where dirt, poverty and wretchedness exist, the population in the bulk for comfort of circumstances will compare very favorably indeed with the population of any other place. The death rate in the town is, for a manufacturing town, comparatively low. This may to a large extent be attributed to a splendid water-supply and a system of sanitation which inspectors of the English and American Governments have acknowledged to be "unsurpassed."

The working people of Rochdale are a people of sturdy independence and of forethought and thrift, a people who have worked upwards, and who no doubt will continue to work upwards. Two years ago I made inquiry into the provisions which the working classes of the town made for old age, the days of scarcity of employment, sickness and death. The information then obtained was considered conclusive evidence of the virtues mentioned. The following information is similar to that obtained two years ago, only it is, if anything, a little more ample:

PAYMENTS TO MEMBERS DURING THE YEAR ENDED DECEMBER, 1892.

	£	s.	d.
Local Friendly Societies having their Registered Office or Meeting-place in the Town of Rochdale:			
Total Payment for Sickness	20,716	7	10
" " Funerals	4,027	10	0
Trades Unions or Local Branches having their Meeting-places in the Town:			
Total Payment for Sickness	1,297	0	11
" " Funerals	432	6	0
" " *Out-of-Work, &c	5,388	11	5
Industrial Assurance Societies and Companies doing business with the Working People in the Town:			
Total Payments by Societies which have supplied information (nearly all death claims)	19,493	19	9
(Several large Societies have refused to state their Payments).			
Total	£51,355	15	11

*Had the year been made up from March to March, this amount would have been much heavier because of a dispute in the cotton trade.

INVESTMENTS.	Total amount owing to Depositors at end of December, 1892, including Share Capital and Loans.		
	£	s.	d.
Post-Office Savings Banks (Rochdale Town Branches)	111,200	0	9
Yorkshire Penny Bank, Rochdale Town Branches	12,428	18	4
Co-operative Stores, Juvenile Banks	5,726	15	1
Children's Bank at Board Schools	445	4	8
Co-operative Stores (members' claims)	515,932	6	0
*Rochdale Corporation	36,730	0	0
*Limited Companies which have supplied information (4 of the largest Companies have stated their inability to furnish figures)	186,480	0	0
*Building Societies exclusive of Loans	41,831	0	0
Total	£910,774	4	10

*1890 Returns.

The figures given have been obtained either from published accounts or from chief officials, and refer to working people.

Care has been exercised to limit the information as far as possible to the town of Rochdale. It may be taken, therefore, that the figures given pertain only to residents within the town and adjoining district.

From the investments have been excluded such as are not the investments of individuals, *i.e.* investments of stores, working men's clubs, and sick societies are excluded.

Information of amount standing to the credit of Rochdale depositors in the ordinary banks not ascertainable.

The local friendly societies and the various concerns in which investments are made are financially sound.

Population of the town, 71,458.

To the above information may be added another item which speaks for the sturdy independence and forethought of the working people of Rochdale. From the 7th November, 1892, to the 25th March, 1893, a conflict between the masters and the workpeople in the cotton trade raged more or less throughout the cotton manufacturing centres of Lancashire.

This conflict was the severest that has ever taken place in the Lancashire cotton trade, and it is said to have involved both sides in the loss of upwards of two million pounds. Rochdale was not so much affected as were some of the other cotton manufacturing districts; nevertheless it was very appreciably affected. An estimate carefully computed by the trades union officials shows that in the town and its immediate vicinity the workpeople employed as cotton operatives drew about £70,000 less in wages than they would have done had the dispute not occurred and had all the mills been working full time during the twenty weeks the struggle lasted.

This loss of wages meant privation in hundreds of homes, yet during the half year which embraced the whole period of the dispute, the outdoor relief granted by the Poor Law Guardians was only £419 in excess of the amount given in the corresponding half of the previous year. The increase in the number of workhouse inmates was but slight; while the relief given by the local Charity Organization Society was only £28 0s. 11d. in excess of the amount given in the corresponding period of the preceding year. Even these small increases were not altogether occasioned by applicants who were cotton workers. Had it not been, though, for the spirit of independence amongst the operatives, and the helpful resources of the trades unions, which the unionist workers were able to draw upon as *their own*, immensely more poor law relief and charity would have been called for than was the case. The question may be asked, "Did the workers keep themselves from being recipients of parish relief and charity by being allowed to run into debt with tradesmen?" To such a question the answer may be made that Rochdale, in bad times as well as good, excels as a ready money trading town.

II. *The Administration of the Poor Law.*

In dealing with poor law administration it is well to remember that in England the boards of Poor Law Guardians, in dispensing poor law relief, whether indoor (workhouse) or outdoor, are subject to the orders and regulations issued by the central (Government) authority. As regards outdoor relief, there are two classes of unions, viz: (1) unions where the "outdoor relief prohibitory order" is in force, and (2) unions where the "outdoor relief regulation order" is in force. The "outdoor relief prohibitory order" directs by Article 1 that

"Every able-bodied person, male or female, requiring relief (from the Guardians) shall be relieved wholly in the workhouse, together with such of the family of every such able-bodied person as may be resident with him or her, and may not be in employment, and together with the wife of every such able-bodied male person, if he be a married man, and if she be resident with him; save and except in the following cases:

1st. "Where such person shall require relief on account of sudden and urgent necessity.

2nd. "Where such person shall require relief on account of any sickness, accident, or bodily or mental infirmity affecting such person, or any of his or her family.

3rd. "Where such person shall require relief for the purpose of defraying the expenses, either wholly or in part, of the burial of any of his or her family.

4th. "Where such person, being a widow, shall be in the first six months of her widowhood.

5th. "Where such person shall be a widow and have a legitimate child or legitimate children dependent upon her, and incapable of earning his, her or their livelihood and have no illegitimate child born after the commencement of her widowhood.

6th. "Where such person shall be confined in any gaol or place of safe custody, subject always to the regulation contained in Article 4.

7th. "Where such person shall be the wife or child of any able-bodied man who shall be in the service of Her Majesty as a soldier, sailor or marine.

8th. "Where any able-bodied person, not being a soldier, sailor or marine, shall not reside within the union, but the wife, child or children of such person shall reside within the same, the Board of Guardians of the union, according to their discretion, may, subject to the regulation contained in Article 4, afford relief in the workhouse to such wife, child or children, or may allow outdoor relief for any such child or children being within the age of nurture and resident with the mother within the union."

Article 4, referred to, directs that:

"Where the husband of any woman is beyond the seas, or in custody of the law, or in confinement in a licensed house or asylum as a lunatic or idiot, all relief which the Guardians shall give to his wife, or her child or children, shall be given to such woman in the same manner, and subject to the same conditions, as if she were a widow."

It will be seen from the foregoing extracts from the "outdoor relief prohibitory order" that where the order is in force the Guardians cannot give, save in the exceptional cases set out under Article 1, outdoor relief to able-bodied persons.

The "outdoor regulation order," however, permits the Guardians of the unions where the order is in force to give outdoor relief to any resident destitute person, subject to the restrictions that the Guardians cannot establish an applicant for relief in trade, nor redeem from pawn tools, implements or other articles belonging to the applicant, nor purchase tools or implements for any applicant, nor pay the expenses of an applicant's conveyance to any place (unless when conveyed in accordance with legal provisions), nor pay wholly or in part the rent or lodging of a pauper, save temporarily in a case of sudden necessity. The order lays down the further restrictions that relief shall not be given "to any able-bodied male person while he is employed for wages or other hire;" and that every able-bodied male person (save in case of sudden urgent necessity, sickness or death in the family, or the husband being in prison or absent), if relieved out of the workhouse, shall be set to work and kept employed by the Guardians "so long as he continues to receive relief." And further that one-half at least of the relief given shall be given "in articles of food, clothing, or in other articles of absolute necessity." Rochdale is one of the unions where the "regulation," and not the "prohibitory order," is in force.

As regards pauperism, the union stands better than the average of the Lancashire unions, and Lancashire as a county stands better than England and Wales as a whole. Taking the returns of pauperism for the 1st January last year, when there was not any exceptional distress, the proportion of paupers to the population was in this union 1 in 74, in the county 1 in 61; and in England and Wales 1 in 41. From these figures pauper lunatics in county asylums are excluded, as also are vagrants—of whom Rochdale has more than enough, owing to one of the great highways of the country running straight through the town.

The statistics attached to this paper show the class as well as the number of persons relieved by the Guardians on the 1st January, 1892, and on the 1st January, 1872, there being a freedom from exceptional distress at both dates; and they prove that the pauperism of the union within the twenty years has been fairly reduced, even allowing for the fact that the Charity Organization Society was at work in 1892, while it was not in existence twenty years previously.

In the proportion of indoor paupers to outdoor paupers, Rochdale does not stand as well as Lancashire as a whole, but it stands better than England and Wales taken as a whole. On the 1st of January, 1892, the proportion of indoor to outdoor paupers in Rochdale was 1 to 2.38; for Lancashire the proportion was 1 to 1.58; and for England and Wales 1 to 2.61. As before stated, Rochdale is a union where the "out-relief regulation order," and not the "prohibitory order," is in force, and this may be accepted as a reason why there is not a higher proportion of indoor to outdoor paupers at Rochdale than there is. Still, the Guardians are making more use of their workhouse than formerly; and there is every reason why they should, for the workhouse is a modern one, and has been admirably planned. It affords accommodation for about 900, and has a full and efficient staff. The infirmary is detached from the main building, and there are also detached buildings for the insane, for the children and for vagrants, as well as self-contained cottages for the aged married couples.

There are two classes of indoor poor, viz., the sick (embracing the insane), and the children, as regards whom the Guardians' management has been greatly improved during late years. The old condition of things, when the sick inmates of the workhouse were left chiefly to the care of other pauper inmates, and the children had not sufficient special care, has gone, and is not likely to return. The sick and insane inmates of the Rochdale workhouse are now attended through the night, as well as through the day, by paid nurses and attendants, who have been well trained for their work. And as regards the children, such as are at the workhouse, besides being kept apart from adult pauper inmates, are brought as much as possible in contact with the better influences of life outside the workhouse walls. Up to quite recently these children were instructed in the workhouse, but now they go out unattended, with the freedom of the children of the artisan, and dressed, not in garb which is uniform and carries the pauper look, but as other children, to the public elementary schools in the neighborhood of the workhouse, and on Sundays to the church, or chapel, and Sunday school belonging to their religious denomination.

It would, perhaps, not be amiss at this point to state that the legal provisions which are in force in England enable Guardians to deal with pauper children in a variety of ways at the expense of the rates. For instance, children may be maintained in workhouses or in separate schools, or they may be maintained and educated in voluntary schools certified by the central poor law authority for the reception of pauper children; or, if of age, they may be placed in service or apprenticed, and if orphans or deserted, they may be emigrated to Canada or boarded out with artisans, or the Guardians may allow them to be adopted by suitable persons willing to do so. Some Boards of Guardians have a preference for one way of dealing with their workhouse children, and some prefer another, but the wiser course is to make as free use as possible of all the provisions named, according to what is found to be best for the children individually.

The following figures show that the Rochdale Guardians have of late years made pretty ample use of the various provisions which relate to pauper children.

> Placed in service since the year 1880, including children adopted, 249
> Boys sent to be trained for sea service since the year 1880. 26
> Placed in voluntary certified schools since October, 1890. 56
> Emigrated to Canada since 1889.. 13

The children who have been adopted and placed in service have on the whole turned out remarkably well, and this accounts for the reluctance which the Rochdale Guardians have always felt against availing themselves of the "Boarding-out System," which is the system of boarding orphan and deserted children out in the homes of artisans and paying so much per week to the foster parents for the children's maintenance and schooling.

And here let it be said that the proper treatment of the sick poor in the workhouse infirmaries is a policy which must pay well. Proper treatment breaks down the reluctance of the sick poor to enter the workhouse, for they know they will be better seen after than they possibly can be at their homes, though perhaps the full and comfortable provision made at a properly appointed workhouse infirmary lends itself to the danger of encouraging persons, whose circumstances do not warrant them in seeking parish relief, to seek admission when sick to the workhouse infirmary for the benefit of the treatment found there; but that danger may always be carefully guarded against by vigilant relieving officers. It is equally true that it must in the long run pay well to deal with pauper children in a thoughtful and generous manner, in a manner which not only does not begrudge the children a future free from the taint of pauperism, but which goes a long way towards making such a future for them. The pauper children of to-day will a few years hence be grown men and women. To help them to become free men and women is to ensure a permanent reduction in the pauper roll and an increase in the number of honest toilers and worthy citizens; but to neglect them means continual accession to the ranks of adult paupers and an increase in the number of the idle and the dissolute, who make society their prey.

Before passing on from the administration of the Rochdale Board of Guardians, another feature in their administration may be mentioned. It is that they not infrequently afford aid, where they may legally do so, at the expense of the poor rate, to persons who, while they are above the stamp of the usual applicant for parish relief, are greatly in need of assistance. Sometimes the aid is in finding the wherewithal to send some such persons to a convalescent home or hospital for special cases; sometimes it is by undertaking the cost of maintenance and training of a blind child or adult, or a dumb child, or an imbecile child, in a special institution. Within the last few years the Guardians have sent 10 cases to institutions for training the blind at a cost of £20 per case per annum; 9 cases to schools for deaf mutes at a cost of £20 per case per annum; and 5 cases of imbecile children to a special institution for educating such children, at a cost of £29 10s. per case per annum.

III. *Charities.*

There are several endowed charities in Rochdale, mostly founded during the last century. Roughly speaking, they cannot in the aggregate be worth less than £17,000. They are charities which were founded principally for the schooling of poor children, but one of these charities, viz., Kenion's Charity, which is the most valuable one, having over £8,000 invested, was founded for "placing out poor children as apprentices;" and another, viz. Gartside's Charity, which has a fund of about £6,000, was founded that the annual income from the fund might, after the annual payment of 20 shillings for a yearly sermon at the parish church, be applied in buying clothing or corn for distribution among the poor on Christmas day. Both the Kenion's Charity and the Gartside's Charity are at present administered according to the directions of the founders, but as there is a growing disposition that these charities—and all such endowments—should be applied in founding exhibitions and scholarships at institutions for secondary and technical education, it is within the range of possibility that they may lose at no distant date their present distinctive features as charities; so it would be best here to leave them out of reckoning. Besides the endowed charities above referred to, there are in Rochdale the undermentioned recognized charitable societies and institutions, viz :—

(1). The Benevolent Society, established in the year 1807, for the temporary relief of the poor and sick of all denominations.

(2). The Ladies' Charity, established in the year 1817, to afford assistance to poor married women in childbed; and to widows whose husbands have died leaving them pregnant.

(3). The Rochdale Dispensary (now Infirmary and Dispensary), instituted in the year 1831, to afford medical and surgical aid to the poor.

(4.) The Good Samaritan Society, established in the year 1832, for the relief of the sick poor.

(5). The Ashworth Chapel for the Destitute, established 1858, and embracing a nightly shelter for homeless females and a mission for teaching the blind.

(6). The Poor Children's Aid Committee, formed in 1878, for sending poor and sickly children to the sea-side, which committee has now an excellent Home for Children at St. Anne's on-the-Sea.

(7). The Charity Organization Society, established in 1879, for the repression of mendicancy, and for securing adequate relief for really necessitous and deserving cases.

These seven recognized charitable societies and institutions depend for a continuance of their operations on voluntary donations and subscriptions; and though the Ladies' Charity has £1,200 invested in Corporation stock, the Good Samaritan Society £400 invested, the Benevolent Society £400 invested, and the Charity Organization Society £260 (as an emergency fund) similarly invested, yet if the voluntary subscriptions and donations ceased, the work of the societies would soon come to a standstill.

The value of the aid given in food, money, and clothing by four of the seven charities, namely, the Benevolent Society, the Ladies' Charity, the Good Samaritan Society, and the Chapel for the Destitute, during last year amounted to about £265, and the cases dealt with would probably be between four and five hundred. In connection with the infirmary and dispensary, 253 in-patients and 1871 out-patients were treated during the year, while the Poor Children's Aid Committee sent 110 children for a few weeks' stay to the Home at St. Anne's on-the-Sea. The Charity Organization Society, which is the only charitable agency in Rochdale which keeps a paid officer for the purpose of receiving applications and investigating the circumstances of the applicants, received during the year 1161 applications for assistance, of which 659 were recurrent applications. Of the 1161 cases, 882 received relief, the total value of the relief being £224 18s. 8d., exclusive of 195 hospital letters distributed, which were valued at £60 12s. 3d. As to the remainder of the cases, 46 were recommended to other agencies or to private persons for assistance, while 110 cases were dismissed as undeserving, and the rest were refused assistance as being cases which should be left to the Poor Law, or were rejected on other grounds. It may safely be taken that the foregoing figures relating to the relief given by the seven charities during the past year are fairly representative as the figures of an average year. The work of the Charity Organization Society, I feel, deserves more extended mention than is given by the summarized figures of one year, and having that feeling, I append hereto an interesting report with diagrams prepared by Mr. Alderman J. R. Heape, J. P., Hon. Secretary of the Society, on the work done by the Society during the years 1880 to 1891.

IV. *Co-operation between the Poor Law and the Charities.*

It would be untrue to state that there is a thorough and an all-round co-operation between the administration of the Poor Law and the administration of the charities in Rochdale. That there ought to be such a co-operation may at once be admitted. That there is not may be set down to want of thought. The Guardians are ready to co-operate with the charities, and do co-operate with the Charity Organization Society by appointing representatives from their Board on the Society's committee of management. The relieving officers of the union and the inquiry officer of the Society also keep well in touch about their cases. That there is not a thorough and an all-round co-operation, and co-operation with the general public as well, cannot be laid to the blame of the Charity Organization Society, as the following extracts from the constitution of the Society will show :—

The objects of the Society shall be (1st) to investigate thoroughly the cases of all needy persons in the district coming before the committee. with a view to (*a*) forwarding such cases to the poor law authorities or other charities (to be brought if possible into mutual co-operation), or (*b*) relieving them through the funds at the disposal of the Society, or (*c*) referring them to private benevolence. (2nd) To repress mendicancy within the sphere of the Society's operations by prosecution or otherwise.

The Society shall be under the management of a president, vice-presidents, treasurer, one or more honorary secretaries, and a committee (with power to add to their number), constituted in the following manner: one representative from each charitable agency and relief society working in the district; one representative from each church, chapel, or other place of worship in the district (not otherwise represented); two or more representatives from the Board of Poor Law Guardians; and other persons able and willing to devote time to the work. The Mayor of Rochdale shall be *ex-officio* president of the

Society. All the other officers and members of the committee shall be annually elected.

One or more properly accredited charity officers shall be appointed by the committee, who shall be responsible for the investigation of all cases coming before the committee, and shall be in communication with the relieving officers and agents of the various charities in the borough.

The charity office shall be open to applicants at such stated hours as the committee shall determine, and a charity officer shall be in attendance during those hours to receive applications.

Tickets bearing the address of the charity office shall be supplied gratuitously to householders in the district, and the cases of all applicants presenting themselves at the charity office shall be investigated and reported to the committee.

All cases properly belonging to the Poor Law shall be at once referred to the Guardians, and the committee shall not supplement the relief given by the Guardians, except under special circumstances.

All cases that can appropriately be dealt with by any existing charity within the borough shall be, after due investigation, referred to such charity, and assistance shall only be granted by the committee in cases which cannot properly be dealt with by any other agency.

Information regarding the scope and operations of the charities of the district shall be collected, and kept at the office for the information of residents, and the books of the committee shall be at all times open to those legitimately interested in particular cases, or in the welfare of the poor generally.

A register of persons willing to dispense charity privately shall be kept at the office.

In face of the foregoing extracts it is scarcely conceivable that there should not be perfect co-operation between the Poor Law and the charities in Rochdale. The lack of co-operation is owing, as above suggested, to want of thought; two or three of the charities keep entirely to themselves and to what they consider to be nobody's business but their own. Thorough and all-round co-operation with the Charity Organization Society, however, will, I am inclined to think, be brought about in the near future, for the subscribers to the various charities are beginning to see the need of proper investigation into cases; and already several of the subscribers to one charity or another hand over to the Charity Organization Society for distribution the "letters" which entitle them as subscribers to recommend cases to the charities to which they subscribe. With advantage to all concerned the Benevolent Society and the Good Samaritan Society might at once be merged into the Charity Organization Society, and I do not see why one or two of the other charitable agencies should not be so merged.

GENERAL OBSERVATIONS.

In concluding this paper, I would point out that if the population of any town or district was mainly a population of thriftless persons who cared not how or by what means they were sustained in the flesh, so long as they were left in the enjoyment of indolence and the vices which indolence is so fruitful of, there would be an ever present need for the application of the best corrective measures and influences. If corrective measures and influences were not brought to bear upon such a population, the condition of things would ultimately become too frightful to describe. Admitting this, it would be consummate folly to allow that there is not an ever present need for the application of the best corrective measures and influences where the population is mainly a population possessing great virtues. In the opening part of this paper I have stated, and given facts in support of the statement, that the working people of Rochdale "are a people of sturdy independence, and of forethought and thrift—a people who have worked upwards, and who no doubt will continue to work upwards." But although this statement with the facts adduced will bear the strictest investigation, there is need at Rochdale, as there is everywhere, for the application of the best corrective measures and influences, for wherever you go is found a lowest stratum of society, and if it be not wisely seen to, there can never be any guarantee that one of two things may not happen, namely, the quiet undermining of the virtues of the higher by the lower, or an upheaval of the lower to the disturbance and hurt of the whole commonwealth. In England, so long as the Poor Law remains, the wise administration of that law is bound to prove one of the most corrective measures and influences that can be ; and if it be not wisely administered, there is no measure or influence of a corrective nature which is not neutralized. The provision which the Poor Law compels for the relief of destitution is practically a tax upon thrift. If the provision be loosely dealt with, not only is an injustice done to the thrifty, but demoralization sets in, which cuts two ways, the thrifty, except such as have great moral strength, becoming demoralized down to thriftlessness, and the always thriftless becoming more deeply steeped in vice. The poor law administration in Rochdale has not been held up in this paper as a paragon, but it is easy to conceive that if the administration were a loose one, no such figures as have been given showing the provision made by the working classes against sickness, non-employment, and old age could be obtained, for there would not be the same incentive to make that provision.

To a wise administration of the Poor Law I would add organized and discriminating charity as one of the most corrective influences that can be brought to bear where the lowest stratum of society exists. Disorganized and indiscriminate charity is as baneful as would be lax poor law administration. Such charity should be called by some other name, for it is not worthy of the name of charity. It is called " charity," it is true, and it is said "charity never faileth." Disorganized and indiscriminate charity unquestionably never faileth to afford indulgences for the idle and the vicious, which in the interest of their present and future welfare should be determinedly withheld from them. Should it be asked, " Is there a need for charity at all where there is a State provision for the destitute and afflicted?", the answer, so far as relates to England, is that the limitations to the Poor Law, as indicated in the " outdoor relief prohibitory order " and the " outdoor relief regulation order"—limitations which could not be prudently removed—and the disabilities which poor law relief carries with it to the adult recipient, create the need for charity. In spite of their forethought and thrift, people are sometimes pushed down under the surface, submerged by sheer misfortune. It is for charity to bring them up again; and when charity, with its hand of strength and kindliness, lays hold of them, then in the sense that is highest and noblest it "never faileth." But the " charity" that so never faileth must be organized, discriminative, co-operative, and investigative. It is a mistake to think that charity is not charity if it investigates. The wounded will gladly bare themselves to the physician; it is the impostor who covers up and when questioned shrinks away.

ROCHDALE UNION.

Statement of the Numbers of the several Classes of Paupers Relieved in Workhouse
(exclusive of vagrants) on the undermentioned dates.

INDOOR.

DATE.	Adults Mar'ied Coupl's Males (1)	Females (2)	Other Males (3)	Other Females (4)	Illegitimate Children (5)	Other Children (6)	Mar'ied Coupl's Males (7)	Females (8)	Other Males (9)	Other Females (10)	Illegitimate Children (11)	Other Children (12)	Orphans or other children relieved without Parents (13)	Lunatics Males (14)	Females (15)	Children under 16 (16)	Summary Adults Males	Females	Children under 16	Total
1st January, 1872	...	...	2	4	2	4	3	2	150	87	2	14	29	34	55	2	189	148	53	390
1st January, 1892	...	...	52	54	2	7	3	3	151	61	1	8	62	39	49	2	245	167	82	494
Increase	...	...	50	50	...	3	...	1	1	...	...	...	33	5	...	...	56	19	29	104
Decrease	...	...	...	...	...	...	...	...	...	26	1	6	...	...	6	...	...	...	...	...

ROCHDALE UNION.

Statement of the Numbers of the several Classes of Outdoor Paupers
(exclusive of Lunatics in Asylums and those residing with relatives) relieved on the undermentioned dates.

DATE.	Able-Bodied, or the Families of Able-Bodied.																Not Able-Bodied.					Summary of Preceding Columns.			
	Adult Males (married or single) relieved in cases of sudden and urgent necessity.	Adult Males (married or single) relieved in case of their own sickness, accident or infirmity.	Adult Males relieved on account of sickness, accident, or infirmity of any of the family, or of a funeral.	Adult Males (married or single) relieved on account of want of work, or other similar causes.	Families of Adult Males in columns 1, 2, 3 and 4.			Widows.	Children under 16 dependent on Widows.	Single Women without Children.	Illegitimate Children and their Mothers.		Families relieved on account of Parent being in Gaol, etc.		Families of Soldiers, Sailors, and Marines relieved.		Resident Families of other non-resident males relieved.				Children under 16 relieved with Parents.	Orphans or other Children under 16 relieved without their Parents.	Males.	Females.	Children.	Total.
	1	2	3	4	Wife. 5	Children under 16, resident with the Father. 6	7	8	9	Mothers. 10	Children. 11	Wives. 12	Children. 13	Wives. 14	Children. 15	Wives. 16	Children. 17	Males. 18	Females. 19	20	21				
1st January, 1872	45	...	8	3	40	115	80	245	17	12	16	5	20	...	2	62	134	205	525	10	51	261	741	592	1594
1st January, 1892	22	...	1	18	34	101	73	214	13	4	6	...	2	...	2	39	72	145	388	16	26	186	552	439	1177
Increase	...	...	...	15	...	...	...	...	...	...	...	...	...	...	...	...	...	...	...	6	...	...	...	...	...
Decrease	23	...	7	...	6	14	7	31	4	8	10	4	18	...	...	23	62	60	137	...	25	75	189	153	417

ROCHDALE UNION.

Statement of the Numbers of the several Classes of Paupers Relieved in Workhouse
(EXCLUSIVE OF VAGRANTS) ON THE UNDERMENTIONED DATES.

INDOOR.

DATE.	Number of the several Classes of Paupers in the Workhouse.													Lunatics, Insane Persons, and Idiots.			Summary of the preceding Columns.			
	Adults.						Children under 16.	Not Able-bodied.							Males.	Females.	Children under 16.	Adults.		Children under 16.	Total.
	Married Coupl's		Other Males.	Other Females.	Illegitimate Children.	Other Children.		Married Coupl's		Other Males.	Other Females.	Of Parents not able-bodied, being inmates. Illegitimate Children.	Other Children.	Orphans or other children relieved without Parents.				Males.	Females.		
	Males.	Females.						Males.	Females.												
	1	2	3	4	5	6		7	8	9	10	11	12	13	14	15	16				
1st July, 1872....	...	...	...	21	60	...	2	1	...	...	106	64	2	6	35	32	63	2	138	128	48	314
1st July, 1892....	...	...	...	21	60	14	1	1	1	1	153	70	2	6	62	31	49	2	206	180	88	474
Increase....	...	...	...	...	...	13	1	1	1	1	47	6	...	...	27	...	...	...	68	52	40	160
Decrease....	...	...	...	...	...	...	...	...	...	...	...	...	...	...	...	1	14	...	...	...	...	...

ROCHDALE UNION.

Statement of the Numbers of the several Classes of Outdoor Paupers

(exclusive of Lunatics in Asylums and those residing with relatives) relieved on the undermentioned dates.

DATE.	Able-Bodied, or the Families of Able-Bodied.																Not Able-Bodied					Summary of Preceding Columns.			
	1. Adult Males (married or single) relieved in cases of sudden and urgent necessity.	2. Adult Males (married or single) relieved in case of their own sickness, accident, or infirmity.	3. Adult Males relieved on account of sickness, accident, or infirmity of any of the family, or of a funeral.	4. Adult Males (married or single) relieved on account of want of work, or other similar causes.	5. Wife.	6. Children under 16, resident with the Father.	7. Widows.	8. Children under 16 dependent on Widows.	9. Single Women without Children.	10. Mothers.	11. Illegitimate Children and their Mothers.	12. Wives.	13. Children	14. Wives.	15. Children	16. Wives.	17. Children	18. Males.	19. Females.	20. Children under 16 relieved with Parents.	21. Orphans or other Children under 16 relieved without their Parents.	Males.	Females.	Children.	Total.
1st July, 1872	41	3	3	...	27	91	89	260	21	5	6	3	10	4	6	50	114	178	495	21	46	222	694	554	1470
1st July, 1892	10	3	13	...	23	72	57	184	13	3	6	1	4	...	2	35	88	142	397	10	33	169	529	399	1097
Increase	...	...	13	...	...	...	...	...	...	...	...	...	...	...	...	...	...	...	...	...	...	...	...	...	...
Decrease	31	...	...	...	4	19	32	76	8	2	...	2	6	4	4	15	26	36	98	11	13	53	165	155	373

ROCHDALE UNION.

Total number of Indoor and Outdoor Paupers (exclusive of Lunatics and Vagrants) on the dates mentioned below, together with the Population of the Union.

	1873, 1st January.	1883, 1st January.	1873, 1st July.	1873, 1st July.	Population of the Union.	
					Census 1871.	Census 1891.
Indoor	390	494	314	474	109,829	123,910
Outdoor	1594	1177	1470	1097		
	1984	1671	1784	1571		
Proportion of Indoor to Outdoor Paupers	1 to 4·08	1 to 2·38	1 to 4·68	1 to 2·31		
Proportion of Total Number of Paupers to Population	1 in 55	1 in 74	1 in 61	1 in 79		

Mr. Alderman Heape's Report on the Work Done by the Rochdale C. O. S. during Years 1880—1891.

The Rochdale Charity Organization Society has now completed twelve years of work, and in addition to the usual statement recording what has been done during the past twelve months it is proposed to analyze briefly the reports of each year from the commencement of the Society.

Taking a broad view, it may be said that there has been a most striking continuity in the procedure of the weekly meetings of the managing committee, and the lines upon which it was at the first decided to conduct the Society have proved to be thoroughly satisfactory, yet there have been developments in certain directions and modifications in others, which experience has dictated, and which it is worth while noting.

The annual volume issued by the London Charity Organization Society, containing the reports of all the affiliated societies in the kingdom, shows their number to be steadily increasing, and it is curious to observe the very different lines upon which they are conducted; it is hoped that a statement of the various modifications which have proved to be desirable in the course of twelve years' work in a manufacturing town may not be without interest as a contribution to that volume.

On pages 342 and 343 below are a number of diagrams in which each curve shows the progress of some particular phase of the society's work for twelve consecutive years.

Curve number 1 gives the number of applications that have been dealt with by the committee. The first year these reached a total of 996; the Society was then of course a novelty, and following close upon the exhaustion of a relief fund that had existed for eight months, it was to be expected that large numbers of the indigent, and especially of those who flock to any centre where public relief is being dispensed, would apply to the new society to see what could be got out of it. Thorough investigation proved that nearly half the applicants, 41½ per cent., were unsuited for pecuniary help, and the effect of their disappointment is seen in the diminished numbers of the next two years, when the applicants were only 752 and 456. After three years the Society's aims became better understood, and there was a gradual increase in the number of cases, until in the year 1886 the applications reached 1,016. This was due to the fact that during the winter of 1885 a good deal of distress existed in the North of England; in several manufacturing towns special relief funds were organized. Here such a course was not thought necessary, the existing organizations and private charity being capable of dealing with the emergency. In the two following years trade became better, and the cases fell from 1,016 to 839. In the succeeding year there was some amount of short time in the cotton trade, which had its effect upon the number of cases, but in the report for that year the increase is stated to be due more to the fact of the Society's becoming better known both by the deserving poor, who found their way directly to the office in increasing numbers, and by householders making freer use of the Society's tickets. This statement holds good as a partial explanation of the rapidly ascending curve of the last two years, but another factor must be taken into account which has largely affected the result. In the year 1883 a new departure was commenced in collecting special subscriptions for a particular case, which it was not considered desirable should be constantly assisted from the funds of the Society. From that time the number of these cases has steadily, and of late rapidly, increased, as is shown in curve number 8. During the last year there have been 320 grants to nine of these cases, and this of course swells the total of the number of applications. This branch of work did not exist during the first four years, but it seems likely to be one that will be permanent, as it has certainly been proved to be useful and important. The cases for which these weekly pensions are organized are generally those of invalids incurably and hopelessly ill, or in some instances, old people who receive a small sum weekly from the Guardians. These could not be constantly helped from the funds of the Society, but where the friends of the recipients are wishful to supplement their little income the agent collects the subscriptions and hands forward each week the stipulated sum. Altogether £370 has been collected and disbursed in this way.

These pension cases also affect curves 2 and 3, which show the number of cases that come each year for the first time, and those that come more than once. The curves are tolerably synchronous, the percentage of recurrent cases being about one-half the first applications until the year 1886 is reached; then for two years they are practically identical, but the curves cross, and now the recurrent cases largely exceed the first applications, a result of course mainly due to the pension cases.

The curves No. 4 and No 9, which must be looked at together, are of considerable interest. No. 4 shows the number of cases dismissed each year as 'not requiring relief,' 'ineligible,' 'undeserving,' or 'vagrants.' This curve follows roughly in its main lines that (No. 1) giving the total applications, but it can be seen at a glance that it recedes farther away from the main line each year. The full significance of this is shown by line number 9, which gives the percentage that these cases bear to the whole number each year, and here it is seen, with one very trifling exception, to be a steadily diminishing proportion each year, the extreme figures being 41.5 per cent. in 1880 and 13.7 in 1891. This is a very striking proof of the discrimination of the professional loafer and vagabond. He has learnt that it is no use pouring forth his most heart-rending tale into the ears of the agent at 32 Water street, unless it is founded upon fact, for his words are merely taken for what they are worth, and thorough inquiry is sure to be made as to their truth. There is no doubt that knowledge of this fundamental rule of the society is now pretty widespread in the town.

Some of those who solicit charity from door to door refuse to accept the enquiry tickets for various alleged reasons, and of those who accept them only a proportion present them at the office. It would be a matter of interest could it be ascertained what proportion of the tickets accepted are never used. Householders are again urged to refer each case of which they have not full personal knowledge to the office for enquiry. The necessary information is acquired in a sympathetic, and not in any inquisitorial manner. Those who need and deserve helping do not resent investigation, and each year's work but further proves its necessity.

Curve No. 5 tabulates the amount of employment that has been given each year at the workyard of the society. For the first two years, as might be expected, good use was made of it as the best way to assist men out of work, and as a test of the willingness of applicants to do something for themselves. For the next three years the figures are but small, an increase takes place in 1885, and in 1886 there is a sudden rise to 162; this is due to the fact before referred to, that in the latter part of 1885 (the period covered by the report of 1886) there was a scarcity of employment in the town, and aid being given to men out of work, much use was made of the yard. From that time the curve comes rapidly down to lower figures. It may, in fact, be considered as being, as far as it goes, an indicator of the general state of employment afforded by the various industries of the town, for when relief is given to a family in which there is an able-bodied man, some portion of the help is almost invariably given in the form of work for which the man is paid.

The next curve, No. 6, illustrates a phase of work that has increased in importance each year, 1886 being considered as exceptional, and shows how experience gradually determines the most useful channels in which aid can be given. The curve indicates the number of instances in which help has enabled applicants to receive the benefits of the Southport Convalescent Home, the Rochdale Infirmary, and other institutions. This number has gradually increased from one case in the first year to 123 in the current year. The wonderful advantage that it is to convalescents to have the benefit of three weeks' residence at the Home at Southport is most strikingly proved each year. The complete freedom from home cares and surroundings, and the change of air and diet, generally result in the patients returning fit to resume work. That the committee are able to deal with so many of these cases is due to the liberal help afforded by the governors of the Cotton Districts Convalescent Fund in Manchester; to suitable cases they grant a remission of a portion of the usual charge, and the committee would again express to them their thanks. The greatest number assisted are those who have received recommendatory letters to the Rochdale Infirmary. Subscribers have sent their letters to the office for the use of the Society, and the committee are able to ensure their reaching suitable recipients. The cases sent to various institutions during the year are as follows: Rochdale Infirmary, 69; Convalescent Hospital, Southport, 40; Devonshire Hospital, Buxton, 6; Ladies' Charity, 4; Manchester Royal Infirmary, 1; Rochdale Children's Home at St. Anne's, 1; Hospital for Consumption, Bowdon, 1; Dr. Hodgson for eye examination, 1.

Curve No. 7 shows how much the work of the society has increased in granting aid in cash and food tickets. The curve commences at the figure 270, goes as low as 188 in the year 1882, and terminates in the figure 736 for the past year. When it is remembered that each of these 736 cases has been thoroughly investigated, and found to be needing monetary help, it is evident that a great deal of the temporary poverty of the town receives timely and efficient help through the medium of the society. It is not with chronic pauperism that it is sought to deal, but principally with those who have stumbled in the way, who require a friendly hand to lift them up and to steady them on their feet until they are again able to walk alone. The very large increase in this year's work is, therefore, rather indicative of much more help being given in this way through the genuine cases reaching the society, than of greater poverty in the town.

The average amount of relief (exclusive of hospital letters and clothing) given weekly to each case assisted is 5s. 0¼d. against 5s. 2½d. last year.

Fewer loans have been made during the past twelve months than the average of previous years. From the commencement of the Society £100 19s. has been lent, in sums varying from a few shillings to £10, to 42 borrowers. Of this amount £73 1s. 9d. has been repaid, £6 0s. 10d. has been written off, and £21 16s. 5d. is still owing. This the committee regards on the whole as very satisfactory. To some of the borrowers the loans have been of great use, and they have been repaid with commendable regularity; but it is a form of help that is liable to abuse, requires great care and discrimination in its exercise, and frequently a persistent pressure to ensure repayment that it is not pleasant to exert.

Such then is a brief résumé of the work of the Society, which has commended itself to the judgment of a committee most widely representative, and of which the members are frequently changing ; it is clear that the work falls into no narrow groove or stereotyped method; that course alone is taken which experience shows to be the best, and the committee again with confidence commend the Society to public approval and support.

DIAGRAMS

ILLUSTRATING 12 YEARS WORK OF THE ROCHDALE CHARITY ORGANISATION SOCIETY.

1. Number of applications.
2. First applications.
3. Recurrent cases.

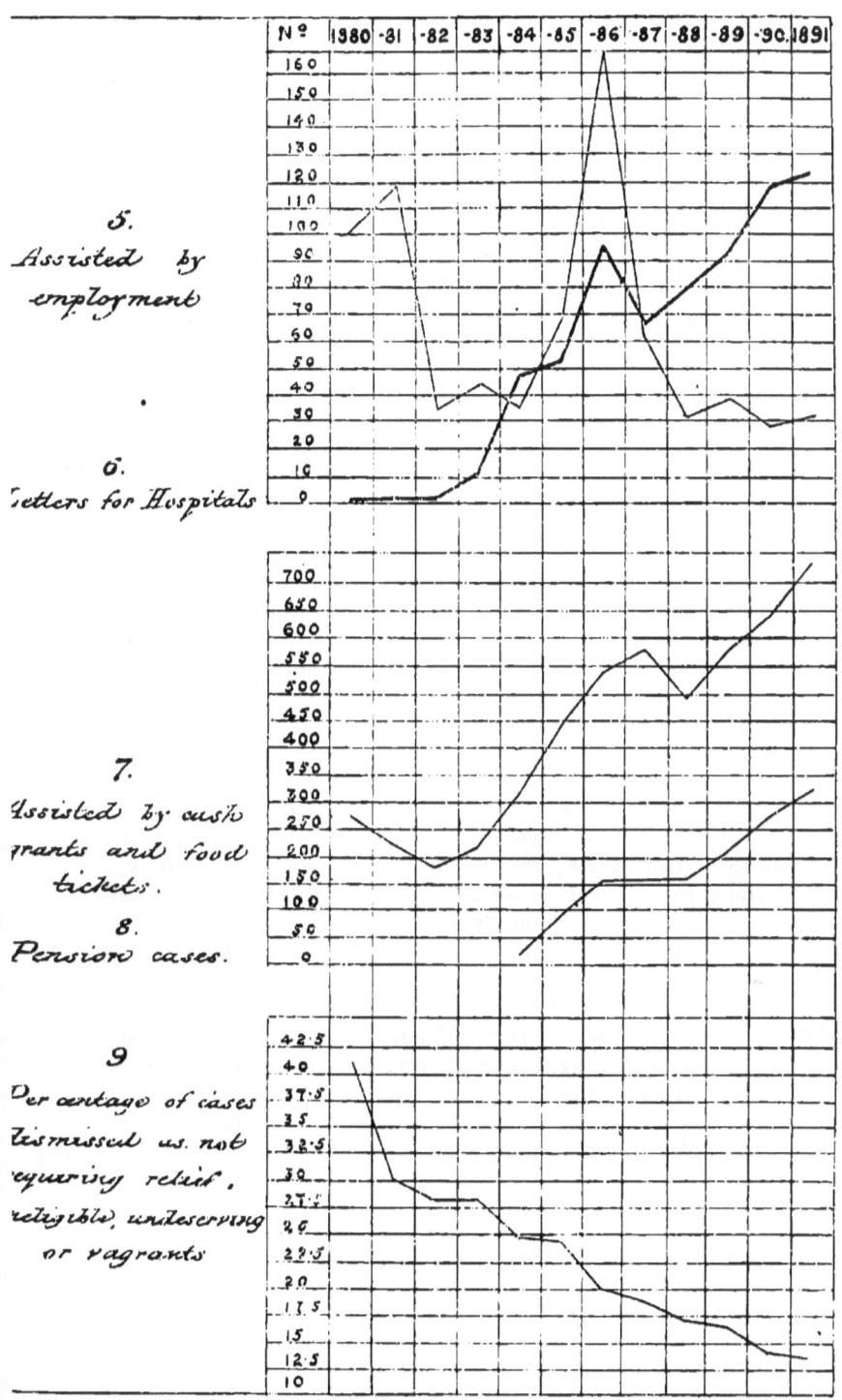

HELPING THE POOR IN ABERDEEN.

BY GEORGE MILNE, SECRETARY TO THE ABERDEEN ASSOCIATION FOR IMPROVING THE CONDITION OF THE POOR.

Aberdeen is a city of 125,000 inhabitants, situated on the east coast of Scotland about 135 miles north north-east of Edinburgh. It may be reckoned the capital of the North of Scotland, and is the seaport of a large agricultural district.

Unlike many of the large towns in England, or Dundee in Scotland, it has no single industry that overshadows every other; and being far removed from the coal and iron mining districts it is less liable to those industrial disturbances that paralyze these trades and plunge vast multitudes of workers into sudden idleness with its attendant evils.

Of manufactures Aberdeen has a little of many, including flax, jute, cotton, wool, combs, paper; and among the other industries of the place are the iron, granite monument, fishing and preserved provision works. The town has within the last thirty years been to a considerable extent rebuilt and greatly enlarged, a circumstance which accounts for the steadiness that has usually prevailed in the various branches of the building trade.

These conditions render Aberdeen a place of comparatively steady social circumstances, never suffering from the excitement of a boom nor from the depression of a general collapse. One other characteristic may be mentioned, namely, the comparative absence of the wealthy and leisured class, and of the most wretchedly poor, who are so frequently to be met with in our large cities. It is thus favorably conditioned for giving a fair trial to the principles of charity organization.

THE POOR LAW IN SCOTLAND.

Prior to the year 1845 the relief of the poor throughout Scotland was committed to the Kirk Sessions of the parish churches, and the necessary income was derived from a voluntary assessment, though as far back as 1576 a statutory assessment could have been enforced, had the circumstances of any parish required it.

In the year 1843, however, the formation of the Free Church resulted from the disruption of the Church of Scotland, and in nearly every parish in the country a sharp ecclesiastical division took place which materially affected the relations of the people to the parish Kirk Sessions.

In 1845 a special act of Parliament was passed placing the care of the poor in the hands of parochial boards, with powers of assessment for their relief, and that act continues in operation to the present day.

The legal objects of relief are:—

1. Persons who are disabled by sickness or accident, who are not dependents of able-bodied parents.
2. Women (although able-bodied) having two or more dependent children, or one child under one year old.
3. Persons above seventy years of age.
4. Orphans.
5. Lunatics and Imbeciles.

No able-bodied men, nor able-bodied women without dependent children, are legal objects of parochial relief.

The City of Aberdeen now includes the parish of St. Nicholas, the greater part of the parish of old Machar and parts of the parishes of Banchory-Devenick and Nigg. The population of the city was in 1851, 71,973; 1871, 88,125; 1891, 124,943; and at the same periods the number of paupers was in 1851, 2,082; 1871, 1,991; 1891, 1,519.

In addition to this legal provision for relief of the poor, Aberdeen possesses many private charities, medical, educational, and alimentary, which are managed by boards of directors in terms of the deeds by which they have been severally constituted.

THE ASSOCIATION FOR IMPROVING THE CONDITION OF THE POOR.

It was felt that there was room for an organization that would bring help to the struggling classes, not only by the distribution of money or goods, but by personal intercourse.

Accordingly, in 1870, the "Association for Improving the Condition of the Poor" was established, with the following objects:—

1. To obtain accurate information respecting the condition and circumstances of the poor in the city of Aberdeen and neighborhood.
2. To prevent the poor from sinking into a helpless condition of poverty, and to endeavor to recover such as have sunk.
3. To discover, and as far as possible remove, the temptations and hindrances in the way of an improvement in the condition of the poor.

4. To encourage and foster, in every available way, the efforts of the poor to form temperate, frugal, industrious, provident, and cleanly habits.

5. To discourage mendicity, and the indiscriminate distribution of charity, whether by individuals or societies, and to give such information as may enable these to administer their charity to deserving and suitable objects;—

6. To encourage and promote co-operation amongst all the charitable institutions in the neighborhood, so as to secure better classification of objects, prevent unnecessary overlapping, and thereby secure economy in the distribution of their charitable funds.

For carrying out these objects, the city was divided into fourteen sections, and these again into sub-sections and allotments, such as could be overtaken by individual visitors, without involving anyone in a burdensome amount of labor. The section committees are composed of leading citizens, many of whom also share in the work of visitation. The whole visiting staff, who are all volunteers, numbers about 200.

With a large body of volunteers there is usually some difficulty in keeping them all up to the standard of sound principle in the discharge of duties requiring so much tact, judgment and human sympathy, and to help towards this end the following instructions were issued to visitors sometime ago:—

1.—Only cases of temporary necessity are contemplated for relief from the funds of the Association.

2.—Every case should be carefully considered at the outset. If it be evident that the case will require ultimately to be taken up by the parochial board, it should be handed over to that body at once. If, however, there seems a strong probability of it again becoming self-supporting, although somewhat protracted, it may nevertheless be persevered with by the Association.

3.—Cases of acute illness should have the advantages of treatment in the Royal Infirmary pressed on their attention. The chances of a speedy and complete recovery will thereby be increased, and the household relieved so far of the patient's maintenance.

4—Other existing local charities should be utilized for the benefit of cases, the resources of the Association being made available where others fail or are insufficient.

5.—Information about the local charities will be supplied by the secretary.

6.—Cases in which exceptional treatment seems desirable will be considered on their merits by the section committees.

When relief is granted out of the funds of the Association, it is usually in the form of provisions, clothing, &c., rather than in money, and in periodic allowances at short intervals of a week generally.

If a personal opinion were permitted in this connection, it would be of a critical kind, the result of twenty-one years' experience and observation of the influence of charity on its recipients.

The conviction is forced upon us, that charity, under its most favorable conditions, "creates much of the misery it seeks to relieve, but does not relieve all the misery it creates."

The touch of charity should be as momentary as possible, and hence it is our belief that more good and less harm would be done if, instead of attempting to mitigate *many* cases of distress, we were to set ourselves resolutely to cure the curable. By the adoption of such a policy the work of our voluntary charities would tell more effectively than they do, even if the number of cases were greatly diminished.

ABLE—BODIED OUT OF WORK.

It will be observed that the Poor Law of Scotland does not recognize able-bodied persons as entitled to legal charity, even when they find it impossible to obtain work. And this necessarily affects the policy of such associations in Scotland, in a direction in which the English charity organization societies have no experience.

In Aberdeen we had to meet this difficulty at a very early period of the Association's history. Applicants were numerous who pleaded utter destitution from want of work, and the parochial boards could render them no assistance. A labor test, therefore, became necessary to protect the Association from imposition. The kind of labor provided could not be of such a description as required skill. Any one who could use his hands at all must be able to accomplish the task if he be willing to do so. Timber chopping for men and knitting for women were introduced and have answered the purpose of helping the willing, and o getting rid of the mere loafer.

ORGANIZATION.

When this Association was established there were already in existence, many institutions for relieving the different necessities of the poor, each acting largely in ignorance of what the others were doing.

Early in its career this Association set to work in the direction of charity organization and co-operation, and in the report which was prepared on the subject at the time (1874,) the following statement appeared, viz:

"In the subjoined statement of the amount annually expended in Aberdeen by the various public charities, which, through the kindness of those connected with them, the committee are enabled to present, there is a sufficient argument for the necessity of such co-operation as would enable each one to know what the other is doing, and thereby to check unnecessary overlapping and imposition."

	Persons.	Amount Expended.	TOTALS.
1. Poor Rates (for both Parishes).	2,368	£25,438	
Less—For stranger poor residing in the above Parishes, the amount of which is repaid.		4,245	
			£21,193
	Cases.		
2. Voluntary Alimentary Funds*	1,810	£3,613	
Medical Charities	13,200	7,345	
Congregational Funds†....say,	1,000	1,800	
Miscellaneous	5,000	2,152	
Exemptions (complete or partial) from Poor Rates	8,028	1,943	
			16,853
	Inmates.		
3. Hospitals (Educational)	1,500	£15,390	
			15,390
Totals	32,906		£53,436

* Including the Association for Improving the Condition of the Poor.

† "Exclusive of the amount contributed by the congregations of the six city churches, which is otherwise accounted for."

"As stated in the above table, about £25.000 (including £4,000 repaid for stranger poor), consists of poor rates. From £19,000 to £20,000 is revenue derived either from invested capital or from Government grants for industrial schools; while from £12,000 to £14,000 is raised by voluntary subscriptions. But the facts to be considered are, that on the books of the institutions included in the above table, which, although very diverse in their character, still come within the category of charitable and benevolent institutions, there are about 33,000 names, and that the annual expenditure is upwards of £53,000."

The approaches then made to the various bodies for information to facilitate the preparation of the foregoing statement, have been followed by a gratifying amount of co-operation between this Association and the municipal and parochial authorities, as well as most of the more private charities.

The co-operation takes various forms. In some cases, the chairman of our Association has been made an ex-officio member of the board or committee of management; in others, the secretary is invested with the powers of an administrator, giving assistance in the investigation and disposal of applications, while his recommendation of cases is uniformly accepted, and in every case the representations of the Association receive the most sympathetic and respectful consideration.

MENDICITY.

In the repression of mendicity the Association has sought to instruct the benevolent in sound principles of almsgiving, but still the tide of beggars flows on and will continue to flow so long as begging meets with the success which it does. The evil can be cured only by making it less profitable to beg than to work.

INTEMPERANCE.

In the work of the Association during the twenty-three years of its existence the evils of intemperance have forced themselves into prominence as chief of the hindrances to the prevention, mitigation, and cure of poverty. If poverty sometimes leads to intemperance, intemperance much more frequently leads to poverty. Better social conditions may do something to lessen intemperance, but the fact that there are many whose social condition is known to have been no safeguard leads to the conviction that not in one direction, but in many, must we look for the improvement of the condition of the poor, which we desire and are striving to bring about.

THE PROBLEM OF POVERTY IN AN ENGLISH RURAL UNION.

BY H. G. WILLINK, CHAIRMAN OF THE BRADFIELD BOARD OF GUARDIANS, BERKSHIRE.

Charity can scarcely be "organized" in the country in the same way as in a town. There is not the same need. People's circumstances are better known, and the amount of real distress is not so great. Moreover, persons who accept "charity organization principles" are rarer, and distance would in any case hinder joint work. "Overlapping" is probably one of the greatest evils, and no country committee could really stop that. As a matter of fact, the writer is not aware of any really rural union in which charity organization, as understood in towns, has been successfully attempted.

Nor is this very much to be regretted if the term "charity" is rightly comprehended by individuals. The letters £ s. d. do not spell "charity," and there is perhaps no kind of help more capable of being really helpful than that which country neighbors can give. A sensible broad minded rector or farmer, thoroughly in touch with rich and poor, can do as much as any committee.

The administration of the Poor Law in rural unions stands, however on a different basis. Officially centralized, in official contact with every parish, endowed with large discretionary authority, a Board of Guardians has almost unlimited powers of good and evil. Too often it is an obstacle to the growth among the poor of those very habits which charity organizationists most desire to foster. It can set an example of indiscriminate dole-giving, and promote indolence, improvidence, envy, deceit, dependence and selfishness. It can, by inadequate, unsuitable "relief" leave starvation unalleviated while stimulating greed. It can demoralize him that gives as well as him that takes. It can tempt the rich to evade their proper responsibilities, and can introduce log rolling into the dispensation of other people's money. It can in short do everything which the founders of the Poor Law intended that it should not do.

On the other hand, a board can do an almost infinite amount of good. And the object of this paper is to give some account of an English rural union in which has been accomplished during the last twenty years a piece of poor law administration that may fairly be regarded as having been essentially in harmony with charity organization principles, no less by bracing up the spirit of self-reliance than by tending to strengthen those ties of kinship and neighborly feeling between man and man, which are the very bonds of true charity.

Would that he who was mainly instrumental in the work, Mr. Bland-Garland, late chairman of the Board, were still alive to describe it.

The Bradfield Union comprises 62,650 acres, situated five-sixths in Berkshire and one-sixth in Oxfordshire, to the west of Reading, having a total rateable value in 1892 of £136,979. The population, which in 1871 was 15,853, had in 1891 risen to 18,017, in spite of the transfer in 1889 to the Reading Union of a portion containing about 1600 inhabitants. There is not any large town, and the villages are mostly small and scattered, there being in 1891 only one parish (which has two villages) with a population exceeding 3000; all the other 28 parishes have less than 1500, and only 5 of them more than 1000.

The occupation of the laboring classes is chiefly agricultural, except as regards such trades as brewing, brickmaking, building, forestry, corn mills, shop keeping, &c. In some parishes there is a considerable number of resident well to do landowners, while in others there are large extents of moor and rough ground occupied in places by small farmers and by cottagers descended from squatters. On the high lands the subsoil is chalk, or gravel on London clay, the lower ground being principally clay or, in the valleys, river gravel.

It is impossible to state shortly the rates of farm wages with any exactitude, but they may be taken to range at present from 15s. a week for the better kinds of laborers to 10s. for the lower kinds. Women earn 6s. as a rule at field work; charwomen of course get more. As regards men, however, these rates do not usually include the very common additional advantage of a cottage rent free, or at a low rental, generally with garden, nor the considerable earnings receivable at certain seasons in respect of harvesting, haymaking and piece work, ranging from 14s. to 25s. nor the "Michaelmas money" of £2 or £3 according to the class.* On the whole it may be said that a man

---

* The old custom of yearly hiring, wages being paid throughout, rain or fine, sick or well, has been largely superseded by written agreements providing *inter alia* that wages shall cease to be payable during disability caused by sickness or accident. Michaelmas money is not paid to laborers who are earning extra money at harvesting, haymaking or piecework.

in regular employment at a nominal 12s. a week really gets something more like 17s. a week on a year's average, without taking into account the produce of gardens and cheap allotments, the latter being rented usually at from 1½d. to 3d. per pole, including rates, tithe, &c. In many households, of course, the boy's earnings form a substantial addition to the family income.

Other wages run, roughly speaking, as follows, viz., building trade from 36s. to 18s. 6d.; brick kilns from 25s. to 18s.; breweries from 25s. to 15s. with 3 pints of beer per day; corn mills from 24s. to 18s. and often a cottage rent free; railway laborers about 18s. Another large field of labor is afforded by the wood lands, the weekly earnings averaging about 14s. to 16s., with the advantage of being earned at seasons when other work is scarce.*

Cottage rents vary as much as do wages, the highest rented cottages being by no means necessarily the best, for, as usual, the small landlords and small farmers can generally least afford to be liberal. From 3s. 6d. to 1s. 6d. or even lower, is probably a fair statement of the extremes; 1s. 6d. is an average rent for a cottage and garden on the larger estates. As above stated, there are some cases where squatter cottages exist. These are either held at low rentals, or are practically freehold. They are, for the most part, wretched little one-story, ill built tenements, often sadly overcrowded and sometimes falling into decay. The people, however, are attached to them, and indeed in many instances prefer them to the better-constructed dwellings erected by good landlords, which are probably as good as the same class of habitation all over England.

The character of the district having thus been stated in general terms, the reader will be better able to appreciate the following account of the poor law administration.

On 1st January, 1871, there were in receipt of poor relief 999 outdoor and 259 indoor paupers, (exclusive of lunatics in asylums and vagrants), a total of 1258, or one in thirteen (7.7 per cent.) of the then population. The total poor law expenditure for the year was £10,865, and the poor rate stood at 24½d. in the pound, entailing a cost of 13s. 8½d. per head of the population.

On 1st January, 1893, the corresponding figures were as follows, viz., outdoor paupers 22, indoor 99, total 121, or 1 in 148 (0.67 per cent.).

---

* In Appendix A will be found a more detailed statement of the wages in the various trades.

expenditure during the preceding year £1995, poor rate 3½d., cost per head of population 2s. 2½d.*

These figures (the scope of which is perhaps more clearly seen from the diagram in Appendix C) do not, remarkable as they are, suffice of themselves to show that the change of system has been successful in the true sense of the word. If they signified that there had merely been a blind withholding of needful relief, and that in 1892 the poor were actually worse off by £9000 than in 1870, they would point rather to failure than to success. If, again, it could be shown that the £9000 had been distributed in alms instead of in poor law relief, the outcome would appear to have been little more than a displacement of burden from public responsible shoulders to those of private individuals; though there would be something to be said even for this result, since charitable gifts are less pauperizing than poor law relief, inasmuch as they do not create a feeling of claim as of right.

But if the reduction of relief has been gradually made, and no applications have been refused without careful investigation ; if, as is generally admitted, the present condition of the poor is no worse, but decidedly better than under the old system, and bears comparison with the condition of the poor in other similar districts ; if while there may have been some increase of individual voluntary aid, such increase includes increased assistance from non-chargeable relatives, and from other persons (such as employers), upon whom there are only moral claims ; if, as is certain, there has been a marked growth of friendly societies, doctor's clubs, savings bank accounts, and other signs of thrift, then it cannot be denied that the poor law figures do represent a real advance, and that they testify to the success of a work which by raising the poor to a position of greater independence is in accordance with the principles of true charity organization.

It is sometimes objected that the work would have been impossible but for the general prosperity of the country and greater cheapness of living. This may possibly be quite true ; at any rate the general improvement of circumstances has been a factor which must not be forgotten.† But this only shows, if it shows anything, that other unions

---

* For statistics as to neighboring unions, see Appendix B.

† Agricultural wages seem to have risen but little, if at all. Labor in other trades is better paid. The prices of most necessaries have fallen, e. g. the 4 lb. loaf cost 7d. in 1873, in 1893 it cost 4½d. On the other hand, the standard of living is higher than it used to be.

could have done the same, not that Bradfield has been wrong or has not done anything.

Unfortunately there is some difficulty in getting exact statistics as to absence of hardship. The case must rest upon the statements of persons living in the district, and their opinions will vary according as they approve or disapprove of outdoor relief. There always will be people who would like to have out-relief if they could get it, as well as people who would like to be saved the trouble and the direct expense of taking an active part in trying to help their kinsfolk and neighbors. And there are still some people who honestly think that public relief is in itself better than private charity. Moreover there is, no doubt, as there has always been and always will be, a certain amount of real poverty in the union. So long as men, especially young men, spend all they get, so long as people marry before they can afford it, so long as there are bad workmen, and so long as drink maintains its attractions, there must be poverty. Consequences will follow causes. But poverty is not more likely to come when men realize that they can themselves provide against it;* and that if they do not do so they cannot reckon upon others saving them from the results. It is a significant fact that the late chairman's successor was elected upon the express understanding that the policy of the board should be continued, and no suggestion has since been made that that policy should be changed.

The present condition of the union may be judged in various ways. To take as a sample one parish, the population of which was 1327 in 1891, there were on 1st January, 1893, in the workhouse 12 persons belonging to the parish (5 being above 65 years of age, and 3 being children), and on the out-relief list 4, all these latter being survivals from the old times. It is not possible to give detailed statistics of any firm value as to the numbers and condition of the rest of the poorer classes, or the causes of their poverty. But of those persons (widows, widowers or old married people) who are unable to support themselves, there are, beside those known to be receiving more or less substantial help in charity, many who are practically supported by their own relations. There are several endowed charities, viz., one of about £25 a year applicable to the apprenticing of boys to some useful trade; one of about £3 10s. applicable in donations for special

---

* See Appendix E.

cases; two others of about £12 each, distributed once a year in doles among 10 poor men and 10 poor women; and lastly, almshouses capable of accommodating 3 old women.

There are a clothing club, a boot and shoe club, and a coal club. A medical club has long been in existence, the members of which, numbering over 100, are by a yearly payment of 5s. for adults and 2s. for children entitled to attendance free. A parish nurse is just completing her first year, and there has not been one instance in which difficulty has been made as to payment of her small fees, though, of course, the expenses are chiefly met by private subscriptions. An Oddfellows Lodge, of many years standing, now has about 145 members; it is entirely self-managed without the aid of the gentry, except that one acts as treasurer, and has more than £900 invested in sound securities. A schools penny bank has about 150 subscribers, with a total balance of about £80 deposits, in the Post Office. Interest at 1d. on each complete pound per month is allowed. The number of private savings bank accounts cannot be stated, but the writer knows of several. There are three voluntary schools, two of which are supported to some extent by a voluntary rate, the third being endowed. There are two village and one junior cricket clubs. There is a Horticultural Society, at whose annual show the cottagers and allotment holders compete in large numbers. Allotments in three or four different places are to be had at from 1d. to 2d. per pole according to situation. A workingmen's club, self-managed, is in a prosperous condition. It is not teetotal, but for a long time there has been no complaint. Lastly, at a recent sale of cottage property, chiefly of the squatter class before mentioned, no less than fourteen were purchased by cottagers, money being borrowed for the purpose in (it is believed) only four cases.

If it is said that this may be an exceptional parish, as being the one in which the late chairman of the board lived for twenty years, the writer can only say he does not believe it is exceptional, at any rate as regards the general condition of the people, though the smaller parishes can probably not show quite so good a roll of special advantages.* In other parishes there are similar signs of a healthy independence. For instance, a group of three small contiguous parishes, numbering together only 1100, has possessed for very many years a benefit society which

---

* In Appendix D will be found some tabulated information as to other parishes in the union.

has, with a present membership of 103, no less than £1230 invested, and has recently been pronounced by a competent actuary to be on so sound a basis that part of the fund may be applied towards provision for old age. In some parts of the union the Oddfellows, in others the Foresters, in others the Hearts of Oak, in others the Berkshire Friendly Society predominate: but there can be few, if any, in which thrift is not apparent in some form. Even the public house clubs, bad as they are (and they are giving way to better), point to a habit of living within income. Not that thrift implies every virtue; but its absence makes the practice of others very difficult among the poor.

The real danger, perhaps, lies in the direction of an exuberance of private alms-giving with the accompanying evil of mendicity, or at all events expectation of alms. The parishes where there are fewest rich residents are not always those which furnish the largest number of paupers in proportion to their population. There is in some places a tendency among benevolent people to relieve the merely "poor" from the duty of providing the necessaries of life. It is quite right that individual cases of real distress should be liberally helped, with care and discrimination. Nor can it be wrong for the rich to assist the poor to obtain certain advantages which, while not strictly necessaries, are nevertheless of real benefit to them and would otherwise be beyond their reach. For instance, a trained nurse cannot possibly be maintained solely out of the fees which poor country people can afford to pay. Yet so long as they do pay something her services may wisely be secured, not only for the sake of the comfort which they bring, but because of the teaching which insensibly accompanies them. Again, a well managed horticultural society can do so much to encourage proper gardening and husbandry, that money spent in supporting it cannot do anything but good. On the other hand, funds raised to enable whole classes of poor to purchase at less than cost-price articles (such as coals, clothing, or food), which would otherwise have to be bought in the usual way, are open to the objections against benevolent trading. And the same is true, in its degree, of the practice of subsidizing interest on savings. The most that can be said for these things is that they are less harmful in proportion to the amount contributed by the recipients, and that in so far as they induce self-denial by extracting periodical deposits, or as they bring rich and poor together in the transaction of necessary business, they do have a good effect. But these merits are not peculiar to these forms of action; and it must not be forgotten that there is difficulty in confining the dispensation of these funds within proper limits ; so that there is always a tendency to admit to participation in them individuals who ought to be able to do without them. It is in the direction of a wise ordering of these kinds of assistance that the influence of those who aim at promoting the well-being of the poor in rural districts may be applied. The object of charity is to relieve not the giver but the receiver, and so to relieve as to remove the causes of distress and not to perpetuate them.

But to return to the Bradfield Union. Another test of the working of its system may be applied by analyzing the indoor pauperism.

Of the 99 indoor paupers on 1st January, 1893, 59 were male and 40 female; 33 were children under 16, and 36 were old people over 65, 28 of whom were males and 8 females. Of the children 2 were orphans having lost both parents, 3 deserted by both or the only surviving parent, and 8 illegitimate. Of the total number of inmates 17 were in the infirmary on the doctor's book and 8 others were imbecile. There were 10 classed as able-bodied, 9 women, 1 man. This man, aged 44, who has since gone out, is of the casual class and unmarried ; his father and uncle were then in the workhouse. Of the 9 women, 5 had illegitimate children, 3 were weak-minded or subject to fits, and the husband of 1 was in gaol.

Again, these inmates may be regarded in the light of families, not individuals. Viewed in this way, the indoor pauperism reduces itself to 74, and even these 74 families were to some extent inter-related, and in several cases are of pauper descent or connection. It is hard to believe that any poor law administration could produce better results on a total population of over 18,000.

To sum up, unless it can be shown (*a*) that the poorer classes are worse off in Bradfield than elsewhere, or (*b*) that if not, private charity has reached an excessive pitch and is a worse form of assistance than outdoor relief, there can be no doubt that the board have proved themselves true guardians of the poor.

As to the latter point, those who hold charity organization principles, and consider that reliance upon State or rate funds is fatal to independence, will agree that private charity must indeed be badly and lavishly bestowed if it can do as much harm as out-relief; while as to the former point, this paper will have failed in its object if it has not convinced the reader that the laborer's position in the Bradfield Union

is not below the average standard of comfort in that part of England *
from youth to age, and that in the absence of great social or commercial disturbances everything points to a progressive amelioration of the present satisfactory conditions.

* Before this paper is printed will be published the Bluebooks containing the Report of the Assistant Commissioner upon the condition of the agricultural laborer. Bradfield was not among the unions selected for investigation, but the adjoining union of Basingstoke and the union of Wantage were visited, and the Reports will no doubt be full of information. They can be obtained from King & Son, King Street, Westminster. There are about 12 series, each costing from 1 to 2 shillings.

APPENDIX A.

CURRENT WAGES IN BRADFIELD UNION, 1893.

Agricultural: Per Week.

Carters, 13/ to 15/ + cottage + harvest and extras, equivalent altogether to about............ 17/ to 20/

Under carters, 9/ to 13/ + harvest and extras, equivalent altogether to about............ 12/ to 15/

Stockmen, (young men generally) 12/ to 14/ + cottage + harvest and extras, equivalent to about....... 17/ to 19/

Mill men and machine men............ 16/ to 22/

Farm laborers, first class, 15/ + harvest and extras, (sometimes cottage)............ 16/ to 18/

Field hands, 12/ to 13/ + harvest and extras............ 14/ to 16/

Rickbuilders and Thatchers............ 16/ to 17/

Building: Per Week.

Bricklayers.	7d. per hour, equivalent say to	32/	
Stone masons,	8	"	"	"	36/8
Plasterers,	8	"	"	"	36/8
Carpenters,	7	"	"	"	32/
Plumbers,	7½	"	"	"	34/3
Painters,	6½	"	"	"	29/9
Plumbers' mates.	4½	"	"	"	20/6
Laborers.	4	"	"	"	18/4

Chiefly Summer Work.

Brewing:

Tunmen,
Enginemen,
Coopers,
Head Maltsters,
} from 20/ to 25/ per week, also 3 pints per day

Ordinary laborers,
e. g., Cleaners,
Draymen, &c.
} from 15/ to 18/ "

Cornmills:

Foremen, 30/ + cottage, equivalent (say) to........32/6 per week.

Purifiermen, Rollermen, 24/ + cottage, equivalent (say) to............26/ "

Carters, 20/ + cottage............22/ "

Sack carriers and general millers............18/ "

Brick Kilns ....from 18/ to 25/

NOTE.—During the last 20 years wages have not varied much as regards agricultural labor.

In the brewing and cornmilling trades they have risen 10 per cent.

APPENDIX B.

Percentage of Indoor and Outdoor Poor (excluding vagrants) on the population of twelve Berkshire Unions.

UNION.	Population 1891.	Percentage of Indoor poor on the Population.	Percentage of Outdoor poor on the Population.
Abingdon	19,612	0.80	1.73
Bradfield	18,017	0.61	0.14
Cookham	20,468	0.86	2.91
Easthampstead	13,717	0.78	2.03
Faringdon	13,544	0.80	2.37
Hungerford	17,017	0.63	3.22
Newbury	21,677	0.90	1.97
Reading	60,054	0.85	0.28
Wallingford	14,706	1.01	0.66
Wantage	16,544	0.57	2.80
Windsor	35,649	0.75	1.13
Wokingham	17,347	0.72	2.01
Total	268,352	0.79	1.50

APPENDIX C.

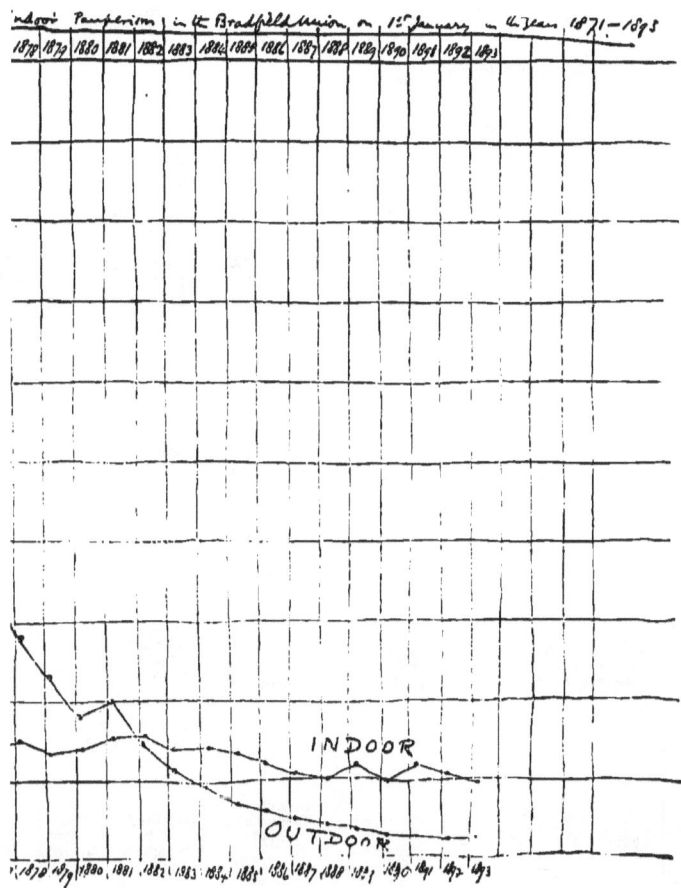

Indoor Pauperism, in the Bradfield Union, on 1st January, in the years 1871—1893

APPENDIX D.

Four Parishes in the Bradfield Union.

Parish.	Area in Acres	Population 1891	Paupers 1 Jan., 1893. In-door.	Paupers 1 Jan., 1893. Out-door.	Other poor dependent on relatives or friends or charity.	Endowed Charities.	Clothing, coal and similar Clubs.	Doctors clubs.	Parish Nurse.
A	4237	1127	12	4		i. £25 a year for apprenticing lads. ii. £10s. spec'l cases iii. £2 annual dole. iv. £1 annual dole. v. Almshouses for 3.	Clothing club. Boot and shoe club. Coal club. (All subsidized slightly.)	One. 5s. per head per annum for adult 2s. for children. Membership over 100.	One. Paid out of (a) fees (b) subscriptions.
B	1175	277	1	0	4 of whom 2 are certainly supported entirely by relatives.	i. Annual dole bread and clothes. ii. " " coal. iii. " " " iv. £20 a year for the school.	Clothing club.	One. Much same as above.	No.
C					The district really forms part of a larger parish, though it is for most purposes distinct, and there are no separate returns *	38 (over 65) of whom 15 are certainly supported by relatives.	i. Rent of parish land applied in coals. ii. Almshouses for 3.	Clothing club. Coal club. "Relief club."	One.	No.
D	989	159	1	0	2 (widows); one is supported entirely by relatives.	a. £12 a yr. School and Poor. b. £1 10s. Calico.	Clothing Club. Subsidized.	One. 6d. per quarter. 8 members	No.

*The returns for this large parish are as follows: Area 4848, Pop. 3154, Paupers, Indoor 27, Outdoor 1.

APPENDIX D.—Continued.

Friendly Society.	Penny Bank.	Schools.	Cricket, &c. Clubs.	Horticult. Society.	Workingmen's Club	Allotments.	Remarks.
Oddfellows. Membership 145. Invested Funds over £900. *Berks Friendly.* Membership 8.	In all schools. Membership about 150. Balance in hand over £80.	Three all voluntary. Total children on books about 300.	Three and a Junior.	Yes, very well supported.	Yes. Non-teetotal, self managed.	Yes. In 3 or 4 places, from 1d. to 2d. per pole.	Occupation chiefly agricultural and forestry. A straggling parish, 3 or 4 good sized, and 6 or 7 smaller, gentlemen's houses, 1 large flour mill. Cottage rents from 1s. to 3s. 6d. A good many small freeholders.
A joint Society common to three small Parishes. Membership (all 3 Parishes) 103. Invested Funds over £1200	Started in Dec. 1801. Membership about 40.	One. Voluntary. Children on books about 60.	One.	No.	No.	None.	Occupation chiefly agricultural. One good sized brewery. No freehold cottages. No squatters. Only one large house & the rectory
Foresters. Membership 200. Invested funds about £600. *Oddfellows.* G. W. Railway Benevolent Society. Juvenile Foresters and other clubs.	Yes. Doing well.		One senior, one junior and a football club.	No.	Yes. Non-teetotal.	Yes, at 3d. per pole, but not all taken.	Five good farms, brick kilns, market gardens. Many men work in Reading, or on the railway or river. Cottage rents from 1s. 6 to 7s. 0.
District Benefit Society. 21 Parishioner members. Total No. of members about 250. Total funds £1000.	No.	Voluntary, 30 on books.	No.	In neighboring parish, a few parishioners exhibit.	No.	About 5 acres at 1d. per pole.	Occupation agricultural. Two farmers. Three freehold cottagers. No squatters. No gentry besides the farmers and the parson. Cottage rents from 1s. to 1s. 6d. a week.

APPENDIX E.

Table showing means available for providing against sickness and old age, (the figures being only selected specimens from a number of various tables.)

Oddfellows:

A young man joining at the age of 18 may by weekly payments of 6½d. secure a sick allowance of 12/ per week for the first 6 months of sickness and 6/ per week afterwards, with £12 on death, and £6 on death of his wife.

Berkshire Friendly Society:

Such a man may by payments of 7d. per month during his life secure a sick allowance of 4/ per week at any time during his life. For 1/ per month he will be entitled to 6/ per week in sickness up to 70 and a pension of 3/ per week after that age.

Private Saving:

A lad beginning to save at 17 may by putting away weekly sums increasing gradually from 3d. to 1/6 find himself at 25 in possession of £25, without including interim interest receivable. By saving sums rising similarly from 6d. to 2/6, he would have accumulated £43, exclusive of interest, by the same age.

CHARITY ORGANIZATION IN RELATION TO VOLUNTARY EFFORT.

BY THE REV. BROOKE LAMBERT, M. A., B. C. L., VICAR OF GREENWICH, LONDON.

A cynic has told us that when the virtues met in a better sphere, Charity asked to be introduced to Gratitude ; they had never, they said, met before. The cynic is wrong, as cynics generally are. He has mistaken so-called Good Nature for Charity, and as for Gratitude, which he tells us elsewhere in the History of Human Weakness is the expectation of future favors, he has not seen her. Yet I should like to make his parable true by saying that Charity and Commonsense were strangers till they met at 15 Buckingham Street.*

In saying this I am by no means claiming for the Charity Organization Society any more than I claim for any other good movement. The genesis of all movements which are destined to prevail is the same. First, there is the voice of one crying in the wilderness, and some few go out to hear him. But he dies the martyr's death. Then his big message is caught up by minor prophets, till by degrees the conscience of mankind is awakened. Then there comes a movement which gives voice to half formed, half expressed notions. Such has been the story of charity organization. It is the result of many prophets' work. It has succeeded at last in introducing Commonsense to Charity. Charity so-called had long sought to better mankind, but Charity such as we know is human, and therefore fallible. She needed to learn of Him who visited a pool at Bethesda and saw a multitude of sick folk, and healed only one. Commonsense met her and explained this apparently eccentric exercise of mercy, showed her that poverty like disease had many causes, and that it was mere waste of power to help those who would afterwards fall back into the same condition. Commonsense made her understand that there was a "worse thing" even than thirty-eight years suffering, that character was more precious than comfort, that self-restraint was cheaply purchased at the cost of suffering. For commonsense is educated judg-

* Office of Charity Organization Society. London.

ment, and is not to be mistaken for that empirical instinct which often breeds nonsense.

I learn that in other papers which are to be presented to this Congress it will have been laid down that there is a sphere for voluntary effort. I presume that it will have been shown that there is a sphere in which it can profitably work, that there are cases which must be left to legal treatment, which if equitable is stern. To use the parallel of medicine, some cases must be treated in hospitals and asylums.

I learn, too, that it will have been asserted that there is a special sphere and scope for the work of the churches. I hope it will have been emphatically asserted that when the churches take up a case they must treat it thoroughly and fully. Again using the parallel of medicine, they must see that the patients have food as well as physic, and must not because the case is burdensome provide the one, and leave the other to haphazard.

I learn, further, that it has been laid down that there is a sphere for individual munificence. I suppose a distinction will have been drawn between organization and relief. Organized charity is not selfishly eager to treat the case for the satisfaction of being credited with the cure. Again using medicine to guide us, the patient will be sent to that doctor, that climate, that "cure," where the case can be best treated. I am asked to wind up the discussion with some words on the mutual relation of these agencies. I write in the dark, not having seen the other papers. Some remarks on the subject of charity organization will, I hope, illustrate the subject.

Whatever may have been said : 1. It is the purpose of charity organization by calling in the aid of all society agencies to quicken individual sympathy. The charity of the multitude, that which the cynic miscalls charity, may be expressed in the words "Send her away for she crieth after us." Poverty is so unpleasant, let us get rid of it. A gift of money will stop the cry, a gift of clothes will cover the rags. The Charity Organization Society says to those who call themselves benefactors, to the individual givers, you must throw yourself like a doctor into the case, determined to cure, not simply to palliate the suffering. This is further the message it gives to voluntary societies. Only that society can be said to be doing the work it ought to do in which the care of the individual is not lost in the thought of the association. The society must beware of routine and treat each case individually.

2. This will be the message of charity organization to the churches. The great object of charity organization is to produce better conditions of life. When the doctor has to treat a case he does not nowadays attempt only to alleviate symptoms, he tries to restore the system. Diet does as much as drugs. You, it says to the churches, have been thinking of one remedy mainly, and in your effort to make people take that remedy you have often increased the disease. Without self-respect the sufferer can never recover. In your effort to make men take the nostrum on which you rely, you have mixed up charity and religion in a way which has destroyed self-respect. When you fully realize that your agency is only one among many, when you have ceased to regard your proselytes as worthy of more attention than any others, then you will have learnt that true charity regards the need and not the creed. Then perhaps you will understand why He, whom you profess to follow, was so constantly pointing out that Samaritans and heathen were not so completely outside the pale as your representatives in these days affirm. You will learn the difference between faith and a creed.

3. The Charity Organization Society holds up to the individual donor the two truths which it has tried to enforce on volunteers and on churches: individual contact; the bettering of the general conditions. It will show him that this agency offers the munificent donor a way of coming into contact with those who need his help, new to him. If he listens to the tale of the man who knocks at his door, or makes the postman his ambassador, he will find himself often deceived. If he will spare an hour a week to go down to the Society's office and read through the case papers, he will find abundant occasion for munificence. His charity account will be like his private account. There will be big and little sums in it. He will not always be spending. He will often find it well to reserve himself for a big occasion. He will find there is a spring and an autumn, a time for spending, a time for saving. Generally the result of his experience will be that, whereas before he gave ten pounds or shillings to ten cases, and found these cases to be recurring decimals, he will now give £10 to one case, and find that by the gift he will have put the person out of need of distress. He will understand the incident at the pool of Bethesda, and see that perfect charity must leave certain cases untouched. Meanwhile he will have learnt what a millionaire may do. The meaning of poverty will have been revealed to him, he will of necessity become a philanthropist.

Not content as once to leave orders when he is away to draw on him for heavy cases, he will use his leisure and his brains to do away with the causes of poverty. Some of these are as remediable as those sanitary defects which made epidemics plagues. He will learn that legislation can come to the aid of sympathy. In removing the sources of evil, in supporting efforts to develop thrift and self-reliance, he will do much to diminish pauperism, if he cannot annihilate poverty. Money spent to help forward such projects will be as real charity in his eyes as direct gifts to the poor. Then, too, perchance there will be born in him the spirit of the old Greeks. He will feel that to undertake a λειτουργια, to be the means of furnishing public recreation in providing for the people parks and libraries is a privilege. He will know that this expenditure of money will be more profitable than that employed in controlling syndicates, or in supporting a personal state which is food for penny-a-liners. He will feel that his own art treasures and pleasure grounds minister to a much higher purpose when he holds them in trust for the good of others. His own personal satisfaction will be multiplied just in so far as he shares with others that which once had only the value derived from exclusive and solitary possession. This will be the message of charity organization. As men listen to it they will become acquainted with the sweet virtue Charity, who is always accompanied by her sister Gratitude, because she does not, like the Charity of the cynic's story, patronize, pauperize, or humiliate her clients.

FRIENDLY VISITING.

BY MISS F. C. PRIDEAUX, WOMEN'S UNIVERSITY SETTLEMENT, BLACKFRIARS ROAD, LONDON.

The organized scheme of friendly visiting which I am about to describe had its origin rather more than two years ago in the minds of Miss Octavia Hill and others, who were keenly alive to a need which it is intended to fill. This need is described by Miss Octavia Hill herself in the Nineteenth Century Magazine for August, 1891. It may be briefly characterized as the need for the union of two people in one, the ordinary district visitor and the charity organization visitor, or perhaps it would be more correct to say, the union in one person of the methods of the ordinary district visitor with the principles of the charity organization society visitor. These two had for the most part been strangers so far, and not infrequently regarded one another with something of the suspicion bred of ignorance. But this was not a necessary state of things. Miss Octavia Hill felt how much might be gained by the really friendly and systematic visiting of a group of families by one who came with no gifts in her hand and who would therefore be valued as a friend or not at all, visiting not only in times of special pressure or distress, but constantly, and so gaining some knowledge of the family under all circumstances. What she wished to see was the periodical house to house visiting and the personal knowledge of a few peoples pecially committed to her charge, that is, the method of the ordinary district visitor, combined with those principles on the subject of material relief and other questions which we may call generally "Charity Organization Society," and which the ordinary district visitor is in the habit of disregarding. It is impossible for the visitors from the charity organization committees to fill this need. Their time must be occupied for the most part with visiting the cases actually applying for help; and after the decision has been arrived at and the family helped or not, as the case may be, the visits in the nature of things will drop. Where a pension is regularly allowed, there will certainly be scope for a friendly weekly visit, and that the value of this visit is recognized is shown by the fact that most committees make a point of the pension being taken by a visitor rather than fetched from the office by the pensioner; but such cases form a very small proportion of the whole, and even in them perhaps the friendliness of the visit is a little spoiled by its being inseparable from relief. Evidently then, visiting from a charity organization society's office could not meet the want, though close co-operation with the local charity organization committee was an essential element in the idea. It was clear that some fresh organization was wanted and this organization, as then planned and now practised, I will here attempt to sketch.

The central idea being to have a body of visitors who would each undertake to visit regularly a certain group of families, the two questions which first arose were naturally how should the visitors be found, and whom should they visit? Miss Octavia Hill's connection with the Women's University Settlement in Southwark led her very readily to an answer to the first question. Here were already a few women who should be fitted and would certainly be willing to undertake the work, while beyond those actually living in Southwark was the association which supported the settlement and included many who would be glad to give one day weekly to something of this kind. And so it came about that the organization started with the settlement as its basis, and ever since the connection between them has been of the closest possible nature. In the first place the warden of the settlement naturally became the head or directress of the visitors. As all applications for work of whatever kind at the settlement are made to her in the first instance, she was thus able to select for this visiting work those who seemed likely to succeed best with it, and these visitors understood that they were responsible to her. It was impressed upon them that when anything seemed to need attention in the circumstances of the people they were visiting, this was to be reported at once at the settlement, special report forms being provided for the purpose. Among those circumstances that should be and are reported are such as destitution, unsanitary condition of the house, neglect of school, chronic illness or special physical affliction of any kind in any member of the family, as well as occasional events, such as temporary illness or accidents of any description. These reports it is the care of one of the resident workers at the settlement to receive and attend to at once. The advantage of this is obvious, as the resident worker being always on the spot there is no unnecessary delay, which could not be avoided if the visitor herself, living as she often does in quite another part of London, tried to do all that is required. But as far as possible, she is associated with the resident worker in what is done for the cases reported by her. Often where she has the requisite experience she is able to carry the whole matter through herself, and always the aim is not to take it out of her hands more than is necessary. When a report has been received it is made into a case much after the fashion of the Charity Organization Society case papers, and every week at a fixed time the warden and the worker in charge of the cases,—secretary for the district visitors as she might be called—go through all the cases, discuss the best means of dealing with them, and record their suggestions as to how it should be done on the case paper. The visitor at her next weekly visit comes to the settlement to see what this suggestion has been and acts upon it, always supposing that her judgment coincides, as it is not at all wished that she should look upon it as an arbitrary decision.

But it was felt that this system of reports would not quite suffice for the visitor, who might easily desire advice about some of her people without having any special need of theirs to report upon. It was thereford arranged that each visitor should have an opportunity monthly for talking over her district. To this interview she brings her book in which are entered the names of all those whom she visits, with as many particulars about them as she has been able to gather, the families are gone through and the difficult points which are sure to arise in her intercourse with her people can be discussed. But a need for something more than this even was recognized, if the work of the visitors was to be all that it might. Beside advice on special points, which could only be given separately to each, there was much knowledge of a general nature which would be useful to all and which could be given to them collectively, local knowledge as to the resources of the neighborhood in the way of education, amusement, relief in sickness, etc., or knowledge on such points as the working of the Poor Law, elementary education, friendly societies and so forth. It was therefore decided that the best way would be to have monthly meetings at the settlement to which all the visitors should be invited, and at each of which a paper was read or an informal lecture given on one of the subjects mentioned above or the like. These monthly meetings were held for more than a year and only discontinued as their place was taken by courses of lectures on similar subjects given at the settlement to other workers besides the district visitors. It had been felt for some time that education for philanthropic workers of every kind was becoming more and more important, as the complexity increased of the problems which, however seemingly simple their work, they must inevitably come across. To meet this demand to some small extent these lectures were started at the settlement, specially with a view to the district visitors and other workers in Southwark.

So much for the organization of the visitors; now for the question as to whom they should visit. Possibly it may seem as if this question could hardly present a difficulty, considering the great numbers of the poor massed together in South and East London, and the comparatively small number of those who have any desire to visit them. But it must be remembered that the parochial machinery, though inadequate for the most part for want of workers, is still at work and that wherever the settlement district visitors began to visit it must be in somebody's parish, and that at least the leave of the vicar, if possible his co-operation, must be obtained. Fortunately for the new scheme the vicar of St. Paul's, Westminster Bridge Road, was ready to welcome as a band of helpers the visitors from the settlement.

A certain part of his parish was apportioned off to be visited by them and the connection of these visitors with himself and the other clergy of the parish was and is still maintained by means of the parochial relief committee held weekly, at which the warden or the secretary to the district visitors is always present, and reports are exchanged. Nothing of moment, therefore, can happen in any district without its being reported to the clergy at the weekly committee, or if their help be urgently needed, they are communicated with by the secretary without any delay.

There are now 15 visitors all with two or three exceptions working close together in this parish of St. Paul's.

I have said that co-operation with the local charity organization society committee was one of the essential elements in the idea of the scheme. This co-operation is very closely maintained, for the secretary for the district visitors is also a member of the charity organization committee. She there takes special charge, as it were, of all cases which apply from the districts and works them entirely. The warden is also a member of the charity organization committee, and the fact that these two are on both the parochial and charity organization committees secures the most complete co-operation possible. It was hoped that not only might the charity organization committee help the visitors, but that occasionally at any rate the visitors might help the charity organization committee by being able to supply information about applicants living in one or other of their districts of a more detailed and dependable kind than could be obtained from a single visit or the accounts of the neighbors. But, of course, the help is chiefly on the other side. Whenever a case reported by a visitor at the settlement seems to be of such a nature as to make help by the Charity Organization Society desirable, it is referred to the committee, and the person in need is told to apply; or sometimes the intermediate step of reporting the case at the settlement is not necessary and the person is sent straight to the charity organization office. Almost all cases except those of temporary sickness are by the decision of the parochial committee referred to the Charity Organization Society, which, therefore, becomes the usual channel of relief. But the visitor may be and generally is the means by which the relief is given; as if it be the question of a loan granted by the committee, she would be the natural person to collect it at her weekly visit, and to distribute the pension or temporary relief which had been allowed to any of her people.

Effort is also made to maintain co-operation with all other wise local agencies for the good of the people; with one especially, perhaps, it is well that the visitor should be in close touch, namely, the Metropolitan Association for Befriending Young Servants. Sometimes certainly, very often possibly, she will come across young girls in her district on the lookout for places, first places perhaps. She will feel the great importance of this first place turning out successful, but will not have the requisite time or opportunities for finding it herself. By referring the girl to the free registry of the Association she knows that all she would like to do will be done and done more efficiently by them.

One word might here be said as to the rules for visitors to guide them in their work. They are of course expected to visit regularly, and to make note of their visit in the book of which mention has been made. Appended is a specimen sheet from one of these visitors' books, showing the sort of information that is to be obtained where possible, and, of course, only by degrees. Very often there may be no special remarks to record, but just the date and the fact of the visit having been paid should be entered. This system of keeping a written record has been found of great use both by the visitors for reference for themselves, and also specially when a district has had to be handed on from one visitor to another. But there is one rule, and one only, on which much stress is laid, and that is one which really follows from what has already been said about the connection with the Charity Organization Society, namely, that no relief of any kind be given by the visitor on her own responsibility alone. One great point in the whole scheme was this, that the visitor never being looked upon as the source from which material relief in the shape of tickets or money would flow, her visits might be valued by the people for just what they were worth in themselves; the help that she was to give them was to be just that which her own nature made it possible for her to give, and as experience has shown, this means a great deal from some people, if but little from others. And it need hardly be pointed out how much she herself gains from this rule; if she is welcomed, she knows it is not for the sake of what she brings with her, and at any rate one obstacle to her getting to know the people as they really are is removed.

Perhaps it may be thought that a good deal has been said about what the visitor may not or cannot do, and very little about the positive side of her work. It must be remembered in the first place that friendliness is to be the characteristic of these visits, and we may have a very friendly feeling for a person for years, and add something, however, inconsiderable, to their pleasure in life by this feeling, without being able to do them one single act of service worthy of record, much as we should like to. It was felt by the starters of the scheme that friendliness was a thing of growth which if it were to be worth anything would not spring up at a word; it would, however, be very desirable to give the visitor some regular excuse for calling on the people whom she was to try to know, some *raison d'être* for her visits until such friendly relations should be established as to make excuse unnecessary. The distribution of tickets or tracts, the traditional district visitor's resource, was out of the question, and the exactly opposite course was decided on, the district visitor should not distribute, she should collect. She should suggest to and make easy for the people the habit of putting by something weekly, by taking round with her a number of stamps and post office forms, selling the stamps to those who would join her bank, and then starting them with their post office savings bank book when the necessary shilling had been saved. Thus she not only gained an introduction to her people, but began her acquaintance by a real, if small, act of service, introducing them to the great State-aided system of saving, and helping them in the little formalities which often seem so formidable to them as to deter them from belonging to the Post Office Savings Bank. And the acquaintance once established, opportunities for other acts of service are sure to come sooner or later in the course of the family vicissitudes. There is at the settlement a small library from which books can be taken by visitors and lent to their people; there are often notices of evening classes, entertainments, exhibitions or the like, to which she can invite those for whom they are suitable; she can urge upon the girls to join a benefit society established in the district, and in many other ways can she be the link which is often all that is wanted to bring together the people of a neighborhood and the advantages, educational or recreative, all ready for them.

And now to conclude, as this scheme has been in force nearly two years it may fairly be asked has it been a success? The answer must be I think that where the right person has been at work the scheme has been distinctly successful: everything depends here, as elsewhere, on the individual worker, and the difference between what some have achieved when compared with the results obtained by others is most marked. But speaking generally, I should say that so far as succeeding in getting on friendly terms with the people goes, the visitors as a body have been more successful than might have been hoped, though perhaps not as much is done in the way of collecting savings as was expected at first. And as among ourselves one friend will have far more power of helping and influencing for good than another, so one visitor will be able to make her friendliness much more fruitful than another, yet the mere fact that a feeling of friendliness exists at all must be so much to the good and is well worth any efforts that have been made to advance it. But not too much of even this must be looked for by any who might think of taking up work of this kind. Again what we find in our intercourse with friends and acquaintances of our own class will hold good here. With some we seem to have by nature that inexplicable sympathy which makes it possible for us to influence and even help them sometimes, while with others it is just the contrary; without any fault exactly, our two natures do not harmonize and we can do each other no good. So in our districts, we must not reasonably expect to influence all alike, perhaps with some we may never "get on" at all. Of one thing we may be sure, that there will be very little to show or to talk of as the result of our work; it will be very indefinite, intangible, so that we ourselves may often doubt whether we are doing any good at all. But the "growing good of the world is partly dependent on unhistoric acts," and that friendliness and mutual interest should be awakened is surely something towards the "growing good," though the acts that go to bring it about are unhistoric and insignificant indeed.

SPECIMEN SHEET FROM VISITOR'S BOOK.

(RIGHT HAND PAGE)

Name,		Address,		Floor,	
CHRISTIAN NAMES.	AGE.	OCCUPATION OR CHILDREN'S SCHOOL.	SAVINGS OR CLUB.	REMARKS.	
				Only remarks of permanent interest to be entered under this head.	

(LEFT HAND PAGE)

DATE.	DEPOSIT.	VISIT.	DATE.	DEPOSIT.	VISIT.

ENGLISH POOR LAW.

BY BALDWYN FLEMING, GENERAL INSPECTOR OF LOCAL GOVERNMENT BOARD FOR COUNTIES OF DORSET, SOUTHAMPTON, SURREY AND WILTS.

The memories of sixty years ago have grown so dim that it is difficult to realize the terrors and the miseries which led to the introduction of the "New Poor Law" in 1834. Much may be learned from the most logical and powerful report of the Poor Law Commissioners upon which that act was founded; but it is necessary to dig deep into local records and the passing literature of the times to appreciate how completely the comfort and convenience of the well conducted sections of society were at the mercy of vicious, insolent, and rapacious idlers.

In the more quiet days which have come for us it is difficult to understand a state of affairs under which employers of labor were obliged to part with old and trusty servants, in order to find room for the able-bodied loafers allotted to them by the parish.

It is hard to believe that if any single woman declared herself to be pregnant, and charged any person with being the father, it was lawful for any justice of the division to issue his warrant for the immediate apprehension of such person, and his committal to gaol unless he gave security to indemnify the parish.

Grumble as we may at the rates imposed upon us, it is difficult to picture to ourselves the reality of a time when they were in many places 10s. and 12s., in several places over 20s., and in at least one place over 30s., in the pound.

It is difficult now to realize the absolute despair of employer and employed in the times when night after night through the southern counties of England the sky was reddened with the flames of the burning food of the people, and the landowner or the farmer scarcely dared to lay his head upon the pillow.

We have almost forgotten the tragedy of the special assize issued to deal with the rioters of Berkshire, Hampshire, Wiltshire and Dorsetshire, when prisoners were tried by the hundred and sentenced to death by the score. Public opinion revolted against the execution of such a crowd of victims. But although in a few cases only was the capital sentence carried into effect, the wretched men were torn from their homes to transportation and imprisonment, in numbers which represent so appalling a sum of suffering that even now it can be recalled only with shuddering horror.

The problem to be solved by the Poor Law Commissioners was twofold: (1) the reformation of the laboring classes who had become absolutely demoralized by the then Poor Law; (2) the salvation of the country from financial ruin.

The Commissioners spared no effort to obtain every information upon every branch of the complications which they were set to unravel, and as the evidence was sifted and compared, it was found all to point in one direction only—that the evils which had assumed such portentous proportions were distinctly traced back to one great economical error, the unlimited grant of outdoor relief to the able-bodied. The whole tenor of the elaborate report of 1834 may be summed up in the foregoing sentence, and the cause having been made clear the remedy was equally apparent. Outdoor relief to the able-bodied must be abolished. This alone would not, however, complete the reform that was imperative for the restoration of order and prosperity. It was essential that all able-bodied destitution should be tested, and that, in one form or another, the test should be work in return for the relief afforded.

The Poor Law Acts and Orders do not prohibit out-relief to the sick, the widow, the orphan, or the aged and infirm, but only to the able-bodied; and even for that class there are many exceptions and modifications to meet emergencies and prevent hardship. The great principle of the English Poor Law as it now exists is that outdoor relief shall not be given to those who are able to work, and that all who are able to work and receive relief, whether under ordinary circumstances in the workhouse, or in exceptional cases out of the workhouse, shall have their destitution put to the proof by the enforcement of a labor test. In working out this principle another great object has been kept in view—that the position of the pauper should be less eligible than that of the independent laborer.

A comparison between the England of to-day and the England of sixty years ago will show at once how sound were the conclusions arrived at by the Poor Law Commissioners in 1834, and how large a measure of gratitude is due to them from their descendants. In one sense the present position of pauperism is undoubtedly disappointing. The prevailing sentiment which underlies the "New Poor Law" is the abolition of outdoor relief, and although the law has been more than fifty years in operation out-relief continues to be granted to a large, and in some parts to an enormous extent.

It was apparently the hope and the intention of those who framed the Act of 1834, that the withdrawal of out-relief from the able-bodied, and the closer restriction of all relief outside the workhouse, would create habits of thrift and independence, which would result in provision for sickness and old age without recourse to the degradation of relief from the rates. It may be argued that the large amount of out-relief still granted is proof that such hopes and expectations have proved to be unfounded. But it would be very wrong to assume that such an argument is correct. Many considerations must be weighed before any conclusion can be attempted, and it is doubtful whether even yet experience is old enough to warrant a reliable decision as to the final effects of the Poor Law as at present constituted. One thing is certain, it was inevitable that the aged and infirm who are now upon the rates, either in or out of the workhouses, should come upon the rates when they had outlived their own generation and their wage-earning power. Neither they nor their relations had the facilities for thrift which are so freely offered to the younger generation, and it was the almost unavoidable consequence of their position that such as survived to old age would find themselves compelled to come to the Poor Law for maintenance during the ending of their days. This fact, however, should not put us out of heart, and society to-day can afford to grant with a very sympathetic hand such relief as may best meet the necessities of those whose burdens are the outcome of the stormy times in which they were bred. It by no means follows that succeeding generations will be equally needy. On the contrary there are many hopeful indications that the present phase of old age pauperism is a passing one, and that the laboring population are taking full advantage of the opportunities for maintaining their independence.

The enormous development of friendly benefit and kindred societies, the steady increase in the savings banks deposits, the greater prudence with regard to marriage, the intellectual advancement of the people, the evergrowing facilities of transport, the extension of free libraries, the means of obtaining instruction in every branch of education, and the constant decline of pauperism, all give evidence that the working classes are willing and able to provide for themselves when they are not demoralized by mischievous offers of maintenance without work.

The test of destitution by work has been proved to be the only sound principle upon which relief can be afforded at the public cost. This principle is at once the justification of the workhouse, and the condemnation of outdoor relief. Indoor relief can be tested; outdoor relief cannot. Indoor relief is sufficient; outdoor relief must be insufficient. Indoor relief is shown to be required by the fact that it is accepted; outdoor relief affords occasion for endless fraud and imposition. Indoor relief is safe as regards the interests of the poor and of the ratepayer; outdoor relief is equally dangerous to both.

The large amount of out-relief still granted, although not so indefensible as it may at first sight appear to be, does most certainly give ground for anxiety—all the more so, because it has been over and over again proved to be unnecessary, notwithstanding all that may fairly be urged in its favor. Wherever the Guardians have made an intelligent and continued effort to diminish pauperism by restricting out-relief, they have been successful. The object to be aimed at is not the abolition of out-relief, but the restriction of out-relief to the smallest legitimate amount. This has been tried under every variety of circumstances in unions of the most different descriptions, Atcham, Bradfield, Brixworth, Manchester and Whitechapel are but a few of many, where sound administration has worked as beneficially for the poor as for the ratepayers. If the good example of such administration had been universally followed, the condition of the laboring classes would give less cause for doubt than it does at present to those who most desire to elevate them above the necessity of recourse to rate relief. The very fact that the Poor Law stands between the individual and actual destitution must have an adverse influence upon thrift and self-help, and that influence becomes the more powerful as the limits of rate relief are widened.

The influence itself may be submitted to in order to protect the community from greater mischief, but clearly it should be kept within the narrowest possible bounds. It is a mistake to urge that indoor relief is more disgraceful than outdoor relief. Both are unfortunate necessities, and it is a false philanthropy to minimize the evils of pauperism; but in a comparison of in with out-relief the latter is the worse of the two.

The recipient of indoor relief submits to the fullest test of destitution and gives the fruits of his labor in return for the relief afforded to him. The person who obtains out-relief, submits to no test of destitution and gives nothing whatever in return for what he receives. That indoor relief is distasteful may be admitted, and it is fortunate that it is so.

The reluctance to enter the workhouse is the best inducement to make provision for the later years of life, and operates powerfully to enforce the obligation upon the members of a family for their mutual support. As regards life in an English workhouse there is very little to which reasonable objection can be taken. Speaking generally, the accommodation is good, the diet is sufficient, the regulations provide for every comfort subject to the enforcement of necessary discipline, the sick are carefully tended, the children well educated, and the inmates well treated.

In 1834 the able-bodied poor created the difficulty to be met. Since then the number of the able-bodied and the children in workhouses in the rural districts, and to a less degree in the towns, has gradually diminished, and now the unions are filled with the aged and the infirm who were young during the thirties. This change in the character of the workhouse inmates has rendered it possible to introduce a less rigid enforcement of discipline than when the inmates were drawn from classes requiring stricter treatment. We have reasonable grounds to hope that as those who are now aged and infirm pass away, the amount of pauperism in the country will diminish.

The deterioration of laboring class morality, which reached its crisis in 1830, had sunk far too deep to be quietly eradicated. The Poor Law then introduced has been unevenly, and not always loyally administered. Although it is a sad fact to be faced that there are still more than 750,000 paupers in the country, costing over £8,000,000 a year, it is well to know that much of this vast amount is amenable to the sounder administration which is gaining ground; that we may look for a gradual diminution of the large proportion now resulting from old age and infirmity, and that the good influences at work for encouraging thrift and independence are daily acquiring a firmer hold upon the classes whom they are designed to benefit.

Large, and to a great extent unnecessary, as is the burden borne by the country on account of this vast weight of pauperism and expenditure, when the proportion of pauperism is spread over the population of England and Wales, it is well under 3 per cent., and the cost upon rateable value is less than 1s. 2d. in the pound. Even to those who feel most keenly how imperfect much of the poor law administration still is, there must be a feeling of grateful satisfaction in the comparison between these figures, and the state of the poor and the expenditure prior to the passing of the Poor Law Amendment Act.

That the principles of the English Poor Law are thoroughly sound has been demonstrated by all experience since the great reform of 1834. That those principles have not been more uniformly and consistently applied has prevented the much greater good which might have been gained. Those, however, who seek to depreciate what has been done, and to deny the future possibilities for good, are blind to the lessons taught us by the past.

In the first three decades of this century England went through a struggle during which the administration of the Poor Law had brought absolute ruin within the near future unless measures could be taken to cope with the general distress and disorganization. The Poor Law Commissioners ascertained and applied the remedy. Many and many a time since then the working classes in this country have suffered periods of stress and difficulty. They have emerged from them without serious detriment, however great the local and temporary suffering may have been. Often the Poor Law has been abused, and suggestions in every conceivable direction have been made for its modification or amendment, but always it has stood strong and firm to bear the burden imposed upon it, to give maintenance to the destitute on the one hand, and on the other to save the people from an expenditure, which had nearly brought them to ruin sixty years ago.

It is not feasible within the limits of this paper to do more than advert in the most general terms to the past and present position of pauperism in England. The many and interesting collateral influences and effects have necessarily been for the most part left aside, but it may truly be said that the actual good obtained by the Poor Law Act of 1834 is small in comparison with the far reaching indirect, but consequent influences, which have been at work in furthering the interests and well being of the non-pauper population, and in keeping large numbers who would otherwise have been paupers in a position of independence.

The great growth of benefit societies is one of the most striking symptoms of improvement. Upon this important subject there is still a considerable lack of definite information. The best of the societies are making strenuous efforts to place themselves upon a thoroughly sound footing, and the immense numbers of members prove that their hold upon the public confidence has been well established. It is impossible to estimate their enormous power and influence for good, and they carry with them the hearty "God speed" of all who care for the true interests of the working classes. Unfortunately there are still extant many societies which are not sound and which may in the future add to the distrust consequent upon failure.

There are no data upon which it is practicable to state what proportion of the population have made efforts to provide for themselves more or less completely by this description of thrift. The number of members of benefit societies is known to be very large, and it is also known that very large numbers are not counted in the recognized returns. Although the proportion of members and those dependent upon them to population cannot be given, it certainly may be reckoned by millions and is constantly increasing. An additionally satisfactory consideration is the fact that this increase is chiefly among the great and well managed societies, and that the small and unsound ones appear to be gradually disappearing.

The wiser use of charitable funds, the provision of institutions without end to meet the varied necessities of the poor in sickness and in want, the growth of kinder feeling between class and class; these and many other things which have for their object to render the life of the working classes better and more wholesome, owe much indirectly to the law which has laid down the right principles upon which pauperism should be dealt with.

When we look back through the half century since the present Poor Law was enacted we have reason to be grateful to it for the remedy of terrible evils, the removal of many dangers, and the active benefits it has conferred. Having regard to the dark past and the comparatively happy present, our prayer should be that no temptation may induce those who will administer it in the future to abandon the sound line of action which has brought us to the calm of to-day out of the wild storm in which the Poor Law Amendment Act was launched sixty years ago.

SCHOOL SAVINGS BANKS.

BY CHARLES HENRY WYATT, CLERK OF THE MANCHESTER SCHOOL BOARD.

In response to the request conveyed to me by Mr. C. S. Loch, Secretary of the Charity Organization Society, I have pleasure in laying before the Congress the following particulars relative to the School Savings Bank movement and its development and extension by the School Boards, and the managers of public elementary schools.

The object of the banks which are carried on in England, Wales, and Scotland, may be said to be two-fold:

First. By the practical method of instruction to inculcate habits of thrift and the husbanding of resources;

Second. To enable children and their parents to save small sums of money which are not received by the Post Office Savings Banks carried on by the Government.

These school savings banks are valuable auxiliaries for supplying depositors to the Post Office Banks and must be of extreme value in bringing into the homes of the people, particularly those of the lower classes, a fuller and more intelligent acquaintance with the various facilities which are now offered by the Government for the safe deposit of money in connection with the savings banks, which have developed into such a gigantic business in the United Kingdom during the reign of our present Gracious Sovereign.

Englishmen lay claim to a great many virtues, some of which they do not possess; but the most devoted Anglo-Saxon would scarcely say that thrift is one of them. We know that the working classes of this country are probably as well off as those of any other part of the world, and yet the less reputable parts of the great cities and towns of the United Kingdom will match for squalor, depravity, and poverty, with centres of population in other countries which lay no claim to such advances of civilization as mark Great Britain. It has been very wisely said that, like many other good habits, the husbanding of our resources is an art which may be acquired, and if the wasteful improvidence of the working classes is to be combated, it must be very largely by the tuition of the children in attendance at our public elementary schools in the proper use of money and the economical expenditure of earnings. Such teaching will also have a very valuable effect in the furtherance of the temperance movement and of all that tends to the lessening of the evil arising through the drinking habits of a large portion of the working class community of large cities.

I will now proceed to explain as briefly as possible the mode in which school banks are carried on in English public elementary schools, taking for example the case of the City of Manchester with which I am most intimately connected, and where the system has achieved the highest success.

We have 130 of these school banks in Manchester under the control of the School Board. They are open each Monday morning for the receipt and withdrawal of money. The work is entirely a labor of love on the part of the teachers, who do all the necessary bookkeeping; it is of course made as light as possible. To ensure accuracy the Board have the books audited twice a year. I should like to say in passing that in dealing with the savings of the working classes every care should be taken to give confidence to the minds of those whom it is wished to attract as depositors. Every thing connected with the banks must be like Caesar's wife, "above suspicion." Monday morning is found to be the best time for holding the banks. This, however, does not hold so strongly now as when the banks were established, one reason for the choice of the day having been that the savings could be brought in with the school fees; but the general adoption of free education in England limits the argument at the present day. The money is collected each week from the schools and deposited at the bank of the School Board. We have not found it practicable to allow interest in our school banks in Manchester, but when a depositor has saved twenty shillings he is encouraged to have the amount transferred to the Post Office Savings Bank where he is allowed interest at the rate of 2½ per cent. per annum. It is always well to encourage these transfers, but it cannot always be managed, as many of the parents prefer that the deposits should remain in the school banks thinking that the money can be more easily got at in case of emergency. The books required are:

1. Depositor's Pass Books,
2. Cash Book,
3. Ledger.

The officials who conduct the business of the bank are:
1. Cashier,
2. Secretary, or Bookkeeper.

The banks should be open only on the day and at the hour appointed in the rules (see Rules, p. 389), and no business can be transacted with depositors at any other time. Each depositor on opening an account receives a pass book showing his number in the ledger, his initials, and the amount of his deposit. The full name of the depositor appears at the head of his ledger account. The initials only are inserted in the pass book so that in case the pass book is lost, any fraudulent attempt on the part of the finder to withdraw the money may be rendered more difficult. The name of the bank, and the place and time when it is held, are printed on the cover of the pass book together with the names of the officials of the bank. An abstract of the rules of the bank are printed on the back of the pass book. The pass book is produced every time business is transacted with a depositor. The cashier receives and pays all moneys, and enters each transaction in the cash book giving the depositor's number, his initials, and the amount either deposited or withdrawn. The cashier also enters the date and the amount in the depositor's pass book, which is then passed over to the bookkeeper, who finds the account in the ledger, and enters the date and amount, copying these particulars direct from the pass book, after which the pass book is returned to the depositor. All entries in the pass books and ledger are initialed by the person making the same. At the close of business the cash is at once counted, and the cash book added up in order to see that they correspond. The cash is then forwarded to the offices of the Board with an advice note, signed by both the cashier and bookkeeper, authenticating the day's transactions, in order that the officer of the Board who has the oversight of the school banks may lodge the amount in the general account at the bank. As pass books are repeatedly lost by the depositors, it is customary to charge a small sum (one penny) for supplying a new book, the balance to the credit of the account being duly entered in the new pass book, and a note made in the ledger that a new book has been issued, so as to prevent fraud. When any depositor has £1 in the school bank he may have an account opened in his own name at the Post Office Savings Bank and he will then receive interest on the same. Before making such transfer the bookkeeper enquires whether the depositor has a pass book with the Savings Bank; if he has, he is requested to bring it; if not, one of the forms prescribed by the Savings Bank in the case of new depositors is filled up, in order that a pass book may be procured. All transfers are effected through the office of the School Board. When a transfer is made care is taken to write off the amount in the school bank pass book, and also in the ledger account of the depositor. Transfers are entered in the cash book after the re-payment. The books are balanced on the 20th November in each year. Each ledger account is added up, and after the balances due to the depositors have been checked, a list is made and a total arrived at. This list is copied in the cash book and follows the last week in the year. The correctness of this list is found by comparing it with the cash book. Should there be any discrepancy between the total of the balances due to the depositors taken from the ledger, and the annual statement made up from the cash book, a rigid examination is always made until the cause of difference is discovered. The teachers are advised to try the accuracy of their books (say every three months) by a trial balance. This is easily done by adding up the various accounts in pencil in the ledger, and comparing the total with the cash book summary, which should be regularly posted up week by week. According to the rules, a week's notice is required for the withdrawal of money; but we do not insist upon the rigid construction of the rule, the teachers re-paying any money that may be required from the money in hand, so long as they are able.

We began this work of school banks in Manchester in the year 1877. We had then 3 banks and the total amount deposited during the year was £93 5s. 3d., the number of depositors being 921, and the number of transactions 5,157.

In order to show the way in which the work has grown, I will quote the figures for the last year (1892), when we had 133 banks, and the amount deposited was £16,415. The number of depositors was 21,257 and the number of transactions 584,453. Since the establishment of the banks we have received altogether £112,740 6s. 7d. In order to show the very small risk connected with the carrying on of the work, I may state that a £5 note would cover the whole of the money which has been lost, mislaid or stolen. With regard to the safe care of the money in the banks, the Board have all deposits collected from the schools weekly and paid to an account which is open in the name of their treasurer at their own bank. We know pretty well the amount of money likely to be required, and also the amount beyond which the withdrawals are not likely to pass. I may say that such a thing as a panic in connection with our school savings banks is unknown. Our principal withdrawals are at the great Lancashire holiday of Whitsuntide, and again at Christmas. There is no doubt that many thousands of children in the City of Manchester are provided with new clothes and new shoes at these annual festivals through the aid of the banks.

We calculate the amount of money required to be kept at our bankers for the purpose of working the banks, and the balance is invested in government securities, *i. e.* consols. The interest upon these consols and upon the money lying with the Board's bankers is carried to a reserve fund to meet any necessity that might arise, and at the present time this reserve fund amounts to £1,043 15s.

In order to develop the work of the banks as far as possible we advertise them by means of handbills, and we have also found it a capital plan to issue picture cards to the children. The first time these cards were issued some 25,000 were distributed. The business of the banks the following week was nearly double what it had been before the issue of the cards, and the business has since continued to increase.

Such briefly is the mode in which this work has been carried on successfully for many years past in the city of Manchester, and it is the conviction of all who have had to do with the work that a very large amount of good has been done, not only in giving lessons of restraint, but in arming the children with weapons of defence against the innumerable tendencies which may work to affect their misery and ruin in after life. But the banks are also very valuable to the schools themselves. Though we have compulsory attendance at school in Great Britain, it does not follow that every child attends perfectly, and it is found that these school banks contribute very much to regularity of attendance and to a large extent stop the capricious migration of children from school to school. An account in a school bank is a wonderfully good anchor.

I believe that such banks, wherever established, if carried on with system and properly supervised, are likely to be among the greatest benefits that school managers can confer upon the rising generation.

I esteem it a high honor to have been invited to send a paper to the Congress upon this subject. I hope the day will soon come when there will be facilities in all civilised countries for children to have bank accounts at their schools and so learn to save their small sums of money

> "Not for to hide it in a hedge,
> Nor for a train attendant,
> But for the glorious privilege
> Of being independent."

SCHOOL BANK RULES.

1. The bank is held in the school premises every Monday at nine o'clock in the morning.

2. Any sums from one penny upwards will be received.

3. No money will be received or paid out without the production of the pass book. The depositor is requested to see that the sums deposited are correctly entered in this book.

4. If the depositor loses the pass book, a week's notice must be given, and a new pass book will be supplied for one penny, in which the balance of the account will be shown.

5. As soon as any depositor has deposited £1, an account will be opened in his or her name in the Post Office Savings Bank, and interest will be allowed. The school bank will continue to receive future deposits from such depositor, but does not allow interest.

6. In the event of the death of a depositor, such money as may stand to the credit of the deceased in the hands of the trustees of the school bank, will be paid to the parents, guardians, or other representatives. The trustees will pay the same to the person whom they believe to be the legal representative of the deceased child, but will not be responsible if the money is paid to the wrong applicant in error.

7. The index number and initials of the depositor are written on the pass book.

8. Twice every year the books of the school bank will be audited, and four times in each year, viz., on the second Monday in February, May, August, and November, every depositor will be required to leave his or her pass book at the school for comparison with the ledger. The pass books will be returned to the depositors on the following Monday.

INDEX.

Aberdeen, Scotland, helping the poor in, 344-349.
Alford, B. H., 250, 253-257.
Almsgiving, indiscriminate, x, xvii, 44, 49; *see* Begging.
Almshouses, 34, 59, 62, 75, 84; *see* Workhouse.
Ames, Miss, 35.
Apprentices, homes for. Dresden, 241.
Austria, charity in, 218.
Ayres, P. W., 15, 30, 35

Baltimore, charities of, 92, 129.
Barbour, Levi L., v, vii, 4, 34.
Begging, suppression of, 49; in France, 156; in Italy, 169, 183; in Germany, 213, 219; in Russia, 244; in Great Britain, 254, 285, 349; *see* Almsgiving.
Belgium, charity in, 135, 162-167.
Bemis, E. W., 12.
Benevolent trading, 356.
Berlin, organization of charity in, 217.
Birtwell, Miss Mary, 19.
Bland-Garland, Mr., as administrator of poor law, 301, 302, 351.
Böhmert, Victor, xiv, 210-243, 215.
Bolles, Commissioner, quoted, 131.
Bonaparte, Charles J., v, vi.
Booth, Charles, xxvi, 253, 263.
Booth, William, quoted, 85.
Boston, charities of, xii, 17, 19, 28, 44, 47, 49, 53, 91, 99, 108.
Brabazon experiment, 293.
Brackett, Jeffrey R., 15, 17, 22.
Bradby, E. H., 251, 258-267.
Bradfield, England, charity in, 350-364; *see* Tables.
Brinkerhoff, Roeliff, 32.
Bristol, charities of, 312-318.
Brooklyn, charities of, 44, 48, 90, 125, 127.
Brooks, John Graham, v, vii, xv.
———- Phillips, tribute to, 56.
Buffalo, Charities of, 10, 14, 44, 47, 48, 51, 93.
Bureaux de Bienfaisance. 154, 156, 179.
Burial clubs, 306.
Burlington, Iowa, charities of, 26, 48.
Bury, Mr., as administrator of poor law, 302.
Buzelle, George B., tribute to, 56.

Cedar Hill farm labor colony, 77–79.
Central Bureau of Poor Relief and Charity, Dresden, 220.
Charities aid associations; *see* State charities, etc.
——— building in Boston, 44, 47; in New York, 47.
Charity organization, general principles of, viii, xvii, xxiii–xxxii; in Italy, 182; in Russia, 244–247.
——— —— section of Congress of Charities, etc., committee of arrangements, ii, v–vii.
——— ——— ——— societies, in America, 43–57, 87–119; history of, 43–55; lapsed societies, 45; relief given or withheld by, 45, 46, 53; finances of, 47; organization and work of, ix, 48–55; friendly visitors of, *see* friendly visiting; registration by, 50, 99–107; agents of, 112; co-operation of with public relief, 50, 114–119; educational work of, ix, 186; Great Britain, 249–368, 372–374; West London, 253–257; East London, 258–267, 299; Shoreditch, 268–277; St. Olave's, 278–282; Islington, 283–289; St. George in the East, 299–303; Manchester, 251, 307; Bristol, 316–318; Rochdale, 328, 338–343; Aberdeen, 345; co-operation of, with poor law, 255, 270, 285, 290–303, 317, 329; difficulties encountered, 263, 288, 316; repressive work of, 254, 285, 332, 339; organizing work of, 254, 273, 288, 317, 330, 348, 365–368; relief granted by, 286, 297, 339, 340, 373; educational work of, 287; objects of, 290, 329, 367.
Charity, the problem of, xix–xxxii.
Chicago Relief and Aid Society, 53, 89.
Children, homes for, 63, 67, 72, 121, 127, 325; poor law schools for, 306, 325; placing out, 11, 325; boarding out, 326.
Church charity in England, 273, 280, 287; France, 136–141, 160; Italy, 169; Russia, 244.
Churches, charities of, 5, 7, 8, 11, 18, 29, 125, 367.
Cincinnati Associated Charities, 48, 93.
Clark, A. W., 11.
Colston societies of Bristol, 313, 314, 318.
Committees of State Charities Aid Association, duties of, 59.
Compulsory relief, 117, 150, 162, 166, 187, 214; from children, 310.
Confrères, 139, 140.
Congregazione di Carità, 182, 218.
Congress of Charities, Correction, and Philanthropy, vi, xix; officers, ii; section on organization of charities, committee of arrangements, ii, v, vi.
Convalescent home at the sea side, 308.
Co-operation, ix, xvii; between voluntary and official bodies, 14, 33, 68, 114–119, 210–227, 290–303; *see* Public and private charity, Charity organization societies, Organization of charities, State charities aid associations.
——— industrial, at Rochdale, 319, 321.
Country week for children, 274, 279, 328.
County visiting committee of State Charities Aid Association, 60.
Craig, Oscar, 32.
Crozier, A. O., 12.

Dawes, Miss Anna L., v.
Decentralization of poor relief, 200, 221.
DeForest, Robert W., v, vi, 3, 4, 8, 22, 31.

Dépôts de mendicité in France, 156.
Deserted wives, 305.
Directories of charities, 106, 161.
Dispensaries, private, with public support, 129, 156, 162; provident, 302. 308.
District Provident Society of Manchester, 307-309.
Dooly, John, 77.
Dresden, organization of charity in. 219-225; People's Club of, 228-243.
Drexel, Joseph W., supporter of Cedar Hill labor colony. 77.
Dugdale, R. L., quoted, 85.
Dupuy, E. J., 37.

East London, charity organization in, 258-267.
Educational work, *see* Charity organization societies; of People's Club, Dresden, 238.
Elberfeld system of public charity, xxix, 5, 113, 185, 187-209; in Elberfeld, 191, 225; in Hamburg, 196; in Freiburg, 203; in Crefeld, 207, 225; overseers, 191, 197, 202, 209; district board, 191, 197, 202; central board, 192, 201; business department, 194, 198; unpaid service, 193; temporary grants, 194, 205; application in large cities, 195; circuits, 197; conditions of relief, 201; paid agents and inspectors, 204, 207, 208; its shortcomings, 113, 203. 207; adaptation to American towns, xxix.
Electric sewing machine rooms of Baltimore, 92.
Emergencies, 53, 223.
Employment bureaus, 241.
Endowments, charitable, 136, 143, 165, 169, 182, 275. 279. 283. 312. 327.
Epileptics, care of, 67, 70, 292.
Evening entertainments of People's Club, Dresden, 229-233.

Farming out the poor, abolished in New York, 63.
Feeble minded, care of the, 292, 294.
First aid to the injured, 64.
Fitch Crèche, Buffalo, 47.
Fleming, Baldwyn, 377-383.
Foundling hospitals, 150.
France, charity in, 5, 37, 135-162; history, 135-148; public assistance, 149-157; private charity, 157-162.
Friendly societies, 280, 320, 355, 363, 382.
―――― visiting, discussion of, 15-31; papers on, 15, 108-113, 369-376; in Aberdeen, 346; Boston, xii, 17, 19, 28; Burlington, Iowa, 26; Galveston, 23, 31; London, 10, 286, 369; Manchester, 302; Minneapolis, 26; New York, 22, 24, 67; Philadelphia, 27; by districts or by families? xxix, 25, 113, 191, 197, 202, 346, 370.
―――― visitors, conferences of, 112, 191, 371; education of, 19, 28, 346, 371; enlistment and introduction of, 29, 108, 370, 374; suggestions for, xxxi, 15-31, 109-112, 373-376; as almoners, 27. 373, 374; as collectors of savings, 374; in tenement houses, 28; in cases of intemperance, 111, 276; from churches, 29; from colleges, 29; of Association for Improving the Condition of the Poor, 24, 346; of St. Vincent de Paul, 30; of the Women's University Settlement, 369-376; *see* Elberfeld system, overseers, etc.

Georgievsky, H., xvi, 244-247.
Germany, charity in, xxix, 187-243, 200; see Elberfeld system.
Gilman, Daniel C., v, vi, viii, xviii, 3.
Girls' Home of People's Club, Dresden, 241.
Gladden, Washington, 7.
Glenn, John M., v, vii, 33.
Grand Rapids, Mich., poor relief in, 12.
Green, David I., vii.
Grey's hospital, London, 278.

Harrison, C. C., v, vi.
Hartford, charities of, vii, 48, 95.
Hayes, Rutherford B., v, vi.
Hayes, Mrs. R. H., 23, 31.
Heape, J. R., 329, 338-343.
Henderson, Charles R., 7.
Hill, Miss Octavia, 68; her plans for collecting rent, 287; for friendly visiting, 369, 370.
History of charity, in Belgium, 162-167; in France, 135-148; of charity organization in the United States, 43-57.
Hodge, H. Lenox, tribute to, 55.
Holt, George D., 26.
Home libraries, 111.
——— of Industry of Brooklyn City Mission, 91.
Hôpitaux and *hospices* in France, 150.
Hopkins, Mrs. M. A., 19.
Hospital Book and Newspaper Society of New York, 63.
Hospitals, in England, 278, 326; in France, 138, 150-154; reformation of, 59, 75.
Hôtels-Dieu, 139, 142.
House of the Good Shepherd, Chicago, 128.

Improving the Condition of the Poor, Association for, Aberdeen, Scotland, 345-349; New York, 24, 38.
Indianapolis, charities of, 48, 56, 94.
Individual treatment necessary, 108, 190, 275, 366.
Industrial School for Girls, Chicago, 128.
Inebriates, institutions for, 111.
Infirmary, Poor Law, of Manchester, 306.
Insane, state care for, 65.
Instruction, college, in charities and correction, 55.
Intemperance, visiting cases of, 111, 276; a cause of poverty, 80, 349; Society against, Dresden, 229, 233.
International treatment of charity questions, 185-186.
Investigation, x, xvii, 50, 194, 255; of hospital applicants, 308; success of, at Paddington, 302.
Islington, charity organization in, 283-289.
Italy, charity in, 5, 168-184; *see* Tables.

Jails in the United States, 84.
Jenks, Prof. J. W., v.
Jews, in Whitechapel, 259, 266.

Johnson, Alexander, xiii, 33, 114-119.
Jones, J. Lloyd, v.
Juvenile reformatories of Maryland, 128, 129.

Kellogg, Charles D., xi, 43-57.

Labor question distinguished from pauper question, 210.
——— in almshouses, 34.
——— colonies, 33, 35, 77-86.
——— homes, 38, 91.
——— tests, 38, 87-98, 378, 380.
Laicisation of charities, 5, 152, 157.
Lambert, Brooke, 365-368.
Larner, C. P., 278-282.
Laundries, 88-98; in France, 37; training schools, Brooklyn, 92, Newark, 93.
Lazar houses in France, 138.
Leach, R. A., 252, 319-337.
Lewis, Charlton T., 74.
Licenses for disguised begging, 49.
Liquor traffic, 26.
Literature of English charities, 250.
Little Sisters of the Poor, 120.
Liverpool, joint collections for charities in, xxvii.
Loch, C. S., vii, xvi, 250-252.
Lodging houses, 36, 37, 49, 55, 65, 87-98; in London, 260.
London, charity in, 16, 249-303, 369; *see* Charity organization societies.
Low, Seth, quoted, 127.
Lowell, Mrs. Charles R., v, vi, xii, 33, 77-86, 122.

McCulloch, Oscar C., tribute to, 55.
McDougall, Alexander, 251, 304-311.
Mackay, T., xvi, 251, 290-303.
Maison hospitalière, 37.
Manchester, poor law relief and charity organization in, 304-311; school savings banks, 385.
Mansion House relief fund, 298.
Marshall, Alfred, ideas of, concerning co-operation with poor law, 296, 300.
Mayo-Smith, Richmond, v, vi, 3.
Medical relief, *see* Relief, medical.
Mendicancy, *see* Begging.
Metropolitan Association for Befriending Young Servants, London, 373.
Milne, George, 252, 344-349.
Miramion, Madame de, 141.
Mittweida, charity organization in, 215.
Moderation of the poor in seeking private relief, 296.
Morse, Miss Frances R., xii, 99-107.
Mumford, Mrs. Mary E., v.
Municipal lodging-houses, 37, 55, 65, 91, 93, 97; *see* Lodging-houses.
Münsterberg, Theodore, xiv, 187-199.
Mutual benefit societies, 161, 167; *see* Friendly societies.

Necrology, 55.
Newark, charities of. 49, 93.
New Haven, charities of, 44, 51, 94.
New Jersey, State Charities Aid Association, 72-76.
New York City, charities of, 22, 24, 38, 47, 54, 57-71, 88, 99, 121, 122, 127
——— State Charities Aid Association, 57-71.
Nicholls, Sir George, as a reformer of the poor law, 303.
Nicholson, C. N., 268-277.
Nurses, for the insane, 64; for the poor, 355, 356; schools for, 62.

Old age pauperism, 161, 379.
Omaha, charities of, 11, 48, 93.
Organization of charity, viii, xviii; *see* Charity organization societies, Elberfeld system, etc.; in Austria, 218; in France, 161; in Germany, 215, 219; in Great Britain, 250-252; in Italy, 182; in Russia, 244; its necessity, x, xxvii, 186, 211, 273.
Outdoor relief, private, 25, 246, 256, 279, 296, 313; *see* Charity organization societies, etc.
    public, 10, 12, 14, 44, 48, 116, 154, 168, 179, 201, 378-381; in London, 255, 269; its abolition desirable, 296, 301, 379-380; see also, Elberfeld System, poor law, etc.
    wages lowered by, 271, 294, 315.

Paine, Robert Treat, v, vi, 17, 30.
Panorama of charitable work in many lands, viii-xviii.
Paton, John, 24, 38.
Paulinengarten, Dresden, 236.
Pauperism, decrease of, in Bradfield, 361; in Bristol, 315; in Manchester, 303; its causes and cure, 80, 226, 293, 295; statistics of, *see* Statistics.
Peabody, Francis G., v, vi, xi, xix-xxxii.
Pellew, H. E., quoted, 100.
Pensions, by private charity, 256, 279, 280, 309, 339; old age, 161, 379; U. S., 14.
People's Club, Dresden, 228-243; club houses, 233; entertainments, 229-233; gardens, 237; home for apprentices, 241; home for girls, 241; journal, the "*Volkswohl*," 240; lectures and class instruction, 238; library, 239; women's meetings, 240.
——— Home, Dresden, 233-238.
——— Palace, London, 228.
Philadelphia, charities of, 9, 27, 44, 46, 50, 89, 129.
Playgrounds, Dresden, 237.
Police powers in private hands, 9.
Political influence in public charity, 114, 124, 126, 130, 157, 281, 314.
Poor-house, *see* Almshouse, Workhouse.
Poor law, Amendment Act of 1834, 294; its history and influence, 377-383.
——— commissioners, report of, 377.
——— relief in England, co-operation of, with private relief, 255, 270-273, 290-303, 317, 329; in a rural union, 350-364; reform of, 255, 294, 299, 301, 305; rules of, 269, 305, 322-327, 378; shortcomings of, 272, 281, 284, 293; in Scotland, 344.
Poor laws, U. S., 116.

Poor relief in Austrian Cities, 218; in German Cities, 215.
Portland, Oregon, charities of, 49, 96.
Post Office savings banks, 291, 384.
Preston, Vicar-General, tribute to, 56.
Prideaux, Miss F. C., 15, 369-376.
Prison reform, 74, 84.
Private charities lack responsibility, 117.
Provident dispensaries, in Manchester, England, 308; Provident Medical Society in Kent, England, 302.
——— efforts and institutions, 52, 53, 111, 161, 167, 287, 291, 302, 307, 308, 320, 355, 363, 374, 384-389.
Public and private charity, co-operation of, 33, 50, 57, 68, 114-119, 205, 210-227, in German cities, 215, 219-225; their relation, 31-33, 57-76, 185; respective fields, 4-15, 121, 257, 293; in Belgium, 162-167; England, 269; France, 135-162; Germany, 187-227; Italy, 168-184; *see* Poor law relief.
——— control of private charity, 132, 148, 159, 182, 213; in Austria, 218; Germany, 214, 223; Russia, 244.
——— subsidies to private charities, xiii, 120-132; in the District of Columbia, 120, 124, 129; Pennsylvania, 123; Illinois, 128; New York City, 121.

Quinze-Vingts, in Paris, 152.

Reform schools, 166.
Registration and information, ix, xi, xvii, 50, 99-107; in England, 330, 339; Germany, 216, 220, 224; Russia, 226.
Reitzenstein, F. Frhrn. von, xiv, 185-186.
Relief, *see* Almsgiving, Outdoor relief, Poor law relief, Poor relief.
——— by work, x, 33, 49, 77, 87-98, 324, 339.
——— medical, 129, 156, 162, 166, 181, 278; in England, 302, 306, 307, 308, 326, 328, 355, 362; see Hospitals.
——— special, 298.
Rescue work, 11, 36, 37, 38, 91, 307.
Rice, Mrs. W. B., v.
Richmond, Miss Mary E., 13, 33.
Rochdale, England, poor relief in, 319-343; administration of poor law, 322-327; co-operation between the poor law and charities, 329-331; industrial and general characteristics, 319-322; private charities, 327-329; *see* Tables.
Rogers, Miss A. P., 36.
Roman largesses, 168.
Rosenau, N. S., v, 7.
Rossi, Egisto, xiii, 168-184.
Russia, charity in, 244-247.

Saint Vincent de Paul, 30, 141.
Salvation army, work of the, 38, 78, 85.
Sanitary inspection, 205.
Savings banks; *see* Provident efforts.
School savings banks, 384-389; benefits of, 388; rules of, 386, 389.
Schuyler, Miss Louisa L., v, xi, 31, 57-71.
Scotland, poor relief in, 344-349.

Sectarian institutions, public appropriations to, 123, 128.
Self-respect developed by friendly visiting, 110.
Servants, 241, 373.
Settlement, laws of, in Belgium, 164, 166; in Italy, 183; in Germany, 187, 214.
Settlements, university, 370.
Seyffardt, L. F., xiv, 207-209.
Sharpe, Miss L., 283-289.
Shoreditch, London, charity organization in, 268-277.
Sisters of Charity in France, 141, 152, 157.
Smith, Miss Frances, 15, 28.
—— Mayo-, Richmond, v, vi, 3.
—— T. Guilford, 13.
—— Miss Zilpha D., 11; quoted, 104.
Societies for general welfare, Germany, 229, 236.
Society for Poor Relief and Charity, German, 215, 217.
—— for Prevention of Abuse of Spirituous Drinks, Dresden, 229, 233.
—— for Prevention of Pauperism, Dresden, xv, 219.
—— for Prevention of Poverty in Berlin, 217.
Sociology in university courses, 55.
Spencer, Herbert, 7.
Starr, Miss M. E., 26.
State boards of charities, 32.
State Charities Aid Association of New Jersey, 33, 72-76; law creating, 73.
                            - of New York, xi, 31, 57-71; county visitors, 60, 68, 70; law creating, 70; legislative work, 61; organization, 58-60; publications, 60; results of work, 61-68; standing committees, 59.
Statistics:
    appropriations to public and private charities, 121, 122.
    Cedar Hill Farm, 78.
    charities of Aberdeen, 348; Bradfield, 352, 362, see Tables; District of Columbia, 121; Dresden, 222, 225; France, 149, 154; Italy, 172-182, see Tables; Manchester, 305; New York, 122; Rochdale, 328, 333-343, see Tables; St. Petersburg, 246.
    friendly societies, 320.
    pauperism, 51, 318, 324, 333-337, 360-364, 381.
    school savings banks, 387.
    working class savings, 291.
Sterilization of the unfit, 33.
Strikes, industrial, 321.
Sturge, Miss Elizabeth, 312-318.
Suffrage lost by accepting public relief in Germany, 211.
Supervision of public charities, unofficial, in co-operation with official boards, 32, 57-71, 72-76.

Tables:
    Aberdeen Charities, 348.
    appropriations for public compared with private charities, in District of Columbia, 121; in New York City, 122.

Tables:—*Continued*.
  Bradfield Union:
    outdoor and indoor pauperism, 1871-1892, 361.
    ——————— ——————— poor in twelve Berkshire unions, percentage of, 360.
    sickness and old age, provision against, 364.
    social statistics of four parishes, 362, 363.
    wages, 359.
  Cedar Hill Farm, 78.
  deposits of working class savings in England, 291.
  Dresden Municipal Bureau of Information for Poor Relief and Charity, 225.
  Italian Charities :
    capital invested in Government bonds, 178.
    classification according to the principal object of each, 1880, 172.
    expenditures for charities by the provinces and towns, 1889, 180.
    financial statistics, 1880, 174.
    patrimony and income, 1861 and 1880, 176.
    real estate, value of, 1861 and 1880, 177.
  Manchester, outdoor and indoor relief, 305.
  Rochdale charities and institutions :
    classification of outdoor paupers, January, 1872 and 1892, 334; July, 1872 and 1892, 336.
    classification of workhouse paupers, January, 1872 and 1892, 333; July, 1872 and 1892, 335.
    diagram of the work of the Rochdale Charity Organization Society, 342.
    investments of working class, 321.
    payments to members of friendly societies, 1892, 320.
    total number of indoor and outdoor paupers, 1872 and 1892, 337.

Tenement-house reform, 67.
Thoma, Dr., xiv, 200-206.
Thrift, *see* Provident efforts.
Training schools, for nurses, Bellevue, N. Y., 62; *see* Laundries.
Tramps, 34, 35, 49, 51, 64, 156, 166; *see* Labor tests, Laundries, Relief by work, Woodyards.
Trading, benevolent, 356.

Uncomplaining poor, 222.
Unemployed, 34, 79-86, 97, 265; causes of lack of employment, 80.
Unpaid administration of poor relief, advantages of, 193.

Vagrancy, *see* Tramps.
Valleroux, Herbert, xiii, 135-167.
Vincent de Paul, Saint, 30, 141.
Visitors, friendly, *see* Friendly visitors; official, *see* Elberfeld System, overseers.
Visitors to charitable institutions, 32, 57-71, 72-76, 98, 183.
Volkswohl, Dresden, xvi, 228, 240.

Wages lowered by outdoor relief, 271, 294, 315.
Wages, rates of in Bradfield, England, 351, 353, 359.
Walk, J. W., 8, 11, 27.
Warner, Amos G., v, xiii, 5, 33, 120-132.

Washington, D. C., charities of, 93, 120, 129, 130.
West London: S. Marylebone, charity organization in, 253-257.
White, Alfred T., v, vi, xii, 87-98.
Whitechapel, London, 259.
Wilcox, Ansley, v, 14, 31, 39.
Williamson, Mrs. Benjamin, xii, 33, 72-76.
Willink, H. G., 252, 350-364.
Wines, Frederick H., v, vi.
Wolcott, Mrs. Roger, xii, 15, 108-113.
Women, *see* Laundries, Relief by Work, Workrooms.
Women's meetings of the People's Club, Dresden, 241.
Wood, Mrs. Glen, 18.
Woodyards, 36-39, 88-98; self-sustaining, 90, 95; *see* Relief by work.
Work, x; *see* Labor, Laundries, Relief by, Woodyards, Workhouses, Working-rooms.
Workhouses, 34, 89, 212; in England, 306, 324, 326, 333, 357, 381; in France, 156.
Workrooms for women, 36, 91, 92, 93, 94, 95.
Wyatt, Charles Henry, 384-389.

www.ingramcontent.com/pod-product-compliance
Lightning Source LLC
Chambersburg PA
CBHW051734300426
44115CB00007B/560